WITHDRAWN

JAPAN AND HER DESTINY
My Struggle for Peace

Tojo Kai Kan, Tokio

Mamoru Shigemitsu

JAPAN
AND HER DESTINY

My Struggle for Peace

MAMORU SHIGEMITSU

EDITED BY
MAJOR-GENERAL F. S. G. PIGGOTT

TRANSLATED BY OSWALD WHITE

E. P. DUTTON & CO., INC.
NEW YORK 1958

DS
890
S513
A23

© Mamoru Shigemitsu 1958

Printed in Great Britain

Contents

Acknowledgments	9
Author's Preface	11
Editor's Note	13
Introduction	17

BOOK ONE

THE 'MANCHURIAN INCIDENT' (1931–32)

Wakatsuki and Inukai Party Cabinets

I	Effect on Japan of First World War	25
II	The First Abortive *Coup d'état* (1931)	32
III	The 'Manchurian Incident' (Part 1)	37
IV	The 'Manchurian Incident' (Part 2)	42
V	The 'Manchurian Incident' (Part 3): The Army Acts	54
VI	The Second Abortive *Coup d'état* (the 'October Incident')	68
VII	The Last Party Cabinet: the Inukai Cabinet (1931)	72
VIII	The First Battle of Shanghai (1932)	74
IX	Assassination of the Aged Prime Minister	80

BOOK TWO

THE REVOLT OF FEBRUARY 26TH, 1936

Navy Cabinets of Saito and Okada

I	The Navy Cabinets (1932–36)	85
II	Failure of Naval Disarmament Talks	89
III	Military Aims in Japan and in Manchuria	93
IV	Hirota's Three Fundamental Principles	97
V	The Revolt of February 26th, 1936	102

CONTENTS

BOOK THREE

EXPANSION TO THE NORTH OR TO THE SOUTH?

Hirota and Hayashi 'Weak' Cabinets

I	The Hirota Cabinet	111
II	Was Japan's Next Move to be Northward or Southward?	113
III	Tactics in North China	117
IV	The Anti-Comintern Pact	122
V	The Defence State	127

BOOK FOUR

THE 'CHINA INCIDENT'

The First Konoye Cabinet, 1937–1939

I	Prince Konoye	133
II	The 'Marco Polo Bridge Incident'	136
III	The 'China Incident'	139
IV	Peace Efforts	144
V	The Navy on the Move Southward	148
VI	The Tripartite Alliance (Part 1)	150
VII	Plan of Action in China	154
VIII	Changkufeng	158

BOOK FIVE

A 'COMPLICATED, QUEER' SITUATION!

The Hiranuma Caretaker Cabinet

I	The Hiranuma Caretaker Cabinet	163
II	Wang Ching-wei (Part 1)	165
III	The Tripartite Alliance (Part 2)	168
IV	Nomonhan (Border Dispute)	172

CONTENTS

BOOK SIX

THE ARMY PUSHES ON

Abe and Yonai Military Cabinets

I	An Opportunity to Change Course	177
II	The Yonai Navy Cabinet	181
III	A Scene That Will Go Down in History	187
IV	Japan's Inexcusable Foolhardiness	189

BOOK SEVEN

THE TOKYO–BERLIN–ROME AXIS

2nd and 3rd Konoye Cabinets

I	Prince Konoye and Matsuoka	195
II	The Imperial Rule Aid Association	198
III	Wang Ching-wei (Part 2) (His Government set up in Nanking)	201
IV	The Tripartite Alliance (Part 3)	202
V	Matsuoka's Policy	206
VI	Matsuoka's Visit to Europe (Part 1) (Russo-Japanese Treaty of Neutrality)	211
VII	Matsuoka's Visit to Europe (Part 2)	215
VIII	Negotiations Between Japan and U.S.A. (Part 1)	218
IX	Council Before the Throne (Part 1)	235
X	My Advice on My Return	238
XI	Negotiations Between Japan and U.S.A. (Part 2)	241
XII	The Sorge Spy-ring	244
XIII	Council Before the Throne (Part 2)	246
XIV	The Last Days of the Konoye Cabinet	249

BOOK EIGHT

THE WAR OF GREATER EAST ASIA

The Tojo War Cabinet

I	Formation of War Cabinet	255
II	Attitude of the U.S. Towards the Problem of East Asia	260

CONTENTS

III	Opening of Hostilities	262
IV	Japan's Plan of Campaign (Part 1)	270
V	Japan's Plan of Campaign (Part 2)	274
VI	A New China Policy (Part 1)	279
VII	A New China Policy (Part 2)	286
VIII	The New Policy in Greater East Asia	291
IX	War-time Diplomacy (Part 1)	295
X	The Quest for Peace (Part 1)	299
XI	U.S. and Britain at War	303
XII	Fortune of War Turns Against Japan	308
XIII	Fall of the Tojo Cabinet	311

BOOK NINE

THE WAR OF GREATER EAST ASIA (*cont.*)

Koiso-Yonai Coalition Cabinet

I	The Koiso Cabinet: Supreme War Council	319
II	War-time Diplomacy (Part 2)	326
III	The Quest for Peace (Part 2)	334
IV	Deterioration of the War Situation: Fall of the Koiso Cabinet	340
V	The Problem of Prisoners of War	343

BOOK TEN

SURRENDER

Suzuki and Prince Higashi-Kuni War-end Cabinets

I	The Suzuki Cabinet: Final Stages of the War	353
II	The Quest for Peace (Part 3)	356
III	The *Coup d'état* that Failed	364
IV	The Task of the 'Cabinet of the Imperial Family'	368
V	Signature of the Instrument of Surrender	371
VI	After the Instrument of Surrender	375
	Envoi	382
	Index	383

Acknowledgments

I should explain that the translation of the Author's Preface is not by myself but by Major-General F. S. G. Piggott and Koichiro Asakai (former Minister-Counsellor of the Japanese Embassy in London) in collaboration. I reproduce it, by permission, from *Bulletin* No. 8 of the Japan Society.

The text of the book has been translated by myself. But while I accept full responsibility for any errors that may have crept in, it would not be right that I should fail to record my deep sense of gratitude to General Piggott for the assistance he has given me. Aware of his great knowledge both of the Japanese language and of the people, and banking on a friendship which has endured for half a century, I had no hesitation in appealing to him to assist me. Right nobly has he responded. As the work progressed, I submitted successive portions to his judgment and criticism. Together we have threshed out many knotty problems. It has been of inestimable benefit to me to have had him at my side throughout as guide and mentor.

I should like also to record my gratitude to a former colleague of mine—G. Burnham Braithwaite. When I have, frankly, been defeated by some, to me unusual, Japanese idiom, I have turned hopefully to him and have never been disappointed.

Another of the numerous friends whom I have consulted is F. J. Daniels of the School of Oriental and African Studies. In particular I am indebted to his translation, with commentary, of Mr. Shunsuke Tsurumi's monograph on 'The Amuletic Use of Words' (*see* under '3. Nationalist Theories', p. 19).

Oswald White

Author's Preface

The events which took place at home and abroad during some twenty years of the *Showa*[1] Era formed the most turbulent epoch in the history of Japan; combined with her defeat in war, they brought about a revolution unprecedented since the opening of the country. This revolution still continues.

The storms and unrest were, from first to last, mainly in connection with the problem of China. As Minister at the outbreak of the Manchurian Crisis, and, later on, during the war as Ambassador, I represented Japan in China. Subsequent to the Manchurian Crisis I held posts whence I could observe clearly world tendencies: for three years at the nerve-centre as Vice-Minister for Foreign Affairs; from 1936 to the end of 1938 as Ambassador to the Soviet Union, the mainspring of world disturbance; then, until June 1941, as Ambassador in England, the political focus of Western Europe; and finally, after Japan's entry into the war, for two years as Foreign Minister.

Following on Japan's defeat I stood my trial for two and a half years at the International War Crimes Tribunal in Tokyo; during that time, day after day, I had the opportunity of listening to a great deal of evidence by the Prosecution, and rebuttals thereto by the Defence Counsel. Included in these exchanges were incidents of which up till then I had not known; also developments of many others which I had not previously fully understood and which became clear for the first time. If this was the case with me, who, throughout the whole turbulent period was in a position of considerable responsibility, both in home and foreign affairs, so much the more was it so with those without direct responsibility; they could not possibly comprehend the development of many of the internal and external events during these years. I believe that it is not only a matter of interest to myself to classify and unravel the evidence produced during the two and a half years of the Trial as objectively as possible; I am convinced also that the storms of *Showa*, being unique events in our history, should be studied carefully by my countrymen, for they contain much food for thought in connection with the future rebuilding of our country. These Memoirs are

[1] Name of the present era which began in 1926.

mainly based on knowledge acquired during my past appointments, supplemented by notes made at the Trial, and from memory. They contain also very valuable material heard from those of my fellow countrymen directly responsible for leading Japan in the past, who lived with me in prison for four years.

It is not easy to apportion fairly the responsibility for the turmoil in the *Showa* Era. I think it will be necessary for skilled historians to devote much time to the matter in the future. It is unnecessary to say that I am not attempting myself to make a considered historical judgment: I merely think it is my duty, as a participant in these events, to record accurately my own beliefs and to add some observations thereon, as a contribution to history.

The Tokyo War Crimes Tribunal was, of course, a military trial of the vanquished by the victors, one-sided, partisan and conducted by those against whom it was submitted that Japan had committed international crimes. The majority of judges recognized she had done so, but the minority (excluding the Philippine judge) in their judgment took an entirely contrary view; the Indian judge, Mr. Pal, in particular, considered the actions of Japan as being fully justified. As regards the Tokyo Trials themselves, world opinion has already been formed. Students of history must not overlook the minority judgment and concentrate merely on the decisions of the majority; furthermore, as regards the evidence at the Trial, it is important that full attention be paid to the submissions of the Defence Counsel, whether they were accepted by the Court or not.

The more the causes of the storms of *Showa*, their course and their influence on Japan are studied scientifically, the better it will be for the future of my countrymen.

March 1st, 1950
In Sugamo Prison

Editor's Note

The sudden death of Mr. Mamoru Shigemitsu at the end of January 1957, when the translation of *Showa no Doran* was almost complete, has naturally affected much of the preliminary work in connection with the publication of this book. In 1955, when he was Minister for Foreign Affairs, my daughter and I were his guests for three weeks in Tokyo, and it was then that the contract was signed which stipulated that I should be the Editor, and Mr. Shigemitsu and I agreed that *Japan and Her Destiny* was the most suitable title for the English edition, rather than *The Disturbed Years of the Showa Era* or some such literal equivalent.

By a fortunate and happy turn of Fate, some months later I was able to secure the services of Mr. Oswald White, C.M.G., formerly a Consul-General in the old Consular Service in Japan, as translator. His exceptional knowledge and experience, coupled with sustained accuracy and determination, has made my own task far easier than I could have imagined. Our association, begun over fifty years ago in Tokyo, and continued to the present day, with intervals due to exigencies of time and space, has ripened into warm friendship and mutual regard during the past eighteen months of close collaboration. Perhaps the following extract from a recent letter he wrote to me may be quoted here:

> The news of Mr. Shigemitsu's death came as a great shock to me. Although I never knew him personally he had become a very real person to me from reading and translating his book. I had hoped that when he saw the translation it would give him pleasure to feel that he was understood in this country.

Mr. White may rest assured that it would have done so; and I have little doubt that the author would have approved the sub-title, 'My Struggle for Peace', that Mr. White and I have added—words that are literally and absolutely true.

Showa no Doran was first published in Tokyo, by the Chuo Koron Co., in the spring of 1952, and some explanation is necessary to account for the interval of over five years before the translation is ready for press; especially so in view of the fact that a few chapters in English appeared in the *Nippon Times* within twelve months of publication of the book. First of all a tribute must be paid to the advice and help given to Mr. Shigemitsu by a former member of his staff at the London Embassy, Mr. Toshikazu Kase, recently Ambassador to the United Nations at New York, and the author of *Eclipse of the Rising Sun*. After the return to public life in 1952 of Mr. Shigemitsu, the continually increasing demands on his time, and on Mr. Kase's, inevitably resulted in the delegation to others of the translation: the resulting manuscript was, in fact, a compendium by more than one hand of the original Japanese text. In spite of its value as such, it was felt by the publishers that this unique historical record by a famous world figure could best be presented to the American and British public by an entirely new translation. How this has been accomplished is told in Mr. White's Introduction.

I have no hesitation in stating that in my opinion, as a close personal friend of the author, and as a result of many conversations with his nephew, Mr. Akira Shigemitsu, until lately First Secretary at the Japanese Embassy in London, this book of his, *Japan and Her Destiny: My Struggle for Peace*, not only does full justice to a great patriot, but is an invaluable contribution to the history of those restless years during which he was always at the front of the stage, and often the principal actor. It was he, indeed, who signed the Instrument of Surrender that ended the war that he, as much as, and perhaps more than, any other Japanese had striven so hard first to prevent, and then to stop.

Mr. Shigemitsu kept a diary, *Sugamo Nikki* (Bungei Shunju Press), a day-to-day account of his four years in prison, with details of visits from members of his family, conversations with other prisoners, progress of the war trials, and even the weather; and, like others, he found the writing of poetry a special solace. He also wrote *Gaiko Kaisoroku*, 'Diplomatic Memories' (Mainichi Press), a record of his career since the outbreak of the First World War and his attendance as a junior Secretary at the Versailles Peace Conference. His service in China, his appointment as Vice-Minister of Foreign Affairs in 1933, promotion to Ambassador at Moscow three years later, and finally his transfer to London in 1938 (ending on the melancholy note 'My Mission fails'), are full of interest. Neither of these books, however, affect the main theme of *Showa no Doran*, which is an explanation, not a vindication, of Japan's actions. As he says in his Preface, it is written for his own countrymen, to be studied carefully, for the events described 'contain much food for thought in connection with the future rebuilding of our country'. The book's transparent honesty, his endeavour always to see 'the other man's point of view', descriptions of the inner working of Japanese politics, and accounts of important events in his own career, all written in graphic and restrained language, give the reader a clear picture of the man himself.

The circumstances of his release from prison, especially the negotiations leading up to this event, are described in detail by the Rt. Hon. The Lord Hankey in his book *Politics, Trials and Errors* to which the reader is referred; it has been translated into Japanese, *Senhan Saiban no Sakugo* ('Mistakes of the War Trials'), and had a wide circulation in Japan.

One final scene: as Mr. Shigemitsu drove back to his home and freedom, accompanied by his devoted American Counsel, George Furness, the car stopped opposite the Imperial Palace, and he descended —that lame, dignified and gallant figure—to make obeisance towards his Emperor. This typical act of loyalty, exemplifying his faith, may fittingly close this Editor's Note, which is, in effect, a salute to the memory of an illustrious statesman whose name will surely live always in the hearts of his countrymen and of some others, too, as the years unfold.

Introduction

I felt it a great honour to be asked to translate Mr. Shigemitsu's book—an honour and yet a serious responsibility. It was not merely the obvious difficulty of translating from an oriental language that gave me pause but also the added difficulty that exigencies of space made it necessary to reduce the length of the book by half. I have solved the difficulty in two ways. In the first place I have omitted sections dealing with events with which I might suppose the reader to be well acquainted —e.g. Hitler's rise to power—or which have already been much written about—e.g. the Chinese Revolution. Since this would still have left the book too long, I have, I hope judiciously, compressed the text slightly wherever it was possible to do so without altering the meaning or the emphasis.

I need hardly say that to a conscientious translator it goes very much against the grain to do violence to the author's text. I can only plead extenuating circumstances! But I have unfortunately to plead guilty to another sin. A few of the headings in the original text have, owing presumably to errors in proof-reading, little relation to the text. Many more, while entirely intelligible to a Japanese reader, would convey little or nothing to a foreign reader coming fresh to the subject. It has seemed desirable that such a reader should be able to gather from the table of contents what he was likely to find in the book. I have, therefore, taken the liberty of altering a number of the headings. Here again, however, I have given no heading that is not justified by the text. In other words I have not at any stage added any interpretation of my own of the events described.

Readers cognisant of the Japanese language, who may wish to compare the translation with the Japanese text, should experience little difficulty, since I have throughout followed the original order. Omission of parts of the book, however, for reasons explained above, has entailed a re-numbering of the sections in places (the numbering of the chapters is my own since they are not numbered in the original).

To assist those readers who have not made a close study of Japanese politics, I explain below certain points that may prove stumbling blocks:

1. POLITICAL TERMS

These must be read against the Japanese political background. A LIBERAL was one with democratic leanings who had studied the political systems of other countries beside his own. Without necessarily accepting Anglo-Saxon political ideals as entirely suitable to Japan, he advocated representative government, which Japan had in name but not in fact. In his attitude to foreign relations he hoped that Japan would live on friendly terms with other nations. Shigemitsu himself may be taken as a typical Japanese liberal.

Ranged on either side of the liberal were members of the RIGHT and LEFT WINGS. Right-wingers, if the term may be allowed, were dyed-in-the-wool conservatives. Though feudalism was abolished in the second half of the nineteenth century, feudal ideas still maintained a strong hold on the minds of the Japanese people, who followed leaders rather than principles. With them politics were the task of the ruling classes. The right-winger believed in what used to be called paternal government. He considered Japanese institutions to be superior to those of other countries, and tended to regard liberal arguments as 'un-Japanese'. One of the leaders of this school was Baron Hiranuma, who figures in this book. His main thesis was the *Kokutairon*—the theory of the constitution (polity) of the country. Briefly the theory assumed the divine right of the Emperor with its corollary, the duty of obedience of the subject. The Japanese Army and Navy may be assigned to the right wing, and the officers were mostly strong imperialists. A bone of contention between them was whether Japan's advance on the continent should be northward or southward, involving a possible conflict with Russia in the one case or with China in the other. The Army favoured the former, the Navy the latter.

The left wing repudiated the monarchical system. Their leaders had been trained in China and had acquired communism at second-hand. A curious feature of the political scene was that the methods employed by self-styled 'reformers' frequently combined right- and left-wing teachings.

2. THE DIVINE RIGHT OF THE EMPEROR

(The phrase is used here in the general sense of sovereign rights that were in theory unrestricted.)

The old Constitution of 1889 gave the Emperor supreme powers—

the Constitution itself was his gracious gift to his people : he issued laws, he commanded the Army and Navy, he contracted treaties, he declared war and he made peace. It is reasonable to suppose that it was not intended that he should exercise these powers and in practice he never did (only at the close of the war did he exercise what may perhaps be called the 'casting-vote' in favour of peace). Of the Emperor's prerogatives the one that attracted most attention was that of the Supreme Command. This power was usurped by those who should have been his military and naval advisers. The fact that the system lent itself to this abuse caused the Allied Powers to insist that it must be amended, if not abolished. The system was frequently discussed in allied countries towards the end of the war under the title of the 'institution of Emperor' or 'Emperorship' (*cf.* Cordell Hull's *Memoirs*, pp. 1591 *et seq*).

It should be noted that at the beginning of a new reign a name is assigned to the era and on the Emperor's death he becomes known by that name. The present era, known as *Showa*, began in 1926. The personal name of the Emperor is *Hirohito* but after his death he will presumably be known as the Emperor *Showa*.

3. NATIONALIST THEORIES

These stemmed from a belief that Japan was a country set apart from other countries—by its divine origin. With an utter disregard of history the nationalists maintained that Japan's form of government had remained unchanged since the Creator and Creatress summoned the country out of the deeps, and descendants of the Sun Goddess came down to rule it. How far they believed these myths it is impossible to say. One suspects that they considered their fairy tales suitable for the indoctrination of the masses. They used a number of catch-phrases that sound impressive but on examination prove to be well-nigh meaningless. A recent writer, Shunsuke Tsurumi (referred to above), has labelled them '*o-mamori-teki*', that is to say, of the nature of a charm. A favourite word was *Kokutai* (already mentioned above), which should mean the national polity but really summed up the theories lightly touched on above. Other similar words occur here and there in the text. If the reader does not understand them let him not worry. He may murmur '*abracadabra*' and pass on.

4. THE GENRO OR ELDER STATESMEN

A peculiarly Japanese institution. It was their duty to advise the Emperor at all times and in particular to recommend a Prime Minister when a new Cabinet was formed. In the period covered by this book, the only surviving *Genro* was Prince Saionji, who died in 1940. No successor was actually appointed in his place but his duties seem to have devolved on Marquis Kido, Lord Keeper of the Privy Seal. He instituted the practice of convening an informal committee of surviving past Prime Ministers to assist him. The peculiarity of the system was that, in the choice of a Prime Minister, the duty of the Genro began and ended with the recommendation of the right person. Since the country's policy was not the Genro's concern, the choice usually fell on the person most likely to maintain harmony in the Cabinet between the military and the civilian members. Once the Genro had made the recommendation his responsibility ended.

5. THE MILITARY HIERARCHY

Foreign commentators on the 'incidents' that occurred in Japan, Manchuria and China between 1930 and 1941 tended to ascribe them to the machinations of the so-called 'young officers', as distinct from senior officers.

The author carries this grouping a stage further by interposing a third group, whom he calls the *chuken* officers. The word indicates that they were the officers who were considered to be the mainstay of the Army. They held key positions—in Tokyo they were in charge of bureaux in the Ministry of War and in the General Staff Office, on service they formed the staffs of commanders of divisions or higher formations. Though it is not expressly so stated in the book they seem roughly to have held the rank of Lieutenant-Colonel or Colonel, with possibly a certain number of Majors. We thus get roughly three groups:

(a) Young officers—2nd Lieutenants, Lieutenants and Captains;
(b) Lieutenant-Colonels and Colonels; (c) Generals (Majors belonging to (a) or (b)).

According to the book the (a) group were hot-headed youngsters with little experience. Their one idea was to remove all who stood in the way of 'reform' by assassination. The (b) group seem to have exercised an influence that was still more sinister in the long run. They connived at the excesses of the young officers because they hoped that the resulting disorders would further their own ends. They planned to establish military government by means of *coups d'état*. Though their attempts in Japan failed in their immediate object, they so weakened the central government that in the end they got their way. In Manchuria they succeeded at the second attempt. In China their actions eventually involved Japan in a major war. For want of a better term I have called the *chuken* 'senior staff officers' in this translation.

The author groups naval officers in a similar way.

6. MILITARY INCIDENTS

In order to minimize the gravity of these subversive activities, Army leaders were wont to describe these startling events as 'incidents' (*jiken*). Government spokesmen had no option but to follow suit. In this book they are described as *jihen*, a word that can be variously translated as 'disaster', 'upheaval', 'uprising', emergency'. None of these words is quite apposite. I have, therefore, retained the word 'incident', which should here be regarded as meaning 'detached event exciting general attention'.

7. THE CODE OF MILITARY HONOUR

I make no apology for devoting space to this subject since it provides a constantly recurring theme in the author's narrative of the Pacific War.

In Japan poets and romantic writers likened the warrior to the cherry blossom. The cherry tree was cultivated not for its fruit, but for its flower, which the Japanese have taken to their hearts as the symbol of purity, of loyalty and of patriotism. Its beauty is short-lived. One moment the tree is decked out in ethereal beauty. The next a wind arises and the petals flutter to the ground. But there is no cause for tears because next year the tree will present the same brave display. The life of the warrior was like that of the cherry blossom. It was dedicated to his country and when the time came it was laid down without hesitation.

In the last war this poetic fancy was transformed into a similar analogy. The duty of the soldier and of the sailor was summed up in the word *gyokusai*—the 'broken gem'. But so to translate it conveys nothing, for it is merely the key-word of a proverb which may be rendered 'better be a gem that is smashed to atoms than a tile that is whole' (the word translated 'gem' originally referred to objects that were rounded but in compounds it has come to be used of anything that is perfect of its kind). Paraphrased the term may be taken as meaning 'strive for perfection even if you die in the attempt. Better so than to live without ambition like a roof-tile'. Translated into terms of the duty of a subject, it meant that, when his country was in danger, he must 'prefer death to dishonour'. To the soldier 'surrender' and 'dishonour' were synonymous. Even when the country was defeated, he maintained that it was dishonourable to surrender, and, if he had had his way, would have condemned the whole nation to immolation.

In translating *gyokusai*, when it appears in the text, I have not scrupled to vary the rendering according to the context, only indicating the word in a footnote towards the end where the refrain becomes more insistent.

8. POLITICAL PARTIES

There were at this time two—the Seiyu and the Minsei. They had no settled political principles, though the former tended to represent agricultural interests and the latter financial (the country *versus* the towns). The old Constitution seriously restricted the powers of the Diet. If I may be allowed to interpolate a personal opinion, it would be that many of the defects in the Japanese political system arose out of this denial of all real power to the Diet.

OSWALD WHITE

BOOK ONE

The 'Manchurian Incident' (1931–32)
Wakatsuki and Inukai Party Cabinets

CHAPTER ONE

Effect on Japan of First World War

1. ARMAMENT REDUCTION AFTER THE WAR

At the close of the First World War (1914–1918), the League of Nations came into being under the Treaty of Versailles. The First World War was a war to end war. Accordingly, the League made an attempt to destroy the seeds of discord by the reduction of armaments. At the Washington Conference, a naval treaty determining defence limits in the Pacific area was established under which 'capital ships' of the three great sea powers—the U.S.A., Great Britain and Japan—were agreed at a ratio of 5:5:3 (1922). Political questions were settled against this military background. As a result the Four Power Pacific Treaty and the Nine Power Treaty in regard to China, together with attendant resolutions, were agreed, the Anglo-Japanese Alliance was abrogated and China's aspirations were recognized.

In the hope of stamping out war a Treaty was made in Paris that forbad the use of war to further political designs (August 1928). This is what is known as the Kellogg-Briand Pact or the Anti-war Treaty. All these were attempts to keep international relations unchanged and were based on the idea that an existing treaty would command respect. After the Washington Treaty the League of Nations tried its hand at a reduction of armaments that should include armies within its scope. In post-war Europe the crux of international problems was similarly arms reduction. That any country should possess powers of defence adequate for its own protection is a necessity. Nevertheless it is reasonable to plan reduction of *excessive* armament. To some extent the tide setting towards reduction of armaments was augmented at the time by a world peace agitation that unfortunately went too far. It was a time when, at the close of one war, in the West and in the East alike, a desire for peace and tranquillity was widespread.

The idea of armament reduction should of course demand acceptance; as a policy nothing can be a greater source of danger than the possession of military strength greater than required. In Japan, in the wake of naval reduction, the Army also, under two Ministers of War, Yamanashi and Ugaki, who succeeded him, carried out successive reductions in the Army, in compliance with the wishes of the Party Cabinet.

The atmosphere of armament reduction at once engendered in the public mind a wave of contempt for the fighting services. For this the shallowness of the arguments of the common man must take most of the blame. In the forces the average officer disliked armament reduction so much that his feelings were violently inflamed against his seniors, who had countenanced it. Resentment against the political parties also became intense.

2. JAPAN ON THE CREST OF THE WAVE

Japan took part in the First World War as in duty bound under the Anglo-Japanese Treaty. She attacked and seized Kiaochow Bay, leased by Germany in Shantung Province, China. She despatched a powerful destroyer squadron to the Mediterranean; she guarded transport routes in the Indian Ocean and she assembled her productive capacity to afford economic aid to the allies. But this economic aid meant also for Japan herself the extension of her markets abroad and a rapid growth of foreign trade. Now Japan was acquainted with free trade but she had had no experience of controlled economy. So it happened that her light industries, which had been gradually developing, paid little heed to the fact that they were playing havoc with world markets, with the result that Japan sowed the seeds of a universal boycott of her goods after the war. But, apart from this, her war prosperity spelt wealth, not only to the financial magnates such as Mitsui, Mitsubishi and Sumitomo, but also to a number of small traders in Tokyo, Osaka and Nagoya, who suddenly accumulated great riches. Thus appeared in Japan the phenomenon of a swarm of *nouveaux riches.* Much of this wealth was lost in the world-wide financial collapse and in the Yokohama earthquake[1] but most of the financial magnates still survived and prospered, to flaunt the insolent tyranny of newly acquired capital. The evil done to society baffles description. National morality declined, manners were corrupted, selfishness was carried to extremes and materialism

[1] So described abroad at the time. Actually it devastated the whole of the Tokyo–Yokohama district.

was rampant. It was only natural that money should grasp control of the administration.

3. BEGINNINGS AND DEFECTS OF PARTY GOVERNMENT IN JAPAN

From *Taisho* (1912–1926) onwards, the *Meiji*[1] clan government had been giving way to a system of party government based on democracy, and liberalism had made a marked advance. None the less Japan did not succeed in throwing off her old practices. The *Meiji* Restoration[2] itself had preserved the privileged treatment of the nobility under the feudal system. Thus the Japanese did not forsake their old habits; it was not principles or logic that decided but rather clan interests or sentiment. Since the First World War ended in a victory for the democracies, the world raised a hymn of praise for democracy. In Japan, however, it was only the evils of democracy that were imported. The political parties, which should have acted as the representatives of the people, spent their energies in pursuing their own advantage. All too often they put the welfare of the country second in their aims. They went a stage further, when they sought political funds from the hands of the financial magnates. The prosperity of the world of finance itself was not due to the normal development of capitalism but had grown out of the alliance between the regime of those times and the clans as they grew in strength. The plutocrats, who owed their rise to the co-operation of the state and the nation, united with the political parties, manipulated them and converted them into moneyed interests, the immense wealth of which was but rarely used for the public benefit. Instead it was mainly used to further political ambitions or the extension of political power. The tide of worship of mammon, that swept the nation, ended by penetrating to the furthest corners of the administrative system. Problems arising out of the extremes of wealth and poverty were aggravated; farming villages were impoverished. Evils caused by the misuse of wealth sprang up overnight. Not only did the two great political parties, the Seiyu and the Minsei,[3] fail to fulfil their duty to point the way to democratic government, but the alliance between the parties and the moneyed interests finally became the main cause of political corruption.

---

[1] The *Meiji* era covered the period 1868–1912.
[2] The usual rendering, but the term includes the meaning of 'renaissance'.
[3] See 'Political Parties' in the Introduction.

4. FALSE PRIDE OF THE JAPANESE

As a result of the First World War, Japan came suddenly to rank as one of the five, if not of the three, major world powers, and she attained the responsible position of leader of the Western Pacific. Japan's standing in regard to world peace was important and her responsibility towards the civilization of mankind was an onerous one. But the future development of the Japanese State, the advance of the Japanese themselves, could have been furthered only if they had fully realized their responsibility. So far from doing so, the Japanese let themselves drift with the tide of new-found prosperity, they thought only of their own *amour-propre*, though what was within, their own merits, did not keep pace. The standing of Japan had improved but they forgot the simple truth that Japan, whether the individuals or the state, could attain greatness only in a spirit of humility and by unremitting effort. They lacked the voice of conscience to teach them what constituted lasting peace and what should be the ideals of the individual and of the state. This was the cause of the '*Showa* upheaval'.[1]

5. CONTEMPT SHOWN FOR THE MILITARY

The military caste had grown out of the former strength of the clans which from time immemorial had held the reins of power in the administrative organization. But in proportion as the spirit of a free democracy gathered force, the political parties strove to overthrow the military caste just as the military on their side strove to stave off their own decline. After the war the political parties, which had long suffered under the arrogance of the military, seized the opportunity to cut down military expenditure. Thus they proposed to destroy the power of the military, and leaders of the political parties openly denounced the Army in the Diet. The nation in general jumped to the conclusion that to show their contempt for the military by stripping them of their privileges, something they had never dared to do before, was itself to breathe the air of untrammelled freedom. A narrow-minded desire to pay off old scores also played its part. It was the manifestation of a people that had emerged from feudalism via clan government to a capitalist era of which it had no experience; it was indicative of the gap between the Government and political power on the one side and the nation and public opinion on the other. As for the military, they considered them-

[1] '*Showa no Doran*' (the Japanese title of the book).

selves a privileged class, and they purposed to retain the power they had enjoyed under clan government. The political parties, again, ignored the fact that their mandate came from the people; they were engrossed in the task of extending their own influence and advantage. Both parties were inured to old habits acquired under clan government. They failed to appreciate the concept that in common with others they themselves were a section of the state and the nation. They failed to see that it was their duty to fulfil the charge laid upon them.

So the military became a target for insults wherever they went. They were made to feel small when they got on the trams in uniform. They had to listen to such remarks as 'What use are spurs in a tram-car?' or 'Big swords are a nuisance to fellow passengers.' The Army were indignant. Whatever their rank, they came mostly from farming villages, which formed their background. And it was these villages that were impoverished and withering away because of the prosperity and corruption of the towns. The claim gathered strength that they could not stand by and watch the foundations of military caste being destroyed.

6. YOUNG OFFICERS FORM THE 'SOCIETY OF THE SWORD OF HEAVEN'

The fighting services felt that it was they that defended the state. This contempt for those who were in simple loyalty building the foundations of the empire arose out of the high-handedness of the political parties and the self-assertion of the moneyed interests. Their claims of liberalism and capitalism were in fact the direct cause of the corruption of society. That being so, it was necessary to cure the disease from which the state was suffering by removing the elements that were poisoning the system. Could there be any hesitation in killing such traitors?

Such were the thoughts that little by little began to fill the minds of Army and Navy officers. In the upper and middle ranks of the General Staff Offices, of the War Ministry, even in the Staff College, there were not wanting those who preached such ideas. The blood of the cadets in the Military Academy and of young officers boiled.

Many years ago the Reform of *Taikwa*[1] had been effected when Prince *Naka-no-Oye* had drawn the 'sword of heaven' and cut down *Soga-no-Iruka* in the Palace of the Emperor. In order to effect the Reform of *Showa*, should there be any hesitation to resort to emergency

[1] A.D. 645. A turning-point in Japanese history, when the nation, emerging from barbarism, turned to China for guidance.

measures? Such action was rather the supreme act of a loyal patriot. The time had come to lay down one's life in order to save the country.

So ran the thoughts of the high-spirited young officers. The summons went forth from Tokyo to every headquarters and formation in the country: gather together fellow-thinkers united in the aim of killing traitors and reforming the Government. Many young officers of every Division and of the naval depots signed in blood as they joined the pact and swore to sacrifice their lives as volunteers in the task of reforming the state. This secret society of young officers, that planned direct action,[1] took to itself the title '*Society of the Sword of Heaven*'.

It is lamentable to think that the idea of reform in the *Showa* era should have gone back to reactionary principles and adopted as its means the lesson of *assassination* learnt from historic times 1300 years previously.

7. YOUNG OFFICERS BECOME THE TOOL OF THE SENIOR STAFF OFFICERS

These 'young officers' were all subalterns, probationary officers and cadets. One and all held the simple desire to serve their country. And that being so, most of them put aside the traditional Japanese idea of marrying and settling down. Without radical reform, Japan, they thought, could not be saved. They themselves, therefore, would pay the sacrifice and settle the matter. The brains of the Army viewed the trend with some disquiet but none the less they used it for their own ends, so that it became a driving force that fostered the high-handedness of the military.

The object of the young officers was to cure the national malady by direct action, to be pushed to the bitter end—a simple destructive operation that was to be the spear-head of reform. As to a plan to build up after the destruction, they had none. Nor had they the power. They would have to rely on outside sources for constructive plans. They intended to hand over the work of building up again to seniors whom they could trust to do it. This fact was utilized by the senior staff officers to formulate and carry out the Army's own particular plans.[2]

---

[1] 'Direct action' as used here and elsewhere by the author has frequently a sinister meaning.
[2] The attention of the reader is drawn to a note on this subject in the Translator's Introduction.

8. 'IKKI KITA' THE REVOLUTIONARY

The man that provided the most powerful ideological background to the conduct of the '*Society of the Sword of Heaven*' was Ikki Kita. He was a born revolutionary, a planner and executor of dark sordid plots. In youth he had drifted to China where he threw in his lot with the revolutionary movement.

The basis on which stood his plan for revolution, 'Principles governing a measure for the Reorganization of Japan', is itself clear enough. The ultimate aim is obscure but the plan itself can be readily recognized as a mixture of right and left thinking.

That what he wrote on the reorganization of Japan constituted a text-book for the young officers of the Society and of revolutionaries in the Army cannot be gainsaid. For them his parlour was a forcing-house of revolutionary thought. The hold he maintained over the minds of the young officers became manifest later at the time of the February 26th revolt (1936).

CHAPTER TWO

The First Abortive *Coup d'état* (1931)

1. THE FORCES OF REACTION

AFTER the First World War current ideas in Japan for a long time swung violently between right and left extremes and, so long as the pendulum was swinging, a certain factor, derived from the political social organization, proved a great source of danger. And this was the fact that Japan's political leaders failed to keep pace with developments in the international situation.

In the post-war times, when thoughts of free democracy flourished, Soviet revolutionary ideas were imported under the guise of a system of liberalism and there was a vogue for Marxism. From the period (1925) during which relations were established with Soviet Russia, communist cells were established throughout Japan and Red influence grew apace. Reaction led to the fall of the Yamamoto 'Earthquake Cabinet' and grew to its height after the attack by Daisuke Namba on the sovereign at Tora-no-mon.[1] Nationalist thought[2] came into prominence and behind the scenes a struggle ensued between left and right wings, which went on for some considerable while. It was at this time that the *Kokuhonsha*[3] was formed under the leadership of Baron Hiranuma.

In this era of chaotic thought no personality capable of wisely leading Japanese thought in the stream of world conditions and culture appeared. Even logical principles, that should respect the dictates of reason, were spurned. The spectacle was presented of a mad rush from extreme to extreme, ever seeking what was fresh and original, in a state of pure confusion, devoid of deliberation or self-examination. Prompted by shallow propaganda that it was entirely due to the evils of liberalism

[1] A well-known district in Tokyo where in January 1924 a maniac attacked Hirohito, the present Emperor, but at that time Regent.
[2] The term implies a form of fascism.
[3] Lit. '*Foundation of the State Association*', a 'right-wing' society.

that Japan had fallen into such a state of confusion, the cry arose for counter-reform. In their attacks on the left wing, the nationalists saw nothing to choose between communism and liberalism. For them the Imperial House existed as an Absolute, loyalty to the Emperor was an essential to the survival of the state; to submit these theories to argument was itself 'dangerous thought' and a failure in one's duty to the country. It was argued that the thought of liberty was dangerous the moment it reached this point, the middle path counselled by liberalism was thrust aside and it came to be said that reform must start from the rejection of liberalism.

Communism strove to accomplish revolution by destroying the organization of society at the roots. The reactionary nationalist campaign in its opposition ended by adopting the self-same methods. It gradually brought pressure to bear against liberal middle-of-the-road advocates in its guidance of a people inexperienced in government.

When Japan emerged from the days of feudalism and national isolation under foreign pressure, she entered on an age of international intercourse and progress. As a system of liberty of thought she hurriedly adopted the principle of individual freedom without having had adequate opportunity to test it out. So it is unquestionable that the Japanese people, dragged into the rough sea of a capitalist society, never had sufficient time to accumulate the training in democracy, which should be buttressed by strong public opinion based on the sound judgment of each section of the people. In Japan public opinion, such as it was, merely applauded vigorous argument and rejected moderation. It thereby paved the way to the inevitable upheaval.

2. THE CAMPAIGN FOR REFORM

From the *Meiji* Restoration seventy or eighty years had passed. The tide of *Showa* reform was something that Japan could scarcely have avoided, faced as she was with the world-wide disruption that followed in the wake of the First World War. Both the Reform of *Taikwa* and the *Meiji* Restoration were dominated by existing world conditions and Japan's advance was achieved in conformity with the progress of mankind as a whole. Reform depended on the efforts made by her culture, untutored because of insular isolation, to catch up with a greater, outside culture. That a tragedy would occur if the state of affairs in Japan was too much out of line with world conditions was inevitable.

After the First World War the Japanese were puzzled to discover the direction in which civilization was moving. Although, in the light of the collapse of German militarism, world trends were clearly advancing in the direction of democratic liberalism, they mistrusted liberalism and came to the wrong decision that they must look elsewhere for the driving force of reform.

At the time it seemed that the world was divided into the two camps of democracy and totalitarian dictatorship or, if the latter were subdivided into communism and state socialism, into three. It resulted that, instead of being guided on the road of democracy, Japanese ideas were tinged with a colouring of German military totalitarianism so that Japan chose to revert to the ways of an earlier age. This it was that formed the groundwork of the upheaval of the *Showa* era.

It would be fair to say that, if the Nazi was, as Churchill said, the deformed child of communism, then the Japanese military, who dreamed of a *Showa* reform, might be called a cross-breed between the Nazis and Japanese feudal autocracy.

3. 'SHUMEI OKAWA', ANOTHER REVOLUTIONARY

The intellectuals, who perceived the need of reform, studied how best to achieve it, and members of the Imperial Household Department set up the temporary University Bureau, to which civilian thinkers were invited to give lectures. For the Confucian doctrine of the golden mean Seitoku Yasuoka was put in charge; for general concepts there was Professor Shumei Okawa, for international history Kametaro Mitsukawa. Then for military affairs, on the recommendation of Professor Okawa, there was Chikara Nishida (afterwards executed for complicity in the revolt of February 26th). The University Bureau was soon discontinued but Okawa and others had in the meantime got in touch with the military and formed the Taikokai[1] which aimed at the actual fulfilment of reform and provided the motive power for the reform campaign.

Professor Okawa had for many years been in charge of the research department of the South Manchuria Railway, where he had carried on research into various internal and external problems. As a thinker he had written a number of books. According to what he says therein, he had started as a left-wing thinker but it seems that eventually he crossed over to nationalism and had made up his mind in favour of a totalitarian state based on the military. None the less his attitude had a different significance from that of Ikki Kita (*vide* Book One, Chapter One, s. 8). The latter proposed to secure a grip on the ingenuous young officers, to remove any obstacles to reform by the direct method of assassination,

[1] '*The Society of Great Deeds*'.

then to set up men whom he believed to be suitable to achieve the desired ends. Okawa proposed to join hands with the senior staff officers who held the actual power in the Army, to stir them up to carry out a *coup d'état* in which the Army was to be the prime mover, then without delay to form a military government and effect a Nazi type of reform. It is this campaign to reform Japan within and without by means of a military *coup d'état*, engineered by the senior staff officers, that is the subject of what has been called the '*Showa* upheaval' in this book. Senior staff officers looked upon their superior officers as robots, set their powers at naught and did not shrink from seizing the reins of power from them.

4. THE 'MARCH INCIDENT', 1931

At the War Ministry General Ugaki was Minister, Lieutenant-General Sugiyama Vice-Minister and Lieutenant-General Koiso Head of the Bureau of Military Affairs, while General Kanaya was Chief of the General Staff, Lieutenant-General Ninomiya Vice-Chief and Major-General Tatekawa Director of the Second Section of the General Staff Office.[1] The senior staff officers, with the connivance of their superior officers, formed a secret association called the Sakurakai,[2] professedly to study the state of affairs (1930), and proceeded to deliberate exhaustively on a *coup d'état* which should have as its object the renovation of internal and external administration together with the establishment of military government. The ringleaders of the plot were Koiso, Tatekawa, Shigefuji, departmental head, and various similar ranks, besides Kingoro Hashimoto, Nagao and others of the senior staff officers constituting the Sakurakai. Lieutenant-Colonel Hashimoto had been Military Attaché in Turkey, had witnessed the revolution of Kemal Pasha and had returned lost in admiration of it. The members of the association worked in closest co-operation with Okawa's reform association.

In the hope of carrying through a *coup d'état* by means of the Army, which was to liquidate the evils of political parties and moneyed interests and to renovate the administration in all its branches, they considered that there was nothing for it but to dissolve the Diet and to put up General Ugaki to form a military government and, therefore, Professor Okawa, having secured the consent of Koiso, urged General Ugaki, both verbally and in writing, to lead the van.

[1] Roughly the equivalent of the D.M.I. in Britain.
[2] Lit. '*Cherry Society*'.

This is what is known as the 'March Incident'. The plan was:

In March 1931 on the day on which a Bill relating to Labour Unions was to be presented, according to the plan of Shumei Okawa, 10,000 civilians belonging to left and right wings were to be mobilized to make a demonstration against the Diet; the headquarters of the Seiyu and Minsei Parties and the residence of the Prime Minister were to be blown up. But, though the explosive power of the bombs was to be great, they were to be such as to cause a minimum of bloodshed. (Taken from the Court Record of judgment in the trial of the 'March Incident'.)

The First Division and the Imperial Guards Division were to be sent to surround the Diet and to dissolve it, the Wakatsuki Cabinet was to be forced to resign, General Ugaki was to be put in control and a select body of high-ranking officers were to fill the various key positions.

The plan failed, since fortunately General Ugaki refused his consent and eventually the secret leaked out. Similarly there were other such plans directed towards the realization of military government, as planned by the senior staff officers. In essentials they were the same though the details varied.

Thus at home the reform campaign based on a *coup d'état*, planned by Okawa's associates in collusion with the military, ended in failure. But abroad it was carried out in Manchuria by the Staff of the Kwantung Army. This was the so-called 'Manchurian Incident'.

CHAPTER THREE

The 'Manchurian Incident' (Part 1)

1. JAPAN'S FORWARD POLICY ON THE CONTINENT

SINCE the days of *Meiji* Japanese home and foreign policy had swung from side to side under the influence of two opposing currents. One school had been converted by French revolutionary thought to the doctrine of the sovereignty of a free people, to wit democracy; this was later named the Anglo-American school. Its ideas had permeated the Court, political parties and the people. The apostle of democracy in *Meiji* times was Yukichi Fukuzawa, and in political circles its ideas were represented by the anti-clan party of Okuma and Itagaki, who built the foundations of the political parties of a later day. The second school had learnt its lesson from the German military caste government. Under the guidance of Marshal Yamagata, military circles and one section of officialdom had formed a powerful militaristic body standing apart in its ideas. In the Navy the impetus had originally been supplied by the Satsuma[1] school, growing to manhood under Admiral Gombei Yamamoto, just as in the Army the force had been supplied by Choshu,[1] perpetuated by the descendants of Marshal Yamagata. Since the Navy had been taught by the British, it took a different line from the Army taught by the Germans. But in its ranks were few that understood Anglo-American democracy.

The clan government of *Meiji* times had adopted a policy of expansion known as the principle of 'a wealthy country (backed by) a powerful army'. Under the existing circumstances Japan could in the long run expand only in the direction of neighbouring regions, i.e. the continent of East Asia. As a result of the wars with China and with Russia, Japan succeeded in extending her influence via Korea into Manchuria. This was also one means of solving the problem of Japan's population.

[1] The daimyos of Satsuma and Choshu had led the revolt against the Tokugawa Shogunate.

Manchuria was an outlying district belonging to and colonized by China. Here Russian influence extended from the north and Japan's influence from the south. At the same time the economic policy of the Americans, British and others, that were engaged in expanding their trade and commerce, displayed greatly increased interest in East Asia.

Thus Japan's continental expansion could not but be directed towards China as its main objective. But China's anti-foreign movement had profited by the racialism[1] preached in Europe during the First World War. It had been influenced by the Soviet Revolution and had become acute. How Japan was to reconcile her continental expansion with China's anti-foreign racialism was for her a most serious problem.

Manchuria was in fact the touchstone.

2. ORIGIN OF JAPAN'S RIGHTS IN MANCHURIA

The preservation of the rights she held in Manchuria was to an island country like Japan, that was short of food supplies, was deficient in natural resources and under existing world conditions had nowhere to send her surplus population, veritably a question of life and death. The question how to protect those rights had haunted the minds of successive cabinets since the Russo-Japanese War.

Manchuria was a sparsely populated, backward country on the borders of China. By operation of the rights that Japan inherited from Russia, viz. the Kwantung[2] Leased Territory (in which are situated Dairen and Port Arthur) and the South Manchuria Railway, the country was by degrees opened up until presently one million immigrants were flowing in yearly from China Proper, most of whom settled in Manchuria. Since it was Chinese territory, the more the number of Chinese increased, the greater grew the strength of the administration, until it thrust aside foreign rights, which it aspired to take under its own control. Here can be seen the origin of the clash of interests with Japan.

It had been assumed that the term of the lease of Kwantung Territory was, as in the case of other such leases in China, ninety-nine years, but when Japan took over the official documents from Russia, it transpired that the lease was merely for twenty-five years, little of which was left. Japan hoped by some means or other to obtain an extension of this term.

---

[1] Self-determination.
[2] Also known as Liaotung (not to be confused with Kwangtung Province in South China).

3. WHAT BRITAIN THOUGHT OF JAPANESE RIGHTS IN MANCHURIA

In the Okuma Cabinet, formed before the First World War, Takaaki[1] Kato was Foreign Minister. Before this appointment he had been Ambassador in Great Britain and, when leaving London, he had called on Sir Edward Grey, then Foreign Secretary, to take farewell, and at that interview had discussed various problems of East Asia.

When the conversation turned on Manchuria, Ambassador Kato touched on the question of the term of the Lease. He stressed the importance of these rights. Japan, he said, had already introduced arrangements of a permanent nature. She had afforested the hills, and bare hill-tops were no longer to be seen. In reply, Foreign Minister Grey said that it was not merely a question of planting trees in the Kwantung Territory: Japan had sown her blood in Manchuria and it was reasonable that she should attach the gravest importance to the problem of Manchuria.

On his return to Japan Ambassador Kato looked for an opportunity to solve the problem.

4. THE '21 DEMANDS', 1915

Shortly after the formation of the Okuma Cabinet, the First World War began. Japan came into the war as an ally of Great Britain and in due course attacked and captured the Leased Territory of Kiaochow Bay owned by Germany in Shantung Province. Foreign Minister Kato proposed to take the opportunity to solve the problem of Manchuria and entrusted the drafting of a plan to Chozo Koike, Head of the Bureau of Foreign Affairs, who had served under him when he was Ambassador in London. In the event he committed a serious blunder that had an irretrievable effect on Japan's future path. It left a blot on the name of the Okuma and Kato Party Cabinets that could not be wiped out. It did grave damage to the credit of party government.

Koike had drawn up a list of demands incorporating the wishes of the military and other parties interested in China. This, Foreign Minister Kato instructed our Minister in Peking to present to the Chinese Government. The items included related to Manchuria and Shantung in particular and to China in general. Not only were specific rights demanded in Manchuria and Shantung: in China also, taken as a whole,

[1] The 'characters' with which this name are written are sometimes read Komei.

Japan was to acquire a form of pre-eminent status. It has to be admitted, however, that presently these undefined demands in regard to China Proper were treated as 'desires' and in the end were withdrawn by Japan.

The Chinese Government secretly informed both the British and American envoys and foreign correspondents of these demands which, known as the '21 Demands', inflamed world opinion and added fuel to Chinese anti-Japanese resentment. Negotiations in regard to the extension of the term of the Leased Territory in Manchuria were soon favourably settled. But in regard to the other questions relating to China Proper, such as those involving Shantung, and in particular the undefined demands now called 'desires', the Chinese attitude was firm, while world opinion at large condemned the Japanese method of negotiating. Though Japan on her side sent a final statement[1] and conducted negotiations in a high-handed manner for some time, she gained little. The points agreed on were very incomplete rights in Manchuria, together with certain questions in regard to China, but Japan had to withdraw the 'desires'.

As a consequence of these negotiations Japan's credit fell disastrously. Even Sir Edward Grey, Britain's Foreign Secretary, went so far as to warn Inouye, Japanese Ambassador in London, that Kato should not overstep the mark. By virtue of these negotiations all that Japan gained in the end was some privileges in Manchuria and in Shantung, while the disclosure of her ambitions in regard to China cost Japan her international credit and caused a wave of anti-Japanese feeling among the Chinese people. The Chinese question was no longer one between China and Japan alone. It had become an international question. For the U.S.A. the essence of American policy was summed up in the doctrine of the open door and the preservation of China's territorial integrity by means of equal economic opportunity for all. She displayed an all-embracing sympathy for Chinese racial aspirations and usually put herself in opposition to the active policy of other countries whatever the reasons involved.

5. MISTAKEN POLICY TOWARDS CHINA

During the First World War, when China was awakening to racial consciousness, Japan should, in deciding her policy, have appreciated general world trends and abandoned her traditional, short-sighted policy towards China ; she should have converted it to one of goodwill

[1] Not quite an ultimatum, rather the last step before one.

and co-operation between the two countries. Thus, she might have returned Shantung to China and, as a *quid pro quo*, China might well have satisfied Japan's hopes in Manchuria. Nor, in the light of existing circumstances, should it have been so difficult to establish some such comprehensive China policy. Instead, in the negotiation of the '21 Demands', her approach to China was made from strength, the limits of which were revealed. And yet, under the Terauchi military cabinet which followed, she persisted in using strength against China. Japanese statesmen were deficient in the insight needed to appreciate the significance of the World War, as well as the international trends that would follow it.

Most of Japan's leaders were ignorant of world conditions, nor had they the perception to understand the significance of the struggle for liberation of the Chinese people. To them 'China was China'. They still had a vision in their minds of the crafty China of the eighteenth century and they were intent on immediate gain. The Cabinet of General Terauchi, who came from the Choshu clan and was much admired by the military caste, appeared on the scene after the Okuma Cabinet and perpetrated blunders quite on a par with the negotiations over the '21 Demands'. They added further to the burden of Japanese discredit. Such, for instance, was the Cabinet's policy of assistance to Tuan Chi-jui[1] by means of the several hundred million (yen) Nishihara Loan. This was a manœuvre to win rights in return for assistance to the Anfu[2] military faction that was powerful at the time. The Chinese revolutionary movement reacted violently and in consequence anti-Japanese agitation became chronic.

Neither the negotiations over the '21 Demands' nor the policy of assistance to Tuan brought any radical solution to the problem of China, a problem that lingered on to occupy the stage when the policies of Tanaka and Shidehara took over.

---

[1] Nominal head of a clique that planned to take over the Government.
[2] Anhwei and Fukien Provinces.

CHAPTER FOUR

The 'Manchurian Incident' (Part 2)

1. TWO SCHOOLS OF DIPLOMACY VIS-À-VIS CHINA

IT has already been related that in the *Taisho* era[1] there were the two schools of nationalists and of liberals. This fact placed in opposition political parties to clan factions, civil officers to military; at a later stage, in the sphere of diplomacy, the same opposition was represented by the Shidehara policy, as against that of Tanaka. It need hardly be said that, though it is possible to speak thus of two schools, the term merely evidences certain characteristics, for it was natural that there should have been some interchange between the two, some intermingling, so that the line was not always clearly drawn. At the same time it is true that there was a radical difference in ideas and a still greater difference in policies arising out of the divergence between their respective reading of the international situation.

The liberal policy, represented by Shidehara, based the national policy on co-operation with Britain and the U.S.A., as the representatives of democracy, in the service of humanity. It rejected direct action and proposed to rely on diplomacy. Accordingly it accepted post-war organizations such as the League of Nations and the findings of the Washington Conference. Not only so. It believed that Japan's prosperous advance could be achieved only by co-operation. Its attitude was that, making use of co-operation and persuasion in the international sphere, it could act on the basis of mutual agreement. As regards its policy towards China, therefore, it would not treat Manchuria as distinct from other Chinese territory nor would it adopt a system of local defence in the case of Japanese communities.

The policy of action represented by Tanaka diplomacy was that the international machinery brought into being by the First World War was merely an instrument for the maintenance of the existing rights

[1] 1912–1926.

42

held by the powers. Neither the League nor the Washington Conference made any attempt to deal with the main causes of international strife. Even though the question of East Asia had become extremely onerous as a result of the Soviet Revolution, no careful thought had been given to the matter. Naturally Japan respected international treaties, but the anti-Japanese fever in China had become increasingly violent since the Soviet Revolution. China went on infringing Japanese rights but there were absolutely no signs to be seen of international measures to redeem the situation. The international machinery of the League had not the least enthusiasm for active fulfilment of right and equity. It was no more than an instrument of Britain, France, etc., aimed at the preservation of the existing state of international capitalism. But Manchuria was Japan's own particular problem, which could be settled only by Japan herself. And thus Tanaka diplomacy approved a policy of active self-defence. It maintained that as a practical policy towards China, Manchuria should be regarded as a special region of China and as such should have distinct treatment. Japanese communities in China should be defended on the spot.

2. SIGNIFICANCE OF THE WASHINGTON CONFERENCE, 1921-22

The forward policy in China, adopted by Japan during the war, was liquidated by the Washington Conference (1922). This was the time of the Hara Party Cabinet. The Anglo-Japanese Alliance, which had for many years been the mainstay of the policy of both countries in East Asia, was discarded and Japan subscribed anew to internationalism in the League Covenant, the Four Power Pact and the Nine Power Pact. By the Naval Armament Reduction Agreement, Britain, the U.S.A. and Japan fixed the ratio of big ships at 5 : 5 : 3 and each country was forbidden to build defence works in the Western Pacific. China's racial aspirations were recognized and each country agreed to assist her in their fulfilment. In accordance with the Treaty of Versailles, the rights taken over by Japan from Germany at Kiaochow Bay in Shantung Province were restored to China. It was also decided to abolish Japanese Post Offices in China. Japanese rights in Manchuria alone were not so much as mentioned.

As a result of the Washington Conference Japan, not spontaneously, it is true, made a radical change in her policy towards China. From her traditional policy of development, featuring China as the objective, she had moved on to a policy of the good neighbour, featuring herself as the fellow-worker. The view on which it was framed was that, if Japan were to accomplish anything worth while, it would not do for her to stand in opposition to China; she must work in concert with her. Only by establishing good-neighbour relations for the sake of co-prosperity, and with this as the rock on which to build, would it be possible to discover a solution to the problem of Manchuria. No true solution could be discovered otherwise.

For the first time Japan awoke to her mission in East Asia. In such wise Japan was to extend her influence, progressing steadily on an unhindered path. Thus could she advance as a natural stabilizing force in East Asia and attain the position of leader.

The Japanese leaders that took over from Kei Hara, who was assassinated, should have pressed on with all their might, at home and abroad, employing the great political powers they possessed, in this new, just policy. For the purpose, and in order to broaden popular knowledge of international conditions, they should have set up influential machinery to enlighten the people. They should have striven to lead them on the right path.

3. SHIDEHARA'S POLICY ENTERS TROUBLED WATERS

In compliance with the Washington Treaty a conference on customs duties and an international conference of the extra-territoriality committee were opened in Peking (1925). The latter was held with the object of terminating extra-territoriality, as desired by China, the former with the object of restoring to China customs autonomy. At this conference Ambassador Hioki, the Japanese Ambassador, proposed at the outset that Chinese customs autonomy should be recognized; he made it clear that the Japanese Government proposed faithfully and consistently to carry out the spirit of the Washington Conference. The restoration of Shantung had previously at an earlier stage made substantial progress towards fulfilment under negotiations between Ambassador Obata and Wang Chen-ting[1] (1922).

The negotiations for the return of Shantung and the Peking customs duties conference were the first steps taken by Shidehara to initiate his foreign diplomacy. One person that was closely connected with this policy was Sadao Saburi, who a little later became Minister to China.

The conference of the powers in Peking (1925) was held during the dictatorship of Tuan Chi-jui based on the red army of Feng Yu-shang. In China the struggle of the War-Lords had been going on without intermission. Meanwhile the Chinese revolutionary movement made

[1] Generally known as C. T. Wang (not to be confused with Wang Ching-wei).

THE 'MANCHURIAN INCIDENT' (1931-32) 45

rapid progress and Chiang Kai-shek had started his northward campaign from Canton. The dictatorship collapsed and Peking was left without a government. The international conference was dissolved.

In Japan criticism of the Cabinet and of Shidehara's diplomacy had been growing in volume. China itself was plunging further and further into disorder, the criticism ran, and could by no means be saved by foreign help. Shidehara's diplomacy, that was to satisfy Chinese wishes, was not doing so. Chinese disorder was chronic. All that Japan was doing was to stand aside and watch the loss of her rights.

The northern progress of Chiang Kai-shek was succeeding. At the same time, at each stage it raised problems. Under a policy that favoured communism and was linked up with Soviet Russia, army units, trained by Soviet advisers, had turned Bolshevik, foreign rights had been trampled on and local magnates were ground under. As a result both Hankow and Nanking were thoroughly looted. At Nanking the scene was harrowing (February 1927). British and American men-of-war opened fire on the now thoroughly disorganized Chinese forces. But the Japanese men-of-war refrained from firing, even in the face of looting and violence at the Japanese Consulate. Afterwards Naval Second Sub-lieutenant Araki, who had been charged with the defence of the Consulate, committed suicide by disembowelment, taking upon himself the blame for failure to discharge that duty.

Japanese public opinion was enraged. One and all ascribed the shame suffered by the Japanese to Shidehara's foreign diplomacy, and criticism of the Government rose to fever heat. The opposition Party denounced the Government policy with its doctrine of non-resistance. It maintained that Japanese communities must be properly protected on the spot and, if needs be, troops should be sent for the purpose. It went on to argue that any step such as that of withdrawing the settlers from danger spots would let down our prestige and sacrifice our rights.

So the Minsei Party Cabinet resigned and a Seiyu Party Cabinet appeared, with General Tanaka duplicating the posts of Premier and Foreign Minister (April 1927).

4. THE ALLEGED 'TANAKA MEMORIAL'

General Tanaka was the popular hero of the Choshu clan. In early age he had filled important posts in the Army. From the time he had been on the Staff he had occupied key positions and had seen visions of himself becoming a latter-day Elder Statesman. At the time of the Siberian Expedition at the close of the First World War (August 1918), he had held the post of Vice-Chief of the General Staff and had led it in person. But when he stepped forward to assume charge of an active policy towards China, he did so as President of the Seiyu Party and as such formed a Cabinet in succession to the Minsei Cabinet. The Seiyu Party, whose foreign policy had for so many years been liberal, now switched over to the militarist diplomacy of General Tanaka.

The latter duplicated the post of Foreign Minister, but he appointed as Vice-Minister Tsutomu Mori, an influential member of the Party noted for his fighting qualities. Mori held very far-reaching positive views on policy towards China, associated himself with extremist elements in the Army, and preached the doctrine of the strong arm in Manchuria.

About this time Chinese newspapers began to publicize the 'Tanaka Memorial'. This received wide advertisement throughout the world as the 'Tanaka Memorandum', an alleged secret document on the subject of Japanese paramount policy, which purported to be a memorial to the Throne expressing General Tanaka's views on Japan's foreign policy. It mapped out, stage by stage, a plan whereby Japan was to occupy Manchuria and then set in motion a military campaign, starting from North China and pursued throughout the whole of East Asia, culminating in the conquest of the world. At first sight its style gave the impression of a genuine Japanese document. At the same time it contains factual mistakes at various points.

In Japan no one doubted the existence of some such document; no one supposed that it was merely a piece of malicious propaganda. Abroad, and particularly in China, it was believed to be a document describing Japan's real designs.

At the time I was stationed in the Foreign Office and investigated the provenance of this document, as also the existence of anything resembling it. But not only was I unable to lay hands on anything of the nature, I was able to satisfy myself that in the first place such a document did not exist in the original and in the second the contents were not the views of General Tanaka himself. None the less it may well be that among the extremists in the Japanese Army there were those that harboured similar designs. It is credible that a written expression of some such irresponsible person may have come into the hands of one who re-wrote it and made use of it for purposes of propaganda. In short there is nothing to hinder anyone from supposing that the 'Tanaka Memorandum' is the joint effort of right and left extremists. It may be added that the subsequent course of events in East Asia and the incidental behaviour of Japan produced conditions just as though the 'Tanaka Memorial' had been taken as a text-book, so that it is now difficult to wipe out foreign suspicions as to the document.

5. GENERAL TANAKA TACKLES THE MANCHURIAN PROBLEM

General Tanaka's line of action was to regard Manchuria as a special region of China, to treat it as a separate entity from China Proper and to seek a settlement of its problems on the spot in negotiation with Chang Tso-lin, its actual ruler. Accordingly he had not taken kindly to the idea that Chang should extend his ambitions to central China and go up to Peking. He hoped that, with Japanese support, Chang would entrench himself in the Three Eastern Provinces[1] in virtual independence so that, acting without reference to the central government, he would set up separate relations with Japan and settle Manchurian problems in the way that Japan wished. For that matter, Chang had already in 1933 proclaimed the independence of the Three Eastern Provinces (May 14th). With regard to China Proper, on the other hand, General Tanaka intended to assist the Kuomintang[2] and Chiang Kai-shek to accomplish their aims, in return for which aid he hoped to obtain the latter's acquiescence in the proposed relations between Japan and Manchuria.

For the purpose General Tanaka kept in touch with Chiang Kai-shek during his northern campaign and even when the latter took refuge in Japan, after the capture of Nanking, gave his approval of the northward advance. In the meanwhile Chang Tso-lin had advanced to Peking whither, however, General Tanaka despatched General Yamanashi, a former Minister of War, in order to advise Chang to withdraw without delay and to devote his energies to the maintenance of law and order in Manchuria. That was a time when Chang had already assumed office as Commander-in-Chief in Peking (June 18th, 1927) and had been installed Chief Executive of China. His response to General Yamanashi was to turn on him with the words: 'I myself have advanced to Peking and am waging war on communist influences. My war is Japan's war. What am I to make of Japan's good faith when, in spite of this fact, Japan is assisting Chiang Kai-shek, who has gone Red, and is advising me to return to Manchuria?' General Yamanashi had no reply to make. Indignant at Chang's arrogant attitude, he returned to Tokyo and made his report. It aroused bitter feelings in the minds of the Army against Chang.

Minister Yoshizawa also discharged an identical mission to that of General Yamanashi under instructions from General Tanaka. This was carried out on May 18th, 1928. If, in disregard to General Tanaka's

[1] The Chinese term for what we call Manchuria.
[2] The Chinese Nationalist Party.

advice, Chang Tso-lin gave battle to the Kuomintang and were forced to withdraw to Manchuria, the Japanese Army were taking the strong line that they might stop him at Shanhaikwan.[1]

6. THE SHANTUNG EXPEDITION, 1928

In spite of General Tanaka's approval of Chiang Kai-shek's northern advance, a clash occurred between Japanese and Chinese troops.

Inspired with communist ideology, Chiang's army indulged in an orgy of violence and looting wherever they went, trampling on foreign rights in the process. In Tsinan, Japanese settlers were killed and Japanese rights were endangered. General Tanaka at once sent troops, which passed through Tsingtao to Tsinan, where they came in conflict with the Kuomin[2] Army. As a result they occupied Tsinan (May 1928). This is known as the 'Tsinan Incident'. It ended without further extension because, on an understanding with Japan, Chiang was able to resume his advance by circling round Tsinan. Chang's Army withdrew from North China and, in response to Prime Minister Tanaka's strong recommendation, Chang Tso-lin retired to Mukden.

The despatch of Japanese troops to Tsinan caused a recrudescence of anti-Japanese feeling, and the benefit of the efforts made by Shidehara's diplomacy to improve Sino-Japanese relations at the Customs Duties Conference was wiped out. A gale of anti-Japanese agitation swept through the whole of China. At that time there was no more powerful weapon with which to strike the foreigner than the antiforeign drive and Chiang Kai-shek did not scruple to use it. The Chinese anti-Japanese boycott at once brought Japanese financial circles under pressure. Led by the financiers, an outcry arose against the China policy of the Cabinet. The Premier began to consider earnestly how best to settle the 'Tsinan Incident' without delay and get Sino-Japanese relations back on the right track. At the end of 1928 he sent Minister Yoshizawa to Shanghai to arrange a settlement of the affair with Foreign Minister C. T. Wang. By Yoshizawa's exertions the incident was settled in Shanghai in March 1929. Thereafter the Nanking and Hankow incidents also were settled by Yoshizawa. At the same time Japan recognized the Chiang Kai-shek regime, i.e. the Kuomin Government, as the *de jure* government of China and established diplomatic relations therewith.

[1] Frontier station between China Proper and Manchuria.
[2] Nationalist.

This proved the last act of the Tanaka Cabinet.

After the Peking Customs Duties Conference, I resumed my official connection with the problem of China at Shanghai and at Nanking, after, that is to say, the negotiations over the 'Tsinan Incident'.

7. ASSASSINATION OF MARSHAL CHANG TSO-LIN, 1928

To revert to Chang Tso-lin. At the time the latter made his excursion into Peking, he was behaving in a high-handed manner. He had gone so far as to attempt recovery from Soviet Russia of the Chinese Eastern Railway and rights in the Three Eastern Provinces. He was in no mood to become the puppet of the Japanese Army. He acted in fact as though there was no such thing as the Kwantung Army.[1] Meanwhile, as a result of the report of General Yamanashi, the Japanese Army was feeling the utmost resentment against him. The Kwantung Army had by now come to the conclusion that a solution of the problem of Manchuria was impossible unless they were rid of Chang.

On June 3rd Chang had left Peking in compliance with the strong recommendation of Premier Tanaka. His train was just about to arrive at Mukden Station when, as a result of a plot by Colonel Kohmoto of the Staff and others, he was killed by a bomb explosion together with many of his attendants (June 4th). His one Japanese adviser, Colonel Machino, had alighted at Tientsin on the way back and thus escaped.

Chang's son, the young Marshal Chang Hsueh-liang, succeeded as governor of Manchuria. The fact that the assassination of Chang Tso-lin was the work of the Kwantung Army Staff was made public for the first time in the evidence at the Far Eastern International War Tribunal in Tokyo, but Chang Hsueh-liang knew it at the time so that from henceforth he must live under the spell of the curse on him who suffers the murderer of his father (in his case Japan) to exist on the same earth with him.[2]

The Emperor had very much disliked the active China policy of the Cabinet and he impressed on Premier Tanaka the necessity of enquiry into both a settlement of the 'Tsinan Incident' and the true facts of this assassination. When the Emperor learnt that the assassination was due to a plot by the Kwantung Army, he ordered that the culprits should be rigorously punished so that at least international good faith should be saved. As already related, the 'Tsinan Incident' had been settled, but rigorously to punish those responsible for Chang Tso-lin's death was

[1] The Japanese Army in Manchuria.
[2] Laid down in the Chinese Book of Rites.

impracticable owing to the opposition of the Army. On the ground that to make the affair public would have an unfortunate effect on the control of subordinate officers, the Army ultimately administered no public punishment. Instead they whitewashed the incident by placing the culprits in the First Reserve. The Emperor's confidence in General Tanaka fell to the ground and thereafter he declined to listen to him in Audience. The Tanaka Cabinet had already lost the confidence of the Diet and finally had no option but to resign.

It should be carefully noted that ultimate acquiescence in the Army action in thus whitewashing the incident of Chang's assassination lent an impetus to the '*Showa* upheaval'.

8. DEIFICATION OF THE EMPEROR

The will of Japan's Chief Executive, the Emperor, in regard to the disposal of the assassination incident was as clear as crystal. The views of the Genro[1] were also definite (*Harada Diary*). It was clearly laid down in Article 11 of the old Constitution that the Emperor possessed the authority to control the Army and the Navy. Even though the Supreme Command was a thing apart from other general state matters, its subordination to the Emperor was clear. If the Emperor had exercised his powers and had formally demanded that the competent Supreme Command (in this case the Army) should publicly announce the responsibility for the assassination of Chang Tso-lin, it is possible that a plain, straightforward settlement could have been effected. But it was contrary to precedent that the Emperor should thus directly exercise his prerogative. It had always been the practice that in matters involving the administration the Emperor should maintain the position of a constitutional monarch and dispose of them through the Prime Minister acting as his adviser. It was up to the Prime Minister to carry into effect the will of the monarch through the intermediary of the War Minister, who in turn represented the department in control. How much more did this practice apply when the Prime Minister of the moment was General Tanaka, who was recognized as wielding considerable influence in military quarters!

At the accession of the Emperor the surviving Genro was Prince Saionji, who had absorbed many of the ideas underlying the French Revolution and as a thinker was a liberal. The theory of emperorship that he counselled was that the Emperor should in all affairs of state assume the position of responsibility. He should act in all political affairs

[1] See Translator's Introduction.

with the assistance of the competent Cabinet Minister and in matters concerning the Supreme Command should await the advice of the Military and Naval Chiefs (Chiefs of the Army and Naval General Staffs) before acting. Needless to say, this advice was in conformity with the intention of the Constitution to prevent the emergence of an absolute monarch. The Emperor in fact did faithfully follow it, that is to say he never issued positive orders of his own volition. This was the truly admirable attitude of a constitutional monarch. None the less it resulted that in practice the Emperor was entirely isolated from the administration and his position ended by becoming that of a deity, while all matters of state were decided in accordance with the advice of those responsible as his advisers or aides-de-camp. This was the practice of a British type of administration but unfortunately Japanese administration had not advanced so far as had British democracy. The Government was not in direct contact with the people, it was directed by a power standing between the sovereign and the people. The contradiction arose that in order to command the fighting services, the sovereign did not issue orders to them but awaited their advice before acting, which meant that control of the fighting services was impossible. The text of the Constitution having thus become a dead letter, the inevitable consequence was that the problems in themselves affected the very life and death of the state. The deification of the Emperor was just what those that planned to act on the Emperor's authority desired.

The deification of the Emperor came about from the sincere loyalty of the Genro, and the upper circles that formed his entourage, who desired nothing other than that no harm befall the immemorial Imperial House. Because the Genro, who was supposed to accept responsibility for the Emperor, had no responsibility under the Constitution, he reviewed affairs of state from behind the scenes instead of standing before the people in all his prestige and openly giving them a lead on the right path. The supreme power laid down in the Constitution was not personally exercised by the Emperor but laid on the shelf, and power gradually slipped away elsewhere. No clearer information on the point is to be found than in the record entitled *Harada Diary* (Relations between Prince Saionji and the political situation). The development of democracy in Japan lagged and the power of the political parties was small. So between a constitutional monarch of the British type and the nation there was room for an interloper to drive in a wedge.

This state of affairs was welcomed most by the Supreme Command, which functioned independently of the Government and the Diet. During the '*Showa* upheaval', on many important occasions, they enforced their views in opposition to the will of the Emperor, who was in theory the Supreme Commander. The Emperor did no more than endorse the views of the Supreme Command, learnt before or after the event. Such deification of the Emperor had produced in earlier ages government by the great military houses; in more recent times it produced government by the Supreme Command. Thereby the military were released from the highest and final restraint, intended to keep them under control. In order to grasp the actual power, they preached the independence of the Supreme Command and the doctrine of nationalism, the theory that the Emperor was an organ of state was rejected and the entourage of the Emperor were even persecuted. They planned *coups d'état* and finally resorted to assassination. It might not be right to say that they were consciously implicated in these occurrences but, inasmuch as they aimed directly and indirectly at the realization of military dictatorship, the fact is that the continuation of such measures brought about the accomplishment of their aims.

When the fundamental laws of a state, such as are embodied in the constitution, have become a dead letter, the state is indeed in danger. However idealistic and splendid a constitution may be, unless the country's upper and lower constituents, that is to say the people, put it to practical use in their daily existence, and are prepared to defend it with their lives, the constitution will sooner or later lose grip. That the disturbances of *Showa* should have derived from the paralysis of the constitution should be a lesson for the future of Japan. In the nature of things the source of the national will is impalpable. Again, rifts in the national will, equally with a too strong concentration in one direction, spell considerable danger to a state. Since ancient times the fortunes of the country have frequently wavered from the straight path.

9. INDISCIPLINE IN THE ARMY

Despite the will of the Emperor that those responsible for the assassination of Chang Tso-lin should be severely punished, Premier Tanaka lacked the power to put it into effect because the leaders of the Army obstructed. The state of affairs in the Army had become such that it lacked sufficient control to uphold the cause of loyalty; discipline had disappeared. Moreover, since the ill effects of the assassination on international relations were taken as a reason for glossing over the affair, the impression was made on the military mind that the correct thing to do, whenever there was a plot that might injure international relations, was for the country to ignore it, even if it had actually been carried out. If an international plot succeeded, the perpetrator was a national hero and, if it failed, the country must shoulder the blame. The dangerous idea that the individual performing the deed should not be brought to justice became unwittingly entrenched in the military mind.

Government by the military houses having passed, from the time of *Meiji*, into clan government, the military powers of the soldier under the Supreme Command tempted him to try to carry his own views by force. Immediately after the Restoration a cry for a punitive expedition against Korea was heard. After the establishment of the General Staff, the plan was mooted that the Commander-in-Chief in Formosa, Kodama, should carry the campaign on to the mainland. The Siberian campaign when Tanaka was Vice-Chief of the Staff Office was of the same nature. In the case of the Chang Tso-lin assassination, Premier Tanaka could do nothing with the Army; he was incapable of carrying out the Imperial wish. The Army had accustomed itself to the idea that, in its desire to fulfil its own plans, even the Emperor was not to be feared.

CHAPTER FIVE

The 'Manchurian Incident' (Part 3): The Army Acts

1. REVIVAL OF SHIDEHARA POLICY AND DEATH OF SABURI, 1929

FOLLOWING the Seiyu Party Cabinet of Tanaka, the Minsei Party Cabinet of Hamaguchi took over (June 1929). That meant the revival of Shidehara diplomacy. Saburi (Chapter Four, s. 3) was now appointed successor to Minister Yoshizawa and I became his assistant.

Foreign Minister Shidehara had two important tasks. One was the China Problem, the other was the London Naval Retrenchment Conference. Both were knotty problems to solve that might be considered as carrying the Washington Conference a stage further, for one, a ticklish undertaking, was to restore Sino-Japanese relations to the straight track envisaged by the Washington Nine Power Treaty, while the other was to determine the ratio of warships other than capital ships, whose ratio had been settled at 5:5:3 by the Washington Treaty. The Naval Conference furnished urgent matters for preliminary consideration and Foreign Minister Shidehara became immersed in their study.

In China Chiang Kai-shek's northern campaign had been crowned with success (June 1928). At once the remains of Sun Yat-sen were sent from Peking to Nanking where a stately service marked the installation of his departed spirit in a mausoleum on the 'Purple Gold Mountain'. Each country took the opportunity to recognize the Nanking Government, which at last began to settle down. Minister Saburi, in taking up his duties in a new China that had only just renewed diplomatic relations, proceeded to exchange views with the key-men in the Nanking Government, who were just then intoxicated with the success of the revolution. He made extensive tours of inspection and returned to Japan, fully prepared to offer momentous advice to this government. But the Foreign Office was worked to death with the Naval Conference and had not the time to spare to talk over things with the new Minister. Meanwhile Saburi was kicking his heels in Tokyo and watching the psychological moment for a revision of Japan's China policy slipping away. He went to Hakone and there committed suicide. The world was at a loss to understand the reason but I had it brought home to me that Chinese problems presented a sea of troubles.

2. I AM APPOINTED MINISTER TO CHINA

Public opinion in China, which had welcomed the return to Shidehara diplomacy, was stirred to the depths by the tragic death of Minister Saburi. The fact that he had committed suicide after a prolonged stay in Tokyo caused many to think that it was due to political reasons, that it was in fact because his views had not been accepted. As his successor Japan proposed to appoint Ambassador Obata, who had been concerned in the negotiations over the return of Shantung and had a thorough understanding of 'Shidehara diplomacy'. But the Chinese press opposed his appointment because it considered that Shidehara had turned back and gone over to 'Tanaka diplomacy'. It recalled that Obata, who had been stationed for many years in China, had been Counsellor when Hioki was Minister and had taken up a firm attitude at the negotiations over the '21 Demands'. Finally the Chinese Government refused *agrément* to the appointment of Obata as Minister. The radical Kuomin Government had raised the standard of 'revolutionary diplomacy'. Public opinion was dead set against Japan and anti-Japanese feeling rose rapidly.

Japan had now reached an impasse: she could not formally appoint a Minister. As a way out, Foreign Minister Shidehara conferred plenipotentiary powers on myself as Chargé d'Affaires and put me in entire charge of negotiations. For me there began a stormy diplomatic existence of some years, divided between Shanghai and Nanking, while I strove to restore relations with the Nanking Government. In the interval relations improved and I continued as the substantive Minister. Needless to say, my task was to clear up the confusion caused by Tanaka's policy, to continue Shidehara diplomacy and bring it to fruition.

3. HEYDAY OF THE SHIDEHARA POLICY

For long the powers had enjoyed special rights in China arising out of the Anglo-Chinese Treaty of Nanking (1842); under the 'unequal treaties' they maintained extra-territoriality, customs duties that could not be changed and residential areas (settlements),[1] and these special rights were equally enjoyed by all nations under the most-favoured-nation clause. These rights had accumulated as a result of foreign control of the customs, the stationing of troops under the Boxer Agreement and the establishment of national settlements, until China could scarcely move hand or foot and had fallen into a semi-colonial status. The Council of Ministers of the powers presided over by the British Minister in Peking had acquired the authority of a quasi-Chinese control organ. It was these special rights of the powers from which the Chinese racial, national movement agitated to release China. From time to time it took on a colouring of violent xenophobia. Particularly after the Soviet Revolution, incited by the Communist Party, it assumed an ultra-revolutionary nature.

Although Japan's representative, I did not attend the meetings of the Diplomatic Corps in Peking since I resided in Nanking and Shanghai. In my pursuit of an improvement in Sino-Japanese relations, I tackled a practical solution of the outstanding problems that had accumulated between the two countries. For their part, when the Chinese had realized my attitude, they welcomed my appointment and gave me their complete trust. I devoted myself heart and soul to the adjustment of Sino-Japanese interests and to the development of better relations between the two countries. Among the principal problems, the customs duties question was settled and the question of the disposal of the Nishihara loans, etc., was put on a sound footing. I also devoted attention to extra-territoriality, which stemmed from the unequal treaties. Sino-Japanese relations improved rapidly. Chiang Kai-shek dismissed his Soviet advisers and replaced them with Japanese and engaged drill instructors from Japan. The Kuomin troops brought China, north and south, under one control. Japan, both the Government and the Army, had established good relations with the Kuomin Government. It was felt for the first time that the relations between the two countries were on the right track. Many of the foreign powers began to copy the precedent shown by Japan. For a time the Shidehara diplomacy had come to full fruition

But it was not to endure for long.

[1] Popularly known as 'Concessions'.

4. BRITAIN'S CHINA POLICY

Britain is very conservative but is at the same time very progressive. In China she had many rights and was most powerful. In Peking the British Minister had for long been the virtual head of the Diplomatic Corps. But now that the Kuomin revolution had triumphed and a Kuomin Government had been formed in Nanking, the Japanese Legation had begun to function in central China. Since the national liberation movement had paved the way, the numbers of countries maintaining their Legations in central China had increased. The Diplomatic Corps in Peking was left entirely in the air.

Britain decided upon a new policy. For the purpose it adopted a plan drafted by Pratt,[1] its China expert. Austen Chamberlain, Foreign Secretary under the Conservative Party Cabinet, announced the decision in what was known as the 1929 Christmas Memorandum. In the new policy Britain, reversing its former conservative policy, recognized the Kuomin Government and approved its aims. It would accordingly discuss with it concrete proposals for the revision of the treaties and the restoration to China of the settlements and other rights. In its understanding of China's racial aspirations the policy marked an entirely new departure. The content of the new policy was quite in keeping with the policy that Japan was pursuing. The U.S.A. also and the other European countries fell into step with Britain.

Countries such as Britain, once they establish a new policy, are in a position to act precisely on the lines laid down. Enviable indeed is the excellence of their political, executive machinery! However splendid Japan's policy might be, her organs of government lacked co-ordination. The Army was self-willed in its interference, the political parties were unversed in foreign diplomacy and no solid support was forthcoming from public opinion. So it ensued that Shidehara's policy could not move one step beyond certain fixed limits. Under the pressure exerted by the opposition party and the military, the Minsei Party Cabinet had lost power. The Shidehara diplomacy was curbed by nationalist arguments that were springing up in Japan and the impetus to carry it to its conclusion was sadly lacking. Meanwhile negotiations between Britain and the U.S.A. on the one hand and China on the other had made a rapid advance and revision of the treaties began to take shape.

China used her negotiations with Japan to expedite her negotiations with Britain and the U.S.A. but, so soon as these approached

[1] Sir John Pratt, K.C.M.G.

completion, the situation was under her control and her negotiations with Japan, who was holding back, lost their importance in Chinese eyes.

5. CHINA'S 'REVOLUTIONARY POLICY'

Japan had in her negotiations with the Chinese from time to time put aside the difficult problems bound up with Manchuria and pushed on the question of the revision of the unequal treaties in China Proper. The programme was, thereby, to improve relations generally, and then to settle the difficult problem of Manchuria in the resulting more favourable atmosphere.

This schedule was perfectly well understood by the Chinese, but the moment the negotiations with Britain and the U.S.A. had made favourable progress they at once stepped up the speed with which they prosecuted their tactics for the recovery of national rights.

The Foreign Minister, C. T. Wang, had been an associate of the radical war-lord Feng Yu-shang. Thinking, it may be, that the position at the moment was opportune, he published his own plan of a 'revolutionary foreign policy for China'. According to this, recovery of customs autonomy was to be Stage 1; recovery of sovereign jurisdiction Stage 2; recovery of settlements and leased territories Stage 3; recovery of rights of navigation on internal waterways and of coastal navigation, recovery of railways and other rights Stages 4 and 5. This programme of so-called revolutionary diplomacy aimed to abolish the unequal treaties in the immediate future and bring about the recovery of all vested interests, but if the negotiations with foreign countries were not concluded within the expected period, then the intention was that China should unilaterally denounce the treaties and proceed to recover the rights involved. The features of Wang's revolutionary diplomacy were published in full detail in the newspapers.

Faced with this development, I decided to return to Japan in order that I might warn the Government of the danger to Sino-Japanese relations, and at the same time submit my own views to Foreign Minister Shidehara. As a first step I satisfied myself as to the views of the Chinese authorities and called on C. T. Wang at his residence. This was in 1931, i.e. six months before the beginning of the 'Manchurian Incident'.

In response to my question, C. T. Wang acknowledged that the newspaper report was authentic. He explained that it included Manchuria within its range. It was China's intention to recover the Port

Arthur–Dairen Leased Territory and the operation of the South Manchuria Railway, both in the published order. I was profoundly disturbed; it looked as if all my labours might come to naught.

To the Japanese Army Wang's pronouncements acted as a powerful irritant. To the fulfilment of the Shidehara diplomacy it administered the death-blow.

6. ANTI-JAPANESE FEELING IN MANCHURIA

By virtue of Shidehara diplomacy, relations between Japan and the Central Government of China had been notably improved but the situation in Manchuria, which was quasi-independent and with which Japanese relations were more intimate, had not progressed in the same way.

Chang Hsueh-liang, who had succeeded Chang Tso-lin, was not disposed to come to terms with Japan. During adolescence he had been very susceptible to British and American influences and at the moment he had a British adviser named Donald. Hsueh-liang's ideas were extremely anti-Japanese. This attitude became quite clear when he himself shot Yang U-ting, who was regarded as pro-Japanese. He went over to the Kuomintang and did away with the barrier of semi-independence, pulled down the 'Five Colour Standard'[1] and erected the 'White Sun on a Blue Sky' of the Kuomintang[2] in its stead. The move indicated that he was openly taking up an anti-Japanese attitude and proposed to drive Japanese influence out of Manchuria.

Under such an atmosphere, disputes between the Japanese and the Chinese steadily increased and subjects of discussion between the two parties piled up. The authority of the Nanking Central Government had not yet, it is true, extended as far as Manchuria, but Hsueh-liang shielded himself behind the pretext that it would be *ultra vires* for him to settle Japanese complaints on the spot and declined to negotiate. So negotiations could be disposed of neither on the spot nor in Nanking and pending questions continued to accumulate. Japan had acquired the right to trading marts in Manchuria, whereby the Japanese were entitled to lease land for trading purposes outside the railway zone.[3] But owing to Chinese pressure it was becoming more and more

---

[1] Symbolizing the five races of Manchuria (Manchus, Mongols, Chinese, Japanese, Koreans), and so suggesting the independence of Manchuria.
[2] Nationalist Party.
[3] Both Japan and Russia had built-up towns, which they administered at important stations on the S.M.R. and C.E.R. These, together with a strip of land on both sides of the track, constituted the 'railway zone'.

difficult to maintain even the leasehold rights already owned by Japanese or by Koreans, who had lived there for many years, let alone acquire new leaseholds. A movement to acquire the Manchurian Railways[1] began. The Chinese themselves built parallel lines and entrusted to a foreign company (Dutch) the construction of a grandiose harbour at Hulutao,[2] planning thus to destroy the value of the port of Dairen and the railway operated by Japan.

These portents, as viewed by the Kwantung Army, which was charged with the protection of Japanese rights and of Japanese and Korean lives, roused a feeling that the diplomats were powerless and that there was no way out but the use of military force.

7. JAPAN'S POPULATION PROBLEM IN ITS RELATION TO THE PROBLEM OF MANCHURIA

At that time the Japanese were in a state of nervous tension as they thought of the future of the State and the Race. Japan is a small island comprising only limited cultivable land. Nor has it mineral resources worth mentioning. The population, which at the time of the war with China had been some 30 millions, had grown in the intervening thirty years to 60 millions and was increasing at the rate of one million annually. How was Japan to feed this teeming population? It was a question to shake the foundations of her national policy. Impelled by conditions that made overseas emigration impracticable, Japan tried to solve the problem by developing Korea and Formosa to their utmost limits and, further, by economic operations in Manchuria, and, for that matter, was solving it. At the same time overseas trade was an indispensable factor. But it takes two to do business and it does not always go as one would wish. The problem of Manchuria acquired increasing importance day by day because it affected Japan's very existence. The diligence of the Japanese was a matter of life and death and not an attempt to raise their standard of living.

The League of Nations had denounced war. Its policy was to keep the world static and, as a means of insurance, it planned universal reduction of armaments. But as a solution of the food problem, that was fundamental to human existence, it had nothing better to offer than empty talk of free trade at a time when the world, with the countries of Europe at the centre, was in practice reverting to a closed economy.

[1] S.M.R. and C.E.R. or possibly only the S.M.R. here.
[2] Half-way between Mukden and Tientsin.

THE 'MANCHURIAN INCIDENT' (1931-32) 61

Even Britain, the home of free trade, showed signs of an imperialistic tendency (the Ottawa Agreement was signed in 1932). In their colonial empires, France and the Netherlands were closing their markets to other countries for the sake of their own interests. Thus it was that the policy of the powers, in the extreme nationalistic era that followed the First World War, had travelled far from the principles of free trade. The powers gave no thought whatever to such principles, though these embodied the spirit of the League of Nations. To feed Japan's increasing population her people might work till the sweat dripped, but reliance on the development of overseas trade was becoming useless. Matters had come to the pass that Japan was forced to lower her standard of living.

In this connection it was relations with China that affected Japan most closely. Japanese trade with China had been badly hit by the boycott. The cotton-spinning industry in China, in which Japanese took the lead, was severely obstructed. Li Lu-san, a stalwart communist fighter trained in Moscow, making Shanghai the centre of his operations, fanned the flames of a labour movement among the students and flung himself into the anti-Japanese movement. Japanese interests were at the mercy of the persecution, to which they were subjected not only in China but also in Manchuria. China's revolutionary diplomacy, as enunciated by C. T. Wang, was displaying its prowess throughout the whole country.

Japan possessed administrative rights, not only in the Kwantung Leased Territory but also in the Railway Zone; in addition Koreans dwelling in remote parts of Manchuria numbered about a million. For Japan to protect these local interests, in the midst of an anti-Japanese hurricane, was no easy task. Furthermore, for Japan to be ousted from China Proper, and not only there but from Manchuria also, was calculated to threaten the very livelihood of the Japanese people themselves.

8. GROWING WEAKNESS OF THE JAPANESE CABINET

The state of affairs caused me profound concern. I had tried hard to forestall a conflict between Japan and China. I had hoped to prevent a crisis by making concessions in China Proper in order to pave the way for a solution of the China problem. At the same time I had maintained to my own Government that Japan should explain the confused situation to the League of Nations and make clear her point of view, and I had strongly advised that for the purpose she should without delay establish a thorough-going comprehensive policy towards China. I believed that the time had come when Japan should demonstrate her great powers of statecraft to the world at large.

In April 1931 I returned to Japan and reported the state of affairs to Foreign Minister Shidehara in person. I supplemented and emphasized the advice I had already offered.

After the assassination of Prime Minister Hamaguchi (April 1931), the succeeding Wakatsuki Cabinet did not look like surviving for long, and when it became evident that the Cabinet lacked the will to form a policy and carry it through, I began to lose heart. I had made a contribution to the main body of proposals. I had maintained that settlements such as those at Suchow and Hangchow, which had little value, should be at once returned to China in order to make clear Japan's attitude towards the unequal treaties, but even this suggestion was turned down on the ground that there was no assurance that it would receive the approval of the Privy Council. Among the Cabinet Ministers there were some that gave me cause for circumspection by pointing out that, inasmuch as my atittude was too sympathetic to the Chinese, I might push the Foreign Minister into an awkward situation. The nationalist movement had already extended beyond the fighting services and was invading the opposition party and the Privy Council. The stand taken by the fighting services over the prerogative of the Supreme Command had succeeded and the Government was so worn down by pressure from the right wing that it had lost all power. Even now political circles had gone so far as to play with the idea of assassination. There was no question but that Foreign Minister Shidehara had undeviatingly followed the path of right in his foreign diplomacy but his weak point was that in a matter of life and death for Japan, such as the problem of Manchuria, he had no plan of solution that would convince the Japanese people. With the country's peril before its eyes, the Government yet lacked the courage and the ability to give constructive leadership and ensure a solution. That was the opening scene of the tragedy and it was one great cause of the failure of liberal principles in Japan.

As the situation developed in this way, the problem of Manchuria became acute at home and abroad. A Government that was devoid of statesmanship stood with folded arms, sorrowing over the course of events and doing nothing about it.

9. OUTBREAK OF THE 'MANCHURIAN INCIDENT'

My suggestions to the Government stood no chance of being substantially accepted.

Arising out of the China problem, an international crisis was now at hand. If it were something with which human effort could not cope, then it was incumbent that we should remain steadfast in this hour of trial. In other words it was necessary that the Government should make adequate preparation and stand firm in the eyes of her people and of the world, in order that she might handle any unpredictable upheaval that occurred. The Government, not overlooking the fighting services, should have controlled and checked any insubordination and should with might and main have avoided any aggravation of her relations with China. Withal, she should have sounded the tocsin and used every effort to enlighten the world as to the justice of her attitude. At that moment when China's revolutionary diplomacy had been revealed in the light of day, when Japan had no remedial power in her hands, when it was clear that Sino-Japanese relations had reached an impasse, then, if it were so that Japan had reached a dead end, there was no other way: her diplomatic policy should have been 'In this hour of crisis we stand firm'. By standing firm I mean that, whatever was to happen, steps should have been taken to win over the world to the position in which Japan's diplomacy stood. Taking as my order of the day those words 'in this hour of crisis we stand firm', I myself, however sick at heart I felt, left Tokyo and returned once more to my post of duty; I would still display the will to retrieve the situation.

In Manchuria incidents such as the persecution of Koreans in the interior and the murder of Captain Nakamura, which carried the seeds of danger, had arisen one after the other. Chang Hsueh-liang's attitude towards Japan was firm and contemptuous. In the hope of a radical cure for the deterioration in the relations between the two countries, I consulted with Sung Tzu-wen,[1] Director of Financial Affairs, who was a key man in the Nanking Government, and sought means of lessening the tension in Manchuria. At that time Sung and I were on intimate terms and worked together to improve Sino-Japanese relations and in his company, therefore, I visited Manchuria, carried out a careful study on the spot and discussed possible means of solution. On the way Sung called in at Peking and persuaded Chang Hsueh-liang, who was staying there, to amend his attitude towards Japan

[1] T. V. Soong.

Further, in Dairen Sung and I, sitting in conference with Count Uchida, President of the S.M.R. and formerly Minister for Foreign Affairs, worked out in mutual agreement a basic plan of dealing with the problem of Manchuria.

I received the approval of the Government to this plan and proposed to leave Shanghai in company with Sung on September 20th, bound north by sea. Passage was reserved but the plan proved too late. On September 18th the 'Manchurian Incident' occurred suddenly in Mukden. Refusing to give in, I intended to proceed to Manchuria in company with Sung and endeavour to localize the incident in order to dispose of it. But while I was awaiting orders from the Japanese Government the situation got out of hand like a conflagration spreading through the prairie. Every device had failed. China submitted a complaint to the League of Nations and it became no longer possible to have recourse to diplomatic action.

Passages in a telegram I addressed to the Government at the time of the 'Manchurian Incident' read as follows:

1. The present action by the Army appears to be based on the theory known as the 'independence of the Supreme Command' and to ignore the Government. I have a feeling that all the unremitting efforts to build up our position abroad are being destroyed in a day. I cannot help feeling the utmost concern when I think of the country's future. I earnestly hope that as from now the Government will prohibit arbitrary action by the Army, that the will of the state will be entrusted to the Government alone, that military circles will be prevented from uttering irresponsible and injurious propaganda, that the Government will make its intentions perfectly clear as guide of the country.

2. The Chinese Republic, recognizing the seriousness of the situation, while retaining its usual doctrine of non-resistance so far as concerns military action, is resorting to every other possible means of retaliation. Not only is the guidance by the Party[1] and the Government solid but every thoroughly well-trained anti-Japanese organization is going into action. Severance of financial relations has not yet been enforced but student activity everywhere, which remained unmoved by the Korean incident, is having great effect. Anti-Japanese resentment is even greater than at the time of the 21 Demands[2] and is regarded as likely to become still worse. Situation is such that the outbreak of an unfortunate incident at any moment

[1] Kuomintang.
[2] *Vide* Chapter Three, s. 4.

THE 'MANCHURIAN INCIDENT' (1931-32) 65

in Manchuria or elsewhere cannot be ruled out. In this connection it is hoped that the Government will warn our Navy to exercise special caution. If by any chance army advances into north Manchuria, an immediate conflict with Russia may be expected and situation would become still graver.

3. Republic has at once adjusted internal quarrels. With strength united, traditional strategy of using the barbarian to control the barbarian[1] will be followed. Incident will first be reported to the League of Nations (recently relations have been made closer through connections of Sung Tzu-wen) and to parties to the Kellogg-Briand Pact. U.S. assistance will be invoked and under the influence of propaganda at home and abroad, plans will be adopted to compel the withdrawal of the Japanese Army, just as at the time of the restoration of Shantung. From now on the arrival in the Republic will not be allowed of officials that may be appointed to attempt to come to a satisfactory agreement about the problem of Manchuria or to enter into negotiations for the purpose. As a result of this incident we must be prepared for a virtual severance of diplomatic relations, which will endure while the Republic carries on with its scheme to expose the incident to the opinion of the world. (From the record of the International Tribunal.)

Japan's international credit, which had gone on growing from the time of *Meiji*, had been great. In one day our international status had crumbled and our credit was fast dwindling to nothing. To one who was engaged in the diplomatic sphere the thought was intolerable.

10. THE KWANTUNG ARMY TAKES OVER

Among the middle and upper ranks in the Army the move to reform the state both at home and abroad had gathered momentum in spite of the failure of the 'March Incident' (Chapter Two, s. 4). The Kwantung Army Staff, with the connivance of Nagata, Director of the Military Affairs Bureau in the War Ministry, secretly took a Port Arthur siege gun and placed it in position at the Mukden barracks of the Kwantung Army. At the same time propaganda by Shumei Okawa and his associates demanding direct action to solve the problem of Manchuria was stepped up. Colonel Doihara marked time in China. Kwantung Army manœuvres were pursued urgently night

[1] Old China regarded all foreign countries as barbarian.

E

and day, for the military had by now made up their mind that to defend Japan's legitimate rights in Manchuria there was nothing for it but to take protective action.[1]

The Ministry of Foreign Affairs was well aware that the situation was threatening and was watching developments with the closest attention. In Mukden Consul-General Hayashi had apprised himself of the dangerous situation and in his reports had urged the Government to take suitable action. In turn Foreign Minister Shidehara passed on this information to Minami, the War Minister, and besought his good offices to clean up the situation. Thereupon the latter despatched Major-General Tatekawa to Manchuria with instructions to the Kwantung Army to exercise circumspection. He was in fact directly enjoined by the Emperor to take measures to ensure that the Kwantung Army would not step off the rails. And yet, he called in at the Korean Army Headquarters on the way over and so arrived in Mukden later than the time scheduled. On his arrival, members of the Kwantung Army personnel staff took him off to a restaurant where he remained while the railway line was blown up and the northern barracks of Chang Hsueh-liang's troops were attacked by the Shimamoto detachment. Meanwhile the Kwantung Army were bombarding the Chinese barracks with the big cannon brought up for the purpose. The 'Manchurian Incident' had started.

Consul-General Hayashi and his deputy Morishima reported in detail what was happening and both, in their earnest efforts to prevent the affair getting out of hand, jeopardized their own safety. Consul Morishima called on Colonel Itagaki, high-ranking member of the Staff, and urged the possibilities of a diplomatic settlement, but Major Hanaya (member of the *Cherry Society*), who was present, flew into a passion and, drawing his long sword, threatened Morishima with these words: 'Interfere with the Prerogative of the Supreme Command at your peril!' Faced with the response that, once the Army was in motion, it was not for anyone to interfere, Consul Morishima had no option but to withdraw. At that very moment, under the guidance of Ishiwara, deputy Commander-in-Chief, the Army was fully mobilized and was already going straight ahead.

The Government, which had been unable to punish the assassins of Chang Tso-lin in the manner it had wished, was powerless when confronted with the Army. Once the independence of the Supreme Command had been politically acknowledged and support of the Army had become pronounced in the Privy Council, the military had become completely independent of the Government. What is more,

[1] [*sic*] In effect, to take direct action.

THE 'MANCHURIAN INCIDENT' (1931-32) 67

within the Army itself senior staff officers were pushing aside their superiors, while the Kwantung Army were practically in a position of independence of the Central Army command. The Nationalist movement, in its opposition to the Communist Party, had advanced a stage further than its platform of the independence of the Supreme Command, opposition to Army retrenchment and clarification of the Constitution, and was now preaching the need to establish the Defence State and the Reorganization of the Body Politic. Meanwhile the agitation among active officers and reservists had taken on a political tinge as a result of one section of the Seiyu Party joining forces with the military.

The Wakatsuki Cabinet moved heaven and earth to prevent the incident growing but the Japanese Army had got out of hand. For the authorities to think that the Army would fall in line with Government policy was pure foolishness. In fact the Kwantung Army, disregarding the wishes of the Government, entered Tsitsihar and Harbin in the north and advanced to the Amur River; in the south they took Chinchow and succeeded finally in driving Chang Hsueh-liang's troops from their last foothold in Manchuria. The Kwantung Army indeed went so far as to threaten that if the Government would not support the Army but instead adopted an obstructive attitude, then they would cut adrift and themselves rule Manchuria.

In consultation with Itagaki of the Staff, Colonel Doihara proceeded to Tientsin and persuaded the last of the Ching Emperors, the young Pu Yi, to come to Manchuria where he was installed, first as Chief Executive, and later as Emperor. The state of Manchoukuo[1] was hurriedly brought into being. Meanwhile foreign countries, in their ignorance of the true state of affairs in Japan, could only regard as a camouflaged smoke-screen to conceal military operations the messages, repeated to them by Japanese envoys in Europe and America on instructions from the Wakatsuki Cabinet, that the policy of the latter was to localize the Manchurian emergency.

---

[1] The Chinese name adopted by the Kwantung Army. It means Manchu Country and implies that the area, which we know as Manchuria, had become an independent state. The full title was Manchoutikuo (Manchu Imperial Country), but in general usage the 'Imperial' was dropped. From this point the title Manchoukuo will be used when the Government is intended and Manchuria when the area is seen through foreign eyes.

CHAPTER SIX

The Second Abortive *Coup d'état* (the 'October Incident')

1. THE 'OCTOBER INCIDENT', 1931

THE 'Manchurian Incident' had started and the plans of the Army were going full speed ahead. To add a glorious finishing touch the military thought it desirable to carry out without delay their plans for a reorganization of the Japanese Constitution. The 'March Incident' had failed because undisciplined civilians had been brought in. The *coup d'état* now planned must keep civilians out and be carried through by their own efforts. So, in the 'October Incident' that was planned by Colonel Hashimoto and others of the '*Cherry Society*', the objects were the same—the Government and the Diet were to be ousted, a reorganization of the state was to be carried through; if needs be, the weapon of assassination was to be used and a military administration should be put in power. But one different item was that in place of General Ugaki, Lieutenant-General Araki was to be put forward.

This *coup d'état* also failed, because it came to the ears of Minami, Minister for War, owing to a change of heart of one section of the conspirators (Lieutenant-Colonel Nemoto and others) and was nipped in the bud.

Prominent culprits in both incidents, such as Professor Okawa and Colonel Hashimoto, were arrested and awarded nominal punishment. The attitude of the military was perfunctory and disciplinary punishment had lost all effect. The public in the face of authority looked the other way and thereby aggravated military failings.

2. FORMATION OF THE 'BLOOD BROTHERHOOD'

When details of the 'March and October Incidents' became known within the Army and Navy and among the public, the single-minded young officers of the *Society of the Sword of Heaven* (Chapter One, s. 6) were roused to indignation. The associates of the Society had dedicated their lives to the rescue of their country. But the *coup d'état* planned by the middle group and the senior officers looked more like a plot to secure the personal advancement of those concerned. They were advocating a seizure of the reins of power in order to further their own ambitions. Once in power they were planning to fill the important roles in the Government themselves. In fine they were not possessed of the sacred spirit of reform; they were dreaming in terms of the elder statesmen of the Restoration; all they thought of was to seize power for themselves. Look at them! Day by day they took up their quarters in the red light district and drowned themselves in *saké* and sexual abandonment. The young officers in their indignation vowed they would have nothing to do with such traitors to the cause. They themselves would devote their lives to the rehabilitation of their country. Those that stood in the way of this sacred task must first be liquidated. They appointed themselves the successors to Takayama and the Shimpuren[1] and at the end of 1931 great numbers of them signed an oath in blood to form the *'Blood Brotherhood'*, each member of which was pledged to kill one man. In this way was formed a Body of Assassins under the leadership of a monk named Nissho Inouye.

Under this covenant, in order that the elements endangering the reorganization of the state should be liquidated, each covenanter had one person assigned to him, whom he swore to assassinate. The members ranged from cadets to active young officers; they began operations at once.

Those young officers that possessed the means of direct action linked up with reactionary factions, and proceeded to the work of assassination, causing no small disturbance of the peace and threat to society. At the same time assassination, centred in the Army and Navy, became a terrorizing weapon in the cause of state reorganization.

---

[1] 'Associates of the Sacred Wind' (a band that raised a revolt in Kumamoto in 1876).

3. ACTIVITIES OF THE 'BLOOD BROTHERHOOD'

Victims appeared in succession—Junnosuke Inouye, leader at the time of the Minsei Party, and in the world of finance men such as Takuma Dan, chief adviser to Mitsui. One by one distinguished leaders of liberal thought were assassinated, disquiet grew and business men vied with one another in donning bullet-proof waistcoats.

Though the Ministry of Justice could arrest and punish the assassins, it was unable to root out the basis of assassination, since this had the backing of the military. Legal sanctions against the most serious of all crimes, that of seeking to destroy social law and order, became a mockery in terms under the unscientific, sentimental principle that 'you must take into consideration the spirit (in which the deed was done)'. Those punished were soon discharged from prison and ready to perform yet greater 'tasks'. The great cause, and ethical duty, of law and order were thrown into the utmost confusion. And doubts arose as to whether a form of legalized fascism had not come into existence; public opinion was powerless.

4. DISSENSIONS WITHIN THE ARMY

The prime mover behind the attempt of the young officers of the *'Society of the Heavenly Sword'* to reform the Government of the country had been the Imperial Way School led by Generals of the Nationalist Faction, such as Masaki and Araki.

Members of the Imperial Way School were indignant at the decline in public morals that had arisen out of liberal sentiments and in their ideology placed the emphasis on national spirit. For them the Imperial troops lived a consecrated life—in any moment of crisis it was their duty to lay down their lives. It was accordingly necessary to fix the mind on the essential features of the national constitution, to follow the Imperial Way and to act as guides of public morals. Full of youthful vigour the young officers flocked in as followers of this doctrine. In their solicitude for the welfare of the country and their anxiety over public morals they clamoured for reform and spared not a thought for the anarchy they were causing.

At that time the main executive in the Army, thinking that discipline must be maintained, since these tendencies were occasioning chaos in the Army, did their best to control these extremist elements. In distinction from the Imperial Way School they were known as the

School of Control. At the same time the Army were the heirs of the old system of clan government and were keenly interested in political manœuvres. And so it came about that the Army planned schemes of reform that entailed the establishment of government based on the military and under military dictatorship, a fact that is clear enough from the 'March and October Incidents'. The Imperial Way School, since they advocated reform based on nationalist traditionalism, hated the Communist Party and were naturally anti-Russian. The Control School loved political intrigue as the spring on which the Army moved and, therefore, at the moment were absorbed in plans for dealing with China. Many had resided in China and had associations there. They were known as the China Party while others, that had Russian connections, belonged to what was known as the Russian Party.

So the Army was divided into the Imperial School and the Control School, which were subdivided into sections based on individual influences. Under the stress of clashing interests and sentiments, the habitual short temper of the soldier led to serious dissensions so that the control which should have been exercised by the senior officers was almost impracticable and the revolt of junior officers became ever more violent. The quality of the Army had almost disappeared. There were even soldiers that wished to put forward members of the Imperial Family to stage a revolt under the aegis of the Imperial Standard: such plots were staged by military or right-wing agitators.

Such was the Army. It embarked on the task of national reform linked up in a relationship of mutual interests with outside right and left elements. The result was chaos and anarchy. Taking advantage of this confusion, internal and external schemes to stir up disorder in Japan were given an opportunity of complete success.

CHAPTER SEVEN

The Last Party Cabinet: the Inukai Cabinet (1931)

1. THE CHINA POLICY OF THE INUKAI CABINET

THE Wakatsuki Cabinet fell at the end of 1931. At that time there still lingered on some echoes of former liberal democratic principles and the Genro, in the hope that a Party Cabinet might still save the situation, entrusted the task to Tsuyoshi Inukai, who had become President of the Seiyu Party on the death of General Tanaka. Having only recently come into the Party from outside, Inukai formed his cabinet, with the new star of the Party, Tsutomu Mori, as Chief Secretary. He made Minister for War General Araki, the favourite of the young officers and the so-called head of the Imperial Way School. As Foreign Minister he sent for the Ambassador to France, his son-in-law, Kenkichi Yoshizawa, who had been many years Minister to China and was a mine of experience. Admiral Osumi became Minister for the Navy.

As a known fighter Mori had considerable prestige in the Seiyu Party. In the Tanaka Cabinet, as Vice-Minister for Foreign Affairs, he had worked in with the Army and had stood for an out-and-out forward policy (*vide* Chapter Four, s. 4). He echoed the Army and Navy call for reform and himself nursed the ambition to set up a political dictatorship. He hoped that the 'Manchurian Incident' would develop in such a way that Japan could establish her supremacy in East Asia.

In order to maintain itself in power the Seiyu Party trailed behind the headstrong Mori. Many people wondered anxiously what policy would be adopted by a cabinet with such a man in the key position of Chief Secretary and the focus of their attention was the China problem.

2. INUKAI'S AIMS

Inukai had been a friend of Sun Yat-sen and had no small understanding of the Chinese Revolution. Nor, in view of his past record, did there seem any reason why he should blunder in his estimate of the situation at home and abroad. Moreover, as a politician who had opposed clan government, he had no liking for the military and had indeed in earlier days attacked them in the Diet. He held entirely different views on a China policy from those held by the late General Tanaka. This indeed was the main reason why Prince Saionji had proposed his name. It was his aim to prepare the ground for a speedy solution of the 'Manchurian Incident' and a restoration of relations between China and Japan and, without saying a word to Mori, he secretly despatched a knight errant[1] named Chochi Sugano to Nanking. In this way a situation of oil and water developed in the Cabinet between himself on the one hand and Mori's followers in the Cabinet, together with the military, on the other.

Ambassador Yoshizawa, on his way home via Moscow, studied the Manchurian storm-centre and then assumed his position as Foreign Minister. In Manchuria military operations had been concluded and the question now was the form of government it was to be given under Japanese occupation. To establish its independence the Kwantung Army had sent Colonel Doihara to Tientsin to work on Pu Yi and had obtained his consent to their plans. Armed with a blue-print for the future administration, Vice-Chief of Staff Itagaki had come to Tokyo for a conference and so Yoshizawa spent his days deliberating with the Army on the future status of Manchuria.

But the Government was in no position to reject the views of the Kwantung Army.

[1] Lit. *ronin*.

CHAPTER EIGHT

The First Battle of Shanghai (1932)

1. TROUBLE BREWING IN SHANGHAI

THE 'Manchurian Incident' set alight the anti-Japanese campaign in China, and Shanghai, which was the centre of Chinese xenophobia, was at once caught up in a violent storm of anti-Japanese agitation. The biggest industrial works were the Japanese-owned cotton-spinning mills, which now encountered large-scale strikes engineered by communist agitators. The Chinese Communist Party was straining every nerve to bring about the expulsion of capitalism from China. Compared with former times, the anti-Japanese campaign had a stronger political tinge; the 'Manchurian Incident' was to be expanded to the point of inviting a rupture between Japan and China.

Stationed in Shanghai was the 19th Route Army. It did not pay much attention to orders from Nanking and the troops were left wing and keenly anti-Japanese.

The Shanghai Japanese, who had already suffered for a long time past from anti-Japanese strikes, were in a state of nervous tension. The success of Japanese military operations in Manchuria hardened their views. Even managers of branches of the big companies, who had hitherto maintained a moderate attitude, began to proclaim, in common with old 'China hands', that this anti-Japanese agitation must be met with firmness, and they refused to listen to my arguments in favour of patience and prudence. I continued to advise them not to be taken in by schemes that would only invite trouble but instead they sent representatives to Manchuria to waylay Yoshizawa and ask for my recall. At the same time Chief Secretary Mori openly published wild arguments in favour of vigorous action, giving the impression that the Cabinet was on the point of taking a strong, direct line in China.

Relations between Japan and China showed every sign of approaching a crisis.

2. I TALK MATTERS OVER IN TOKYO, 1932

Not only was I apprehensive as to the policy of the Cabinet; I had no means of checking up on Yoshizawa's aims. I therefore obtained permission to return to Tokyo in order to report the situation in detail and to submit my views. I was prepared, if necessary, to tender my resignation. The time was early in January 1932, a week after Yoshizawa had taken over.

The new Foreign Minister was immersed in the immediate problem of the establishment of a state of Manchuria and had no time to spare over the question of Shanghai, so that in spite of my representations the interview was postponed from day to day. I was strongly advising the Government that the situation in Shanghai was grave, that the attitude of its leading members, which was causing misunderstanding at home and abroad, should be revised and that the Japanese Government should make a public declaration in clear terms explaining the justice of its policy. But the Government had not the leisure to study the problem of China as a whole, since its attention was engrossed by the problem of the new state to be set up in Manchuria.

Whenever the Army took up a strong line in the north of China, the Navy, as it were in a spirit of emulation, stiffened its back in Shanghai. In the squadron there were also members of the '*Blood Brotherhood*'. The commander of the naval landing party suggested to the Navy Department that the anti-Japanese Headquarters near the Northern Station should be raided and forced to close down, and asked for approval. When I heard that the competent officials proposed to give their sanction, I was appalled at their recklessness. Such a step would not only give an excellent pretext to anti-Japanese agitators but the act itself would amount to a clash between the Japanese and Chinese troops. How indeed was a naval landing party of 700 or 800 going to handle the situation to which it would give rise? The project was dropped.

On the score that the situation in Shanghai had deteriorated, I succeeded in getting an interview with Yoshizawa. The new Minister had already received a full report of my views from Tani, Director of the Asia Bureau. With my suggestions he expressed entire agreement and requested me to return at once and use every effort to forestall anything untoward happening in Shanghai. But he decided that the moment was not opportune to issue a statement of the Cabinet policy towards China in an attempt to clear away misunderstanding. Though, therefore, I was returning to China, suspicions that the new Cabinet was going to revert to the direct policy of General Tanaka were not dispelled.

I returned to Shanghai in haste.

During my absence the situation had become acute. Praying and beating the drum, *Nichiren*[1] priests had been going along a Chinese main street regarded as a nest of anti-Japanese agitators when they were set on and knocked down by a Chinese mob. Japanese *ronin*, who had drifted into Shanghai, had snatched up swords and run to the rescue. Such fracas were becoming more and more violent and as the anti-Japanese agitation intensified, so the attitude of the Japanese had stiffened beyond measure.

3. THE FIRST BATTLE OF SHANGHAI

I had joined the *Nagasaki Maru* in Kobe (air services between Japan and China had not yet been opened). Newspapers and radio reported that conditions in Shanghai had worsened and, as the ship left Nagasaki, we learnt that Japanese and Chinese troops had clashed.

When we arrived in Shanghai, it was to meet a deplorable situation. Since there was no telling when law and order might not be disturbed by the high tide of anti-Japanese agitation that was running, foreign troops stationed in Shanghai had agreed to joint measures of defence and had been allotted different areas. The Japanese landing party had taken action in conformity therewith and fighting had broken out between it and the Chinese troops so that a state of war had ensued (January 28th, 1932).

Including relief detachments from the ships lying at anchor, the naval landing party amounted at most to about 1000 'white leggings'. Under the guidance of German advisers, they had built up strong trenches defended by railway guns. But what could they do against the several divisions of the 19th Route Army? However well they fought, they must be annihilated if left to their own resources. And 30,000 settlers and all Japanese property in Shanghai would be at the mercy of the Chinese Army. Great numbers of Japanese settlers crowded down to the jetties in the hope of taking ship. Meanwhile Chinese residents, dragging hand-carts piled up with household belongings, converged on the Garden Bridge near the Japanese Consulate (office of the Legation) in the hope of finding refuge in the International Settlement. The line of defence of the landing party was strained to breaking point; its rear was menaced by guerilas.

[1] Japanese Buddhist sect.

It had come to this, that without reinforcement by the Army the Navy could not discharge its duty of defending Japanese lives and property in Shanghai. Having, therefore, ascertained the views of the Army and Navy, I requested the Government to despatch troops at the earliest possible moment to save the Japanese residents from annihilation.

The Chinese Government proceeded to arraign Japan as the aggressor before the League of Nations and the Council, which was then sitting at Geneva, at once took up the appeal. Since the 'Manchurian Incident' Japan had been placed in a very awkward position and now the outbreak of fighting in Shanghai added to her troubles. But it was out of the question that I should tamely submit to the annihilation of thousands of unarmed Japanese, together with their vast holdings, for it was only right that Japan should defend her treaty rights in Shanghai. The Army acceded to direct requests from Army and Navy representations on the spot and decided to send troops.

4. TRUCE AGREEMENT

The Navy formed No. 3 Squadron under the command of Vice-Admiral Kichisaburo Nomura and, placing on board a mixed brigade of 10,000 from Kurume, sent it post haste to Shanghai. Meanwhile the Army mobilized the 9th Division under the command of Lieutenant-General Kenkichi Ueda and sent him to Shanghai as commander of the forces.

It was considered that rather more than one division accompanied by a specially equipped battery would suffice to redress the balance, but even with this strength the 19th Route Army could not be driven out of the Shanghai area, hard though the Army fought to deploy from its base. Thereupon three more divisions were added and General Shirakawa was appointed Commander-in-Chief. He arrived at the beginning of March and finally succeeded in dislodging the Chinese forces from the Shanghai district and restoring law and order.

I decided that the moment had come for a 'cease fire' and called on General Shirakawa. It took me half a day to persuade him to issue the order but, when he did, it served to prevent the affair becoming an international incident. The General Assembly of the League of Nations opened on March 3rd but the meeting passed off without trouble, fighting having ceased.

The defence of the international city of Shanghai being the joint task of the local forces of the powers concerned, the maintenance of law and order was equally their joint concern. The truce negotiations between Japan and China were, therefore, opened under the good offices of the United States, Britain, France and Italy. Since it was to be a truce agreement, the Army maintained that the Prerogative of the Supreme Command was involved and, accordingly, the Divisional Commander Ueda was appointed our senior plenipotentiary, with myself as his deputy. But both the foreign envoys and the Chinese were accustomed to negotiating with the Japanese Minister alone. So, as matters turned out, the burden of the negotiations fell on my shoulders.

The negotiations continued from early in March to the beginning of May and, what with the Army and Navy taking their stand on the Imperial Prerogative, the surveillance of the League of Nations, and the necessity of negotiating in an international city with representatives of the Chinese and of the foreign powers, my task was no light one. It was a herculean task to bring these complicated, difficult negotiations to a successful conclusion.

When the truce agreement was on the point of conclusion, and the atmosphere in Shanghai was returning to normal, the Japanese Forces carried out a Review on the Emperor's Birthday, April 29th. At the same time the Japanese residents organized a celebration in the New Park, attended by detachments from the Army and Navy, schools and residents and many foreign guests. At the height of the proceedings a Korean named Yun Tae Gil belonging to an independence movement threw a bomb, which caused a shambles—Kawabata, Chief of the Residents' Association, and General Shirakawa were killed; Commander-in-Chief Nomura, Consul-General Murai, Divisional-Commander Ueda and the Secretary of the Residents' Association were all seriously wounded; a woman employee of the Japanese Consulate lost an eye; and I was wounded so seriously as to be brought to death's door.

Refusing to give in, I carried on the final truce negotiations from the hospital and brought them safely to a conclusion on May 5th. The text of the agreement having been drawn up at the British Consulate-General, the scene of the negotiations, the document was brought round to my bed in the hospital, where, racked with pain and in danger of my life, I managed to complete the numerous signatures required. I said then to Chang the Chinese Secretary: 'Relations between Japan and China must now enter a state of amity. I pray that this document may be the starting-point of future good relations between our two countries.' At that moment it was a question whether my life could be saved. The Chinese Secretary returned to the council chamber and in impressive tones disclosed my message. When all the signatures were completed, the operating table was wheeled in and one leg was amputated.

Peace having been restored, the Japanese forces were withdrawn from the Shanghai area and conditions returned to normal.

CHAPTER NINE

Assassination of the Aged Prime Minister

1. MILITARY GOVERNMENT IN MANCHURIA

However much Prime Minister Inukai longed to restrain the military, he could not prevent the Kwantung Army from setting up the Manchurian State. The Cabinet had perforce to agree that Manchurian questions should be taken from the control of the Ministry for Foreign Affairs, a new Manchurian Affairs Bureau (under the control of the War Office) was set up and for all practical purposes Manchuria came under the administration of the Army.

Troops released from the Shanghai area were transferred to Manchuria, where they were used to maintain order. The question of Chinchow had been cleared up and the Great Wall of China terminating at Shanhaikwan was taken as the boundary of Manchuria, from which all unsatisfactory characters had been rooted out. The question whether or not the province of Jehol should be included then arose, and, since it was north of the Wall, the decision was that it should be incorporated, so the Army was on the move again, this time to drive out the Chinese troops from Jehol.

2. ASSASSINATION OF PRIME MINISTER INUKAI, MAY 1932

Like the Wakatsuki Cabinet before it, the Inukai Cabinet could not directly oppose the military plan to occupy Manchuria. Not only so but the Chief Secretary and other members of the Seiyu Party were constantly conspiring with extremists in the Army and Navy and acting in collusion with them. None the less it is true that the aims of Inukai himself were very far from fitting in with the plans of the military. The Prime Minister was a genuine Party man and from an early stage had figured on the black list of the young officers. On May 15th, 1932, a party of members of the *'Blood Brotherhood'*, led by a naval sub-lieutenant, broke into his residence and called him into a Japanese-style room. Saying, 'Let us talk it over,' the Prime Minister endeavoured to win over these strange visitors, who were carrying revolvers, but the last word was with the visitors. At the signal, 'Why waste words, shoot', the pistols were discharged.

Covered in blood the Prime Minister fell on the *tatami*. Japanese democracy had already been dealt a mortal blow by the assassination of Kei Hara, President of the Seiyu Party, the first Party Prime Minister (November 1921), followed by that of Hamaguchi, President of the Minsei Party (April 1931), who had both fallen victims to assassins from the right wing. But the assassination of Inukai, the last of the Party Cabinet leaders, was the most pitiful of all.

With its head the Seiyu Cabinet fell. Mori was later stricken down by illness.

Owing to misunderstanding there were few active list officers among the assassins, of whom however most came from the Navy. The principal naval culprits were sentenced to five years' imprisonment by court martial but the sentences were reduced and they were shortly released and appointed to positions of trust. This was the only punishment meted out at that time to officers on the active list who broke into the residences of Government highest-ranking officials and slaughtered them in cold blood.

That was the end of party government. By terrorism the Government's defences had been breached. There was no longer any direct obstacle to the manœuvres of the military. Not that there were wanting among the upper classes and thinking people generally those that deeply deplored this state of affairs and still hoped that, if the military could not be held in check, their actions might at least be toned down a little, lest they lead the country to ruin. The Genro, for instance, tried to use the strength of the Navy to restrain the Army or trusted to the power of diplomacy to redress the balance. In other words, by alternate manipulation of different political influences he tried to prevent government by extremists. But so far from such temporizing tactics serving to stem the tide, once the flood had broken the dykes the forces of disaster swept on with ever-increasing momentum.

It had been said that at the time of the 'Manchurian Incident' Foreign Minister Shidehara had made an urgent telephone call to Kanaya, the Chief of the General Staff. The fact gave rise to the argument among the senior staff officers that the prestige of the Supreme Command could not be maintained if it were open to the Foreign Minister to summon the Chief of Staff to the 'phone in this manner. Thereupon the

Army appointed Marshal H.I.H. Prince Kanin Chief of the General Staff. The purpose of this manœuvre was to employ a member of the Imperial Family as a robot so that the staff officers could move the Army about as they pleased and use the prestige of the Imperial Family to intimidate the Government and the public. It was of a piece with the deification of the Emperor. Not to be outdone, the Navy made H.I.H. Prince Fushimi Chief of the Naval General Staff. In practice all this meant that the staff officers had acquired still greater power to manipulate the Supreme Command.

3. REFLECTIONS ON THE COLLAPSE OF PARTY GOVERNMENT

The *Meiji* restoration came about when the tide of the outside world beat on the shores of Japan. The 'outside'[1] daimyo of the Tokugawa regime were the mainspring of that change. As a result, in the *Meiji* era there was clan government by the former daimyos of Satsuma and Choshu who had overthrown the Tokugawa. In opposition to it were political party influences, which little by little spread the doctrine of democratic freedom and developed into parties based on the advocacy of particular political theories. Such rapid progress did the parties make that they had begun to measure up to the military, who had inherited the power of the clans. The appearance on the scene of the modern-type political party was round about the time of the First World War.

Taking her place in the general trend of world affairs, Japan had, little by little, developed a political structure based on the nation as a whole. Naturally enough the movement had stirred up a violent reaction, in which liberal thinkers and political parties fought against the reactionaries and the military clans. But the former were found wanting in strength of character and they made mistakes while the people generally lacked political training. So they went down in utter defeat under the direct onslaught of the forces of barbarism. The curtain was rung down on the assassination of Prime Minister Inukai. That was the end of party government.

---

[1] Not hereditary feudatories of Tokugawa, particularly Satsuma and Choshu.

BOOK TWO

The Revolt of February 26th, 1936

Navy Cabinets of Saito and Okada

CHAPTER ONE

The Navy Cabinets (1932–36)

1. FORMATION OF SAITO CABINET, 1932

IN choosing a successor to Inugai, the *Genro* faced the disturbing thought that purely party cabinets merely invited assassination. A counsel of expedience would have been to let the military form their own government but this would have been tantamount to approving 'direct action', which was the last thing desired. The solution was to adopt a Premier who was himself a product of the Navy but was at the same time moderate in his views—the naval veteran Minoru Saito, former Governor-General of Korea. It was thought also that Saito might be able to restrain naval extremists in their attitude to the coming disarmament question. Araki remained as War Minister; Admiral Okada, later succeeded by Admiral Osumi, became Navy Minister. Count Chika Uchida, President of the South Manchuria Railway, was pressed willy-nilly into service as Foreign Minister. Two veterans of the Seiyu and Minsei Parties—Takahashi and Yamamoto—also joined the Cabinet. Subsequent cabinets followed this pattern.

Internationally Japan had become the target of criticism. At home the people, menaced by the threat of assassination, were shaken by a constant stream of propaganda that the country was in danger. The task of the new Cabinet in following a policy of moderation was no light one, since the people lacked democratic training. The country merely followed any strong lead and the voice of thinking people met with little response.

2. SECESSION FROM THE LEAGUE OF NATIONS, 1933

By nature Saito was not a man to initiate action; he took things as he found them. For a moment there ensued a lull. The Kwantung

Army were busy forming the new state, from which question the Government stood aloof. Manchuria might for all the world have been someone else's business. Unhappily Japan's responsibility for Manchuria was *not* someone else's business; military operations were operations by Japan and the Japanese Government itself must shoulder responsibility. According to the *Meiji* Constitution the Prime Minister was simply the servant and adviser of the Emperor. But, since the Prime Minister was no more than the controller of the Cabinet, once the country faced a crisis and a strong hand was required to assume full responsibility for their guidance, this arrangement became unsuitable. How much more then when the question of the new state had escaped from the grasp of the Prime Minister, who could no longer control it!

The Lytton Mission sent by the League of Nations carried out a prolonged investigation on the spot and, after visiting Japan, drew up a detailed report. Meanwhile the foundation of the new state made rapid progress in the hands of the Kwantung Army and Pu Yi assumed the position of Administrator under the title of Chief Executive (March 1st, 1932). So the state of Manchoukuo was born. The next question was that of recognition, which of course the Army desired. But it was realized that recognition by Japan would embarrass her standing with the League of Nations, which had still to debate the Lytton Report. Whether to recognize or not had become a burning question, as to which Foreign Minister Uchida considered the sensible course was to recognize the new state in order to stabilize the local situation and let the Army go ahead. The Foreign Office thereupon bethought themselves of the precedent of Britain's recognition of Iraq and framed a Japan-Manchoukuo Protocol by the signing of which Japan formally recognized Manchoukuo (August 15th, 1932). Japan's attitude was thereby determined.

When the League of Nations took up the Lytton Report, the General Assembly deliberated whether or not to adopt the conclusion that Japan was the aggressor. The Government had sent Yosuke Matsuoka as its representative, but for all his skill in the English language the decision that Japan was the aggressor was a foregone conclusion. Thereupon Matsuoka walked out of the Assembly (January 1933). The Government then announced that Japan had seceded from the League of Nations (February 27th), thereby making it clear that she had committed herself to the foundation of Manchoukuo and that she would stand apart from the comity of nations in her intention to develop that country. This was the most serious diplomatic step that she had taken since the start of the emergency. At the time an Imperial

Edict had been issued, declaring it incumbent on civil and military officials loyally, without deviation, to fulfil the exact nature of their duties and announcing the dominant feature of the policy that the Government would pursue at home and abroad in order to effect a settlement of the Manchurian emergency, as well as to deal with the situation arising out of Japan's departure from the League of Nations. The purpose of the Edict was to advise the people that our international relations were none too good, to urge the military to be circumspect and to direct the country as a whole to devote every effort to bring about a settlement of the 'Manchurian Incident'.

It goes without saying that, if this self-reliant, independent policy was to succeed, it demanded the utmost faith in the justice of the cause and thorough statesmanship. But not only did the Army utterly ignore the Edict but the nation proved itself lacking in both perseverance and discipline, while the necessary guidance and statecraft of the Government were non-existent.

With his task half completed, Uchida resigned on the score of ill-health and Ambassador Hirota on return from Moscow succeeded him. Shortly after I became Vice-Minister.

3. OKADA CABINET COMES ON THE SCENE, 1934

Lurking behind the Saito Cabinet, which all but made a virtue of inaction, were the military and allied reformers, who certainly were anything but inactive. The Kwantung Army were going ahead with work on the foundations of Manchoukuo while at home the reformers stepped up the pace. The secret work of the left wing and the underground activity of the communists were coming into prominence; even among members of the judiciary some signs of Red infection were observable. The case of the Imperial Rayon Company, in which the Vice-Minister of the Treasury was alleged to have received bribes, proved the last straw. The newspapers were filled with the scandal for days until the Government, convicted at least of laxity, fell. (Afterwards it became clear that the driving force behind the case was a plot to cause mischief in political circles.) Admiral Okada, who had played an important part in bringing about the London Naval Agreement, formed a cabinet on Saito's recommendation. The accused in the Rayon case, after several years' violent recrimination in the courts, were all found innocent.

Okada's Cabinet was merely a continuation of Saito's, but with the march of events its mission became more important and difficult.

Foreign Minister Hirota remained, as also General Senjuro Hayashi, who had succeeded Araki. Osumi, too, stayed in office at the Navy.

In its characteristic attitude of the passive onlooker the Okada Cabinet was very like that of Saito, but during the three years of the two Cabinets events occurred that seriously influenced the next stage of development of the Manchurian business. The first was the breakdown of the Naval Disarmament Conference. The second was the inception of activities in North China, resulting in a further deterioration in Sino-Japanese relations. The third was internal discord, which became acute.

CHAPTER TWO

Failure of Naval Disarmament Talks

1. THE WASHINGTON CONFERENCE (1921-22) IN RETROSPECT

BY the Washington Conference (1921-22) the fleets of Britain, U.S. and Japan had been fixed at a ratio of 5:5:3. But Japanese naval experts had been profoundly dissatisfied. For one thing it made Japan inferior to other countries. For another, it imposed on something so changeable as a navy absolute inferiority which there was no means of remedying. Finally the assent to such a ratio was itself considered an infringement of the Prerogative of the Supreme Command as well as of Japan's sovereign rights. The experts were obsessed by the actual figure[1] and paid no attention to the extent of Japan's natural resources and degree of economic strength, in a word to national power. And now the Navy were aroused by the sight of the Army's jubilation over events in Manchuria and their attitude began to run to extremes. In their determination to brook no interference, both the Navy and the Army went straight ahead with their own plans for expansion. In one sense it was a struggle to take the lead in the political arena.

At the Washington Conference the naval technical expert had been Vice-Admiral, later Admiral, Kanji Kato. He had strenuously opposed the ratio. Afterwards, as Commander-in-Chief of the combined fleet and as Chief of the Naval General Staff, he had never ceased his fight against disarmament, emphasizing the theory of the independence of the Supreme Command and claiming that any retrenchment that had not been agreed by the Supreme Command was a breach of the Constitution. His successor, Admiral Suetsugu, inherited his views.

In the Ministry for the Navy, Kato and Suetsugu, had been opposed to the High Command. They represented what was known as the Fleet

[1] 5:5:3. (It was the 3, as against 5:5, that wounded their pride.)

89

School and their views gradually carried all before them in the Ministry. The opposition of the extremists in this school to the moderate views of the High Command gave rise to passion, but on the point of the necessity for expansion there was in practice little difference of opinion. But the question of the ratification of the agreement reached in London (1930) as to the ratio of auxiliary vessels became a serious political issue, when once more the constitutional bearing of the Supreme Command Prerogative became the subject of argument.

2. PROBLEM OF THE SUPREME COMMAND PREROGATIVE

Naval propaganda increased in violence and both the Army and the Nationalists lent their support. In the Privy Council, Miyoji Ito and Kentaro Kaneko and their followers agreed with the naval extremists. They endorsed the view that under the Constitution the prerogative of the Supreme Command was paramount and they hesitated to ratify a treaty that was not approved by the Naval General Staff. It was forgotten that the prerogative was vested in the Emperor.

Prime Minister Hamaguchi and Foreign Minister Shidehara pointed out that the London Treaty had been signed in consultation with the Naval General Staff and that matters such as military numerical strength, which did not come within the Army's Supreme Command (Art. 10), fell within the responsibility of the Government and insisted on ratification, though they were compelled to agree to the theory of the independence of the Supreme Command, which had become a political one.

3. ASSASSINATION OF PREMIER HAMAGUCHI, 1931

In such an atmosphere was Hamaguchi assassinated (April 1931). Baron Reijiro Wakatsuki succeeded him. This was after the attempted *coup d'état* of March but before the 'Manchurian Incident'. Thereafter Army and Navy vied with each other in their common discontent with the existing state of affairs and one incident followed another. Backed by the theory of the independence of the Supreme Command the fighting services came in time to ignore the Government in their actions.

4. DENUNCIATION OF THE NAVAL TREATIES, 1934

The Washington and London Disarmament Treaties (1922 and 1930) were the basis of the conference opened in London in 1935 which was to examine the problem in its broader aspects. In it the Okada Cabinet faced a ticklish issue.

After ratification of the previous London Treaty the strong line advocated by the Fleet School had gradually gathered so much influence that milder counsels were no longer heard. What it was now demanding was that the shackles of the existing treaties should be thrown off. The slogan that 1936 and 1937 would be years of crisis originated in fact in the Navy, which now fixed on abrogation as the immediate objective.

The Cabinet included Tokonami, Yamazaki and Uchida (Nobunari)[1] from the Seiyu Party, but they were there as individuals, who left the Party to join the Cabinet. Since the Seiyu Party itself, under its President Suzuki, acting as the opposition, abetted naval extremists, the political outlook continued to deteriorate. The 'crisis' slogan synchronized with an agitation to denounce Professor Minobe's theory that the Emperor was an organ of state, and the argument that the national structure was divinely inspired and its own justification was blatantly paraded before the people until the weak Government itself was forced more than once publicly to acknowledge this irrational theory. The desire of the Navy to denounce the treaties and the contention of the Foreign Office that the Washington system should be maintained were in violent opposition but the Cabinet silenced the Foreign Office, and in December 1934 issued formal notice of abrogation. At the London Conference in 1935 Japan advanced its suggestion of a 'common upper limit' in men-of-war construction, within the bounds of which each country should be free to build. Britain and the U.S. did not agree and Japan's representatives then withdrew from the conference. Not only had it become impossible to bind Japan in any new treaty but by her notice of abrogation Japan had freed herself of all previous commitments.

5. CONSEQUENCES OF ABROGATION OF NAVAL TREATIES

I have already explained that abrogation was not merely a question for experts on naval construction; it affected the fundamental principles of our national policy. Following as it did on the Manchurian affair

[1] Not to be confused with Count Uchida.

it was a major problem calculated radically to weaken Japan's international standing—something to be undertaken only after the most serious deliberation. And yet the Okada Cabinet, without so much as attempting to rein in the hotheads in the Navy, or placing the issue fairly and squarely before the country, were content to constitute themselves spokesmen for the Navy, merely that they might avoid internal disturbance. The Manchurian question had led Japan to depart from the League of Nations. Now she was denouncing naval treaties that formed the basis on which the Washington organization had been set up. She had cast aside the last defence that shielded her international status. Henceforth she would walk alone and unfettered, but that also meant that she was isolated because she had antagonized the world. Isolation breeds disquiet, it invites a sense of inferiority, of nervous irritation. Hence the constant talk of the 'country in danger' with its rising crescendo of militarism. No longer was there any brake on the Army and Navy, which had gained the upper hand. There was no barrier to prevent completion of military preparedness and total mobilization of the nation. Side by side the Army and Navy pressed forward to the establishment of the Defence State.

Rejection of disarmament had a direct bearing on the China problem. It meant the breakdown of the system set up at Washington. On the part of the Army the feeling arose that any restraint on its continental adventures had been removed. The direct results were to be seen in North China. All these moves were watched by the powers with vigilant eye. But the Army and Navy, for all they were the two wings of national defence, were keen rivals. Their emulation was not confined to their share in the Budget. It took place also in the political ring, where details of internal and external policy were decided. In such matters they claimed parity. What this amounted to was that abroad the Army and Navy had cast off all restraint, while at home there was no one to hold them back.

And now took place the distribution of rewards for the Manchurian affair. The Army insisted and the Government had not the will-power to resist. So those who had violated an Imperial edict, those who had set themselves against the policy of the Government, those who had carried out the Manchurian upheaval in a spirit of revolt, these were the men handed national awards by the Okada Cabinet. There could be no shorter cut to a second and a third Manchurian upheaval type, however the nation might look askance at the conferment of peerages and decorations for such services.

CHAPTER THREE

Military Aims in Japan and in Manchuria

1. PLAN OF STATE REORGANIZATION; THE 'DEFENCE STATE'

IN their origin the Manchurian upheaval and the agitation to reform Japan sprang from the same root. Both borrowed largely from the theories of Professor Shumei Okawa, formerly of the S.M.R. Research Department. In Manchuria his views on the assimilation of the five races, his utopia,[1] his opposition to moneyed interests, all these composite right and left ideas of his were taken up by staff officers in the Kwantung Army and by them put into effect (*vide* also Book One, Chapter Two, s. 3). The *Concordia Society*, which was to guide the country under one party, was formed in imitation of the Nazi organization. Further, an agreement was made providing for economic co-operation between the two countries, on the basis of which the Manchurian Heavy Industries Company was formed under the control of the Nissan Company.[2] This new company, together with the S.M.R., took a leading part in the industrial development of the country.

From its inception the S.M.R. Research Department had stood as the brain of the Kwantung Army. It was a vast organization with offices in Dairen and Tokyo. Its duties were to study and draft plans for all manner of political and economic projects; for a long time Okawa had directed its operations. Staff officers used this department to draft a far-reaching plan of reform. This was their secret source of inspiration. Among the plotters it was known as '*The Book of the Tiger*'. As might have been expected from its author, its contents covered a wide field and took the form of idealized Naziism. Only a few leaders (the senior staff officers) knew the whole of the book. Associates,

[1] Lit. 'Paradise' (on earth) under the rule of the 'Kingly way'. The reference was to the supposed golden age under the rule of the mythical, or semi-mythical, Chinese Kings of the dawn of history.
[2] Japanese company hitherto interested mainly in the production of motor vehicles.

with whom they were secretly in touch, put the ideas into operation, each in his own section of Government departments, in their aim to effect a reorganization of the state. In their actual operations they used left-wing tactics. They supplied the fuse of the Manchurian explosion and in the agitation to reorganize Japan they were at the epicentre.

2. THE CONTINENT AS JAPAN'S FIRST LINE OF DEFENCE

Having occupied Manchuria and founded the state of Manchoukuo, the Japanese Army, which had assumed the joint[1] responsibility for its defence, took a more careful look round and was startled at the seriousness of its task.

The remnants of Chang Hsueh-liang's army were scattered over North China with Peking as their centre, and not only were they supposed to be plotting to recover Manchuria but Soviet Russia, which was engaged on its Five-Year Plan (begun on October 1st, 1928) and was fast expanding its military strength, encircled Manchoukuo on three sides and it was only a question of time before it joined forces with Chinese troops to menace Manchoukuo. The Chinese Communist Army too was growing at its headquarters in Yenan. Obviously the Kwantung Army must lose no time in preparing plans to meet this new situation in East Asia. But when it was engaged in this grave duty, it was intolerable that anything like the existing Japanese Government should be allowed to exist, seeing that it had no conception of Japan's mission on the continent and all too often failed to co-operate. Very well then. The Government of the country must be radically changed and a position prepared in which the Army could fulfil its new mission on the continent—in fine the Army must build a true Defence State.

Such were the views that dominated the Army and overflowed into public discussions, putting foreign countries on the *qui vive*.

For her part Soviet Russia was paying the closest attention to Japanese operations in Manchuria. She foresaw that, using Manchuria as a base, Japan might one day invade the Maritime Provinces and Siberia, and she hastened to take defensive measures. Under the second Five-Year Plan the Far East was to be industrialized, immigrants settled on the land, munitions works established, the railway track was to be doubled and a string of strongpoints round Manchuria constructed. And in case the Japanese Army should ever invade Russian territory, a new Jewish State of Birobijan was founded near to the

[1] In theory; actually it was sole.

military centre of Habarovsk, in order to take advantage of Jewish influence over world opinion (May 7th, 1934). As a counterbalance to the Japan-Manchoukuo Agreement, Russia concluded a joint defence agreement with Outer Mongolia (March 12th, 1936). When the second Five-Year Plan got under way (begun 1933) Russian military establishments in the Far East were extended almost overnight and Manchoukuo was becoming rapidly encompassed by Soviet Russia.

However fast the Kwantung Army pushed on its preparations, therefore, Soviet Russia went one better and began to pass Japan in the race. But flushed with success, the Army was in an exalted mood, convinced that there was nothing too difficult for it to accomplish. Wherever the finger of fame beckoned, egged on by its hotch-potch of right and left theories of reform, heedless of the need or prudence in handling affairs of state, the Army went on stirring up trouble. This was a truly lamentable state of affairs because it provided the Comintern with just the right terrain in which to operate its Trojan tactics of overthrowing the enemy from within.[1] Even before the Manchurian emergency, as early as 1928–29 the Sorge-Ozaki spy-ring was operating in China and Japan.

3. THE PROBLEM OF INNER MONGOLIA

In the defence of Manchoukuo one of the most vital points was the Chinese frontier, i.e. the North China-Inner Mongolian territory. If perchance Russian influence were to succeed in penetrating via Outer Mongolia to a point where it could join forces with the Chinese Red Army in North China, then Manchoukuo would be completely surrounded by Soviet Russia, and China would fall into the Russian sphere of influence. No wonder the Kwantung Army took so serious a view of Inner Mongolia! The task was, then, to entrust power to the hands of those who were not inimical to Manchoukuo. So now the Kwantung Army extended its operations to Inner Mongolia.

The Army's interest in North China was not purely strategic. It was also bound up with the foundation of the Defence State. In order to counter the world movement towards closed economics, a country's resources must be self-sufficient. The Kwantung Army, therefore, asked itself whether Manchuria was adequate. The answer (provided by the S.M.R. Research Department) was that Manchuria alone was insufficient; it was necessary also to tap the resources of North China. The Army brains strongly endorsed this opinion.

[1] Allusion is to the 'Trojan horse'.

The Cabinet, in its desire that the Manchurian imbroglio should not extend beyond Manchuria, had placed its limits north of the Great Wall of China, but the Kwantung Army was not to be bound by Cabinet views. Under the Saito and Okado Cabinets, the fighting services had defied the wishes of the Government. They now used the same tactics to extend the Manchurian trouble into China.

CHAPTER FOUR

Hirota's Three Fundamental Principles

1. THE OPPORTUNITY TO SETTLE THE MANCHURIAN PROBLEM ONCE FOR ALL

THE Manchurian incident had startled the world but it had startled the Japanese also. The nation was alarmed: what would become of Japan? The Government bestirred itself to work out all things for the best but it was no match for the Army, while the staff officers in the Kwantung Army just went ahead with the programme they had worked out. The Commander-in-Chief, Honjo, followed dumbly in their tracks.

In facing the outside world the Japanese Government could do nothing else than accept full responsibility for the doings of the Kwantung Army—it said that the steps taken were justifiable defence measures, which it guaranteed to confine to the minimum necessary. In actual fact it was in the nature of a revolution. The Kwantung Army had taken the bit between its teeth and bolted.

Had there only been some moderation in her acts, Japan's attitude in defying the whole world would have been magnificent. The League and foreign countries might, in time, have sympathized with Japan's excuse that China's violent anti-Japanese agitation had started the affair. While the League was talking, the establishment of a noble-seeming state had taken place. If only operations had been confined to Manchuria, who knows but that the powers might have acquiesced? In Britain there were still many persons of influence in the Conservative Party that thought, with nostalgia, of the days of the Anglo-Japanese Alliance. Then, also, there were many that were keen to prevent the problem of China coming to an impasse. Britain had sent, unofficially, the influential Barnby Mission. And in an attempt to rescue China's finances, the British Government had despatched its leading light in the Treasury, Leith-Ross, who had asked for Japanese co-operation. It was evident that at that moment Britain still set store by her relations with Japan and tried hard to mediate between Japan and China.

China watched Japan's uncompromising attitude with amazement. The world might say that Japan's hardihood would bring the country to ruin but Japan seemed only to find fresh reserves of strength. Revolutionary China studied the source of this compelling force in order that she might herself follow suit. She was in just the same mood as she was after the China-Japan War.[1] Accordingly great numbers of Chinese students flocked over to study in Japan and there was also a sudden increase in visits from Chinese politicians and diplomats. It looked as if, provided the opportunity could be seized, the misfortune that had befallen relations between the two countries might be converted to a happy ending. But, if it were to be so, patience, generosity and self-control were called for. Above all, exercise of the utmost wisdom was requisite.

2. CONDITIONS PRECEDENT TO A SOLUTION: THE AMAU[2] DECLARATION, 1934

The Ministry of Foreign Affairs was quick to grasp the opportunity. But first it must establish the prerequisites: 1. Japan must resolutely forgo any forward move in China Proper and, in order to show that she had no ulterior motives, she should pay special heed to the doctrine of the 'open door' so highly prized by the U.S. 2. The powers must be asked not to encourage China in her anti-Japanese agitation, and refrain from supplying munitions or finance for the purpose. 3. It must be recognized that both countries were threatened by the same calamity of internal disturbances from the machinations of the Communist Party. Roughly speaking, that was the line to be taken. Japan must proceed cautiously, must give the powers no cause to criticize her actions, while the latter should remember that Japan's status was that of a stabilizing influence in East Asia. After all, Manchuria was to China a border region that she had colonized. It had always been semi-independent and had never been an integral part of China. But inasmuch as it would be difficult for China to recognize Manchoukuo at the moment, Japan might, while watching its progress, leave to a later date a request for its recognition. None the less, since Manchoukuo was peopled mainly by Chinese, China for her part should refrain from any action that might exacerbate relations between

[1] 1894–95.
[2] Pronounced Amó and often so written.

THE REVOLT OF FEBRUARY 26TH, 1936

China and Manchoukuo. She should let matters follow their natural course and leave it to time to solve the problem. Japan, again, should make it clear that she had no designs on China Proper. She should meet China's aspirations in a spirit of tolerance.

This policy made great headway. The understanding of the powers grew and opinion at home and abroad welcomed it. But at that time (1933–34) powers other than Japan were making military loans and supplying arms to China, and it was feared that this would injure Sino-Japanese relations and disturb the peace of East Asia. In April 1934 the Chief of the Information Bureau, at his regular meeting with Japanese correspondents, explained the foregoing policy in answer to questions and his statement was published on April 17th as a talk off the record. Malicious use was made abroad of this statement, expanded and misrepresented, whether deliberately or not, as the 'Amau' declaration. It had to do with item 2 above. Its purpose was not utterly to disregard the intentions of the Nine Power Pact, nor yet to shut out other powers from China, but simply to elucidate Japan's serious role in China and to prevent the powers from aggravating conditions in China by their attitude.

In short the intention of the policy was to justify Japan's standing on the continent, to adjust the interests and feelings of Japan, China and other powers in Manchuria and to work for a radical solution. Afterwards it was given out in the Diet as Hirota's Three Principles. It was hoped that in due course the atmosphere would clear and that, just as at the time of the Shanghai trouble, negotiations could take place between Japan and China, with Britain representing other foreign interests.

Experience had shown that there was no means of reaching a settlement of the Manchurian problem unless Britain's sympathy and good offices were obtained (and behind Britain there was the U.S. to be considered). I myself have no doubt that if Japan could have carried out the policy in a firm, coherent manner, the Manchurian problem could have been solved on favourable terms. At a later date, when I became Ambassador in London, I had occasion to confirm this belief. At the Far East War Crimes trial again, the Chinese Prosecutor expressed the opinion that if this policy had been continued, relations between the two countries might have been changed for the better, and that it was in order to prevent this happening that the military plotted the February 26th revolt. Whether this be so or not, the military did in fact thwart this policy by their opposition, for the Government, instead of displaying active statesmanship, attached more importance to inaction, so that they might live from day to day in peace. The military refused to look at an understanding with Britain and the U.S. and vetoed any official undertaking that Japan had no designs on China Proper.

3. THE ARMY BLOCK THE PLAN

In truth the schemes of the Kwantung Army in North China bore no resemblance to the declared policy of the Government, which the Army just ignored. They went ahead with their plans in secret so that the Government and the diplomats were at a loss to keep track of their doings. The Army pretended to approve the Government policy but actually violently opposed it both at home and on the spot.

As a matter of policy the Government raised the rank of the Minister to China to that of Ambassador in the hope that his higher rank would enable him to prosecute the new policy with greater prospect of success. The Army thereupon adopted a threatening attitude and expressed great resentment that they had not been consulted. By now they fully intended to take not only Manchuria, but also China, out of the hands of the Ministry of Foreign Affairs and handle these problems in their own foolhardy way. Nor would they tolerate any curb on their free licence from the Minister of Foreign Affairs or anyone else.

The attitude of the military and their operations provided excellent material for Communist Party propaganda. At that time the influence of the Chinese Communist Party received a setback from Chiang Kai-shek's campaign against them but the Comintern, working in secret, made the fullest use of Japan's unpopularity to stir up trouble.

After Russia's adherence to the League of Nations, Red influence grew therein. The Health Commissioner Reichmann (Polish-Jew and Party member) was sent to China, ostensibly to study the traffic in opium, a fertile source of anti-Japanese criticism. He finally became adviser to the Chinese Government and put in very good work for the Communist Party. The Sorge spy-ring had for a long time been active in China and Japan. The influence of the Russian Fifth Column in Europe and America was exerted all too effectively. So the attitude of the U.S. progressively hardened under the guidance of the principles enunciated by Stimson. He demanded of Japan the observance of the doctrine of the 'open door' and lost no opportunity of pressing home his protests and his opposition. His action stirred up the Army and finally made it impossible for Japanese administrators to carry to fruition the policy for a settlement of the Manchurian affair that they had initiated

If only the U.S. and Britain had approved the plans of Japanese peace-lovers and had accepted Japan's stabilizing influence in the Far East, if they had taken within their sights the political situation in the whole of East Asia, which hinges on that of China, and set themselves to obtaining stability there, world conditions might well have escaped the pass to which they have now come.

CHAPTER FIVE

The Revolt of February 26th, 1936

1. NATIONALIST SCHOOLS OF THOUGHT

How the *'Society of the School of Heaven'* had grown into the *'Blood Brotherhood'*, how the young officers that aspired to reform the state had taken as their idols the leaders of the Imperial Way School and planned with them to carry out the task of reform, how in order to open up the path they decided to liquidate those who stood in the way, this I have already told. When General Araki had become War Minister and General Masaki Vice-Chief of Staff under H.I.H. Prince Kanin, the Imperial Way School had suddenly gained in stature. But when General Hayashi succeeded to General Araki, the struggle between the Imperial Way School and the Control School came into the open and the Army had split into two factions.[1]

2. BLOOD SHED IN THE WAR MINISTRY

General Hayashi felt keenly the importance of discipline; he proposed to punish severely any acts of an alarming nature such as 'direct action' and to suppress dangerous elements. He roused the young officers to a high pitch of indignation by discharging Masaki, Director-General of Military Training, who enjoyed their confidence, and that caused an unpleasant incident.

There was a certain Lieutenant-Colonel Aizawa, who had no direct relations with the young officers' association, but was a single-minded, unbending officer, who held the same views as they. Concluding that the discharge of General Masaki was due to a scheme by Nagata, Chief of the Military Affairs Bureau and belonging to the Control School, to

---

[1] *Vide* Book One, Chapter Six, s. 4. The Control School might be described as disciplinarians.

seize power, he decided to take it upon himself to administer just punishment. In broad daylight, in the office of Lieutenant-General Nagata, he calmly despatched him with his sword. By this outrageous act the dispute in the Army was given its blood-bath.

The act brought the factional dispute to boiling-point. Aizawa's sympathizers characterized the murder as a heroic deed and rose in a body to support him. In the court martial that followed, employing left-wing tactics, they preached their doctrines as though they constituted a defence. Their counsel, Lieutenant-Colonel Mitsui, denounced the corruption of the Japanese administration, laid stress on the need for reform, exposed the evils of favouritism in Army administration and attacked the leaders of the Control School. This factional struggle had a close bearing on the reform campaign of the young officers; under the secret guidance of Kita and Nishida they proceeded to prepare the ground for a resort to direct action.

3. TROUBLE AT THE MILITARY ACADEMY

The Army chiefs cudgelled their brains to discover means of reducing the temper of the young officers. Now these young men, who were genuinely patriotic in their aspirations, were banded together in an association that comprised among its adherents all the brightest students at the military academy. In their antipathy to the Army executive these cadets united in declining to enter their names for that gateway to higher promotion, the Staff College, and preferred to await their opportunity to sacrifice themselves in the cause of reform.

Notwithstanding, there were not wanting members, well fitted to lead them on the right path, such as Lieutenant Muranaka or Intendant Isobe and others, who did seem to listen to the advice of trustworthy seniors. They pledged themselves to abandon the idea of direct action and to become good officers and Muranaka did in fact enter the Staff College and appeared to set himself wholeheartedly to the study of military strategy.

But the political campaign of the young officers showed no signs of slackening and in the Academy great numbers of students were becoming infected. The military authorities, therefore, adopted a plan to excise the cancer and, on the recommendation of Lieutenant Tsuji, a company commander, Major-General Tojo, Chief Instructor of the Academy, had a confidential talk with a student named Sato, who was supposed to be a confederate, and instructed him to spy on the young officers. Sato called on Muranaka and Isobe and others, and, affecting to abuse them for their defection, satisfied himself as to their true intentions. He reported definitely that they had not changed in the slightest; they were still actuated by the desire to reform the state and were only waiting for the right opportunity.

On the basis of this secret report the authorities dismissed from the Staff College all that were implicated and placed them on the retired list. Many students of the Academy also were disciplined. The incident further inflamed the young officers while Muranaka and Isobe burned with a desire for revenge. The hour had struck. With their confederates they perfected their plans. And backing them up were Kita, Nishida and their ilk.

4. ASSASSINATION OF THE SENIOR STATESMEN
FEBRUARY 1936

Suddenly there came to the First Division orders to proceed to Manchoukuo in spite of the fact that it had always been an understood thing that this Tokyo Division would never be moved elsewhere. The young officers at once jumped to the conclusion that this was a plot to get rid of those officers that were looked on with disfavour. They decided it was now or never.

On the night of February 25th, 1936, in a snowstorm, a company of the First Division commanded by Nonaka, together with detachments from the Guards Division, went into action. Under a well-co-ordinated secret plan they split into several bodies and proceeded to assassinate senior statesmen. A main body attacked the residence of the Prime Minister and occupied the districts of Nagata, Kasumi-ga-seki and Tameike. They also took possession of the Metropolitan Police Headquarters, the Home Office, the General Staff Office and the War Office.

Prince Saionji, who was living at Okitsu, received warning in time and escaped. Makino, former Keeper of the Privy Seal, was staying with his family at his country seat in Yugawara; he was attacked during the night but thanks to the devotion of his police guards, who were killed, he also escaped by the skin of his teeth. The Minister of the Household Saito, Finance Minister Takahashi, Director-General of Military Training Watanabe, were each brutally murdered. Suzuki, a Chamberlain, was fatally wounded.

A dramatic episode was enacted at the residence of the Prime Minister, Okada. A cousin, who was remarkably like him, Captain Matsuo, was mistaken for him and killed in his place. Though the residence was surrounded by the rebels, he got out by passing himself off as one of the bearers at Matsuo's funeral.

5. NEGOTIATIONS WITH THE REBELS

The separate detachments, having offered up their blood sacrifice of the country's aged statesmen, assembled at the Prime Minister's residence, which was made the rebel headquarters, while strongpoints were established at the Yamao Hotel and eating-houses in Tameike, and a military cordon was drawn round the neighbourhood. At the same time the rebels despatched telegrams to fellow conspirators in the provinces and urged them to rise. For a moment disquieting symptoms appeared at various centres and troops seemed to be on the point of revolting, but the movement petered out and the country as a whole narrowly escaped a rebellion.

On the outbreak of the revolt, members of the Cabinet and other important officials sought refuge in the Palace compound and took up their quarters in the Household Department. The gates of the Palace were firmly barred and communications with the outside world were cut except for a roundabout passage at the back leading to the Hirakawa Gate, which normally was never used. Home Minister Goto was appointed Acting Prime Minister *ad interim*. But when the escaping Prime Minister Okada emerged a day or two later from the house in which he had been hiding, the appointment terminated.

Since the centre of administration, the Prime Minister's official residence, was in the hands of the rebel troops, and as for some days it was not known whether he himself was dead or alive, the Government making no public announcement as to what had occurred, wild rumours flew around and people began to fear that Japan was in a state of anarchy. Sensible people thought that the Government should put up a flag and say 'This is where the Government is', but when eventually they learnt that not only the Cabinet Ministers but also the Army and Navy leaders were lying hidden, with the Genro and senior statesmen, behind the Palace moats within a barbed-wire enclosure, their disgust was beyond words.

In the midst of this crisis the Cabinet resigned. The Government had dissolved itself and for a time the public had no official guidance whatsoever.

The leading Army generals came out from the Palace to meet the rebel leaders in the War Office, now in their hands, and for days struggled unavailingly to prevail on them to lay down their arms. Meanwhile the rebel army had styled itself the 'Loyalist Army'. To the public they were the 'Zealots', the 'Army of Action', the 'Independents'. When, however, the War Minister Kawashima was received in audience,

His Imperial Majesty sternly enquired, 'Have you not yet put down the rebels?' The terms of this enquiry made it clear that this was to be regarded as a rebellion and the troops were thereafter described as rebels.

Colonel Ishiwara and other staff officers in charge of Martial Law, meeting at the Imperial Hotel, agreed to submit the name of Admiral Eisuke Yamamoto, a member of the right wing, to form a new government. The rebel army at the moment were demanding that a Reform Government should be established, based on the Army and headed by General Masaki. If their demands were accepted, they would disband the troops, submit themselves to judgment and pay the penalty.

6. SUPPRESSION OF THE REVOLT

The formation of a Cabinet was a matter of Imperial mandate and not dependent on the question whether General Masaki would say Yes or No. As the days passed with nothing to show, disquiet grew in the capital. The Navy said that if the Army could not make up its mind they themselves would quell the revolt, and began to fortify the Navy Ministry. But at length troops were assembled for the purpose from the provinces. Headquarters were set up at the foot of Kudanzaka,[1] though the language used by Colonel Ishiwara seemed calculated rather to encourage the rebels than to subdue them, until the public began to wonder what it was he was proposing to suppress.

After days of persuasion by generals such as Masaki and Araki the rebels had for the moment consented to commit suicide, eighteen coffins were carried into the War Minister's official residence and pistols and Japanese swords provided,[2] but Ikki Kita over the telephone opposed the idea and advised instead that the rebels should surrender and deploy their tactics in a court of law. It was then rumoured that the Martial Law Headquarters would open fire on the rebels and at long last the Company Commander Nonaka put a pistol to his forehead in the courtyard of the Prime Minister's residence and shot himself. The other leaders submitted themselves to justice and the troops were returned to barracks. The date was February 29th.

The court martial took place behind closed doors.[3] The leaders, together with Kita and Nishida, were condemned to be shot. General Masaki was incarcerated for one year and then released.

Prince Saionji submitted that Prince Konoye should form the new

[1] Adjoining the Nagata District.
[2] Note that the suicides were to be ceremonial and carried out in a blaze of military glory, i.e. it was to be the death of national heroes.
[3] Thus defeating Ikki Kita's purpose.

cabinet but the latter asked to be excused so, since foreign relations were regarded with concern at the moment, the ex-Foreign Minister Hirota, who had scored a success in the negotiations for the purchase of the Chinese Eastern Railway from Russia, was given the task of restoring the political situation to order after the rebellion.

7. WHAT FOREIGN ENVOYS THOUGHT OF THE REVOLT

The Emperor had declared that the Army stood to him as 'his own hip and thighs' but it was this very support, even down to the Imperial Guards, that had rebelled, had murdered his trusted servants, had seized and held for four days the centre of government. What was this? Were they rebels or weren't they? What was loyalty and what was rebellion? Who was to know? One thing only was clear, and that was that there was something wrong at the heart of the Army.

In any age first essentials are the basis of government. If law and order are to be maintained, the distinction between loyalty and treason must be clearly established. In Japan the doctrine that one must hate the crime but not the criminal has led to over-sympathy with the motives, so long as they are sincere, and right and wrong have been turned upside down. Crimes have been condoned though they confused loyalty and treason and struck at the common interests of society. Rebels have been looked up to as heroes. For a country to reward or punish at the wrong time is to destroy the distinction between loyalty and treason. How many instances there have been since the beginning of the *Meiji* era! I recall that more than once I heard soldiers criticize their Emperor and say that if he opposed reform, then such and such a Prince of the blood would be put in his place. The fighting man presumed to criticize the theory of the so-called 'Emperor as an organ of State' doctrine and reminded me of the arrogance of the military in the olden days.

Soon after the outbreak of the revolt many of the foreign envoys had found their way through the military cordon and come to call at the Ministry of Foreign Affairs. In the absence of the Minister it fell to my lot to receive them. One and all expressed their sympathy but two representatives, the Afghan and the Siamese Ministers, added words to the effect that they hated to think that such a mishap should have befallen Japan, the leader of the Far East. Their eyes were wet with tears as they grasped my hand. And I stood there with my head bowed in shame as I thanked them for their sympathy. In their eyes was reflected the thought that the Japan they revered as a beacon light in the

Far East stood on the brink of anarchy. It was more than I could bear. That is how it would appear to a foreign envoy. Japan, that bore such a heavy responsibility towards the peace of the world! In what direction would she set her course in future? The capital lay buried in snow. Here and there were the stains of the blood shed so copiously by the rebels. The Central Government had for the moment stopped functioning. Even the sound of the trams was stilled. As, left to myself in the reception-room, in a soundless world, I followed with my eyes the retreating forms of those friendly representatives, my heart was filled with thoughts that lay too deep for words.

8. FORMATION OF THE HIROTA CABINET

The formation of the new Cabinet, in the teeth of difficulties raised by the military, was by no means easy. The Army took it upon themselves to appoint Terauchi War Minister, and, accompanied by officers from the Bureau of Military Affairs, he descended on the cabinet office with ever fresh demands. The Army would not have Shigeru Yoshida as Foreign Minister, and Baba, President of the Hypothec Bank, who was said to be closely associated with one section of the Army, stepped into his shoes as organizing chairman. Objection was then raised to the proposed Education Minister so that it was a week before the membership of the Cabinet met with Army approval.

Baba became Finance Minister and Vice-Premier. Under a battle array of Terauchi for the Army and Nagano for the Navy, Arita, recently appointed Ambassador to China, became Foreign Minister. I ceased to be Vice-Minister and my place was taken by Kensuke Horiuchi. Crushed under the burden of the February 26th incident, the Hirota Cabinet was formed to the slogan of 'a transformed government' but in reality it was nothing more than the puppet of the Army. The 'Manchurian Incident' had freed the Army from government control. The revolt of February 26th now enabled it to vault into the saddle and take over the reins in the Central Government.

The Control School now had Terauchi as War Minister and, since it was said that the rebels had hoodwinked the Imperial Way School, its leaders accepted responsibility and retired to private life. The extremists among the young officers were mostly transferred abroad or to the provinces. But the senior staff officers continued to exercise power in the name of their superiors and it was their demands, based on the '*Book of the Tiger*', that were forced on the Government and displayed to the world as the reformed administration.

BOOK THREE

Expansion to the North or to the South?
Hirota and Hayashi 'Weak' Cabinets

CHAPTER ONE

The Hirota Cabinet

1. NATURE OF THE HIROTA CABINET

THE Hirota Cabinet was little more than the tool of the military. But since it was not made to order but merely a makeshift, it never worked satisfactorily.

Prime Minister Hirota, a right-wing product of the Genyosha,[1] had seemed somewhat out of place in the Ministry of Foreign Affairs. He certainly did not approve the policy of the Army, with whom he could not wholeheartedly co-operate, though from the way he talked one would have said at times that he was a reactionary and the advocate of a military cabinet. What he really meant was that those who held the authority to discharge the functions of government should openly shoulder the responsibility and submit their views to the judgment of the people as a whole. If they could not prevent the machinations of those working behind the scenes, government would never be clear-cut; it would lack a sense of responsibility, it would ever be the prey of the schemers. His own character was that of one that had mastered the secrets of *zen* philosophy.[2] He himself would never stir himself to set things in motion. He seemed rather to study what was happening around him and to act accordingly.

His policy was anything but belligerent. He wanted only to maintain amicable relations with the powers and to get Japan back on the right track. Since his appointment as Foreign Minister in 1933, his record had shown this to be so. That is why the Genro decided that he was the most suitable man to clear up the confusion left by the February 26th revolt and to persuade the Army to keep in line with world

---

[1] A reactionary society said to have been related to the '*Black Dragon Society*'. Its teachings were ultra-patriotic.
[2] A Buddhist sect that taught that knowledge came not from reason but from inspiration (enlightenment). It is perhaps significant that *zen* had a great hold on the military mind.

conditions instead of pursuing its mistaken policy at home and abroad.

But the Cabinet was confronted by the overwhelming strength of the Army in a world that had entirely changed. What hope had he of thwarting military plans?

The Party Cabinets of Wakatsuki and Shidehara[1] had opposed the Army, the Saito and Akada Cabinets had looked on, while Hirota and Hayashi, who succeeded him, were powerless and merely paved the way for the next cabinet of Konoye, which was formed in collaboration with the militarists.

2. ARMY AND NAVY MINISTERS APPOINTED FROM THE ACTIVE LIST

It was ironical that the first act of a cabinet pledged to reform was to revive a former practice of appointing Army and Navy Ministers from officers on the active service list. The Army insisted and the Navy followed suit. The ostensible reason was that if generals and admirals, who had been retired as a result of the revolt, were brought back, it might prejudice discipline (actually the Control School did not want the members of the Imperial Way School to reappear on the scene). But it is only too obvious that the revival of the rule consolidated the political powers of the Army and Navy. Meanwhile statesmen retired more and more into the background. What began as ideas and plans in the military mind had become national conceptions, the policy of the country. It was quite over the head of the average man. As for the intellectuals, they were overawed and submissive.

3. INFLATION OF THE ARMY AND NAVY BUDGETS

The Army and the Navy demanded the appropriation of huge sums, the one for defence on the continent arising out of the occupation of Manchuria, the other to provide for the situation caused by the abrogation of the naval treaties. Baba, the Finance Minister, was only too complaisant.

The Japanese budget had always been weighed down by the burden of military expenditure. But from this time the country's finances were based on the theory of totalitarian countries that they could be expanded indefinitely by increased issue of notes, so long as suitable means were devised of calling them in again.

[1] Shidehara had not been Prime Minister but Foreign Minister in five cabinets.

CHAPTER TWO

Was Japan's Next Move to be Northward or Southward?

1. TUG-OF-WAR BETWEEN THE ARMY AND THE NAVY

THE prerogative of the Supreme Command, having been set up as a separate entity freed from government control, was then split into two between the Army and the Navy—a calamity likely to deal a death blow to the country. Now that Manchoukuo had been set on its feet, the Army could not but treat Soviet Russia as its potential enemy, whereupon the Navy felt called upon to place themselves in opposition, for while the Army's impulse was to look northward for its next advance, the Navy's thoughts turned southward. And so Japan, one small island in the Pacific, was going to set as its targets the greatest military and the greatest naval power in the world in order to settle the question. Poor Japan! It was to be torn asunder between the north and the south. The Navy had no liking for either the Manchurian business or adventures in North China. To the Army a southern advance seemed dangerous, the height of folly. Statesmen such as Prince Konoye spent themselves trying to play off one service against the other and ended by capitulating to both.

2. THE ARMY AND THE NAVY COMPROMISE

At the end of each year it was the practice of the High Commands of the Army and Navy to prepare plans of campaign against potential enemies and submit them for Imperial sanction. The plans were a joint effort that required agreement between both parties. Though military in their scope, they reflected the political views of their authors. Both High Commands had their own Intelligence sections, which sent officers abroad, set up the necessary organization and drafted plans for study.

Acting independently, these sections brought forth projects of their own for dealing with foreign countries, a fact not generally known but of profound significance.

The plan for the 'China campaign' was prepared annually. For the 1936–37 term the Navy, mindful of the recent Shanghai hostilities, included in its draft provision for the despatch of troops to the Yangtse Basin and to Shanghai and requested that it be incorporated in the plan. The Army objected. Its main target was Soviet Russia and it attached less importance to China Proper;[1] a small-scale detachment for North China was all that was required. But, with their eyes on the south, the Navy maintained that in the event of a clash between Japan and China, the despatch of a force to North China would be insufficient; a Shanghai force was also required.

When it seemed that the dispute could not be settled by the year's end, the Army produced a compromise, 'Forces may be sent to Shanghai should the need arise', which saved the day. This divergence of opinion serves to explain why, when hostilities broke out at Marco Polo Bridge, fighting went on spreading southward. It provides a clue to problems that arose later. But, since it was always treated as purely a service matter between the Army and the Navy, even the Prime Minister was never brought into consultation and was often at a loss to know what was going on.

3. A BASIC NATIONAL POLICY

During Hirota's tenure of office, a Council of Five Ministers was formed: the Prime Minister, the Minister for Foreign Affairs, the War Minister, the Minister for the Navy and the Finance Minister, meeting to deliberate on a national policy in regard to international problems. For the most part proposals put forward by the Army and Navy formed the basis of discussion. But at the moment the Central Government were concerned to restrain the activities of the Kwantung Army, which had taken too much power to itself since the Manchurian affair, to confine them to Manchoukuo and to keep them from breaking out into North China; the Foreign, War and Navy Ministries were agreed on the point. But whereas the Ministry of Foreign Affairs was hoping to reach a settlement with the Nanking Government, the Army held that the China problem was not a business for the diplomats to

---

[1] Note, however, that the Army was keenly interested in North China, which it planned to detach and form into a buffer state (cf. Book Two, Chapter Three, s. 3 and later chapters).

handle and that, therefore, questions relating to North China should be left to the Commander of the Tientsin garrison. As for the Navy, it devoted all its energies to getting its 'southward advance' adopted as the national policy.

There exists a 'national policy' that was passed on August 7th, 1936. But executive officers, in their wish to polish off 'business', were inclined to concentrate on their immediate terms of reference, with the result that they frequently left the seeds of future trouble, as this document was to prove.

The basis of this national policy was that the Empire was, both in name and fact, to become the stabilizing force in East Asia: 'Foreign policy and national defence must be correlated in order to guarantee the Empire's footing on the continent in East Asia as well as to expand in the direction of the South Seas.' As to the means, the keynote of the continental policy was: 'In order to ensure sound defence of Manchoukuo, as well as to secure the defence of Japan also, the menace of Soviet Russia to the north must be eliminated, while, to provide against trouble from Britain and the U.S., an intimate working understanding as to our economic development must be established between the three countries, Japan, Manchoukuo and China. In furtherance of this policy, attention must be devoted to friendly relations with the powers.' With regard to the Southern Advance: 'Our racial and economic development in the South Seas, particularly on the southern fringe (Dutch East Indies), must be so planned that, while avoiding irritation to other countries, we may hope to develop our influence by peaceful means. Thus, in step with the growth of Manchoukuo, the strength of the country is to be brought to its fullest height and national defence consolidated.'

To provide the means, national defence was to be perfected. The Army must 'bring its military strength in Manchoukuo and Korea up to a point where it is a match for any forces deployed by the U.S.S.R. in the Far East, and able to get in the first blow at forces already stationed there in the event of the outbreak of hostilities....' 'Naval preparedness must be brought up to a strength sufficient to guarantee supremacy in the West Pacific against the American Fleet.' In order to realize the aims of this national policy, a call was made for a diplomatic offensive, a reform of domestic administration and the adoption of suitable financial measures.

Since the Manchurian affair the Navy had been pressing for the southern advance as a recognized national policy to counterbalance the Army's northward advance, and had now got its way. The Finance Minister adopted the attitude that increase in military expenditure was unavoidable, and the Foreign Minister, having stressed the need to do everything possible to smooth relations with the powers, assented. In the budget, the irrational method was adopted of dividing the military appropriation equally between the Army and the Navy.

Oshima, the Military Attaché in Berlin, on receipt of information from the General Staff, had pointed out that the two northern and southern advances scarcely accorded with the terms of reference of the negotiations that had been initiated in Berlin for an anti-communist agreement and asked for instructions. In reply he was informed that the Army still placed the greater importance on the northern advance and that, therefore, the negotiations might be continued as scheduled. None the less the views of the Army were of no avail to check the Navy's plans for an advance to the southward.

CHAPTER THREE

Tactics in North China

1. STARTING POINT OF THE NEW DEPARTURE

IF the Manchurian affair had ended with Manchoukuo, it should not have been impossible to settle it internationally. Or if it had been initiated and planned by a united nation, a settlement might equally have been planned and carried out. But the affair was no more than one symptom of a feverish impulse to reform conditions at home and abroad. The disease was deep-seated and was to cause one trouble after another.

If, again, the Government had been able to limit the trouble to the territory outside the Great Wall, I think that both the Manchurian affair and the problem of China itself could have been settled by diplomatic machinery. But the extension of the adventure into North China was the spark that caused war between Japan and China and eventually brought Japan to disaster.

No sooner had the state of Manchoukuo been set up than the North China adventure was taken in hand. In vain did the Ministry of Foreign Affairs endeavour to find out what was happening. The Government left the matter to the Army. It seemed in fact to prefer not to know.

The driving impulse behind the move was the desire of the Kwantung Army to consolidate the defence of the new state. The General Staff gave its approval in principle because of the desire to tap the resources of North China. The energy thereupon displayed by Japanese forces already stationed there was stimulated by a desire to keep the Kwantung Army out of their own preserves.

2. DANGEROUS NATURE OF THE NORTH CHINA ADVENTURE

With the tacit consent of Army headquarters, but without consulting the Government, the Kwantung Army embarked on what might be described as political manœuvres in the adjoining provinces of Hopei, south of the Great Wall, and Chahar to the north. The latter manœuvre formed part of its policy towards Inner Mongolia, the former was directed towards North China. The aim was to drive out of these two territories any administration that was hostile and replace it by one that was friendly.

On May 31st, 1932, a truce had been signed at Tangku[1] making the Great Wall the boundary between Japanese and Chinese forces, in conformity with which Kwantung troops that had penetrated south of the Wall were withdrawn and normal relations between Mukden and the Peking-Tientsin district were restored, but only on the surface, for the Kwantung Army began its probe into North China and conditions deteriorated.

The bogy in the two territories was the troops of Chang Hsueh-liang, but by inviting their enmity Japan finally succeeded in uniting the whole of China Proper against her. In North China there was always the danger of a clash with the National Army of the Nanking Government, while in both Hopei and Chahar the Army was invading the sphere of influence of the communists, who were backed by the U.S.S.R. Moreover the Peking-Tientsin district was an intricate network of European and American interests. The incursion of the Japanese Army also gave the Comintern the opportunity for which it was looking of fishing in troubled waters.

None the less, acting on instructions from the Kwantung Army (Commander-in-Chief Minami, Chief-of-Staff Koiso, Deputy Chief Itagaki), Colonel Doihara proceeded to set up 'Special Bureaux' in the Peking-Tientsin district and thereby provoked a conflict of jurisdiction with the local Japanese forces.

3. THE LOCAL JAPANESE FORCES IN NORTH CHINA

The Kwantung Army had been growing steadily so that it had become a continental army with a vast organization and great influence. The local Japanese forces in North China on the other hand (Com-

[1] At the mouth of the river on which Tientsin stands.

mander-in-Chief Umezu, Chief-of-Staff Sakai) were a feeble force comprising two battalions, stationed respectively at Peking and Tientsin, but after the Tangku Truce it had gained strength and acquired influence by the addition of a mixed brigade. When, therefore, Colonel Doihara was despatched on his mission, it at once protested that the action constituted an affront to its dignity so that the Kwantung Army was forced to attach Doihara to the local staff and agree that the discharge of duties in the area should be entrusted to a branch office under the control of the local forces. The fact was that Sakai, who was all for action, had made up his mind that he himself was the man for the job. Then there was also another officer, Colonel Takahashi, Assistant Military Attaché in Peking, who was very active and collaborated with Doihara and Sakai.

Major-General Sakai came to Tokyo to talk matters over and gave an unpleasant impression that something was likely to happen in North China. Alone among his contemporaries Sakai had hitherto had no opportunity to distinguish himself. The more sober-minded of them feared the worst.

4. THE UMEZU-HO YING-CHIN AGREEMENT, JUNE 1935

Japanese plans in North China were proceeding none too quietly. The Embassy Military Attaché, Isoya, had contributed to the press an inflammatory statement which was interpreted as conveying the views of the Government. In Chinese eyes Japan was working to detach North China as a second Manchoukuo. Kuomin (Nationalist) troops were despatched to Peking and numerous agitators from several organizations were smuggled in to stir up hostility to the Japanese Army. With both the Kuomintang (Nationalist Party) and the Communist Party working at full blast, it was difficult to distinguish the one from the other. It looked as if hostilities might break out at any moment.

At this juncture Sakai suggested that the Chinese Commander-in-Chief, Ho Ying-chin, should be asked to remove from the district all troops and agitators. The Minister for War Hayashi, having come over to Manchoukuo on a visit of inspection, Commander-in-Chief Umezu went to Mukden to report. When he was leaving, Sakai obtained permission to make such a suggestion verbally and in his Chief's absence called on Ho. Instead of the friendly talk that his Chief had contemplated, he browbeat Ho into withdrawing the Kuomin troops from Hopei. This is what is known as the Umezu-Ho Ying-chin Agreement

(May 1935). It was a severe blow to the prestige both of the Kuomin troops and of Ho himself. (At the end of the war Sakai fell into Chinese hands and was done to death.)

Thereafter the Japanese Army plans to establish a favourable administration in North China came, little by little, to fruition.

5. DESIGNS ON INNER MONGOLIA

In Inner Mongolia the Kwantung Army was left to its own devices.

Inner Mongolia, with Chahar as its centre, is an extensive territory lying north of the Great Wall, midway between Outer Mongolia, Manchuria and North China. It is traversed by the railway running from Peking to Paotow.[1] Here live a tribe of Mongols closely related to the Buriat Mongols (who inhabit an area roughly bounded on the north by Lake Baikal in Siberia and Manchuria to the east). They are the descendants of the Mongols that devastated Asia and Europe in the days of Gengis Khan and dream of a revival of his empire in central Asia. Their headman was 'Prince' Teh.

Inner Mongolia was the junction at which Japanese, Chinese and Russian interests came into contact and clashed. If one sought to seize an advantage, the others would do their best to stop him. But in former times it was a no-man's land, a barren waste over which large bodies of troops could not be moved. The Gobi Desert acted as a natural boundary cutting off Russia from China. Only when armies came to be mechanized did the grasslands north of the Great Wall present suitable terrain for their operations. By then it was no longer an impenetrable political barrier. The situation had changed overnight. Just as Nationalist troops had been persuaded to leave North China, they were now induced to evacuate Inner Mongolia. The Kwantung Army then set up an Autonomous Mongolian Administration Commission at Kalgan, headed by Prince Teh, with Japanese advisers trained in Manchoukuo.

6. A POLICY FOR NORTH CHINA

The Japanese army chiefs in Tokyo wished that the Kwantung Army would keep their hands off North China, which was regarded as the special province of the Tientsin garrison. The latter had produced

[1] In Suiyan Province. The railway skirts the southern boundary of Inner Mongolia.

'Essentials for a settlement in North China' (No. 1) and submitted it for approval. In essence it proposed to convert the Five Provinces of North China into a second Manchoukuo. The Japanese Ministry of Foreign Affairs strenuously opposed the project, the more so that in an endeavour to avoid a clash with Japan the Nanking Government was itself proposing to set up a special autonomous area with Peking as its centre.

On August 11th, 1936, a second project for a settlement in North China was produced into which this proposal was interwoven. Only, both in Tokyo and on the spot it was the military authorities that handled the problem and the views of the Ministry of Foreign Affairs were ignored. The military did as they pleased and that meant that any solution must take as a condition precedent the views as to the 'Northern Advance' propounded in the 'Basic National Policy' (*vide* Chapter Two, s. 3).

The policy that now received the approval of the Hirota Cabinet provided that 'a zone, anti-communist and friendly to Japan and Manchoukuo, shall be established which shall further the acquisition of resources necessary to national defence, as well as perfect communication facilities. Thereby interference by Soviet Russia will be warded off and a basis established for mutual aid and co-operation between the three countries—Japan, Manchoukuo and China.' The project took within the scope of its operations the whole of the five provinces that it proposed to detach from China Proper. It indicated means for guidance of the two autonomous provinces into which Hopei had been divided, as well as of the three provinces of Shantung, Shansi and Suiyan, and in effect it demonstrated how the separate administration of the five provinces was to be carried on and their economy developed.

The Hirota Cabinet had thus accepted, and formally adopted as Government policy, the plans of the Army.

It was these intrigues in Inner Mongolia and North China that led to the head-on collision between Japan and China.

CHAPTER FOUR

The Anti-Comintern Pact

1. RUSSIA AS A MENACE TO JAPAN'S SECURITY

BEARING the grave responsibility for the country's defence on the continent, the Japanese Army were very much on the *qui vive*. At home they pressed on with defence preparations. Abroad they scanned the horizon with anxious eyes.

In its search for warm-water harbours the colossus of Northern Europe and Asia, Russia, turned now west, now east. Since the Revolution she had penetrated into Poland and Hungary. And now the pendulum was swinging to the east. The China problem called loudly for attention.

Russia's next move west or east was bound up with conditions in Europe. As Russia's eastern neighbour Japan could not but watch these conditions closely. Did Russia's western neighbours look on Japan as in the same boat with themselves or did they rather feel that their interests were identical with those of the U.S.S.R.? The question was of importance to Japan. Whether they could be induced to ally themselves in opposition to Russia or would prefer to join with Russia in opposition to Japan was a matter of life and death, not only to Manchoukuo but even to Japan herself.

2. OSHIMA, MILITARY ATTACHÉ IN GERMANY

Japan's modern army had been built on a German model. Nearly all its leaders had studied in Germany and the Army had sent many of its officers to study Nazi Germany. The Army had, accordingly, many authorities on the subject of Germany and felt a special liking for the country. Among the authorities Major-General Oshima was in the front rank. He was fluent in German and he was a brilliant soldier with a broad outlook. As the heir of the Minister of War Oshima, that, working under Marshal Yamagata, had done so much to remodel the Army on German lines, he had studied in Germany and was the happy possessor of a disposition that went down well with the Germans.

On taking up his duties as Military Attaché, Oshima lost no time in suggesting an interchange of Intelligence with the German Army who, however, referred him to Ribbentrop, the Party's diplomatic chief, as the right person with whom to discuss any political matters. Oshima, therefore, established friendly relations, by the good offices of Ribbentrop, with Führer Hitler and the Nazi leaders.

In the early days of the Nazi regime Baron von Neurath had stayed on as Foreign Chancellor, but there had been considerable friction between him and his opposite number, Ribbentrop. Then the latter had been appointed Ambassador to London but, during the years he had spent there, he was constantly on the move between London and Berlin, where he set the Party's diplomatic machinery in motion; he played a great part, therefore, in the discussions and the eventual signature of the anti-Comintern Pact with Japan. In 1937 he succeeded Neurath as Foreign Chancellor and thenceforward openly directed Germany's foreign policy. In the German Foreign Office were still many of the old school that had inherited the ideas of Stresemann; not unlike Japanese Ministry of Foreign Affairs servants, they felt that world conditions had not yet reached a point suitable for a direct alliance with Japan, but under Ribbentrop's guidance the Party's diplomatic section had struck out on its own so that in both countries the Ministry of Foreign Affairs was side-tracked, direct negotiations were instituted with the Japanese Army, and both the latter and Ribbentrop himself were prepared to 'speculate in futures'.

3. MILITARY TIES WITH GERMANY

The discussions that Oshima was holding with Ribbentrop satisfied him that Hitler still held to an eastern move as outlined in *Mein Kampf*, and made it clear to him that Hitler appreciated the need of an anti-communist pact to counter the menace of Soviet Russia. Since Poland, Czechoslovakia and Hungary lay between Germany and Russia, the talks necessarily ranged over a wide political field. Even the Army could not well conceal them from the Government. The question of such a pact had in fact cropped up towards the end of the Okada Cabinet and was now formally presented to the Hirota Cabinet.

The Comintern was at that time inveighing against Japan and

Germany as aggressor nations. The Chinese Communist Party had declared Japan its enemy and was busily engaged in making mischief in North China. Defence against communism seemed, therefore, to accord well with 'Hirota's three principles' (*vide* Book Two, Chapter Four) as an important political measure.

The Government would have liked to take the political discussions out of the hands of Oshima and entrust them to its Ambassador Mushakoji. But since Oshima and Ribbentrop had already made considerable progress, there was nothing for it but to allow them to carry on; in Tokyo it was the Army that drove the Government, in Berlin it was Oshima that drove Mushakoji. The Germans were well acquainted with developments in Japan: the Army were pro-German and anti-Anglo-American while the Ministry of Foreign Affairs respected the British and Americans, but it was the Army that directed policy. For this reason Germany was well content to leave everything to Ribbentrop and Oshima.

In Japan, Oshima's telegrams and reports were highly regarded by the Army. Oshima's views became the basis of the Army's reading of the situation in Europe. They knew little of world conditions. They were answerable to no one for their decisions and it suited them to swallow Oshima's views wholesale. They inclined more and more towards Germany until not only their sympathies but also their strategy marched step by step with her. The Axis policy of the Army, which in turn directed the Government, came eventually to be Japan's fixed course. There can be but few instances of the views of the Government of one country so effectively acting on the views of the Government of another country.

Once more the independence of the Supreme Command had had a decisive effect.

4. ABUSE OF THE SUPREME COMMAND PREROGATIVE

The Army and Navy never slackened their hold on the independence of the Supreme Command, the theory of which it constantly expanded. Not only in political matters, but in ordinary everyday life, they insisted on their privileges. They seemed to divide the nation into soldiers and ordinary individuals or country folk. For the soldier they demanded favoured treatment (pensions and special privileges at Court were only two of many instances). The soldier appeared to think that he belonged to a special class enjoying quasi-extraterritorial privileges. When soldiers marched in their goose-step, they ignored the rule of the road so that civilians had to take the wrong side. Their progress through town or city caused utter confusion and sometimes stopped all traffic for the time being. This senseless arrogance became ever more pronounced until the end of the war and roused bitter resentment among the people.

In foreign diplomacy also the Army and Navy adopted their own particular interpretation of the rules. In any question in which the Supreme Command was involved, they were independent of the control of the Ambassador or Minister, and any officer sent on a mission insisted on negotiating direct. Military and Naval Attachés have, by international usage, diplomatic privilege, but it is understood that they are acting under the supervision and the responsibility of the Ambassador or Minister. But Japanese Attachés, except at ceremonial functions, carried on their duties as though they were independent; they communicated directly with their central authorities. It was as though they had no relationship with the envoy. The Ambassador or Minister did not even know what they were negotiating unless the Attaché or the person with whom he was negotiating told him. Moreover the scope of their duties was determined by the Army or Navy alone and that scope naturally tended to grow until it included the gravest political questions.

In Japan there were now two Governments—the Supreme Command (General Staff) and the Cabinet, each exercising diplomatic functions independently. There was no co-ordination in the will of the country, which spoke with two voices. What could result but disaster?

5. CONCLUSION OF THE ANTI-COMINTERN PACT, NOVEMBER 1936

At the close of Oshima's talks the negotiations for an anti-communist pact were restored to the normal diplomatic channels. At this stage the Germans had no wish to conclude a military alliance; their aim was merely to hold the Communist Party in check. The Japanese Ministry of Foreign Affairs, being of the same mind, the negotiations were carried through smoothly and the agreement was signed as an anti-Comintern pact. The Japanese Army had hoped for more than this and a secret document was signed pledging both parties to adopt no measures that would have the effect of lightening Russia's burden. The fact was that the Japanese Army was obsessed by the fear that Germany would scheme to drive Russia eastward.

It so happened that I had arrived in Moscow as Ambassador to Russia on November 25th, 1936, the day on which the conclusion of the pact was made public. So this was the child of the Hirota Cabinet!

Russia's answer was to decline to continue discussion of a Russo-Japanese Fisheries Treaty.

The Japanese Ministry of Foreign Affairs had never quite gathered how the pact talks had come to be set on foot. They looked on them as a proposed agreement of mutual aid to check the Communist Party's destructive activities. Since the Comintern had always maintained that it had no connection with the Russian Government, there seemed no reason why the pact should injure national relations with Soviet Russia. They argued, therefore, that the secret agreement had no more than a negative significance and could have no very serious political implications. The Army, however, put the emphasis on the secret agreement and regarded the Anti-Comintern Pact as a military agreement. The Germans, on the other hand, presumably put the emphasis on the broader use to be made of Japanese strength; to them the pact appeared as the product of their diplomatic strategy. When, at the moment of crisis in 1939, it came about that Germany signed a non-aggression treaty with Russia, she did not trouble to discuss the matter with Japan. She trampled the secret agreement underfoot.

If we turn to another aspect, having learnt of the course of the Oshima-Ribbentrop talks, Russia interpreted them as signifying a German-Japanese military alliance intended to hold Russia in a vice, and at once took counter-measures. She chose as the centre of her industrial activity the Urals and Western Siberia and paid particular attention in her Five-Year Plan to the realization of this shift.

CHAPTER FIVE

The Defence State

1. THE CAMPAIGN FOR A NEW NATIONAL STRUCTURE:
HIROTA'S RESIGNATION

THE February 26th revolt left behind it a strong aftermath of resentment against the Army, under cover of which certain politicians attacked them in the Diet, hoping thereby to regain the influence formerly exercised by the political parties in the Diet. The Army experienced no difficulty in launching a counterblast. They borrowed freely from left- and right-wing theories, drafted a plan for the Defence State and hurriedly threw it into shape; the Diet based on liberalism was to be dissolved and in its place absolute rule under the backing of a powerful single party was to be established to carry on the Government of the country smoothly and vigorously while building up a totalitarian Defence State.

In their resentment against the Army the political parties attacked the Hirota Cabinet and denounced the Anti-Comintern Pact. Aware of Army hopes of forming a military alliance with Germany they took this indirect method of showing their ill-will, but by doing so they drove the Cabinet into a corner. War Minister Terauchi indicated that he would not scruple to sacrifice the Hirota Cabinet, if it were necessary, in order to realize Army plans, and more than once fell foul of the Diet. He strongly urged Hirota to dissolve it. The Premier chose instead total resignation of the Cabinet. The Army then proposed General Senjuro Hayashi as successor. They planned to set up an absolute military government, to dissolve the Diet and to form a single party on the Nazi model. They advocated that the country should be put in a state of defence against Russia and closer relations cultivated with Germany and Italy.

2. UGAKI FAILS TO FORM A CABINET

On Hirota's resignation the Genro put forward the name of General Ugaki, who, as an Army man well liked by the political parties, was considered the most suitable man to restore a difficult situation. Court circles still hoped to avoid violent change, above all to the right.

Ugaki's nomination came as a shock to the Army, who exerted every effort to prevent his forming a Cabinet. After the First World War, Ugaki had succeeded Yamanashi as War Minister in the Minsei Cabinet and followed in his footsteps in cutting down the Army. The Army thought of him as one who, to curry favour with the politicians, had damaged the efficiency of the Army and set the defence of the country at naught, and were unanimously agreed not to support him. Thereupon, as was the practice, the three Military Chiefs—the War Minister, the Chief of Staff and the Director-General of Military Training—as one man declined to nominate anyone as War Minister. Ugaki gave in, and the Genro was forced to accept General Hayashi, the miltary nominee. There was in fact nothing for it but to choose a member of the fighting services.

3. HAYASHI'S CABINET IS FORMED BUT DISAPPOINTS

In putting forward General Hayashi, the Genro had by no means capitulated to the hotheads. Court circles begged Hayashi to include a sprinkling of moderates in the composition of his cabinet and, accordingly, he appointed Sugiyama Minister for War, Yonai Minister for the Navy and Ambassador Sato Minister for Foreign Affairs, and he rejected Lieutenant-General Itagaki and Admiral Suetsugu and others pressed on his notice by the hotheads.

Now that they had obtained Hayashi, the militarists were disappointed to find that his Cabinet was little different in its nature from that of Hirota; it was, if anything, worse. Ishiwara, Chief of Staff, together with Asahara,[1] called on Hayashi and protested against the composition of his Cabinet. From the beginning the reformers brought extreme pressure to bear on him. They preached that Russia was an explosive charge that might go off at any moment, they declared that the country must be so organized that it was ready for war at any time; in short the air was filled with talk of the need to put the country in a state of defence. So the Government did what the Army wanted, a

[1] A left-wing agitator.

five-year industrial plan was adopted and, in order to prepare the foundations of the Defence State, a Planning Board was set up.

Under such conditions Hayashi's administration was a fiasco. He went against public opinion and quarrelled with the Diet. And yet at the last moment the Diet adopted a conciliatory attitude and passed the Budget, thus enabling the session to end without a crisis. None the less the Government dissolved the Diet without warning and called for a general election. Hayashi had acceded to the Army's demand and was throwing down the gauntlet before the political parties in order to launch out on an uncharted course of national reconstruction, though as yet no concrete plans for the formation of a single party had been made.

The public were on edge. They were being hectored, they had to listen to propaganda, they were given no peace—and all for what? They could not really understand why their views need be ascertained in a general election. Victory went to the political parties, which were returned in their old strength.

Hayashi's handling of the administration had been beyond the understanding of the public. What is more, the Government's 'divinely inspired unity of spiritual and temporal authority', 'univeral affinities' and suchlike slogans only excited their utter abhorrence. The Hayashi Cabinet did not know whether to go on or to give in. A bare few months after it had come on the scene it was forced to retreat.

The Army had, since the days of the Hirota Cabinet, been working for an administration that should unite the country under one party and had, therefore, insisted on the dissolution of the existing parties The senior staff of officers that wielded the power now went ahead with plans to promote as the head of the new party Prince Konoye.

BOOK FOUR

The 'China Incident'[1]
The First Konoye Cabinet, 1937–1939

[1] See note on Incidents in Translator's Introduction.

CHAPTER ONE

Prince Konoye

1. SAIONJI'S THEORY OF IMPERIAL RULE

THE surviving Genro, Prince Saionji, had a good understanding of the principles of constitutional government and of liberalism. It was his view that clan government should give way to democratic government by political parties on the Anglo-American model. After the death of the Elder Statesmen associated with the age of clan administration, therefore, the two political parties enjoyed prosperity for a time.

But now that Saionji was an old man, it was Prince Konoye and Marquis Kido, who in his declining years inherited his prestige in Court circles, attended on the Emperor and shaped his guiding influence in the state. Saionji taught these two young aristocrats to follow in his footsteps and in fact made them his heirs. They, however, were the new men of a new age and their political views differed from his. They recognized that the militarists could not be simply thrust aside, and they thought, therefore, that it was better to work with them and, as far as might be possible, keep their errors down to a minimum. Konoye in particular, unlike Saionji, did not favour democracy of the Anglo-American type.

The Emperor Meiji, at the head of a band of brilliant men, had led Japan out of clan administration into constitutional government. There were great men in his day but the fountainhead of their leadership was the Emperor himself. But, when the structure of a constitutional state had been completed, then it was the written Constitution that set in motion all the organs and systems of government. Saionji counselled Emperor Meiji's successors, as the principle of Imperial Rule, that in all matters they should act on the advice of those responsible under the Constitution. The Emperor Showa, on whom Emperor Meiji's mantle has descended, has displayed wisdom and sagacity from the time when as Regent he was first entrusted with affairs of state. With unclouded will he has discharged all political matters on the advice of those responsible—the Cabinet and the Supreme Command.

Emperor Showa is better acquainted with affairs of state than any of his servants. He has accumulated valuable experience of trends at home and abroad. It may well be that, changing constantly as they do, the views and explanations of responsible officials must at times appear foolish to His Majesty and that he may frequently have pointed out their mistakes to them, but he has never failed to act in accordance with the advice of those who carry the responsibility.

Only when the February 26th revolt had broken the Government, and later, when the country was face to face with disaster at the end of the war, did His Majesty step forward and decisively exercise his leadership. At the end of the war the whole of the responsible officials (including the Minister for War) attached their signatures to the Imperial Edict decreeing the end of the war, so that even here the responsibility of his advisers was formally discharged.

2. PRINCE FUMIMARO KONOYE

In the political arena of the *Showa* era the most important person was, like Prince Saionji, a Court noble. Prince Fumimaro Konoye was quick-witted and clear-minded; he was universally liked and a typical gentleman. In his political views he was open-minded and frank. He was by no means anxious to see government by the militarists, nor was he in sympathy with their aims. That is not to say that he was prepared to reject the views of either the right or the left wing out of hand. Whether in the political world or in his own personal tastes, he had contacts with all shades of thought and was at home with everybody. He had a special liking for politics and loved to see himself playing the leading role on the political stage. As a member of the aristocratic circle most intimate with the Court, he was esteemed by all classes, high and low. Surely such a man was not cast to be the puppet of the militarists; he himself at all events did not think it. And yet that is just the grave responsibility that he must bear. He did in fact become the puppet of the Army.

At the time of the revolt he had been offered the task of forming a Cabinet and had declined it. Only a short while later his name was again put forward and thenceforward he took an active part in the political world. As President of the House of Peers and of the Privy Council he had enjoyed the confidence of the Emperor but in sagacity and depth of character he was not the equal of Prince Ito, on whom Emperor Meiji had relied absolutely. One might fairly say that here was a Court noble who passed his life swimming with the tide.

Konoye's first Cabinet retained Sugiyama as War Minister and Yonai as Navy Minister. Hirota became Foreign Minister, while leading representatives of the political world, of the industrial world, of bureaucracy and of the Army took up positions, whether as Ministers of State or as Cabinet Counsellors. The depository of so many hopes, the Konoye Cabinet, now took up its duties (June 4th, 1937). And the Army hastened to use it to forward military schemes at home and abroad.

CHAPTER TWO

The 'Marco Polo Bridge Incident'

1. TWO FACTIONS IN THE ARMY: THE RUSSIA SCHOOL AND THE CHINA SCHOOL

AFTER the revolt, apostles of the Imperial Way had been rooted out of strategic positions in the Army but two new opposing factions had appeared on the scene—the Russia School and the China School.

In their absorption with National Defence the General Staff placed the emphasis on relations with Russia. Their main problem was that of bringing equipment up to the standard required to meet Russia and most of the highest posts were occupied by members of the Russia School.[1] They had approved operations in North China but they were strongly opposed to their extension southward, since the main preoccupation of the General Staff was to protect Manchoukuo as well as to keep Russia out of North China.

But in the Army, particularly among those connected with the administration and with China questions, more importance was attached to a disposal of the problem of China as a whole. And they were blindly followed by those of the senior staff officers that had already had a hand in Chinese affairs. The desire for honour and glory over a second Manchoukuo had a great deal to do with this.

The China School had its home in the Ministry for War, though it is to be noted that the relations between the General Staff and the Ministry were governed not so much by mere differences of opinion on military policy, as by quarrels engendered by personal feeling. Factional bickering had become a chronic disease.

The military view in regard to China was uncompromising. Its spearhead was wielded by staff officers serving at the front. The Government on the other hand respected the utterances of the Minister for War, which they took as representing the views of the Army.

[1] Also known as the Northern School.

2. MILITARY DESIGNS ON NORTH CHINA PROVOKE ANTI-JAPANESE FEELING

Since the Umezu-Ho Ying-chin agreement, and the similar agreement engineered by Doihara in Inner Mongolia, Japanese military designs on North China had made rapid progress. Along the line of the Peking–Mukden Railway the influence of the South Manchuria Railway had grown. At the same time activities by various Japanese that were cloaked under the title of 'Development of Natural Resources' attracted attention. All this activity naturally provoked bitter feeling: no subject was so favourably received by the Chinese people as anti-Japanese propaganda.

Since the Manchurian affair the Comintern had openly envisaged Japan and Germany as Russia's enemies and the anti-Comintern Pact had aggravated the situation. The Chinese Communist Army had opened hostilities against the Japanese Army and the front extended across most of North China. To throw that area into disorder was the best way to bolshevize the Far East. Fighting between Japan and China would relieve the pressure on Russia.

Military designs on North China had created a situation that could not be resolved without inviting a head-on collision between Japan and China.

3. THE 'SIAN INCIDENT', DECEMBER 1936

Forced out of Manchuria, and later from Peking, Chang Hsueh-liang had taken refuge in the Province of Shensi, where communist troops had set up their headquarters under Mao Tse-tung and other leaders. He had come to an understanding with them and had taken over one flank of their line. As an army the communists were as yet of little account but as a Party their success was prodigious. They extended their influence among the farming classes and their underground drive spread through the whole of North China. Their slogan, 'Liberation of the Chinese People', fanned the fever of hatred of Japan.

At the end of 1936 Chiang Kai-shek, who wished to visit Suiyuan, where he had checked the western sweep of the Kwantung Army, stopped at Sian to see Chang Hsueh-liang. Hsueh-liang eagerly begged Kai-shek to bring together the different internal factions in one united front against Japan but Kai-shek maintained that, before he could meet this foreign enemy, he must deal with his enemies at home;

he wished as a first step to crush the communists. Thereupon Chang Hsueh-liang put him under arrest. In imminent danger, but backed by the Nanking Government, Chiang Kai-shek put up a bold front and, aided by Chang Hsueh-liang's adviser Donald, who later became adviser to himself, he was finally able to return unharmed to Nanking (June 12th, 1936).

From that time on, the Nanking and communist forces, together with those of Hsueh-liang, joined hands in a combined front and when the explosion occurred Chiang Kai-shek, on September 22nd, 1937, announced formally that the nationalist and the communist forces would work in unison. The following day the China Communist Party announced that a combined front had been established (Chang Hsueh-liang did penance in Nanking and for some time was put under a mild form of restraint).

4. WAR BREAKS OUT AT MARCO POLO BRIDGE

The movement to combine forces against Japan had been stimulated by Japanese manœuvres in North China. Japan was ever extending her activities and the danger of a clash constantly increased. One actually occurred at Fengtai (near Peking). A Japanese detachment was carrying out night manœuvres close to the Marco Polo Bridge when they came into conflict with Chinese forces. For a time truce negotiations held out a hope of success but fighting broke out again and the Japan-China War had started (July 7th, 1937).

CHAPTER THREE

The 'China Incident'

1. CHINA MUST BE TAUGHT A LESSON!

JAPAN might well have displayed patience and prudence; she should never have stirred beyond Manchuria. Instead, the incompetence of the Government, and the recklessness of Army intrigues in North China, led her on; the Manchurian affair had its sequel in the North China affair, which grew into a full-scale war with China. If we study the reason, it is that Japan's political system broke down. It is fair to say that the Japanese people lacked the ability to govern themselves. The clash at the Marco Polo Bridge was the spark of a conflagration that brought the Japan of the *Showa* era to the brink of destruction.

North China was an area packed with interwoven dangers. To let loose in it impetuous troops, burning with a zeal to distinguish themselves, was utter folly.

Nationalist troops, withdrawn from the area under the Umezu agreement, came north again with reinforcements from Nanking. One clash led to another. Japanese forces in North China were at first few in number but, glad that the 'day' had come, once they were set in motion they poured forth like an avalanche.

Only recently formed, the Konoye Cabinet, in the hope of clearing up the situation without delay, responded to the demands of the General Staff by deciding to send three divisions, presently increased to five. Thoughtless Cabinet spokesmen dwelt on Japan's stern resolution and now began to describe the affair not as an incident, but as a crisis. The Government made up its mind to localize the affair—and magnified it! Both the Government and the Army declared this to be 'A sacred war of retribution on China'. The Premier advocated a 'New Order' in East Asia.

2. THE WAR IN NORTH CHINA

General Terauchi was chosen Supreme Commander. He was the leading exponent of the strong hand in China but Army expectations that they could dispose of this unfortunate war in a short time proved false. The Army was like a man traversing marshy ground; at each step he becomes more deeply involved. So, from the Peking-Tientsin area the tide of battle spread further and further into the interior. The High Command went ahead, reckless of consequences. Mindful of the bitter experience of earlier cabinets, the Konoye Cabinet outstripped the Army in their stalwart attitude; it may be that they hoped to regain the initiative by showing that they were not this time jogging along in the rear.

Hostilities in the north were at once reflected in central China. Here the great need was to prevent a repetition of the Shanghai battle, since one false step might involve the Army both in central and southern China; simultaneously this could mean the signal for the Navy's policy of an advance southward, and before many months had elapsed war did in fact flare up in Shanghai and the worst had happened.

3. THE SECOND BATTLE OF SHANGHAI, 1937

Shanghai was the financial and cultural centre of China but it was also the focus of communist activity. Any trouble between China and Japan in the north was reflected *sympathetically* in Shanghai, where hatred and contempt of the Japanese reached boiling-point. The question was how far could Japan, taking the longer view, put up with this manifestation.

The truce agreement of May 5th, 1932 (Book One, Chapter Eight), had forbidden the entry into specified districts of Chinese troops in order to maintain peace in Shanghai, for the security of which troops of foreign powers were responsible. But the Chinese claimed that this was merely a temporary agreement and one which moreover infringed Chinese sovereignty. Regardless, therefore, of Japanese protests, they moved troops into the area. As usual the troops were 'Red'—the 29th Route Army. Their anti-Japanese feeling was excited by the fighting in the north and the general situation threatened a clash with the Japanese forces at any moment.

The occasion arose when Lieutenant Oyama of the Naval Landing Party was murdered in the vicinity of a Chinese military airfield.

Fighting then broke out and the resulting situation resembled that which had arisen before; indeed there were those who said that, if the Army started something in the north, you could count on the Navy trying its hand in Shanghai. One thing certain was that on its own resources the Navy was not strong enough to handle fighting of this nature; the first battle of Shanghai had shown that.

4. OPPOSITION TO DESPATCH OF TROOPS TO SHANGHAI OVERCOME; NANKING TAKEN

Yonai, the Navy Minister, demanded the despatch of a military expeditionary force. It was laid down in the agreed plan of campaign[1] that 'forces may be sent to Shanghai should the need arise'. The Army had sent troops before; the Navy could not handle the situation alone. Therefore, thought Yonai, it was only reasonable that the Army should send troops to deal with the land fighting.

The Northern School in the General Staff strongly demurred. To extend the fighting in the north to central and southern China was to divide up Japan's fighting strength. It meant a dangerous thinning out of strength in the north at a moment when national defence had not yet been perfected. Troops actively employed must be kept down to the minimum and they should not be sent elsewhere than to North China, whatever the sacrifice entailed.

The Ministry for War, however, divided in opinion as ever from the General Staff, took the view that at all costs troops must be sent. Fighting had already begun. This was no time to discuss the reason why. The lives and property of many thousand Japanese residents were at stake.

The Government, after consulting with the Army and Navy, finally assembled, as the very least required, three divisions under General Matsui, and despatched them to do battle with Chinese troops burning with hatred of the Japanese.

As a result of these conflicting views the mistakes made in the first battle of Shanghai were repeated in the second on a larger scale. The troops landed at Wusung could not advance in spite of bitter fighting and heavy losses, and were held down in front of Shanghai. In a land, sea and air battle without declaration of war, round an international city, accidents were never-ending and roused hostile feelings against Japan all over the world. The General Staff then reversed its opposition and despatched several more divisions, which landed at Hangchow Bay and

[1] Book Three, Chapter Two, s. 2.

advanced in the direction of Nanking, whereupon the Chinese forces retreated. The new Japanese force, joining up with the Shanghai troops, attacked and took Nanking on December 13th, 1937.

Mainly as a result of the excesses committed by the Nakajima Division, which entered the city, world-wide propaganda—'the Japanese Army runs amok in Nanking', 'the rape of Nanking'—brought the fair name of Japan to the dust.

5. NORTH AND SOUTH CHINA OVER-RUN

Though the Japanese Army had occupied his capital, Nanking, Chiang Kai-shek, who transferred his Government first to Hankow and then to Chungking (December 20th, 1937), showed not the slightest intention of suing for peace, so that, contrary to Army expectations, the war went on extending. General Sugiyama, who had resigned his position as Minister for War, replaced General Terauchi as Commander-in-Chief (North). In the centre General Hata became Commander-in-Chief. The northern army took Tsinan and Hsuchow after hard fighting and penetrated into Shansi Province. The central army made its way up the River Yangtse to Hankow. A southern army under General Furusho landed at Bias Bay and took Canton. In this way, by the end of 1938 the Japanese Army held in its hands Hankow and Canton. It had occupied a vast area of China including the Peking–Suiyuan Railway in the north, the Peking–Hankow, the Tientsin–Pukow and the Lunghai Railways in the centre and the principal towns along the Yangtse. It was forced to maintain its hold on these key points and lines, behind which the Communist Army engaged in guerilla warfare at will.

Meanwhile in July and August 1938 fighting had broken out with Russian forces at Changkufeng (Chapter Eight).

6. ADMINISTRATION OF THE OCCUPIED TERRITORY

As the Army advanced, the South Manchuria Railway Company began to push its way in. It was brought in to operate the railway from Peking to Mukden and at first its industrial experience in Manchuria was invaluable in drawing up plans for the economic development of North China. But merely to run the area as a second Manchoukuo would be to bring it under the sphere of influence of the Kwantung Army and that neither the Government, nor the Army, nor the public in Tokyo, wanted. Instead both Government and private organs vied with one another to extend their own interests in North China.

The eventual decision was to separate business undertakings in China Proper from those in Manchuria and to set up a new organ to operate them. This was the Ko-a-in,[1] which was to control all non-military enterprises in those parts of China occupied by the Army.

---

[1] Asia Development Board. Hereafter so called.

CHAPTER FOUR

Peace Efforts

1. EFFORTS TO REACH AGREEMENT

Now that hostilities had extended to the Yangtse Basin and the situation was going from bad to worse, the Japanese Government were anxious to restore peaceful conditions in China. Even the General Staff, in which the views of the China faction carried little weight, disliked the extension of hostilities to central China and worked for a peaceful outcome. Nor was the Army as a whole averse to peace, provided only that terms were acceptable. The Army, therefore, on their own initiative, tried to get in touch with Chiang Kai-shek through their representatives on the spot. But Chiang did not trust the Army and would not take the approach seriously. The Army then took up with the Government the possibility of Germany's acting as a mediator.

Konoye had, in forming his cabinet, relied on the strength of the China faction and taken Sugiyama as his Minister for War but, having heard that the General Staff favoured peace, he went over to their side and proposed to use them to restrain the Minister for War. The influence of Ishiwara, D.M.O., went up at once.

The British and American Ambassadors also offered Foreign Minister Hirota their good offices. Both these countries thought it expedient to mediate, whether from the point of view of the protection of their own trade and interests in China, or in order to prevent disorder spreading throughout East Asia. The Ministry of Foreign Affairs too was well aware that, without backing from Britain and the U.S., a settlement of Sino-Japanese differences was impossible, whereas German interests in China were quite inadequate to ensure success. But the militarists nursed a grudge against the British and Americans for their continued opposition to the Army's doings since the outbreak of the 'Manchurian Incident'. To them a request to these countries to mediate was tantamount to entrusting Japan's fate to her enemy, and they stood out against it; moreover Konoye himself saw no objection to intervention by the Germans, since they were on an intimate footing with the Japanese Army.

Thinking people understood that the British-American offer afforded the one and only means, both of settling the dispute and of developing Japan's international status in the future, but, seeing that the Army held the reins of power and that British and American assistance would entail changing the direction of Japan's aims, they realized that they could not hope to force such a change in the teeth of Army opposition.

2. GERMAN MEDIATION

The Germans had had a hard struggle to carry on their business in China since the First World War, but surprisingly enough it was the very loss of their treaty rights that proved a factor in the success they achieved. The Chinese Government had engaged German military advisers and planned to buy German munitions. Before Hitler's rise to power the German foothold in China was won by merchants who were, if anything, in opposition to Nazi sentiments and were by way of being business competitors of the Japanese. They resented Japanese action in China and were anxious to see the end of hostilities, which threatened their own business interests. Hitler himself felt that war would drive the Chinese into the arms of the Russians and strongly urged the Japanese Army to bring the fighting to an end. His attitude accorded well with the views of the General Staff, who devoted their efforts to getting the Germans to mediate. A Colonel Manaki acted as their liaison officer and he and Ott, the German Military Attaché, went over to consult with Trautmann, German Ambassador in China. Negotiations were initiated at the end of 1936. The Chinese intimated that they were willing to make peace on condition that (1) Inner Mongolia should be granted autonomy, (2) Chinese sovereignty over Manchuria should be recognized and a government friendly to Japan should be set up.

3. PEACE EFFORTS FAIL

Foreign Minister Hirota now asked von Dirksen, the German Ambassador in Tokyo, to enlist the good offices of Trautmann as mediator. The gist of his proposals was joint action against communism, a stoppage of anti-Japanese propaganda, economic co-operation and the payment of an indemnity. At the same time, behind the scenes, the General Staff was also working for peace and through Ott privately intimated that the payment of an indemnity was unnecessary. Oshima in Berlin had been instructed to arrange that General Falkenhausen, military adviser to China, should assist the negotiations from the sidelines. The Japanese Government itself had no inkling of these activities.

On the other hand the home of the China School, the Ministry of War, throughout took a stronger line. Anything in the nature of appeasement, they said, was out of the question. After the fall of Nanking they became still more uncompromising. Meanwhile Chiang Kai-shek was suspicious of Hirota's offer and, through Trautmann, requested that it should be couched in more detailed concrete form; he made it clear, however, that he had no intention of accepting a request that North China should be demilitarized. Hirota, therefore, sensed that the Chinese Government was not minded to compromise and at an early stage decided that the negotiations offered no prospect of success. The Cabinet agreed and a scheme to occupy China put forward by the advocates of the strong hand at once took shape.

As a result the Government put out the famous declaration 'We will not treat with Chiang Kai-shek' (January 18th, 1938), and began its search for someone with whom they *could* treat, someone of their own way of thinking, by means of whom they could realize their aims in China. In answer to a question in the Diet Hirota explained, amidst loud applause, that Japan's attitude might be considered even stronger than a declaration of war.

4. RECONSTRUCTION OF THE KONOYE CABINET

The General Staff took umbrage and strove to restore the position by a Cabinet reconstruction, together with a change in the War Office. They proposed to replace the Minister for War by Lieutenant-General Itagaki, who had been a close friend of Ishiwara, D.M.O., since the 'Manchurian Incident'. Konoye agreed and carried out a major reconstruction of his cabinet. Itagaki replaced Sugiyama as Minister for War, General Ugaki became Foreign Minister in place of Hirota, General Araki became Minister of Education and Ikeda, head of the Mitsui firm, Finance Minister; Admiral Suetsugu had already become Home Minister. At the wish of the Army Ugaki promoted Oshima to become Ambassador to Germany and appointed Shiratori, a diplomat in close touch with the Army, Ambassador to Italy (Germany promoted Military Attaché Ott to be Ambassador in Tokyo).

The Army, however, got wind of the intended appointment of Itagaki as Minister with Ishiwara as Vice-Minister, and forestalled the second half of the plan by bringing in Lieutenant-General Tojo as Vice-Minister. Intense rivalry resulted between the Manchuria School (represented by Itagaki) and the Control School (represented by Tojo). The Control School wanted a strong hand in China but had no objection to a tripartite alliance between Japan, Germany and Italy. Since the whole Army in fact desired this, Konoye's hope of restraining the Control School by resuscitating the Imperial Way School with its 'northern aims' failed of its object.[1]

Konoye's main purpose had been to oust Sugiyama and Hirota and with them the strong-hand-in-China faction, but an underlying aim had been to reverse the 'We will not treat with Chiang Kai-shek' decision (he now announced his three principles as anti-communism, economic co-operation and the good-neighbour policy). Meanwhile the Army ingeniously contrived to maintain connection with Chiang's associates. These various movements started Wang Ching-wei's split with Chiang but there was little reaction in Chungking and the peace movement made no progress.

The attempted German mediation failed, therefore, but it led to closer bonds between Japan and Germany. Whatever their dissensions the whole Army favoured them and talks for a tripartite alliance took place in Japan, Germany and Italy.

---

[1] *Cf.* Chapter Two, s. 1. The Russia or Northern School seems to be roughly the same as the Manchuria School and the China School to be much the same as the Control School. The leading exponent of the 'Imperial Way' principle now resuscitated was General Araki.

CHAPTER FIVE

The Navy on the Move Southward

1. ATTITUDE OF THE NAVY TOWARDS THE TRIPARTITE ALLIANCE

IN its origin the *rapprochement* between Japan and Germany arose entirely out of their relations with Russia. But in the Far East the war with China had spread southward while in Europe tension between Germany and Italy on the one hand and Britain and France on the other had become acute so that no assessment of the value of the *rapprochement* could ignore relations with Britain and France, and, it may be added, the U.S. In Japan the Navy had in the past opposed a tripartite alliance. But, now that the Army and Navy were co-operating in a southward advance, their joint action caused a decisive change in the Navy's attitude.

2. NAVY'S SOUTHERN DESIGNS

The Navy had not been interested in Army action in Manchuria and North China; if anything it had opposed it. But in Shanghai the Navy had taken on more than it could handle and itself had requested the Army to send troops. It could not very well draw back again. In fact the Army and Navy co-operated in the campaign along the Yangtse and in unison advanced southward and southward again.

South of Shanghai the Navy had taken charge. Under the Hirota Cabinet it had secured for the Navy the post of Governor-General in Formosa, which could be regarded as an offset to the Army appointment in Korea. In Formosa the Governor-General ruled over a race of Chinese and the island had intimate relations with the Province of Fukien on the neighbouring Chinese mainland. Liaison with the Japanese Consulates-General in Fuchow and Amoy and agencies of the Asia Development Board were under the jurisdiction of the Navy. At a later date Formosa was the base from which operations for the capture of the Philippines were launched. Before that the force that landed at Bias Bay was assembled in Formosa. No longer did the Navy look on while the Army acted. Rather it was the Navy that took the leading role. The Navy was committed up to the hilt.

3. EFFECT ON THE U.S. AND BRITAIN

In its southern advance the Navy had occupied an uninhabited archipelago in the South China Seas in spite of French protests. It now planned to take the island of Hainan south of Kwangtung,[1] an action which was bound to raise awkward questions with French Indo-China. One way and another the Army and the Navy were advancing together, sometimes in combined operations, sometimes in rivalry. Their action had a decisive effect on relations with Britain and the U.S. Internationally we were riding for a fall. The situation lent itself to an acceleration of the alliance talks.

---

[1] From which Canton takes its name.

CHAPTER SIX

The Tripartite Alliance (Part 1)

1. CHINA PROVES A BOND BETWEEN JAPAN AND GERMANY

THE Army belief that Germany could assist in settling her difficulties in China had a profound bearing on the political upheaval of the *Showa* era.

The Army had little understanding of Britain and the U.S., whose attitude over Manchuria it deeply resented. Its field of vision was filled with the spectacular rise of new-born Germany. Here was its model, its fellow-worker.

Hitler thought that to earn Japanese gratitude was well worth while and he was prepared to go to great lengths to obtain it. He recognized Manchoukuo. He withdrew the German military advisers from China. He even dropped an earlier request that German economic enterprises there should receive favoured treatment from the Japanese Army.

Britain and the U.S. continued their opposition to Japanese operations in China and came more and more to give her moral support. And, in inverse proportion, Germany showed her sympathy with Japanese aims and did everything to respect the feelings of the Japanese Army. On the military mind the contrast had an overwhelming effect.

2. JAPAN AND GERMANY PITTED AGAINST BRITAIN, U.S. AND FRANCE

At the outset relations between Japan and Germany had as their object to hold Russia in check. Otherwise the two countries had few interests in common. Indeed, in China they were at one time held to be antagonistic. But a great change had taken place. For one thing, Japan had come to rely on Germany to lend a hand in straightening out her troubles in China. For another, as Germany's problems in Europe became pressing, so she was beginning to attach increasing importance to her relations with Japan, the more so that her contacts were made through the military authorities. The views of the Japanese Army, again, had suffered a radical change as a result of the China campaign. The deeper Japan became involved, the further south the Army and Navy penetrated, the more the Army came to be obsessed by the bogy of Britain and the U.S. rather than that of Russia.

For some time past the question of Britain and the U.S. had been the subject of some heart-searching on the part of Germany and Italy, so critical had the situation become in Europe. The Communist Party had thrown itself with zest into the task of stirring up trouble all over the world. In Tokyo Sorge and Ozaki worked hard and reported to the Kremlin that, as matters were tending, the danger from Japan had receded.

For Japan the problem of China had become the problem of her relations with Britain and the U.S. The general conditions, therefore, pointed to joint action by Japan and Germany against Britain, the U.S. and France. And in such a frame of mind the Japanese Army undertook negotiations for the formation of a tripartite alliance. The situation resembled that which had formerly induced them to seek a military pact with Germany after the 'Manchurian Incident'.

3. THE OBJECTS OF THE PROPOSED MILITARY ALLIANCE

As Military Attaché, Oshima had, in accordance with the wishes of his Army chiefs in Tokyo, cultivated friendly relations with the Germans since the signature of the Anti-Comintern Pact. Inasmuch as that pact was designed to counter the efforts of the Communist Party to stir up trouble abroad, it was one to which any country feeling itself endangered by such activities could reasonably adhere. Italy, for one, had lost no time in joining to make it a Three Power Pact (November 1937). Similarly Spain and other satellites of Germany and Italy had one by one subscribed.

So, Japan, Germany and Italy were already allied in so far as concerned the Anti-Comintern Pact. But, geographically, Italy was in a totally different position to Japan and Germany. Accordingly the secret agreement attached to the pact was limited to those two countries; Italy, therefore, and other parties, had no cognizance of it. But a military alliance intended to put teeth into the pact could scarcely exclude Italy as matters stood, nor would conditions in Europe allow its sole objective to be Russia.

From the point of view of political strategy, Italy's objective was Britain since, under Mussolini's guidance, her ambitions clashed with British interests; Mussolini's plans contemplated the expulsion of British influence from the Mediterranean, and the establishment of Italy as paramount in her place.

In self-defence Britain opposed the spread of fascism while, if she was to maintain her leadership in the adjoining European countries, she could not afford to connive at Hitler's eastern drive. France was in the same position. As the situation developed, therefore, Germany regarded Britain and France as her main objective and, in view of relations between Britain and Italy, she could not exclude the latter from the negotiations.

Japan's position was different. Thinking people realized that to conclude a military alliance aimed at not only Russia but also Britain and France (and ultimately the U.S.) might draw Japan into a world war and was an act of folly calculated to bring the country to destruction.

4. PRELIMINARY TALKS

As already explained, the talks between Oshima and Ribbentrop were originally to have envisaged no more than an extension of the Anti-Comintern Pact, bringing in Italy and converting it into a military agreement, thereby strengthening the bonds of union between the three countries. The Cabinet was unaware of the negotiations. Outside one section at Army Headquarters no one thought for a moment that any country other than Russia was under consideration. Apart from the Army the traditional feeling of respect for Britain and the U.S. was still deeply rooted. Even after the war with China had developed no one could seriously contemplate war with the two countries, nor was there any discussion of the subject except in tendentious propaganda by naval extremists. It was thought indeed, reasonably enough, that the quickest way of causing second thoughts about a tripartite alliance was to demonstrate that it might result in making enemies of Britain and the U.S.

But after Germany's attempt at mediation in China had failed and the Army had lost confidence in its ability to solve the problem of China on its own resources, it looked elsewhere for a culprit and found one in the three countries, Britain, U.S. and France. It was entirely due to their obstruction that a solution was impossible! They supported Chiang Kai-shek and egged him on to continue the war. In fact Japan's enemy was not China at all. It was the British and Americans! Army propaganda such as this gradually began to have its effect. Public opinion veered round against the British and Americans. That such propaganda, which spelt the gravest danger to the fortunes of the country, was able to prevail in this way passed the bounds of reason.

In his talks with Ribbentrop, Oshima found that the latter's ideas had changed and now went further than Japan had envisaged. They included a provision that, if one ally were attacked without provocation by any country, then the other ally would at once come to her assistance. Thereupon Oshima despatched Major-General Kasawara to Japan to sound the central authorities and obtain fresh instructions.

5. PREPARATIONS MADE FOR THE PROPOSED NEGOTIATIONS

Itagaki, the War Minister, was only too well pleased at the prospects of the alliance and brought the proposal before the Council of Five Ministers (Prime Minister Konoye, Foreign Affairs Ugaki, War Itagaki, Navy Yonai, Finance Ikeda). The Council assented and, as on the previous occasion, took the negotiations from the Military Attaché and handed them to the Ambassador as representing the Government. But, shortly afterwards, Oshima was promoted to be Ambassador and once more took over the negotiations. Minister Shiratori, who advocated the alliance, was transferred to Italy where as Ambassador he could second Oshima's efforts. In reverse of customary procedure, therefore, it was now the envoys in Europe whose main aim was to guide the home government.

Prince Konoye made these arrangements in compliance with the wishes of the War Minister. Diplomatic representation was now complete and there was every indication of a successful prosecution of the negotiations.

All this took place about the end of 1938.

At the same time I was sent to London to replace Ambassador Yoshida.

CHAPTER SEVEN

Plan of Action in China

1. ESTABLISHMENT OF IMPERIAL HEADQUARTERS: FORMATION OF ASIA DEVELOPMENT BOARD[1]

Now that Japan was committed to a full-scale war with China, Imperial Headquarters were set up in the Palace. General political administration was becoming merely a branch of the High Command, the Northern School had lost all power and the China School was in charge.

The Army had got its plans for the occupation of China cut and dried. China was to become a second Manchoukuo, with the Army in control. Political matters were to be taken out of the hands of the Ministry of Foreign Affairs and transferred to the Asia Development Board, which was to be given authority of administration. There was here a direct conflict between the theory that the handling of international questions was the province of the Ministry of Foreign Affairs and the military theory that relations with Germany and the administration of China were their affair. Abandoned by the Army and opposed to the Development Board, Ugaki resigned and was replaced by Hachiro Arita.[2] He was the third Foreign Minister since Konoye had formed his Cabinet. His ideas were not in line with those of the Army and in the diplomatic field the Konoye Cabinet had come to a dead end.

Section 1 of the Board handled political questions and Section 2 economic. Agencies were established at Peking, Hankow and Canton (Army supervision), Tsingtao and Amoy (Navy supervision) and Shanghai (joint supervision). These agencies were to direct the Japanese and the Chinese of their areas in administrative, cultural and economic matters. Diplomatic organs remained merely as a façade made up to look like international establishments.

[1] *Cf.* Chapter Three, s. 6.
[2] A foreign service diplomat.

To direct economic undertakings the North China Development Company was formed in Peking and a Central China Business Promotion Company in Shanghai. Both were Japanese juridical corporations. They were the parent companies to a host of great and small companies that were joint Sino-Japanese undertakings. Existing concerns were brought within the fold. All were to be under the supervision and control of the Development Board. Further, federal reserve banks were established in Peking and Shanghai,[1] which issued banknotes and acted as central financial organs.

Roughly the area north of the Yangtse was divided into two parts, Peking as the centre in North China and Shanghai the centre in central China. The division was artificial but the two halves had an air of being different countries, in neither of which the currency of the other circulated. In North China the railways were run by the South Manchuria Railway, in central China by the Japanese Government Railways (I.G.R.). Chinese administrative organs were subject to the dual control of the Development Board and the Japanese Army.

These measures were worked out during the time of the Konoye Cabinet and thereafter hurriedly put into effect. As the Army continued its southern advance, similar measures were adopted in the territories occupied.

2. EMERGENCE OF WANG CHING-WEI

Since Chiang Kai-shek would have no dealings with the Japanese Army, the latter thought to set up a Government of its own contrivance. Wu Pei-fu and other former war-lords were sounded without success.

Then suddenly it became known that a serious rift had developed in the inner councils of the National Government in Chungking. One of the senior members of the Kuomintang,[2] Wang Ching-wei, attacked Chiang's determination to carry on the war. He proposed a break with the communists and an understanding with the Japanese.

In the Army there was some opposition to accepting Wang, since it would prejudice any chances there were of agreement with Chiang, but the general feeling was that it would pay to win him over. Wang made his escape from Chunking and came to Tokyo. This occurred during the time of Hiranuma's Cabinet,[3] but the Army's manœuvres in China were carried on as the Army thought best, regardless of cabinets.

[1] The titles were different but the functions were similar.
[2] The Chinese Nationalist Party.
[3] Book Five.

3. PROVISION OF EMERGENCY MILITARY EXPENSE ACCOUNT

Since the Government's nerve-centres were keyed up to a state of war, military expenditure strained ordinary budget resources to breaking point. Following the practice in former wars, a system of extraordinary military expenditure was adopted, which set no limit on the sums paid out. Healthy finance disappeared without a trace and the printing of paper money took its place. The Army and Navy vied with each other in demanding huge sums. Not only had they to pay for war expenses. The Navy had to build ships to compete with Britain and the U.S. The Army had to hurry on with the defence of Manchoukuo, action which was likely to provoke Russia.

Unlimited expenditure dealt a severe blow to the internal economy. Since domestic sources could not keep pace with the demand, commodities ran short and prices soared. The country had to go over to a drastic system of control. Shut off from world markets, the field of Japanese economic activities shrank to one corner of the Far East and Japanese finances wilted. Economic demands on the occupied territories then became more and more stringent. The Army sent orders to collect necessary goods and raw materials on the spot and the Federal Banks were forced to print unlimited quantities of notes. To fill the gap Japan exported gold and manufactured goods. But these did not go far, for Chinese merchants bought up the goods that had been exported. As a result of the note issue inflation occurred and for a time it was profitable to purchase Japanese currency with Chinese notes at the fixed rate of exchange and remit to Japan. When this practice was prohibited, Chinese currency slumped and inflation became worse. There were shortages of goods both in Japan and in China. So, in proportion as military operations expanded, Japanese economy in the Far East dried up. The political harm done to the occupied territories by these financial expedients can scarcely be imagined.

At the finish the position in Japan was that, even if the military funds were there, the goods were not; they had been exhausted. But military defence must go on and so the Army took to buying up goods intended for the public. Japan's economy was gradually withering. She was on the road to bankruptcy.

4. KONOYE'S RESPONSIBILITY; SORGE-OZAKI ESPIONAGE

The plans of the Konoye Cabinet for changes at home had for a time been arrested by the outbreak of war but military schemes for a Defence State had in the meantime made considerable progress. Konoye himself had set up several unofficial study organizations such as the Showa Research Institute and other semi-official, semi-private organs for the investigation and planning of national policy. Together with existing organizations, these new study groups worked in close conjunction with the Army, held discussions and drew up plans. Left-wing intellectuals participated and representatives of the senior staff officers were much to the fore. There was little suggestion of the need to preserve national secrets. Government secrets were in fact freely debated.

It is to be noted that one of Konoye's 'brains' was Hozumi Ozaki, who was a member of the Communist Party and a Russian spy. He was engaged in espionage in company with the Russian Communist Party member Sorge. From Konoye and his associates he picked up top secrets. His assignment was to divert Japan from a northern to a southern move, steer her away from a clash with Russia and direct her on a path that would bring her to a conflict with Britain and the U.S.

Konoye's Cabinet must bear the grave responsibility that its *laissez-faire* policy led Japan to the brink of disaster. It was during Konoye's first tenure of office that was set on foot the Tripartite Alliance, which was the direct cause of the Pacific War.

CHAPTER EIGHT

Changkufeng

1. THE 'CHANGKUFENG INCIDENT', JULY 1938

CHANGKUFENG is a mountain in the Chientao area north of the River Tumen and close to the frontiers of Korea, Manchuria and the Maritime Provinces. It looks down on the railway running from Ranam (Rashin) to Hunchun. To the east it peers through the mists to Vladivostok and across Possiet Bay.

The incident arose out of the disputed interpretation of an old treaty that determined the frontier. The Russians relied on the Russian text and the Japanese on the Chinese, both of which were accepted as official. The Russians contended that the boundary ran along the Changkufen ridge; the Japanese maintained that Changkufeng lay inside Manchoukuo and that the line ran along its eastern flank. One basic fact was that the local people on the Manchurian side came and went with their flocks pasturing on the sides of the mountain.

In the summer of 1938 Russian frontier guards suddenly took possession of the peak of Changkufeng, dug trenches and surrounded them with barbed-wire entanglements. The Japanese were up in arms at once; this was a strategic point from which the Russians could dominate North Korea. At the same time a Japanese soldier was fired on and killed on the grassland north of the mountain.

As Ambassador in Moscow I received strict instructions to negotiate for the withdrawal of the Russian troops on the ground that their occupation of Changkufeng constituted a violation of the frontier. If they were not withdrawn, it was intimated that anything might happen.

2. DIPLOMATIC NEGOTIATIONS

The negotiations that I conducted with Litvinov proved extremely difficult. Litvinov said that Japan had no grounds for complaint since the boundary line followed the ridge and, therefore, the action of the frontier guards was within their treaty rights, in proof of which he was willing to show me the maps attached to the treaty. But I replied that what was all-important at the moment was to forestall a clash between Japanese and Russian troops. The Japanese believed that under the treaty Changkufeng lay within Manchoukuo. The Japanese Army had the right and the duty to defend Manchurian territory. Even supposing, for the sake of argument, that the peak of Changkufeng was the boundary, for one side to fortify that point was irregular. To prevent a clash, the Russian troops should be withdrawn for the time being. A mixed commission could then be appointed to make a careful study of the treaty and the maps and finally delimit the frontier.

But Russia declined to withdraw her troops and, while the negotiations were deadlocked, the clash occurred. The Japanese Army attempted to recover the ground by force; the Russian Army retaliated by attacking our rear in great strength, mustering mechanized units and using tanks and planes, and threatened our lines of communication. The assault troops came from the Korean Army[1] and included members of the senior staff officers that had been sent away from Tokyo; they were led by a member of the *Cherry Society*, who had taken part in the Manchurian affair from the beginning. The Japanese forces, totalling one division with artillery, attacked, but in face of the full-scale Russian preparations they could make no headway. The situation was grave. Was Japan to treat it as a frontier affray or was it something more serious that must be met by large-scale preparation?

Itagaki, the Minister for War, asked for an Imperial edict authorizing him to provide adequate forces to meet a possible offensive by the Russians, but the Emperor reproved him for setting aside the Government decision to settle the question by diplomatic machinery.

The Moscow negotiations were with difficulty brought to a successful conclusion; both armies ceased fighting on the lines they then occupied. I was told that the Japanese Army recovered the peak, but whether this was true or not, I never learnt. There were certain features in the Government's attitude that I found hard to accept but my line of argument was consistent from start to finish. It was simply that fighting should be stopped, that the opposing troops should be separated, that the boundary line should be justly delimited and the dispute settled. There was indeed no way of succeeding other than to take one's stand on an argument that was just and to persist in it. I have a shrewd suspicion that Russia knew that their troops had reached the boundary line they claimed and later the Japanese forces voluntarily withdrew

[1] The Japanese Army in Korea.

from the battlefield so that in effect the boundary in use conformed to the Russian claim.

3. SIGNIFICANCE OF THE CHANGKUFENG CLASH

The International War Tribunal, comprising representatives from eleven countries including Russia, decided by a majority that Japan was the aggressor in this Changkufeng clash. Whether the judgment was just or not must be left to future historians and jurists. But this at least is true. Neither the Japanese Government nor the General Staff planned a war of aggression over a spot of so little strategic value. Moreover all classes in Japan watched the development of the incident with the greatest anxiety.

The Army, it may be added, was at the moment deploying a large body of troops in the Wuhan[1] campaign and wished only for peace and tranquillity elsewhere. They had made no provision whatever for an entanglement with Russia. Then, again, it was widely said in foreign countries that the Army attacked because they wanted a trial of strength with the Russian Army. There is not the slightest reason to believe this. The fact was that the Army had already had an opportunity to gauge Russian strength from the invasion of North Manchuria in 1929. They had good reason to know that their own strength was inadequate from the 'China Incident': as a trial of strength the place where the incident occurred would have had no significance. The clash was fortuitous. But, though the incident arose from uncertainty where the boundary lay, it cannot be denied that the Army aggravated it by their reckless action. Such recklessness was a recurrent feature of the '*Showa* upheaval'.

The incident left an unfortunate cloud over Russo-Japanese relations. The importance of frontier defence was disclosed. But there was no slackening in Japan's southern advance.

---

[1] Opposite Hankow.

BOOK FIVE

A 'Complicated, Queer' Situation!
The Hiranuma Caretaker Cabinet

CHAPTER ONE

The Hiranuma Caretaker Cabinet

1. HIRANUMA REPLACES KONOYE

THE Konoye Cabinet might be called a 'cabinet of all the talents' but somehow, though it had been reorganized more than once, the bigwigs seemed only to get in the way. At the outset it had been faced with an upset in China, which developed into an out-and-out war that cast a shadow on the future of the country. Nothing that Konoye did came out quite as he had expected and for the moment he was a little tired of holding the reins. Then the pledges he had so light-heartedly given the Diet had been returned to him dishonoured. As the year 1938 drew to a close, he could not face another session and decided to resign with his whole Cabinet.

The reason given out by Konoye was somewhat vague: the crisis in China had so grown in magnitude that existing plans had come to a stalemate, to end which it was necessary to change the personnel in order to bring in fresh ideas. In that sense, accordingly, the Hiranuma Cabinet, which succeeded him, was generally regarded as an extension of the retiring Cabinet.

Baron Hiranuma was President of the Privy Council when he formed his Cabinet (January 1st, 1939). He was also head of the *Kokuhonsha* (a nationalist society), established after the Tora-no-mon incident.[1] This society was considered a prime mover in the nationalist[2] movement, and as its head, Hiranuma had been an active campaigner. He gave up the position to form a Cabinet. His Ministers were Arita (Foreign Affairs), Itagaki (War), Yonai (Navy), Araki (Education) and Kido (Home Affairs). They succeeded to a legacy of serious problems bequeathed them by Konoye.

This Cabinet was to be followed by those of Abe (Army) and

[1] In which the Emperor, then Regent, was attacked by an insane assailant.
[2] Fascist.

Yonai (Navy). The period of these three Cabinets was one of comparative quiet after turmoil in China, not unlike that of the Saito and Okada Cabinets formed after the 'Manchurian Incident'. The Army was engrossed in its continental plans, which carried the seeds of trouble to come. There again history was repeating itself.

During this interlude problems of internal reform continued to engage attention while the subject of a sphere of co-prosperity to extend throughout the whole of the Far East came into prominence.

The first Konoye Cabinet had signalled the beginning of an epoch. The three intervening cabinets merely marked time while the form of the Tripartite Alliance was under consideration. The solution of this problem was to be profoundly affected by the turmoil in Europe and eventually a decision was deferred until the time a second Konoye Cabinet took it up again.

2. HIRANUMA CABINET: ACTIVITY OF FIGHTING SERVICES

Hiranuma had no sooner taken over than the Navy occupied Hainan. The report took him by surprise. To the Navy it merely formed part of the High Command's policy towards China but it was obvious that this action would stir up political issues with French Indo-China and in South-East Asia. The problem of China was showing signs of merging in the greater problem of the southern advance.

As already related,[1] blame for the failure to reach a settlement with Chiang Kai-shek was laid at the door of the British and Americans and, whereas propaganda against them intensified, the need for a *rapprochement* between Japan and Germany became urgent. Wang's escape from China to Tokyo followed[2] and Itagaki, Minister for War, broke the news to the Premier that he desired an interview. Hiranuma's bewilderment grew. He had been living in a world that knew nothing of the tricks that the militarists were playing.

---

[1] Book Four, Chapter Six, s. 4.
[2] Book Four, Chapter Seven, s. 2.

CHAPTER TWO

Wang Ching-wei (Part 1)

1. WANG CHING-WEI'S ATTITUDE TOWARDS JAPAN

WANG had been an associate of Sun Yat-sen from the beginnings of the Chinese Revolution. In Peking he had been arrested for an attempt to throw a bomb at the Regent of the infant Emperor (afterwards known as Pu Yi) but escaped punishment owing to the good offices of an influential friend (1910). A highly cultured scholar, he ranked next to Sun in the Kuomintang. At Sun's death he had been present at the bedside and later published his last will. As a pioneer of the movement, therefore, he was senior to Chiang Kai-shek.

Wang had lived many years abroad in Japan, France and elsewhere. When Chiang started from Canton on his northern campaign, Wang had taken part in the formation of the Hankow Government. Later he had set up a government in Canton. After the 'Manchurian Incident' he became chief executive under Chiang of the Nanking Government.

In his political views he was definitely of the left wing but as a practical man he had rounded off the corners. His main idea was 'liberation of Asia', his avowed policy 'Asia for the Asians'. He hoped that other nations would co-operate and by their united efforts restore the fortunes of Asia. He keenly hoped to find ways and means by which Japan and China might agree on a common policy. As a left-winger, Wang had originally sought an understanding with the communists but he had drifted apart from them and in the end he had set himself in absolute opposition to China's going Red.

As Foreign Minister he had warmly supported my exertions over the cease-fire at the first battle of Shanghai and thereafter, also, he had spared no effort to bring about an understanding with Japan. At first Chiang had been in sympathy with his aims, but after the Sian incident Chiang's attitude had changed to one of collaboration with the communists. That involved resistance to Japan and a rift developed in their relations.

2. HIS ESCAPE FROM CHUNGKING

Even after the Government had been transferred to Chungking, Wang did not change his views. But though in principle Chiang agreed with Wang, after a long experience of contact with the Japanese he had come to the conclusion that the Army's way of doing things made it impossible to come to an understanding with them. So he saw nothing for it but to lean on American and British support, to co-operate with the Communist Party and fight to the end. Whether Wang's views or Chiang's judgment were correct, I leave it to history to decide.

But, apart from a serious difference of opinion as to the political outlook, irreconcilable grievances were at work. One can sense that Chiang could not altogether appreciate Wang's political background and behaviour, while for his part Wang greatly prized his own prestige as a pioneer of the Kuomintang. In Chungking these differences came out into the open as the war developed until it became impossible for them to work together.

As time went on, Wang decided that not only was it impossible to realize his aims in Chungking but that his life was in some danger. Accordingly he escaped to Hanoi in Indo-China, where he published a statement in response to Konoye's declaration (*vide* the three principles in Book Four, Chapter Four, s. 4) and announced his intention to work with Japan for the betterment of conditions in the Far East. He was met by Major-General Kagesa of the Special Bureau and made his way to Japan to consult with high officials in preparation for the establishment of a united government in China.

3. JAPAN'S PLANS IN CHINA A MISFORTUNE

Wang's patience and energy were taxed to the full to reach an understanding with the Japanese. In Japan all hope of an agreement with Chiang had not yet been abandoned. There were still some that felt that, even with the backing of Wang's name, there was little hope of setting up a new government in China, so that the project was not tempting, especially as it meant saying good-bye to all hope of an understanding with Chiang: better to be satisfied with temporizing measures in the hope that such an understanding might be reached. But, after interviews held by Wang with the Prime Minister and other leaders in key positions as well as with Konoye, whose approval he obtained, Army heads took the view that it would be well to set up a new central government to administer the occupied territory.

But when this point had been settled, there still remained two schools, divided between a policy of firmness and one of moderation. Experts on China maintained that the best plan was to give Wang a chance to work out the schemes he had so long cherished: better, they argued, to give him a free hand in order that he might win over the Chinese people in the manner he wished. But this was the view only of the Government and those capable of taking a broad view of the situation. The view of the Army and the Asia Development Board was just the opposite. With them the over-riding feeling was in favour of a puppet government on the Manchurian model. Besides, if ever there was a time to obtain permanent privileges in China, this was it. And this was the view that gained the day. Military, official and private organizations were only too eager to try their hand at solving the problem of China. As for pledges originally given to Wang, they went by the board.

Wang's government was formed. It was recognized by Japan in the time of the Second Konoye Cabinet following the conclusion of a basic agreement between Japan and China (November 3rd, 1940). The decision to form a government was taken during Hiranuma's tenure of office, the interval of a year being taken up with preparations. Cabinets came and went but the plans of the Army went on without ceasing.

4. WANG CHING-WEI'S EXPLORATORY WORK IN CHINA

Preparatory work in China also was complicated. In Shanghai a Restoration Government, formed under the auspices of a Special Committee and the local Army Special Bureau, had achieved some success. From the beginning it was intended to combine with the new national government. In Peking, however, there was a North China Political Affairs Committee headed by Wang Ku-min, whom Wang Ching-wei met in Tsingtao. Nominally it was taken over by the new government. But behind these existing political organs were numerous Army officers and their protégés, who supported them. The North China Committee, for instance, had done good work and was backed by the Army of North China. In practice it always remained independent.

CHAPTER THREE

The Tripartite Alliance (Part 2)

1. OPPOSITION TO THE TRIPARTITE ALLIANCE

THERE was not wanting opposition in Japan to a tripartite alliance. It centred in the Foreign Office under the Minister Arita and, apart from such diplomats as Shiratori, that favoured the Army, the main body of opinion was dead against Axis diplomacy or any alliance with it. If the purpose of the negotiations was to strengthen the Anti-Comintern Pact, then they must be confined to the possibility of trouble arising with Russia. They should go so far and no farther. If perchance countries such as the U.S. and Britain were included in their scope, then these countries would be regarded as our potential enemies; to make relations with them any worse than they were already was dangerous and should be avoided at all costs.

To anyone that followed our international relations and had any understanding of world affairs, this was mere common sense. Foreign Office establishments at home and abroad were of one mind in the matter. Surely, when the European situation was pregnant with danger, to estrange Britain, U.S. and France and ally ourselves with Germany and Italy was the last word in foolishness. Court circles, also, included many that had not changed their views since the days of the Anglo-Japanese Alliance. They mistrusted Germany and loathed the idea of an alliance with her, implying as it would disregard of relations with Britain and the U.S.

The Navy was anxious to lay its hands on oil and other essential supplies. Hence the southern move. But they had no desire to adopt a policy that would invite war with Britain and the U.S., and moderates such as Navy Minister Yonai, Vice-Minister Yamamoto and other seniors strongly opposed the alliance. Since the Navy as a whole supported the southern move, this attitude was essentially illogical. But it seems probable that the Navy had been dragged into the move by the hotheads. At all events, thoughtful officers, with their eyes on the actual strength of the Navy, not to mention that of the country itself, continued their opposition until the time of the Second Konoye Cabinet.

In Europe the situation threatened war at any moment. At such a time the foolishness of contracting an alliance that spelt entanglement in a European war was self-evident. But thoughtful men took comfort in the knowledge that Court circles opposed it. All too late they found that the force brought to bear by the Army had proved too strong. The attraction exercised by Germany had drawn Japan into a position from which there was no retreat.

2. ON THE HIGH ROAD TO AN ALLIANCE

The Army got its way. In two meetings of the Five Ministers' Council (May 20th and June 4th, 1939) the Hiranuma Cabinet studied the question of basic national policy and decided upon negotiations for a *rapprochement* with Germany. No concrete plans were adopted, nor indeed was there agreement on the point. The Army wanted an unconditional tripartite alliance; the Foreign Office wanted the alliance to be aimed solely at Russia. To the end they never agreed. One has the feeling that personal likes and dislikes were involved.

Ambassador Oshima took up the negotiations for a triple alliance with enthusiasm and advised the adoption of a treaty general in its scope such as Germany herself favoured. At the same time Shiratori, Ambassador to Italy, who had before leaving Tokyo familiarized himself with the Army point of view, lent his good offices, in opposition to Arita's wishes and in defiance of his instructions. The point was raised that these two Ambassadors were exceeding their powers. The Emperor indeed went so far as to admonish the War Minister that the Army should not usurp the Imperial Prerogative of diplomacy under the Constitution.

The campaign for the alliance now came out into the open, with a by-product in the shape of an anti-British demonstration. It looked as though rioting might break out; the Home Minister warned the Prime Minister that, unless steps were taken to control the situation, he could not guarantee the preservation of law and order. The procession, composed of irresponsible right-wingers and scheming left-wingers, forced its way into the British Embassy compound. The people of a great country might well be ashamed that lack of calm judgment should betray them into such an outrage. But both the Army and the populace had unquestionably wrought themselves up into a high pitch of excitement.

3. THE FIVE MINISTERS' COUNCIL DIVIDED ON THE ALLIANCE ISSUE

Whenever the Five Ministers met, the same fruitless arguments were repeated. For the most part the press espoused the Army case and published provocative, tendentious articles and leaders. Since the 'Manchurian Incident', thinking people had gradually retired into obscurity, unlike the newspapers and magazines, which vied with each other in welcoming militarist views. Those who opposed the plan feared reprisals by the Army and shunned the public eye. None the less the influence of the opposition in the background was by no means negligible. The Emperor was strongly opposed to the alliance, while the Genro, Court circles and foreign service diplomats abroad were overwhelmingly antagonistic. In the Five Ministers' Council, which met time and again, Foreign Minister Arita fought valiantly and was ably seconded by the Navy Minister, Yonai.

But by the time the meetings numbered over seventy, the pro-German campaign had become extremely active and the Government was showing signs of yielding to pressure. The Prime Minister sent Hitler a telegram of friendly greeting and the more imminent became the danger in Europe, the more urgent became Ribbentrop's insistence that Oshima should speed up the negotiations.

In its consideration of the views held by Germany, the Japanese Government now had to decide the following question. Assuming agreement to an alliance that was general in its scope, i.e. one which provided that if one ally were attacked without provocation by a third power, the other ally was bound to come to her assistance without delay, was the third power to be Russia only? And, again, were the time, means and form of assistance to be left to the discretion of the assisting ally or could the problem be surmounted by the interpretation of the text of the treaty? Such talk did not satisfy the Germans. The Japanese Army, too, maintained that the conclusion of the alliance was the all-important thing. Whether the third power was Russia or whether it was Britain or the U.S., both of which ever since the 'Manchurian Incident' had been unfriendly and were doing their utmost to assist China, it was only reasonable to ensure that the ally concerned was in duty bound to come to the assistance of the other. Judging from recent events in China, it was quite unnecessary to make any distinction between Russia, Britain or U.S. Even war itself seemed to worry the Army little.

Ambassadors Oshima and Shiratori, to whom the negotiations were committed, quite agreed with the German view that once the alliance was signed, Britain and France would climb down.

Before final agreement had been reached, the explosion in Europe took place. Germany absorbed Czechoslovakia, invaded Poland and made a treaty of non-aggression with Russia, who had been the original objective of the alliance talks. Britain and France declared war on Germany and the talks dissolved into thin air.

Hiranuma, having declared that the political situation in Europe was 'complicated and queer', protested to Germany that her treaty with Russia constituted an infringement of the Anti-Comintern Pact and then withdrew with his Cabinet from the Government. The talks had not given sufficient consideration to the state of Europe; up till now the negotiators had not been able to see the wood for the trees. Thereafter those who advocated the alliance were charmed by early German victories into ignoring the international situation as a whole; one might say that they could not see the mountain for the woods.

CHAPTER FOUR

Nomonhan (Border Dispute)

1. THE MANCHURIAN – OUTER MONGOLIA BORDER DISPUTE

THE territory of Outer and Inner Mongolia consists of grassland backed by the Gobi Desert. Even today the Mongols follow their flocks as they pasture. The boundary between Outer Mongolia and Manchuria is an imaginary line, formerly dividing Metropolitan China from the outlying frontier provinces, which never had any practical significance. But when Manchoukuo came into existence under Japanese support, the boundary between it and Outer Mongolia with its Russian backing became a live issue. Under their treaty agreements Japan and Russia had made themselves responsible for the defence of the two countries, so that a border dispute spelt danger of a clash between Japanese and Russian troops.

A section of the Kwantung Army (later the 6th Army) had been entrusted with the defence of the Nomonhan area south of Hailar. The Japanese contention was that the boundary line of the area was the River Halahen : apart from the river there was no geographical feature that could constitute a boundary line. But under Russian support Outer Mongolia claimed a frontier line running through the plain far to the east of the river. They maintained that that had always been the frontier.

2. CLASH BETWEEN JAPANESE AND RUSSIAN TROOPS, MAY 1939

In May 1939 Japanese forces occupied the line of the river and Russian forces launched a counter-attack. The fighting was violent, the Russians concentrating mechanized units and using their air force. The 6th Army was crushed under the weight of Russian armour and the

23rd Division was annihilated (end of August). The Kwantung Army was enraged. General Ueda, the Commander, and Lieutenant-General Isoya, the Chief of Staff, planned to concentrate a formidable striking force that would hit the enemy hard but they were prevented by an Imperial Order and fighting ended. Both the Commander and the Chief of Staff were withdrawn and placed on the retired list. Umezu was appointed Commander.

Negotiations then took place between Ambassador Togo and Foreign Minister Molotov to settle the matter and an agreement was concluded in Moscow, under which the dead and prisoners were exchanged and a committee was appointed to delimit the frontier (September 15th). The frontier line was established more or less as the Russians had claimed it (August 25th, 1940).

Just as in the case of Changkufeng, foreign countries commented that Japan was trying out the strength of the Russian Army. But at the time the General Staff was absorbed in the task of bringing the Army up to a war footing and clearly had neither the spare forces nor the intention to become embroiled with Russia. In fine the Nomonhan fighting was purely a frontier dispute over a line that was ill-defined. That is not to say that it was not aggravated by the imprudent action of the senior staff officers.

BOOK SIX

The Army Pushes On

Abe and Yonai Military Cabinets

CHAPTER ONE

An Opportunity to Change Course

1. HIRANUMA'S CABINET RESIGNS: A GOLDEN OPPORTUNITY

IN the European arena, Germany and Britain were locked in a struggle for supremacy. What did it mean in terms of world politics? What effect would it have on the Far East and on Japan? These were questions to which it behoved Japan's leaders to give their serious attention, to ponder carefully, for in the East it was Japan that was likely to be most affected by the turmoil in Europe.

The answer was simple enough. What was required of Japan was to revise her policy, for nothing could be more hazardous than her present one. The life and death struggle in Europe meant that European influence in Asia would dwindle while American strength would be fully engaged in Europe. The struggle was likely to be protracted. Altogether, pressure exercised by the powers on Japan in her isolation would be lessened. Here then was a chance for Japan, struggling in the morass in China, to extricate herself with dignity unimpaired. To put it differently, the Fates had been kind. Japan was given the chance to choose the one path that guaranteed her future existence, to return to a just policy, and to advance on the road to security.

Hiranuma had resigned because the Government had pursued futile negotiations for an alliance with a country that made light of the goodwill of Japan, with whom it had already signed one important treaty. Moreover it had become clear that Germany and Japan thought on different lines and that their aims and interests did not agree well together. Just as the Anti-Comintern Pact had been reduced to blank paper, so Japan's commitments had been liquidated. Japan had been given back her liberty so that she could start again. Hiranuma's resignation also meant that the bankruptcy of the pro-German policy had been disclosed. It was in the nature of a protest against the Army, which directed Japan's policy. It seemed at that moment that this was the opportunity for her leaders to set a fresh course to meet a world situation of profound significance.

Hiranuma's reference to a 'complicated, queer' situation meant more than a mere apology to the nation for the fact that the Government's reading of the situation in Europe had been confused. He was suggesting to them the dangers to be encountered if Japan became entangled in such a perplexing situation. The writing was on the wall. Take heed of this serious outbreak in Europe. Let Japan reconsider these adventures abroad into which she had plunged. To me it was impossible to interpret the saying in any other way. This is what I constantly advised when I was transferred to London.

At the outset Japan had been propelled by the arbitrary action of the Army into ventures that were really beyond her powers and she had become a prey to feelings of inferiority and isolation. Committed up to the hilt on the continent, she awoke to find herself wanting in every respect. As she was constituted, where was she to find the qualifications necessary to fill the role of one of the world's Great Powers? And to remedy her deficiencies, she only embarked on new ventures! The fact was that those who had lost faith in themselves attached themselves to the Army, which to all appearance brimmed over with self-confidence and went its way, ever launching out on fresh schemes. The man that is not sure of himself is fretful if opposed and acts without due consideration. He sets himself in opposition, he is boastful, he nurses delusions. Aware of his own inferiority, he over-uses such strength as he has: he goes in for a policy of bluff. So the word went round, 'It is up to us to fend for ourselves'—'Japan can do it alone': until it became a blind article of faith. And all the time the warning bell was pealing out its message!

That was the chance to recover her faith in herself. That was the moment to pause, to reorganize her policy thoroughly, to discover for herself her natural role as a permanent Great Power in the Far East.

2. THE OPPORTUNITY IS MISSED

The decline of imperialism created a vacuum, which Japan should have filled. But, if Japan were to become a true leader, it was not right that she should follow in the footsteps of imperialism. Leadership was not to be acquired by antagonizing the Asians. Only if she became their trusted friend would they accept Japan as a guide. The time when Asia could be treated as a colony by Europeans had passed. Racial aspirations must be fostered and the war furnished the opportunity. If Japan placed herself at the head of Asiatic countries, made herself the champion of the independence and liberation they craved, the Asians would follow her but, if she were so ill-advised as to copy the methods of past European imperialism, the various nations would think that they were living in unpleasant proximity to an aggressor and they would hate the Japanese more than they hated the Europeans and Americans. It was not merely a matter of ethics, nor yet a question of human rights, it was also a question of practical self-interest. Without the spirit of good neighbourhood, what country was going to trust Japan, to open up her resources, to encourage trade and to welcome Japanese goods?

With this as a policy, the problem of China could have been smoothly settled. Why indeed was it that Japan felt inferior and isolated, if not that she could not compose her quarrels with China? Now that Japan was no longer under pressure from Britain and the U.S., Japan could have reached agreement by making certain necessary concessions. When it came to tackling the problem of China, if only she could have devised means of solution that would be readily appreciated, not only by China but also by Britain, U.S. and other countries, that would have been the way, the only way, in which she could have rid herself of those feelings of inferiority and isolation. She would have recovered normal international relations. She would have retained her foreign commerce. That was the key that would have unlocked the gate. Cast aside her old methods, remove unnecessary friction and restore to herself a feeling of security.

That would have been the safest approach whatever the outcome of the war, but, if one attempted a provisional forecast, Germany was the stronger on land, Britain had the upper hand at sea. If neither side showed marked superiority in the air, then the war was bound to be long-drawn-out. The First World War had shown that the U.S. was almost certain to come in on the side of Britain. That being so, the ultimate outcome should have been obvious. Internationally that would have been the common-sense view and it is no more than I frequently said after I came to London. Japan was the guardian of the Far East. It was up to her to prevent the war spreading to the Far East and, to do so, she should have built up a good-neighbour spirit of friendship to all other nations in the eastern part of Asia. She could have found the way to live as a Great World Power.

3. THE WEAK ABE (ARMY) CABINET

But a country directed by a self-sufficient army had no time to spare for a calm assessment of world conditions. Its decisions were based on one-sided, wishful thinking. It pursued wild-cat schemes and careered onward like a horse and carriage drawn by a horse that has bolted. Her leaders paid no attention to the cause of Hiranuma's resignation. They were concerned only with the immediate task of patching up the internal regime and tackled the problem as though it were a matter of daily routine.

So, at a moment of crisis, an Army Cabinet under General Abe, that was so weak that its like had never been seen before, came into being. Balance between the Army and Navy was preserved by appointing as Foreign Minister a naval officer—Admiral Kichisaburo Nomura. The Ministers were all 'ordinary'. A Cabinet built round two well-meaning officers lost a valuable opportunity by doing nothing while conditions were at sixes and sevens, and collapsed within half a year.

The opportunity never returned. Events in China and the southern advance proceeded by sheer momentum as though the cataclysm in Europe was no concern of the Army and Navy. Profiting by the decline of Western power and impelled by insatiable greed, they could not see the mistakes they were making; they thought only, 'Here is the golden opportunity', and proceeded to pursue their policy to still further extremes. They went on plunging deeper into the abyss. That was Japan's calamity. One might say that the Genro had grown old, that the high-handedness of the Army was a distressing national symptom, but fundamentally the fact was that the political consciousness of the people was, judged by the standard of other countries, woefully underdeveloped.

CHAPTER TWO

The Yonai Navy Cabinet

1. YONAI CABINET FORMED, JANUARY 1940

HAD there but been someone with sufficient vision to take the helm! Not in the ranks of the Army, not in the ranks of the Navy, was such a one to be found: the combined efforts, supported by the resolute determination, of the very highest leading classes, were called for. Among these classes was there no one to be found who had the perception to see how the world was tending and what the future held for Japan, no one who had the requisite personality for the task? Can it be that those, who sorrowed for their country, were so stricken with the spirit of defeatism that they dared not come forward?

However that may be, those designated to form the Cabinet were merely 'moderates' from the Army and Navy, appointed to apply the brake. They were not there to stand above the Services and direct the course of the country. The ship of state was committed rudderless to a sea of troubles in the midst of which it plunged on, shaken by the violent agitation of its engines.

Yuasa, Lord Keeper of the Privy Seal, consulted with Admiral Okada, a former Prime Minister[1] and others and put forward the name of Admiral Yonai. The Cabinet had all the hall-marks of a compromise between the Army and the Navy. At the instance of the Emperor, his former aide-de-camp Hata, belonging to the moderate school, remained as Minister for War. The militarists were thoroughly dissatisfied. At a moment of utmost gravity in international relations here was a Cabinet formed merely to achieve equilibrium between the Army and Navy, to carry out a policy of moderation! Accordingly they just went ahead, making no attempt to reconcile their actions to the Cabinet frame of mind.

[1] *Vide* Book Two, Chapter One, s. 3.

Foreign Minister Arita fought hard to get things under control but the militarists had no time for prudence, they were under the spell of what they could see immediately before their eyes. The Chinese upheaval had merged in a southern advance, the 'co-prosperity sphere' was to be extended, like a German *lebensraum*, to the whole of the eastern part of Asia, the Defence State must be Nazified with a single party.

The Yonai Cabinet fell in July 1940. It never formulated an active policy but merely conformed itself to the operations of the Army and Navy. It had wasted a valuable six months, drifting.

2. ADJUSTMENT OF ANGLO-JAPANESE RELATIONS

As Ambassador in London I devoted all my efforts to the achievement of more harmonious relations between the British and Japanese Governments. I had a pleasing vision of bringing about an understanding between the two countries under which the China problem might be solved, if only the opportunity afforded by the war were not missed. Thereby the Far East might be spared the tragedy of war. I believed that this was the only way in which Japan's status could be assured.

There was good reason to feel that Chamberlain's Cabinet, which was formed on the main stream of thought of the Conservative Party, would not be averse to an adjustment of relations and might indeed welcome it, always provided that Japan's attitude made it possible. It depended on the manner in which the Japanese Government transformed its policy on more rational lines.

Foreign Secretary Halifax was friendly in his approach to the question and specially deputed Under-Secretary Butler to confer with me. Influential Ministers such as Lord Hankey and Lord Lloyd frequently consulted with me and threw themselves wholeheartedly into the study. All of them had one wish—not only to prevent the historical relations between the two countries deteriorating, but better still to improve them. Even when the Japanese Army blockaded the British and French foreign concessions at Tientsin and a British man-of-war had searched the *Asama Maru* outside Tokyo Bay and taken off German passengers, both incidents were in the end amicably settled (Ambassador Craigie's great efforts in Tokyo contributed in no small measure). Again Britain met Japan half-way in a settlement of the problem of the despatch, not only of British goods that had been ordered, but also of munitions ordered from Japan. All these matters were satisfactorily adjusted.

Britain's policy towards Japan was continued when Churchill, who had attacked Japan while in opposition, succeeded to Chamberlain. Churchill talked to me frequently and his understanding grew. Ultimately he went so far as to be more than willing to close for a time the Burma Route, by means of which the Chungking Government was receiving help from outside sources, in order that Japan and China should find a means of coming to terms. Churchill assured me that Britain was far from opposing a rational settlement between Japan and China. The critical warnings he had addressed to Japan while in opposition had been directed against her extremely radical policy. He himself had been one of the first to approve the Anglo-Japanese Alliance. He would close the Burma Route for three months round about the rainy season and he trusted that in the interval Japan would try to find a guiding light to settlement with China, which Britain would welcome.

Churchill told me further that he believed that, when one considered the great disparity between the material resources of the U.S. and Japan, and that an attack on Singapore, which was several thousand miles distant from Japan, was much the same as an American attack on Gibraltar, Japan was not a country so foolish as to undertake any such enterprise that would bring her into the war.

The closure of the Burma Route was an event of sufficient importance to arouse considerable criticism in China and the U.S. as well as in Britain. The Chinese Ambassador in London in particular protested against Britain's softening her attitude towards Japan. Only in Japan was there no reaction. The Yonai Cabinet lacked the vitality to seize the occasion and remedy the situation. It was always struggling to cope with the pressure and the plots of the militarists. Since the defeat of France the real strength of Britain was underestimated while the excessive importance attached to German successes obscured the vision of the militarists, whose schemes were now well off the rails.

3. JAPAN'S CHAOTIC POLICY

The driving force in the Army had by now fallen into the hands of the senior staff officers belonging to the China School. As for the Minister for War he had become merely an outward symbol. Under Army direction the Asia Development Board and its agencies, that were to take China under their wing, pushed on its schemes utterly without co-ordination, while the establishment of Wang Ching-wei's Central Government proceeded apace in Lieutenant-General Kagesa's hands.

The Japanese were under the pleasing delusion that the short-sighted scheme of converting China into a second Manchoukuo was succeeding.

As this foolish plan progressed, the Army, aided and abetted by the Navy, was spurred on to advance even further southward. Theory had become reality. As the war developed in Europe, so Japan plunged still further into the mire.

4. SINGLE PARTY GOVERNMENT PROPOSED

It was at this time that the campaign for national reform demanded strongly controlled government under one single party.

In Manchoukuo the *'Concordia Society'* and in China the *Shimminkai* (People's Society) had blazed the trail, it was claimed; in view of the melancholy spectacle presented by the past unseemly scramble for power of the political parties, a single party was essential. The movement had gathered momentum. Military reservists in the provinces were engaged in building up the foundations and the Army now demanded the dissolution of the old parties. For their part the politicians thought that what was required was the amalgamation of the existing parties and joined in the campaign, hoping to preserve their influence in one party resting on the foundations of the former two. Prince Konoye, finding the tide flowing his way, planned one great party with himself in control and won favour by proclaiming again and again that now was the time to act.

The political world was in a state of confusion in which the two opposing reactions of decomposition and re-combination were taking place. On the one hand right- and left-wing agitators were poised ready to seize their opportunity. On the other the power of the politicians was crumbling and the tendency to fall in line with the militarists and to cling on to their coat-tails was gaining the day.

5. EXTENSION OF THE CO-PROSPERITY SPHERE

Meanwhile the theory of *lebensraum* and the study of *geopolitik* were growing popular.

The military resources demanded by the Defence State could only be supplied by countries under Japan's sphere of influence. The world practised closed economies so that the trade which was a life-line to the nation had become impossible. To provide for their needs, as well as to maintain the supply of munitions, Manchoukuo alone was insufficient, so China had to be brought within the 'co-prosperity' sphere. But still this was insufficient. The Navy needed oil. So losses in trade with Europe must be made good in the eastern part of Asia. The argument was plausible.

But, as fast as territory grew, so did Japan's economic demands, until the idea embraced the whole of 'Greater East Asia'. And that meant that the area of conquest must itself be expanded. Like a snowman, the concept of the Japanese sphere of influence just went on growing and growing.

Japan had rejected the rule of right and embraced military rule. The doctrine that in the process of time water will find its own level did not commend itself to the Japanese people. They preferred the sudden swoop: if it meant defeat, better to die gloriously.

Anything more dangerous it would be hard to imagine.

6. REVIVAL OF THE TRIPARTITE ALLIANCE TALKS

A year after Hiranuma had resigned, the Army resumed its alliance talks with Germany. The German argument was that victory was certain and the collapse of the British Empire inevitable. How then could the British and Americans be of any use to Japan? It was Germany that was Japan's friend. The Japanese Army felt all alone in the world. They *must* have someone to help them carry out their plans.

This time, however, the talks were not concerned with theoretical enemies. The Germans pointed out that Germany was engaged in a life and death struggle with Britain and France. If the talks meant anything, it was that Japan must be prepared to take sides with Germany in the war. The Army accepted the argument and demanded of the Cabinet permission to resume the talks. Oshima came back to Japan and Ambassador Kurusu took over in his absence. The Yonai Cabinet objected to negotiations that would make it necessary for Japan to come into the war and the Army set about overthrowing the Cabinet.

7. ARGUMENTS FOR AND AGAINST THE DRIFT TOWARDS WAR

At that time there were two schools of thought. Japan's military representatives in Berlin and Rome maintained that the mighty German Army and the Air Force had already shown what they could do. Germany would win the war in a short time, particularly if Italy came in, and Britain would collapse. Tighten the bonds that linked Japan with Germany and Italy and reap the benefit! This was just the moment for Japan to establish her leadership in Greater East Asia and take her place in the world as a great power, commanding all the resources she required.

The other school was represented by the Japanese Embassy in London (the Naval and Military Attachés concurred). Germany was superior on land, Britain on the sea. The German Air Force could not dominate the British skies nor her submarines complete the blockade of Britain. The war would be a long one and the U.S. was certain to come in. In the end Germany would be surrounded and defeated. If Japan were not misled by present appearances but instead found means to come to terms with Britain and the U.S. during the war, she could clean up her troubles in China, keep the war away from the Far East and designate a neutral area there. At the same time, giving due consideration to the racial aspirations of other Asian nations, she could set up a lasting policy of goodwill towards them and maintain her neutrality from start to finish. This was the way in which Japan could consolidate her position, carry her due weight in world affairs and, when the war was over, take the place as a great power to which she was destined.

From these views I never wavered.

CHAPTER THREE

A Scene That Will Go Down in History

1. THE BRITISH PEOPLE (THE SCENE AFTER DUNKIRK)

THOSE who know the British can imagine how they behaved at a moment of crisis when the existence of the nation was at stake. During the previous World War I had been present in England and had seen them then. It is a national characteristic that the worse things are, the calmer and more confident they become; they make light of difficulties. In that dangerous hour after Dunkirk, the statesman and the man-in-the-street, men and women, the working-man and the nobleman, were united; there was not one that lost confidence in ultimate victory. When others might have been flustered, the British took it in their stride. They went to work as usual. Truly a remarkable people!

Parliament opens. The time has come when, in the most critical moment in British history, the people's representatives must review the situation without delay and inform the nation what decisions have been taken. It is June 18th, 1940. Parliament Building stands in Westminster overlooking the Thames. The day stands out. The attention of the world is concentrated on this one building.

The House was packed. The spectators' seats, the diplomats' seats, the women's seats were filled to overflowing. Preceded by the ushers in their ceremonial wigs and robes, the members came in quietly. When the Speaker had taken his seat, the session opened. First the order of the day was read over formally and then the Assembly waited with bated breath for Churchill to take the floor.

2. CHURCHILL'S SPEECH TO THE HOUSE

And so Churchill began his first report on the war. In dry tones and simply he assessed the defeat. The German Army had achieved a great victory by their brilliant tactics. The Allied Army had fought bravely but had been overwhelmed. The British Army had been forced back to the coast. He pictured the tragedy of Dunkirk; the desperate bravery of the British, the heroic efforts of the French; naught had availed. The calm, courageous recital struck, word by word, to the hearts of the listeners.

And then he continued. If France fell, Britain must fight on. The enemy stood on the opposite coast and might invade at any moment. Britain faced the greatest crisis in her history. He had consulted the experts in the three Services and they had not abandoned their belief in a final victory; the fighting spirit of the British would triumph. Rather than submit to a tyrannical enemy, they would fight to the last man. The Commonwealth was solidly behind them. The issue was Victory or Death—'their finest hour'. Succeeding generations would praise their decision.

No one who witnessed the scene as he resumed his seat will ever forget it.

At that second the House boiled over. Chamberlain jumped up clapping vigorously and waving his handkerchief: Members stood up, stamped their feet and went mad with excitement. What a difference from the calm with which the announcement of war had been received a year earlier! The British have their moments when the emotions surge to the surface.

The determination displayed by Parliament was that of the whole nation. One moment of ecstasy and then the people were calm again. They hastened to their daily task. Government, factories and households resumed their routine duties.

All this I reported to my Government and concluded with the words that this was a scene that would go down in history.

CHAPTER FOUR

Japan's Inexcusable Foolhardiness

1. JAPAN'S COURSE OF ACTION IN THE LIGHT OF GERMAN SUCCESSES

GERMAN victories certainly gave them excellent material for propaganda, which was most effective in the case of Japan. The Army and certain members of the Government were impressed. Assuming Germany to win and the British Empire to collapse, the British Colonies would fall into German hands[1] if Japan stood by with folded arms, and Japan would be worse off than before the war. The Far East would be under German control and the Germans did not exactly stand on ceremony. Those that swallowed German talk were now seized with panic when they contemplated the results of German victory. They could have no peace of mind unless Japan made a pact with Germany beforehand, under which spheres of influence after the war were agreed. There was, for instance, the question of the mandate over the former German colonies in the South Seas. The extension of German might, that was so formidable, to the Far East, must be checked while there was time. Otherwise Japan would always regret it. Better to watch for an opportunity to come into the war and fight side by side with Germany. They hated to think that Japan might 'miss the bus'.

By now Japan had forsaken the calm, realistic view. She believed that Germany would win and thought only what she could do about it. One might have expected that the Army would prove a good medium for German propaganda but that most Japanese leaders should have fallen into the same frame of mind can be recalled only with a feeling of shame.

---

[1] The French and Dutch Colonies are mentioned in similar terms elsewhere in the text.

2. BEARING OF THE CHINA PROBLEM ON THE TRIPARTITE ALLIANCE

Since the Army was credulous enough to accept German talk of victory, they were in a desperate hurry to be on good terms with Germany and Italy. To the military mind, whether it was a question of China, or of ensuring Japan's position in the post-war world, close relations with Germany were all-important. Come to think of it, Germany's treaty of non-aggression with Russia actually improved Japan's relations with that country, for it lessened the danger from the north. It should in fact be welcomed. So there was really nothing to stand in the way of the alliance. Once the Army knew that Germany was going to win, that bogy vanished from sight.

At the same time, it seemed to the Army that the only explanation of Chiang Kai-shek's continued resistance to Japan was the outside assistance he was receiving from Britain, the U.S. and France. Here were goods being smuggled in from Hong Kong, supplies coming in via the Yunnan Railway (from Indo-China) and blood-transfusions via the Burma Route. Outside assistance to Chiang made a solution of the China problem impracticable. It was an insult in the face of the Japanese Army!

3. THE ARMY THREATENS BRITAIN

One Sunday in July, the British Foreign Secretary summoned me urgently to meet him. The interview took place in the Secretary's room overlooking the park. Halifax said that he had received an urgent telegram from Ambassador Craigie. It appeared that the Director of Military Intelligence had sent for the British Military Attaché and requested a cessation of assistance to Chiang in the following terms: 'Britain is already beaten and the British Empire faces dissolution. And yet Britain continues to support Chiang and to encourage him to resist Japan. Japan now is strong. The Army has its batteries trained on Hong Kong and it only requires one word of command for them to bombard the island. Britain would do well to cease assistance to Chiang and to control smuggling from Hong Kong. Today in Japan it is the Army that holds the power. The Japanese Foreign Office, on which Britain relies, is powerless and unworthy of trust. Britain would be well advised to accept this request from the Japanese Army.' Listening to these outrageous words, I could not believe my ears. It appeared that the British were under the impression that an attack on Hong Kong by the Japanese Army was imminent.

'What meaning,' said Halifax, 'am I to attach to this request from the General Staff at a time when you and I are doing our best to improve relations?'

While the Foreign Secretary had been reading the telegram, I was thinking to myself, 'Has the Army really come to this?' and my heart sank. Even as a bluff it was clear that the threat could have no effect on a great power like Britain. I could not bear to think that the Army would destroy such a valuable relationship. If the words were accepted at their face value, it meant the severance of diplomatic relations. I felt that it by no means expressed the true sentiments of Japan. Nor should it do so.

'From whom did the Attaché hear these words,' I said, 'concerning, as they do, a matter of great importance to our diplomatic relations?' 'From the D.M.I.,' Halifax replied. 'But,' said I, 'in Tokyo the only person who is authorized to handle such a question is the Foreign Minister and in London myself. I most deeply regret that a member of the General Staff should have used such language. But it is the bluster of one who has not the authority to use it and it is not an official statement. The policy of the Japanese Government is, as stated by its competent officials, to maintain good relations with Britain. You should not pay attention to the blustering of a member of the General Staff.'

The Foreign Secretary regained his composure and the conversation continued on friendly terms. Thereafter both the British F.O. and I myself continued to work for better relations. A later change in the Government brought in Eden as Secretary. For a long time he was absent in the Middle East and I frequently met Churchill. Eventually Britain tightened up control of smuggling from Hong Kong and closed the Burma Route for three months, thereby clearly indicating her hope that Japan would straighten out her relations with China. Thus was given to Japan the last opportunity to restore her intercourse with China to normal, to improve her relations with Britain, and incidentally with the U.S., and to bring back her foreign policy to the right track.

This was the advice and the warning that I constantly gave my Government.

But looking back, I can see that what the General Staff told the British Military Attaché was only too true—power rested in the hands of the military authorities and the Government was powerless. The concessions made by Britain and my own efforts were pure waste of time.

4. THE ARMY OVERTHROWS THE YONAI CABINET

In their determination to ally Japan with Germany and Italy, the Army gave the Cabinet no peace. The latter had the support of the intellectuals and of Court circles in their opposition but the Army rode rough-shod over their objections.

The Army were not only insistent in their request that negotiations with Germany and Italy should be resumed but also loudly demanded the dissolution of the existing political parties and the establishment of a Nazi-type single party. On the grounds that the Yonai Cabinet was unsuited to the task of handling such a critical situation, they declined to co-operate further with it. Muto, Director of Military Affairs in the War Office, intrigued to force the resignation of Hata, the Minister for War, and the Army refused to nominate a successor.

The Yonai Cabinet therefore resigned.

Previously Prince Konoye had resigned his position as President of the Privy Council. He now established himself as the favourite of the Army by declaring publicly that once the existing parties were dissolved, he himself would establish a powerful single party.

BOOK SEVEN

The Tokyo–Berlin–Rome Axis

2nd and 3rd Konoye Cabinets

CHAPTER ONE

Prince Konoye and Matsuoka

1. SECOND KONOYE CABINET TAKES OVER

THE Japanese people have short memories. What had the Konoye Cabinet accomplished? What had it done for the country? The people had forgotten. Unfortunately they have, generally speaking, little sense of political responsibility. They have not learned that ultimately affairs of state are the duty of the whole country, which is another way of saying that they are the responsibility of the people themselves. Even the statesman thinks that once he has resigned his duty is discharged. The Japanese seem to regard politics as a 'show' put on for their benefit. They applaud good 'acting' but it never occurs to them that they themselves are the players, that it is they that are performing. The statesmen strut on the stage in their brief hour of glory. How many statesmen are there who reflect that it is their duty to be of lasting benefit to their country?

It was natural that the nation should place great hopes on Prince Konoye, seeing that he had already been Prime Minister and had also been President of the House of Peers and President of the Privy Council. Moreover he had won golden opinions by volunteering to establish that 'Great Party', of which there had recently been so much talk. Political circles expected him to curb the Army by means of this wonderful party, and to restore the political responsibility of the people. The Army, however, had its own plans; they proposed to set up single-party government in order to attain their objective of the Defence State. That Prince Konoye should have attracted the complete confidence of all circles and should have been put forward by the Lord Keeper of the Privy Seal and senior statesmen to take upon him the mantle of leadership, so sadly lacking of late, was what might have been expected in the political situation of the day.

At that time Marquis Kido had succeeded Yuasa as Lord Keeper of the Privy Seal.

The first Konoye Cabinet had coincided with one epoch—the bankruptcy of Japan's diplomacy after the 'Manchurian Incident'. His second Cabinet was to coincide with another epoch—Japan's rapid advance on the road to ruin under the Tripartite Alliance. Neither the people nor Konoye himself had learned anything from what had happened before. The cast that took the stage with so much *éclat* included Lieutenant-General Tojo, ex-Inspector-General of Aviation, as War Minister, and Admiral Oikawa as Navy Minister (in succession to Admiral Yoshida). But the outstanding appointment was that of Yosuke Matsuoka, who had been a highly successful President of the South Manchuria Railway. He became Minister for Foreign Affairs.

2. YOSUKE MATSUOKA

Mr. Matsuoka was born at Hagi in Choshu[1] and was brought up in the old clan atmosphere, but he finished his education at Oregon University, where he absorbed American ideas of statesmanship. He spoke English fluently so that he could acquit himself as well in that language as in Japanese, whether in everyday talk or in public address. The American ideas that he had absorbed were neither of a pronounced right or left leaning. The principles he stood for were those of a Japanese patriot.

Matsuoka held strong views on the subject of Manchuria. But at the time of the first battle of Shanghai he had displayed most definite liberal and moderate ideas in the assistance he had rendered me in the truce negotiations. Soon after assuming the duties of Foreign Minister he published his views on the problems of China and the Far East in a statement in which he laid down the principles of 'no indemnities, no annexations, and recognition of sovereignty'. That fact alone induced me to think for a while in my European outpost that now at last, in the association of two liberal thinkers, Konoye and Matsuoka, Japan might keep the militarists in check and get back on the right track again. Matsuoka had valuable experience of our Foreign Ministry. Since then, he had for many years held positions of great responsibility on the continent of Asia both in the political and in the industrial field. Many thoughtful people, including myself, expected great things of Matsuoka.

Alas that conditions falsified our hopes! Matsuoka was very ambitious. He hoped to follow in the footsteps of earlier great men of Choshu—Yamagata, Terauchi[2] and Tanaka—and saw himself as the

[1] The old name of the province. Now part of Yamaguchi Prefecture.
[2] Not the Terauchi mentioned elsewhere in this book, but his father.

architect of a New Japan. Possibly the state of his health made him impatient to seize the chance to achieve his political ambitions while the general trend seemed favourable. In any case the result was disastrous to Japan.

He was in too great a hurry to get results. He wanted to be always in the vanguard, leading the Army, not as their plaything but as one who could mould them to his own uses. In the Cabinet he assumed a role larger than that of Konoye himself. There was no room in the Japanese politicial world for two such outstanding men on the stage at the same time.

3. COMPOSITION OF THE SECOND KONOYE CABINET

Before finally forming his new Cabinet, Konoye had conferred with the candidates for the Army, Navy and Foreign Affairs on his proposed policy and, having reached agreement, proceeded to the actual formation. The policy adopted was an entirely new one that met the demands of the Army—at home the single-party system, abroad the formation of a three-power alliance and the occupation of China.

One section in the Army had favoured Shiratori as Foreign Minister; he became instead Adviser to Matsuoka. Under the strong recommendation of the Army and Navy, Lieutenant-General Oshima was reappointed Ambassador to Germany,[1] Admiral Nomura became Ambassador to the U.S. and Lieutenant-General Tatekawa (who had been involved in the 'March Incident' (1931, Book One, Chapter Two, s. 4), Ambassador to Russia. Needless to say, the Army attached more importance to Germany, the Navy to the U.S.

In the hope of controlling the Army and the Navy, Konoye appointed Admiral Teijiro Yoshida Minister of Commerce and Industry, where he would be in close touch with the supply of arms, and Teiichi Suzuki, an ex-Army officer, Chairman of the Planning Board, to preserve a balance between the two Services. At a later stage Baron Hiranuma also joined the Cabinet as Home Minister.

---

[1] For the time being, however, Oshima remained in Japan and Kurusu carried on as Ambassador in Berlin.

CHAPTER TWO

The Imperial Rule Aid Association

1. THE CAMPAIGN FOR A NEW CONSTITUTION

PRINCE KONOYE was of opinion that it was impossible to discharge the duties of administration smoothly without the backing of a single party; as already related, he had, in demanding the dissolution of the existing political parties and announcing his intention of forming such a party, resigned his position as President of the Privy Council for the purpose. That had been the signal for a political change and the public were pinning their hopes on him. It was now announced that he would assume the post of President of the new party with Marquis Kido as Vice-President. I imagine that he expected to absorb the powers of the fighting services within those of the new party so that he could alternatively manipulate or restrain them.

The Army got to work at once on the formation of the party. The two existing political parties could not but feel aggrieved at the prospect of their dissolution and, when it transpired that the planning was to be in the hands of the Army, they regarded the scheme as being one to establish fascist government and withheld their support. There was indeed at that time a strong current of opposition to fascism, for the dislike of any form of feudalistic government was widespread and it was not only the political parties that opposed the military plans to form the new party.

2. THE DUTY OF A SUBJECT IN PRACTICE

The feeling that the existing political parties did not merit confidence had spread to all quarters. Since the 'Manchurian Incident' their influence had been waning, though they still had the Diet to themselves. But the Army thought that affairs of state should be the province of the whole nation. The Diet should not be a half-way house where politicians confused the issue. Leaders and people must be coupled together, working smoothly in unison. Only if the duty of a subject as defined in Eastern ways of thought was applied to the parliamentary system would there be perfect communion between all classes. Only thus could a subject be of real assistance to the Government. Such an organ should gather into one fold Government organizations, party members, intellectuals, the fighting services, provincial representatives, the press, everybody.

So came into being the Imperial Rule Aid Association (I.R.A.A.), a Japanese feudalistic, political idea moulded into a Nazi pattern, with a huge budget and organization and provincial branches. Count Yoriyasu Arima, a friend of Konoye, became Secretary-General. But the prime mover was the Army, which sponsored it. Japanese theories as translated in this association are hard to follow but the explanations of its progenitors savour strongly of reaction.

In course of time appeared offshoots such as the Youth Association, the Production League, the Patriotic Industrial Crusade, etc., on the lines of the Nazi S.S. or the Russian labour unions. The Association also fostered the expansion of Japanese influence in the East Asian sphere of co-prosperity and as a subsidiary founded the Asia Development League on an ambitious scale.

Though the Association purported to be a Japanese version of the Nazi system, it was really founded on the ideas of the Manchurian '*Concordia Society*', being a hotch-potch of right- and left-wing theories. Control was in the hands of the Military Affairs Bureau. It was no more than a mask for the activities of the militarists. It was utterly unlike the Nazi organization. It had no vitality of its own and in fact its most noticeable feature was the excesses committed by the Youth Association under the shield of the Army.

3. DISSOLUTION OF THE FORMER POLITICAL PARTIES

In order to get internal administration firmly in its hands, the Army urged that the Minister for War should duplicate the duties of the Home Office, but it was baulked by the strong opposition the suggestion encountered. Instead Konoye scored a minor triumph by appointing Hiranuma,[1] who was by way of favouring the Imperial Way School, Home Minister, and Lieutenant-General Yanagawa, an associate in the *Kokuhonsha* and also an advocate of the Imperial Way, Minister of

[1] *Vide* Book Five, Chapter One.

Justice. With scant concern for Army views, Hiranuma declared in the Diet that the I.R.A.A. was not a political, but a public, association: Japan was not going to copy the Nazi system of single-party authoritarianism but to introduce a system under which all the people would support the Government by individually carrying out their duties as subjects in their own Eastern manner.

If this were so, then the I.R.A.A.'s only purpose in life was to busy itself with questions relating to political ideas; it was in fact to be a white elephant. The political parties, cut adrift by these various moves, ended by coming into line and were dissolved.

But if the I.R.A.A. was not a political association, then the ex-party members had no home to turn to. It seemed that Prince Konoye was having second thoughts about the I.R.A.A. and nobody wanted them. But so long as the Constitution was still in existence, the business of the Diet must be carried on. So the former parties put their heads together and formed the Imperial Rule Political Association (I.R.P.A.). It was to command a majority in the Diet and to join hands with the Government in the smooth discharge of affairs of state, just as the Army desired.

The I.R.A.A. was at pains to explain that it had no connection with the I.R.P.A. But much the same people ran both and the names were similar. It was all very well to say that one was a public association and the other a political association but the public were all at sea—not that they greatly cared. Actually the I.R.P.A. included, in addition to former party members, retired soldiers, bureaucrats and business men, but for the most part it was composed of politicians with an admixture of former Army officers and Civil Servants.

That was the end of the power of political parties in the Diet, which became a puppet-show. The Army had swept away all political obstacles to the free exercise of its will. Neither the I.R.A.A. nor the I.R.P.A. ever acquired the driving power of their prototypes in Germany or Russia. They were powerless, amorphous organs manipulated by the Army. The political consciousness of the people withered on the stalk.

CHAPTER THREE

Wang Ching-wei (Part 2)
(His Government set up in Nanking)

BASIC AGREEMENT BETWEEN JAPAN AND CHINA

At the time that Prince Konoye's Cabinet was installed, Wang Ching-wei's Government had already been formed in Nanking. The Kuomintang[1] was retained. The national flag was still the white sun on a blue sky but a triangular, yellow pennant was attached with the words 'peace', 'foundation of the state' and 'anti-communism' inscribed as the mottoes of the new Government. The next step was formal recognition by Japan.

Japan had appointed ex-Premier General Abe special envoy and after protracted labour an involved, grotesque agreement was born. Gone were Wang's dreams of a liberated China. Jumbled up in the text were Army plans of occupation and demands for the grant of special rights. Such was the Basic Agreement between Japan and China, under which Japan recognized Wang's Administration as the Central Government of China, in return for which Japan would be given any necessary assistance for the prosecution of her military operations. Japan, again, recognized Chinese sovereignty and the new Government extended comprehensive rights on a basis of joint Sino-Japanese co-operation. At the same time Japan, Manchoukuo and China issued an identic proclamation that the three nations would henceforward make common cause, that Manchoukuo and China would exchange envoys and would settle outstanding differences for all time.

The agreement was ratified on November 4th, 1940. Major-General Kagesa became Supreme Military Adviser and actually sat in the driving seat. As Supreme Economic Adviser, Kazuo Aoki, a former Finance Minister, was sent with an army of financial experts to guide the new Government. Authority in the Central Reserve Bank was held by a Japanese.

[1] China's 'Nationalist Party'.

CHAPTER FOUR

The Tripartite Alliance (Part 3)

1. PRELIMINARY CONFERENCE OF LEADING CABINET MINISTERS

KONOYE'S most serious problem was diplomatic—how to tone down Army demands. The Japanese version of a Nazi text, the I.R.A.A. served a double purpose. At home it meant national reform, abroad it was related to the proposed tripartite alliance. The Navy no longer opposed it, now that power had passed into the hands of the stalwart Southern School. Matsuoka, who knew nothing about Germany and was very hazy on the subject of European politics, had fallen completely under the spell of the Army. He ignored the views of the country's diplomatic representatives and accepted German propaganda at its face value.

Germany had abandoned its plans to invade Britain in 1940 but did her best to convince the world that they were merely postponed till 1941. That would be the end of Britain. The Japanese Army was told that Japan should seize the opportunity and take Singapore. Then, when Britain collapsed, Japan would be entitled to her share of the spoils. Was she going to lose the golden opportunity, which would never return?

The Japanese were in a receptive mood. The proposal for an alliance had already been accepted at a conference held by Konoye at his Ogikubo residence on the eve of the formation of his Cabinet. At that meeting Konoye, Matsuoka, Tojo and (Admiral) Yoshida had been present. Evidently the Navy still had misgivings at that time, for Yoshida had resigned on the score of ill-health but his successor, Admiral Oikawa, had given his assent to the proposal.

2. NEGOTIATIONS TRANSFERRED TO TOKYO

No sooner had Matsuoka assumed charge than he instructed Ambassador Kurusu to ascertain Ribbentrop's intentions. The latter, realizing that the time had come, despatched his trusted Minister Stahmer as his personal representative to confer, in company with Ambassador Ott, with Matsuoka. It was understood that Germany would take care of Italian interests in the negotiations.

Full of confidence and secure of Government support, Matsuoka took up the negotiations, aided by Saito, Foreign Office Diplomatic Adviser. In substance his proposals envisaged a simple military alliance such as Ribbentrop had suggested earlier. No country that the parties had in mind was specified. The means and the time of assistance were regarded as a matter concerning the sovereignty of the ally and left to her decision.

3. RELATIONSHIP BETWEEN THE ALLIANCE AND SOVIET RUSSIA

Japan's relations with Russia had not improved in the slightest but she was committed to the southern advance and she had come to feel that in her relations with Britain and the U.S. her interests were identical with those of Germany, and that these were the enemies by whom she was confronted. As for the northern danger she believed that she could rely for the time being on the improvement in Russo-German relations.

In reality Germany had merely obtained a breathing space in the East but she assured Japan that the non-aggression treaty had so improved Russo-German relations that Russia now respected German intentions, so that Germany would have no difficulty in persuading Russia to show goodwill towards Japan. For that matter, once the alliance was signed, Germany would see to it that Russia became a party to it.

German pronouncements were well received in Japan and made a deep impression on the Army, which put blind faith in Germany's boastful talk of leading Russia as she wished: the negotiations were continued in that frame of mind. One reason why the name of Russia was expunged from Article 3 of the alliance treaty was that the Anti-Comintern Pact was still in existence. In view of the German non-aggression treaty there was the underlying hope that Russia could be won over.

4. SIGNATURE OF THE TRIPARTITE ALLIANCE; REPERCUSSIONS

The negotiations in Tokyo were concluded and a Triple Alliance between Japan, Germany and Italy was signed in Berlin on September 27th, 1940.

Originally the Emperor had been very much opposed to the Alliance, as was also the Genro, but in the end H.I.M. yielded to the advice and persuasion of Prince Konoye and fell in with the wishes of the Government. An Imperial Rescript then made it clear that henceforward Axis principles would be the basis of the country's policy.

The announcement created a sensation throughout the world, which divided into two camps—the Axis countries on the one side, the Democracies Britain and the U.S. on the other, with Russia occupying the favourable position of neutral. Relations with Britain, the U.S. and France speedily deteriorated. But Konoye, in defiance of common sense, explained to the Privy Council that the Alliance was consistent with an intention to improve relations with the neighbouring countries of Russia and the U.S. Presumably he expected that Germany would assist a *détente* with Russia, while the U.S., as Germany had explained, would be deterred by the might of the three allies from coming into the war. But how could the Alliance be other than an obstruction to friendly relations with the British and Americans or even be a means of improving them ? If such diplomacy was not sheer bluff, what was it ? To those like myself who had consistently opposed the Alliance it passed human understanding.

However that may be, on his way back from a visit to Europe[1] Matsuoka met Steinhardt, American Ambassador in Moscow, to discuss Japan-American relations and said that Konoye would lose no time in opening negotiations with the U.S. in a spirit of goodwill. Matsuoka also telegraphed to me more than once that he was working for a better understanding with Britain, that he would exchange views with Churchill and that he attached great importance to good relations. But I felt that the Alliance had placed Japan in a position from which she could never recover and I was plunged in the depths of despair.

As the war between Germany and Britain developed, the anti-British, pro-German feeling in the Army intensified. Soon after the

[1] *Vide* Chapter Six.

formation of the Konoye Cabinet many British residents were incarcerated by the gendarmerie, with the unfortunate result that Cox, Reuter's correspondent, committed suicide while in their hands. As relations with Britain went from bad to worse, the Army gave the impression that that was what they wanted.

CHAPTER FIVE

Matsuoka's Policy

1. MATSUOKA'S REVOLUTIONARY DIPLOMACY

THE Matsuoka type of diplomacy was something new in Japan; in one sense it might be termed a revolutionary policy. Matsuoka seems clearly to have thought that it was his mission to renovate Japan's political structure. The starting point was to be the Alliance, on the basis of which he proposed to carry out his reforms at home and abroad after the manner of his Nazi 'master'. He felt that the time for a reform based on the Army had come and he intended to lead the van.

Having explained his policy to his subordinates, he proceeded to fill key positions in the Ministry of Foreign Affairs with zealous supporters of the Axis and he dismissed nearly all Japan's former Ambassadors and Ministers. That the working of the overseas missions should be brought to a standstill did not check him. Since he placed complete reliance on the international Intelligence brought him by the Army, his own diplomats were superfluous.

The model of this drastic treatment was shown for all to see in his own Ministry but, curiously, neither the Army and Navy, nor other Government departments, displayed much haste to follow the example he gave them. Having settled Japan's course by concluding the Alliance, having disposed of the problem of China by the basic agreement, Matsuoka now turned his attention to the south at the request of the Army, for in French Indo-China a new development was taking place under the combined efforts of the Army, the Navy and Matsuoka himself.

Matsuoka gambled everything on a German victory; with this as his premise the 'Greater East Asia Co-prosperity Sphere' was to be established, in which Japan's influence was to be firmly implanted. His diplomacy followed the Hitler model. The Tripartite Alliance, the proposed Russo-Japanese neutrality pact, the basic agreement with China, all these manœuvres followed the same fundamental design.

2. NEGOTIATIONS WITH FRENCH INDO-CHINA

Japan maintained that huge consignments were reaching Chiang from French Indo-China via the Yunnan Railway, that Hanoi had become the port of supply of the Chungking Government and that, in permitting this, Indo-China was acting in an unfriendly manner, which should not be allowed to continue (on the China side of the border the army of occupation had now reached the frontier).

The Governor-General de Coux was, at least outwardly, subject to the orders of the Vichy Government, which in turn, being under German protection, was bound to be friendly to Japan. Indo-China could not, therefore, continue what was in effect hostile action. Since Japan needed to satisfy herself that the railway was not being used any longer to supply Chungking, it became necessary to station troops in Hanoi and other key-points in north Indo-China. The Army accordingly despatched Major-General Nishihara to negotiate with de Coux, while the Foreign Minister negotiated directly with Arsène-Henri, the French Ambassador, and with the Vichy Government.

Acting under coercion the Governor-General gave way. His negative, non-co-operative attitude at times irked the Japanese Army considerably but eventually Indo-China agreed to the stationing of Japanese troops in the north of the country.

Thereupon the Army was guilty of disgraceful behaviour. The entry of troops was to have been a peaceful manœuvre but the plan was upset by the intrigues of the senior staff officers. Staff officers of the occupying troops, with the connivance of the Army chiefs in Tokyo, carried out the entry as though it was an occupation by force of arms, and proceeded to control the territory in the manner that had now become second nature to them. The fact was that the officers were dissatisfied with the attitude of moderation shown by Nishihara in the negotiations, and, therefore, just ignored them. The Navy protested strongly but the occupying troops paid no attention. In defiance of the arrangements made they carried out bombing attacks. Later, when the Emperor heard of this indiscipline, H.I.M. expressed grave concern that it should be the Army that had damaged Japan's fair name.

The incident was patched up and the pretence of occupation by mutual consent was maintained. Afterwards a comprehensive trade and economic agreement was concluded.

3. INTERNATIONAL DEMOCRACY: ECONOMIC FREEDOM

If we look back at past history, the European *renaissance* and the Industrial Revolution opened up new worlds to conquer in the Far East. The whole earth was the colonizing ground of the Europeans, who mapped out spheres of influence throughout the world while the native races were still asleep. Only Japan stood out and became a great nation. But the Japanese were completely shut out from the European colonies. In the Philippines, Indo-China, Borneo, Indonesia,[1] Malaya, Burma, not only were Japanese activities forbidden, but even entry. Ordinary trade was hampered by unnatural, discriminatory treatment. These territories were in fact no more than dependencies of the mother countries. In this epoch there was not so much as a smell of democracy to be traced. A curtain of capitalist imperialism had been interposed. If the Eastern races had been liberated, if they had been on a footing of free intercourse, allowed to trade and work together, then there is no knowing what development these countries might have made, how far their standard of living might have been raised, what contribution they might have made to world stability!

In a sense the Manchurian outbreak was the result of the international closed economies that followed on the First World War. There was a feeling at the back of it that it provided the only escape from economic strangulation. To provide for a growing population and safeguard Japan's position as a great power, a space in which to breathe must be found. The pity was that Japan did not know the ways of the world. She was hemmed in between the rigid static doctrines of the League of Nations and the anarchism of the Comintern. She should have looked before she leapt. She should have put forward a dignified claim for the economic emancipation of the Far East, have proclaimed the ideal of international democracy and appealed stage by stage to the good sense of the U.S., of Britain and of the world.

But Japan lacked the understanding and the patience. She was obsessed by the urgency of her immediate problems. She rushed in time and again; she reverted to the methods of European imperialism of the dim, distant past. And so the excessive military reliance on power provoked a reaction from Europe and America, which first manifested itself in the economic war waged against Japan. The straits to which she was thereby reduced were slowly but surely bringing her to death's door. She dashed on blindly to open up just a little more space for herself. In proportion as the pressure of economic controls increased,

[1] Known at the time as the Dutch or Netherlands East Indies (N.E.I.).

so the need for living space seemed to grow. Economic warfare and a mistaken idea of militarism formed a vicious circle, which ended by precipitating her into the Second World War. Reasons were proclaimed and ideologies were preached. American and British belief in the sanctity of treaties was met by the doctrine of self-defence. The policy of the *status in quo* was countered by the co-prosperity sphere. By the time that 'Matsuoka diplomacy' was in its stride, French Indo-China had been invaded and the vicious circle had landed Japan in a position from which there was no escape.

4. ECONOMIC DISCUSSIONS WITH FRENCH INDO-CHINA AND NETHERLANDS EAST INDIES

French colonial policy was far more reactionary than that of Britain and the U.S. From the time France had conquered Annam and Cambodia and made them into French colonies, her policy had been one of exploitation. Independence movements were ruthlessly crushed and the political freedom of the people taken away from them. Economically French Indo-China was entirely dependent on France and the door was shut to other powers. Intercourse and trade with Japan, the country most favourably situated to do business, was severely restricted. Stationed at one corner of East Asia, the country was kept in complete isolation. Indonesia's relations with the Netherlands were much the same. But the spirit of racial emancipation had at long last begun to breathe over East Asia. Now that the home countries were at war or had been occupied by the enemy, the down-trodden races awoke. There were in Tokyo many refugees who had fought for independence. When Japan's influence spread southward and they saw her power with their own eyes, racial movements stirred to life. For that reason the home countries looked askance at Japan and regarded all her economic requests as veiling political designs.

The economic pressure brought to bear on Japan by countries that opposed the stand she had taken made it absolutely essential that she should obtain elbow-room in adjoining countries of East Asia; it was inevitable that she should seek an economic outlet in the colonies of the Western powers. But the door was shut in her face. She then resorted to force and was marked down as an aggressor. In French Indo-China she had initiated negotiations before the Army came in. They were now concluded but on terms that were never satisfactorily implemented.

To the Netherlands East Indies Japan at first sent her Minister for Commerce Kobayashi, and later her former Minister Yoshizawa, to

o

straighten out economic relations. The Netherlands, however, were dissatisfied with the outcome of the talks and irresponsible diehards fanned the flames of international discord caused by Japan's southern advance, so that the talks served only to worsen relations between the two countries.

5. MEDIATION IN FRONTIER DISPUTE BETWEEN INDO-CHINA AND SIAM

The boundary line between Indo-China and Siam, which roughly followed the course of the River Mekong, had always been a bone of contention. The Siamese longed to recover the Cambodia area that France had taken from them by force. On the outbreak of the European War a clash occurred and hostilities broke out. Considering that the peace of East Asia was endangered, Matsuoka made an offer to mediate, which was accepted.

Talks in Tokyo made no progress until Matsuoka suggested terms that were accepted under pressure. Siam was satisfied to receive half of what she had claimed and the line was delimited by a commission headed by a Japanese delegate.

Japanese action was natural and was welcomed by the Privy Council, but after Japan's defeat the former line was restored.

Britain, the U.S., France and the Netherlands resented Matsuoka's political offensive and his threatening tone with its military and naval background. His actions brought these countries together and caused them to concert political and military measures against her.

Britain let the U.S. take the lead in tackling the problems of China and the U.S. came to fill the role of advocate for Europe and America. The other countries also accepted American leadership and a united front was established. Under American guidance Japan's encirclement by the A.B.C.D.[1] powers became formidable.

So soon as he had completed his mediation between Indo-China and Siam, Matsuoka set out on a visit to Germany and Italy (March 11th, 1941).

---

[1] American, British, Chinese, Dutch.

CHAPTER SIX

Matsuoka's Visit to Europe (Part 1) (Russo-Japanese Treaty of Neutrality)

1. MOTIVES OF MATSUOKA'S VISIT TO GERMANY AND ITALY

THE 'brains' of Konoye's Cabinet had no longer any doubt as to world conditions nor as to Japan's future course. The Axis would win the war and Japan had obtained an outline agreement from Germany and Italy as to the subsequent measures to be taken. Japan's position in the new world was, therefore, secure. The moment seemed opportune for Matsuoka to visit Germany and Italy, to establish close relations with their leaders, to study for himself how far the Axis had already gone on the road to victory and to gather data for a decision as to the next steps to be taken by Japan. The Army urged him to make the trip and Matsuoka himself thought it would afford an extremely favourable opportunity for him to consolidate his future political standing.

One further means of ensuring the Axis victory was closer relations with Russia. It was tacitly agreed, and hoped, in the negotiations that Russia could be induced to view the Tripartite Alliance with a benevolent eye. Matsuoka wished to carry the suggestion a stage further.

At the same time, for various reasons, there was some considerable opposition to Matsuoka's trip. In particular the Navy was anxious that, having absorbed military ideas, he should not go out of his way to promise an attack on Singapore, which Germany ardently desired. He was particularly requested, therefore, to make no commitments of a military nature. For that matter both the Army and the Navy absolutely refused to allow anyone else to discuss questions affecting the Supreme Command. So the Foreign Minister set out on his journey, accompanied by military and naval attachés but bearing no *o miyage* in his hand.[1]

---

[1] It is customary for visitors to present gifts, preferably souvenirs of their native place (*o miyage*).

2. MATSUOKA TACKLES RUSSO-JAPANESE RELATIONS

A year and a half had elapsed since Hiranuma had resigned over the Russo-German non-aggression treaty. Conditions had changed and Japan now planned a *rapprochement* with Russia. The idea was a standstill in the north and an advance in the south. Germany had indeed led Japan to believe that this presented no difficulty.

When Matsuoka arrived in Moscow, the new Ambassador Tatekawa had taken up his post. He had already been working on the suggestion of a non-aggression treaty to guard Japan's rear but Russia had demanded various compensating rewards and no progress had been made. Matsuoka again broached the subject of a treaty but he got the same answer and left for Germany empty-handed.

Matsuoka remembered German protestations and still thought that Russia could be won over. He expected that Germany would be willing to assist. After all Japan was only asking that Russia should treat Japan as she had treated Germany. The latter ought to be only too happy to carry out her promise of assistance.

3. TREATY OF NEUTRALITY BETWEEN JAPAN AND RUSSIA, APRIL 1941

In Berlin Matsuoka was fêted by Hitler, Ribbentrop and others and was given opportunities for discussion with the leading men. He also visited Rome (April 1st) and was welcomed by Mussolini and Ciano. After returning to Berlin he stayed there several more days and then set out on his way home.

Matsuoka had invoked Ribbentrop's assistance to bring about improved relations with Russia. He also brought up the question of an agreement with her similar to that between Germany and Russia but Ribbentrop would not be drawn. If anything, the German reaction was hostile.

Returned to Moscow, Matsuoka renewed his proposals but the Russians did not shift from the line they had previously taken. They did, however, say that, while they did not want a non-aggression treaty, they had no objection to a treaty of neutrality, provided that Japan surrendered her oil and coal concessions in North Saghalin. Agreeing to this in principle, Matsuoka expressed the hope that a fisheries agreement might be concluded.

The treaty of neutrality was thereupon signed. The U.S., under

President Roosevelt, was carefully watching the course of events. She regarded Germany and Japan as aggressors and was giving her entire support to Britain as a counter to their plans. She was also striving to bring Russia into the anti-Axis camp, for what the Americans most feared was Russian adhesion to the Tripartite Alliance. The sudden conclusion of a treaty of neutrality with Japan came, therefore, as a great shock. Just as the non-aggression treaty with Germany had been the prelude to the European War, so this treaty with Japan was an invitation to her to continue her southern adventure. The Americans were beginning to think that a catastrophe in the Pacific was inevitable. This opinion still held ground when later Germany attacked Russia. When Matsuoka had met the U.S. Ambassador Steinhardt, an old friend, in Moscow, he had made it clear that Japan's policy was based on the Tripartite Alliance, which, combined with the new treaty, was the weapon by means of which, it was hoped, U.S. might be deterred from participating in the European War.

On Matsuoka's departure, Stalin unexpectedly came to the station to see him off and showed great *empressement*, embracing Matsuoka and declaring that he also was an Oriental. No wonder he was pleased, knowing, as he did, that Germany might attack him at any moment!

4. WHAT REALLY HAPPENED IN BERLIN?

While in Germany Matsuoka had learnt enough to see that relations with Russia had worsened and he had had occasion to note that the German attitude towards Russia had changed, but he did not realize that the two countries were on the brink of war. It might have struck him that his talks in Berlin and what he had accomplished in Moscow had revealed glaring inconsistencies but he travelled home wrapped in dreams of what he was going to do next. He always came back to the same conclusion that the mainspring of Japan's policy was the Alliance. On arrival in Manchuria he learnt that the question of talks with the U.S. was on the *tapis* but, with the demeanour of one who has all the time in the world, he took his time and reached Tokyo at the end of April to receive a great reception from the people, who thought that all danger of a conflict with Russia had been removed.

The Emperor was pleased by the treaty of neutrality. In his account of the trip to H.I.M. and to the Government, Matsuoka dwelt on the details of the treaty talks but made no more than a formal report on his visits to Germany and Italy. The Emperor took note of the point and Konoye was at a loss to understand the reason for Matsuoka's attitude.

The latter displayed no enthusiasm over the talks with the U.S. that had been initiated in his absence.

At the reception in his honour given in Hibiya Park,[1] the Hitler mannerisms affected by Matsuoka in his speech were the subject of bitter criticism by Konoye and his *entourage*; he seemed to think that he was the only one that counted in the political world.

To this day there is no official record in Japan of Matsuoka's visit to Berlin and he died without leaving any memoir of his own. There are, therefore, gaps in our knowledge. For instance, prosecuting counsel at the Tokyo Tribunal, relying on the German record, would have it that Matsuoka promised Hitler that Japan would attack Singapore, that he kept the fact to himself on his return to Tokyo and set to work to overthrow the Cabinet in order that he himself might seize the reins of power; but this seems to be going too far. Again, it appears to have been thought by one section of opinion in Germany that Matsuoka was forewarned in Berlin of the intention to attack Russia and divulged the secret to Stalin as the price of the neutrality treaty, but this is not true.

At the time that Matsuoka set out for Europe, changes that had occurred there had not been realized in Japan, which was still thinking along the same lines as in the days when the Alliance had been forged. Matsuoka set out with this picture in his mind. In collecting data on which to base her judgments Japan merely followed surface indications and indulged in wishful, emotional thinking so that her point of view was always half a year, or even a full year, behind the times. When Germany had already abandoned the idea, Japan still thought that she was on the point of landing in Britain. When Germany had decided to make war on Russia, Japan still believed her former talk of friendship with that country. But the fact that conditions in Europe are 'complicated and queer', that geographically Japan is far distant and finds it difficult to grasp what really is going on there, is no reason why she should have embarked on so serious a policy while still in the dark. It merely goes to prove that she is slow to understand the essential background of world politics. Our Matsuoka certainly did not know his Germany.

---

[1] The 'Hyde Park' of Tokyo.

CHAPTER SEVEN

Matsuoka's Visit to Europe (Part 2)

1. RELATIONS BETWEEN MATSUOKA AND THE SUPREME COMMAND

BEFORE Matsuoka left Tokyo there had been a conference at Imperial Headquarters on the subject of his visit to Europe. As already related, the Cabinet and the Supreme Command were convinced of Britain's impending defeat and Matsuoka had left Tokyo with that belief in mind. According to German documents Germany had proposed to Russia that she should join the Alliance but had been unable to secure her agreement and had so informed the Japanese military authorities in Tokyo. Japan, however, knew no details of Molotov's visit to Berlin and could not believe that Russo–German relations had changed so completely for the worse.[1]

It was at this conference that the Supreme Command had impressed on Matsuoka that he should enter into no undertaking to attack Singapore and his military advisers had private instructions to watch over him to see that he kept the point in mind. In such circumstances Matsuoka must have been on his guard.

2. MY PLAN TO MEET MATSUOKA

The war reports I telegraphed to Matsuoka seemed to make not the slightest impression on his mind. It has always been the practice to circulate copies of reports on the situation from envoys abroad to the Throne, to the Prime Minister and Ministers concerned. But to my amazement I learnt afterwards that my most important telegrams were not circulated but only telegrams from envoys in the Axis countries.

[1] At Hitler's invitation Molotov had visited Berlin on November 12th, 1940 to discuss the subject but the meeting ended unsatisfactorily.

One member of Matsuoka's mission was Toshikazu Kase, who had recently worked under me in London and was well acquainted with my reading of the situation.[1] Perceiving that there was a yawning gap between my opinions and Matsuoka's pet theories, he suggested to him the desirability of our meeting to exchange views. Matsuoka offered to meet me at some convenient point on the continent. War-time travel in western Europe was beset with difficulties but I was prepared to brush them aside. At my request the British Government at Churchill's own intervention gave me special flying facilities. Unfortunately, a curtailment of Matsuoka's travel schedule made a meeting in neutral Switzerland impossible and I declined to go to Berlin. The plan was, therefore, dropped. Shortly afterwards I suggested that I should go to Japan since I was none the less anxious to open up my mind to the Foreign Minister and, having obtained sanction, I left London in June 1941.

Meanwhile, fed solely on military assessments of the situation, Matsuoka was in no state of mind to digest and assimilate even such explanations of the sudden change in relations with Russia as were given him by German leaders in his meetings with them in Berlin.

3. THE QUESTION OF AN ATTACK ON SINGAPORE

Matsuoka was anxious to know the date of the proposed landing in Britain but learnt nothing fresh from the Germans. They wanted to know when Japan was going to attack Singapore, because at the time Hitler had made up his mind to attack Russia and was insistent that Ribbentrop should take steps to make peace with Britain. Ribbentrop thought that the best way was to get Japan to turn the screw on Britain in the Far East (Ribbentrop's evidence at the Nuremberg Tribunal). Oshima had foretold that Matsuoka's *miyage*[2] would be the decision to attack Singapore. Matsuoka, however, brought nothing but an abstract message that Japan's attitude towards Britain had stiffened; he was not in a position to give a pledge. All the same the Germans understood him to have given his own personal undertaking; that at least is what is recorded in German documents. The impression gained is that both parties were at cross purposes.

Stalin had clear warning of German intentions, for the U.S. Government had transmitted intelligence in January 1941. From Tokyo also the spy Sorge had wired reliable intelligence, which he had acquired

[1] *Cf.* his *Eclipse of the Rising Sun.*
[2] *Vide* footnote to Chapter Six, s. 1.

from the German Embassy. Matsuoka's desire for a treaty of neutrality on his way home must have surprised the Russians. Faced with the prospect of a German attack, the Kremlin must have been only too well pleased to have their rear safeguarded. Moreover it was the constant Russian aim to turn Japan's attention southward. It so happened that this fitted in with German policy. Sorge's spy organization and Ott, the German Ambassador, were in fact working on the same lines.

4. WAR BETWEEN GERMANY AND RUSSIA, JUNE 1941

While in Lisbon, waiting for an American Clipper on my way home, I met colleagues stationed in western Europe and was discussing with them how matters stood between Germany and Russia when it was reported that war had broken out (June 21st). Before I left London, Churchill had hinted to me, when I was taking my leave, his feeling that war was not far off.

The news caused general surprise in Tokyo. It came on an evening when Matsuoka was entertaining Wang Ching-wei, Chief Executive of the newly established Nanking Government, at the Kabuki Theatre. He went straight to the Palace to submit the report and, to the amazement of the Emperor, added that it might be necessary for Japan to take up her position side by side with Germany. H.I.M. at once sent for Prime Minister Konoye and requested the view of the Government. The latter relieved H.I.M. by replying that Japan would stand by the treaty of neutrality with Russia and making it clear that Matsuoka's views were merely his own.

The incident gives just one more glimpse of Matsuoka's obsession by the Tripartite Alliance.

CHAPTER EIGHT

Negotiations Between Japan and U.S.A. (Part 1)

1. EFFECT OF THE TRIPARTITE ALLIANCE ON RELATIONS WITH THE U.S. AND RUSSIA

WHEN Prime Minister Konoye and Foreign Minister Matsuoka assured the Privy Council that the Triple Alliance would straighten out relations with Russia and could even lead to a *rapprochement* with the U.S., they were not deliberately deceiving the members; there is no doubt that they were saying only what they hoped would be the case.

Germany, as already related, was full of confidence at the time that she could entice Russia to join the Alliance. Further, it was only natural that Germany should do all she could to keep the U.S. out of the war. To use Japan to pin down American strength in the Far East would make it difficult for her to intervene in Europe. If, again, Japan came into the war before American preparations were complete, declared war on Britain and attacked Singapore, it should dampen the ardour of the Americans and, with public opinion against it, they might lose the opportunity of taking part in the war.

In Japan it was the Army that accepted these German views wholeheartedly. But there were others that thought differently. However, pushed hither and thither by the force of circumstance, they still clung to the hope that intervention in the war might be avoided and that diplomatic relations with Britain and the U.S. might be maintained and improved. These put their trust in the official Government statement that the Alliance was not a sword-point aimed at either Russia or Britain but a means whereby it was hoped that relations might be ameliorated.

Matsuoka's views were those of the Army, that Germany would win and that the alliance with Germany was the pivot on which turned Japan's policy, just as the Anglo-Japanese Alliance had been in the past.

So, when Germany made war on Russia, he maintained that Japan should also make war on her at Germany's side. But the Prime Minister was in the habit of adjusting his tactics to the immediate situation. To him the Alliance was just one more development in his handling of the Army. He, therefore, approved an interpretation of Japan's obligations under the Alliance that they were altered by the fact that Germany had attacked Russia without consulting Japan. In contradistinction to Matsuoka, who placed the emphasis on the aim of the Alliance to keep the U.S. out of the war, he regarded peace with the U.S. as something with which the Alliance had no concern.

2. PROPOSAL OF AMERICAN MISSIONARIES

Many people were unhappy about the state of Japan-American relations. Among them were two American missionaries of the Catholic Maryknoll Mission named Father Drought and Bishop Walsh, who came frequently to the Far East to preach the Gospel. They usually stayed in Kyoto while in Japan and were particularly concerned about this subject. Their religious standing brought them into contact with devout Catholics in the American political and financial world.

At the end of 1940 they brought to Japan a plan for the adjustment of diplomatic relations, which on examination gained approval both in Government and in private circles. Briefly the plan was this. The sphere of influence of the Monroe Doctrine, which was defined as embracing the Western Hemisphere, should be regarded as extending in the Pacific Ocean as far as the International Date Line of 180°; west of this line was no concern of the U.S. and east no concern of Japan. That was the gist of the argument. The Pacific Ocean was to be divided into east and west and there was to be an understanding that the U.S. was not to interfere in the Western Pacific nor Japan on the Eastern side (including Europe). It would not hinder the U.S. from joining in the European War but the U.S. was to drop its traditional Far Eastern policy of, among other doctrines, the open door in China.

Japan showed keen interest in the plan but it was obvious that the U.S. Government baulked at the idea. The plan had not been taken up officially when the two missionaries left, but one section of opinion in Japan got the mistaken impression that it really represented American intentions. During their stay in Japan the missionaries had interviewed Matsuoka and Konoye and had been in close touch with Ikawa,[1] an employee of the New York Finance Bureau.

[1] Appears in Cordell Hull's *Memoirs* as Wikawa.

Ikawa distributed an outline of his talks with the missionaries to many quarters, including military, and studiously preached the practicability of an understanding between the two countries. With Konoye's consent, he got into touch with Colonel Iwakuro, a sectional head in the Military Affairs Bureau (Director Major-General Muto). The Army's preparations for a full-scale war were incomplete and they were not at the moment contemplating war with the U.S. Having studied the proposition, they approved it in principle and took up the question of an understanding with the U.S. enthusiastically. The Navy also were in agreement.

3. MATSUOKA'S INSTRUCTIONS TO NOMURA

Admiral Kichisaburo Nomura had for some time past been urged by Matsuoka to take the post of Ambassador to the U.S. and, on the strong recommendation of the Minister for the Navy, he accepted the appointment and set out from Tokyo on January 23rd, 1941. The previous day Matsuoka handed him the following written instructions. They give a clear account of his duties and of Matsuoka's policy (taken from Ministry of Foreign Affairs archives).

(a) Unless our policy is drastically changed, it would be a pure waste of time to seek an understanding with the U.S. whereby peace in the Pacific could be assured and the two countries could work together for the restoration of peace to the world;

(b) If, further, matters are allowed to drift, there can be no certainty that the U.S. will not take part in the European War or make war on Japan;

(c) If this were to happen, it would mean a terrible world war far more hideous than the last; leading perhaps to the collapse of present-day civilization;

(d) In default of other, direct or indirect, means of an understanding, the U.S. must be prevented from making war on Japan or from taking part in the European War by the co-ordination of mutual assistance between Japan and countries other than Britain or the U.S., even if coercion or intimidation become necessary. Such action would be taken not merely in the cause of the self-defence of Imperial Japan but in fact in the cause of humanity.

(e) It is because it was decided that there was no other method of defending our country and warding off a world war that the Tripartite Alliance was formed;

(f) Once having formed the alliance, our future policy must revolve round it as the axis, just as in former years it pivoted on the Anglo-Japanese Alliance;

(g) Should the contingency contemplated in Article 3 of the Treaty arise, viz. that the three allied governments agree that an attack by a third party has occurred, Japan would of course show her loyalty. There must be not the slightest cause for doubt on the point. So vital a decision would be taken by a Council before the Throne with all due solemnity;

(h) It may be that some of Japan's actions in China may have seemed irregular, unjust or aggressive, but that is a passing phase. Our country will always ensure peace and reciprocity between the two countries. The day will dawn when that great ideal, which has been fostered since the country came into being—the *hakko ichi-u*[1] (the whole world is one family)—will become a living reality;

(i) The Greater East-Asia Co-prosperity Sphere is one manifestation of this ideal. No conquest, no oppression, no exploitation[2] —such is my motto. In fine, Japan aims to establish an area of international goodwill and reciprocity in this sphere that may serve as a model to the whole world;

(j) Putting these ideals aside for a moment, there is a practical everyday problem we have to face. Japan is in the grip of a need to work out means of self-supply and self-sufficiency in Greater East Asia. Is it for the U.S., which rules over the Western Hemisphere and is expanding over the Atlantic and the Pacific, to say that these ideals, these ambitions, of Japan are wrong? Cannot Japan be allowed even this? There is no idea of exclusion in our minds. Let the U.S. come to the Greater East Asia Co-prosperity Sphere and help us to develop it. Any misgiving that we might shut off the supply of rubber and tin that she requires is laughable.

You are requested to communicate *in extenso* to the President, the Secretary of State and other influential persons, official and private, these several points, taken in conjunction with my after-dinner speech to the Japan-American Society and my recent speech on foreign policy in the Diet.

In the above instructions Matsuoka explained clearly the conditions under which the Tripartite Alliance was conceived and instructed

---

[1] The reader will find a number of such expressions sprinkled through the text. They are usually based on premises that are, to say the least of it, debatable, but the Japanese 'man-in-the-street' was forced to swallow them as the complete answer to all his doubts. *Cf.* Note on Nationalistic Theories in Introduction.
[2] In English in the text.

Nomura plainly as to his policy. More, in his closing words he revealed openly and frankly to the American people what he himself thought. He stressed the point that the threat of our Axis policy was to be used to keep the U.S. out of the war. Any idea that concessions might be asked of us was thrust aside.

On his arrival in Washington, Nomura found that anti-Japanese feeling was acute. Roosevelt's anti-Axis policy was undisguised. He was uniting the whole country in preparation for war. American participation appeared to be inevitable. Nomura's predicament, arrived with such instructions in a country in such a state of mind, may be well imagined.

4. TACTICS OF AMBASSADOR NOMURA

In taking up his post, Nomura had requested the Army to appoint an assistant of good standing, since he attached great importance to his military connections. As a result he was assigned Colonel Iwakuro,[1] one of the senior staff officers.

Iwakuro had also received some briefing from Konoye and it was arranged that he should be accompanied by Ikawa[1] as his interpreter. When the two men arrived, they lost no time in getting in touch with Walsh and Drought[1] and proceeded to draft a concrete plan to adjust Japan-American relations. These Japanese and American well-wishers took Iwakuro's outline plan as their basis. They also listened to Nomura's views in completing their draft. Ambassador Nomura completely disregarded Matsuoka's instructions from the word 'go' and furthermore he did not take into his confidence his own staff, though they also were employees of the Ministry of Foreign Affairs.

From time to time Nomura received warnings from Matsuoka as to the activities of men such as Ikawa, who had no official standing. Finally he was strictly enjoined to have nothing further to do with them (March 17th, 1941). But he paid no attention. Not only did he sanction the activities of Ikawa and Iwakuro but he himself took a hand in drafting the plan. The reason of his action seems to be that he took into consideration that Ikawa was in direct communication with Konoye while Iwakuro was an influential representative of the Japanese Army. Moreover he considered that Matsuoka's strong-handed policy was bound sooner or later to land Japan-American relations on the rocks and he honestly hoped to prevent this happening. In other words, the Ambassador on the spot respected the views of the Prime Minister and

[1] *Vide* s. 2.

the Army communicated to him indirectly and privately, rather than the instructions communicated to him directly by his own Chief, the Minister for Foreign Affairs. That the negotiations were doomed from the start is due to these divided counsels. Future historians should pay more attention to the pattern than to the details of the negotiations or the manner in which they were conducted.

5. CORDELL HULL'S ATTITUDE TOWARDS THE 'PLAN FOR AN UNDERSTANDING BETWEEN JAPAN AND AMERICA'

The enthusiasm of the two missionaries infected the Catholics in the U.S. Government and made some impression on President Roosevelt. Postmaster-General Walker ranged himself on their side. So a provisional concrete plan for the adjustment of Japan-American relations produced by the missionaries and Iwakuro in consultation was laid before the President (according to the testimony of Iwakuro at the Tokyo Tribunal he himself drew it up). Roosevelt summoned Secretary of State Cordell Hull and together with him listened to the views of the missionaries.

According to Cordell Hull's *Memoirs* the missionaries declared that, if the plan were adopted, the influence of Japanese moderates would be enhanced and the Government would then be strong enough to carry through a modification of its Axis policy, but he himself had considerable doubts on the point.[1] Whatever the occasion, he followed the principles of American policy. For instance, he held with the Stimson doctrine that a policy of aggression must be opposed and the fruits of aggression must not be recognized. Moreover he retained his support of 'the open door and equal opportunity', a policy that he would not change. His attitude, therefore, was that an understanding was possible only within these limits. His conclusion was that, even if negotiations were instituted, the chance of success was about one in twenty.

None the less the United States was not prepared at that moment to challenge both Germany and Japan. It would seem, therefore, that Roosevelt and the American Government considered it desirable to gain time by an informal discussion that would bring out the point of view of both countries so that they could see where they stood. American defence chiefs wanted above all to postpone a crisis for the time being.

On April 16th, 1941, the Secretary of State invited Nomura to a talk, gave him a copy of the draft proposal and asked if it was true that the

[1] The missionaries had evidently swallowed the favourite argument of Japanese apologists.

Ambassador had had a hand in drawing it up. On Nomura's agreeing, he informed him that, if the draft proposal could be regarded as the Ambassador's, then the American Government would enter on informal, preparatory talks in order to go over the points raised. He meant that diplomatic negotiations could not take place on a draft that was not vouched for by the competent officials. Nomura agreed and promised to report the plan and Hull's views to his home Government. (Taken from Hull's *Memoirs*.)

The plan referred to the following items (telegram no. 234 from the Ambassador):

1. International and national concepts of Japan and the U.S.
2. Attitude of the two countries to the European War.
3. Relations of the two countries to the China crisis.
4. Naval and Air Power and transport facilities of the two countries in the Pacific.
5. Commercial and financial co-operation between the two countries.
6. Commercial activities of the two countries in the S.W. Pacific.
7. Policy of the two countries in regard to political stability in the Pacific.

If an understanding could be reached on these points, President Roosevelt and Premier Konoye should meet in Hawaii to discuss details.

6. NOMURA'S ATTITUDE TOWARDS PLAN

On April 16th, 1941, Nomura telegraphed to his Government. At the moment Matsuoka was still absent and Konoye had assumed charge of the Ministry of Foreign Affairs. In answer to Konoye's request for further information Nomura expressed himself as follows (telegram no. 244, concluding portion):

> To put it briefly, this plan for an understanding, like the Treaty of Neutrality between Japan and Russia, should be regarded as a logical development of the Axis Alliance, which forms the keynote of our national policy and the validity of Article 3 of the Treaty, which forms the basis of the Alliance, should not be affected thereby. As Ambassador my opinion is that if the U.S. be left in her present frame of mind, we must make up our minds that sooner or later the U.S. will come into the war and at the worst war will break out between Japan and the U.S. I consider that it would accord with the fundamental interests of the Axis Powers that we should now negotiate on these lines.

It thus appears that Nomura's views were as follows. The basis of the Tripartite Alliance and of the Axis policy must not be touched. If a bridge to mutual agreement could not be discovered, war was inevitable. It must, therefore, be to the interest of the Axis powers to prevent the U.S. from coming into the war by bringing home to her Government Japan's standpoint. Fortunately, there existed this plan, which he hoped would enable him to attain his object. If the plan failed, then 'Japan-American relations will go from bad to worse, economic sanctions will be tightened and the danger of war will be greatly increased' (*ibid.* point 2).

In other words, Ambassador Nomura was to negotiate to prevent war by using Matsuoka's weapon of the threat of Axis policy. But it is impossible to overlook the fact that Nomura's ideas did not for a moment accord with the point of view of the American Secretary of State. The prosecution of Axis policy and the adjustment of relations between Japan and the U.S. were irreconcilable. For either side to have hoped to achieve the impossible would have been foolish in the extreme. One cannot avoid the suspicion that the Americans were procrastinating in order to complete their preparations while Japan was searching for an opportunity to start hostilities.

7. BASIC OBJECTS OF JAPAN AND THE U.S.A.

In order that a formula should be devised to reconcile the long-standing difference of outlook between the two countries, it was necessary that one or the other should revise the ideas underlying her policy or that the international situation should change radically. If Japan maintained her policy towards China and the 'southern advance', then an understanding was difficult. If, again, the U.S. maintained her economic pressure on Japan, then equally it would be difficult for her to induce Japan to give way. If the negotiations were to succeed, it was essential that the two countries should alter their present course.

President Roosevelt had already made up his mind that Europe and the west coast of Africa constituted America's first line of defence and Britain the outpost. His third election had assured his own position and, without an actual declaration, the U.S. was practically in the war already.

The Tripartite Alliance may have restrained the U.S. from entering the war until her preparations were complete but, to anyone who understood the national character, it was unthinkable that any negotiations could induce her to refrain from taking part in the European War. Still less was it likely that threats would avail. But what was important for the U.S. to know was whether Japan would remain neutral or would declare herself an enemy. The American aim in the negotiations, therefore, was to obtain an assurance that American participation in the war would not bring into operation Japan's obligations under the Alliance. If Japan were willing to see the Alliance emasculated, desist from her 'active policy' and change over to a policy of co-operation with the U.S. and Britain, then the U.S. would not be averse to making concessions, always provided that her principles in regard to the countries of East Asia were not infringed. This was the key to successful negotiations.

It follows that such success required Japan to abandon the Alliance for all practical purposes and to amend her policy of the strong arm in East Asia. For Japan, who had just contracted the Alliance, this was an extremely difficult issue. To Matsuoka himself, who had just visited Germany and Italy as one of its authors but knew only too well what Prime Minister Konoye and others felt about the negotiations, it was a carking care. In ignoring facts and light-heartedly undertaking such negotiations, Japan was involving herself in an encounter from which she could not retreat and of which the stakes were dangerously high.

8. FUNDAMENTAL MISUNDERSTANDING IN THE NEGOTIATIONS

It has already been related that on April 16th, 1941, Cordell Hull had informed Nomura that if the latter were prepared to adopt the plan of the Japanese and American well-wishers as his own, he himself was willing to enter on informal talks taking it as a base.[1] Since it had been produced by the Secretary of State, the Ambassador suggested to his Government the desirability of negotiating. He telegraphed:

> I have been working under cover and sounding[1] the U.S. Government about this plan and have satisfied myself that the Secretary of State has in general no objection. I myself had privately taken part in drafting the plan and, as a result of talks in various quarters, have agreed to adopt it.

The Japanese Government concluded that this was at least an American proposal approved by the Americans, from which the U.S.

[1] English word used in the text.

would not draw back, and that Japan could, taking it as a basis, put forward counter-proposals. Washington was looking at this very same plan but the Americans and the Japanese were regarding it in a very different light. They were in fact at cross-purposes.

Konoye was very pleased. The Government called a meeting of the Liaison Council.[1] The Army, having received a detailed report from Colonel Iwakuro, gave their assent, and both the Supreme Command and the Government being in agreement, there was no hesitation in coming to the conclusion that negotiations should be begun with the U.S. Government. On the other side Hull presented to Nomura what were called his basic four principles and, requesting their acceptance by Japan, enquired whether the latter proposed to abandon her present policy of military conquest. The four principles were (1) respect for the sovereignty of all countries, (2) non-interference in the internal affairs of other countries, (3) observance of the principle of equal opportunity, (4) non-disturbance of the *status quo* in the Pacific. In such way did the Secretary of State make his attitude clear at the outset.

At this stage Matsuoka was in Manchuria on his way home. The Vice-Minister for Foreign Affairs, Ohara, therefore, maintained that such an important decision should be deferred until his return and Konoye so decided.

9. MATSUOKA'S ATTITUDE

On Matsuoka's return Prince Konoye at once summoned a Liaison Council conference, at which, after Matsuoka's report had been heard, the question of the negotiations with the U.S. was considered and it was proposed that they should be undertaken. But Matsuoka, pleading indisposition, said that he would like to think over the matter and withdrew without entering into discussion. Both Konoye and the Army representatives were highly dissatisfied. It looked as if Matsuoka had taken umbrage at such an important question having come into discussion during his absence. Konoye commented that his attitude was inexplicable.

Having exchanged ideas with German and Italian leaders, Matsuoka had returned with his mind full of plans of action under the aegis of the Alliance. He had met with a great reception and had been hailed as the hero who had won the neutrality pact with Russia. He is said to have spent the time crossing Siberia wrapt in pleasant dreams and it was

[1] It is not stated precisely which officers and officials attended meetings of this Council.

supposed that they went beyond the confines of diplomacy and embraced the hope of building a new Japan. On his return he behaved just as though he were another Hitler.[1] Some people indeed supposed that he planned to take over the Government in order to realize his own theories of statecraft. Konoye was sensitive and watched Matsuoka's behaviour with great suspicion. The attitude of each towards the other, therefore, became irreconcilable. To make matters worse, the Army and Navy, who held the fate of the country in their hands, acted as though the diplomatic negotiations were no concern of theirs. The military mind put diplomatic negotiations and military operations in separate compartments. They regarded the first as a supplementary function intended to assist the second.

10. KONOYE AND MATSUOKA AT VARIANCE

Matsuoka's attitude was quite clear. In a meeting with Steinhardt, the U.S. Ambassador in Moscow, he had emphasized the fact that the Alliance was the corner-stone in Japan's policy, and said: 'There is no secret agreement between Japan and Germany, and Japan is under no obligation to enter the war at the moment. But should the U.S. come into the war, that is another matter. Germany has no intention of declaring war on the U.S. and I hope that the U.S. will remain quiet.'

Matsuoka reported this interview to Oshima and stated: 'I urged that the U.S. should pay careful attention to two points: (1) not to enter the war, (2) to advise Chiang Kai-shek to make peace: and added a third point, (3) that not even the semblance of a speck of dust would be allowed to settle on the Alliance. If the U.S. came into the war, Japan would step in at once. I asked Steinhardt to telegraph this as my personal message to the President.' He also prophesied Germany's ultimate victory and urged that American leaders should proceed cautiously.

At the same time Matsuoka professed himself willing to visit the U.S. in order to tackle the task of putting American-Japanese relations on a better footing. There was nothing strange in Matsuoka, who had grown up in the U.S., wishing to do his utmost to improve relations. It was in fact his duty nor could he see how he could be left out of the discussion. But a start had been made while he was away. He had exchanged earlier ideas with Walsh and at first he thought that the plant was growing from the seed he had sown. But when he looked into the matter, he found that this was not so. Others, who thought differently

[1] Lit. 'papier-mâché Hitler'. There is a hint of malice in the use of the term.

from himself, had taken a hand. Konoye and one section of the Army and Navy were working behind his back. They had moved far away from his plan to use the Alliance to keep the U.S. out of the war. He could not agree to the suggestion that Prince Konoye and President Roosevelt should meet to talk matters over.

Matsuoka concluded that negotiations that had emerged from such extraneous circumstances offered little prospect of success, whether viewed in the light of international conditions or considered in the train of Japanese policy up to that time, and he was in a quandary. He could not see how the negotiations could be reconciled with the relations he had just established with Germany and Italy. He himself could not solve the dilemma. Konoye on the other hand had cooled off from his mood of enthusiasm for the Alliance, and could not see any particular difficulty. In his mind and that of the Army and Navy Iwakuro's draft had become a proposition made by the U.S. Government and they maintained that the talks could be advanced to a point where Konoye and Roosevelt could meet. They thought that such an excellent opportunity of adjusting relations should not be let slip. But Matsuoka would not agree. He himself set to work to draft counter-proposals.

Matsuoka telegraphed to Nomura that a fortnight's consideration would be required before Hull's plan could be answered and that put Nomura in a difficult position. He bombarded his Government with requests for action.

Japan was by now pursuing an erratic course. At a conference on May 3rd, it was decided, as a temporary expedient pending a formal reply, that Nomura should be instructed to propose, as an idea of his own, a treaty of neutrality, that he should communicate to American leaders the conviction of German-Italian victory, clothed in an account of Matsuoka's visit to Europe, that he should explain how profitless would be American entry into the war and stress the fact that Japan's standpoint under the Alliance was steadfast and immovable, all this in the hope of restraining the U.S. from taking positive action. But this *démarche* called forth no response from the Americans.

News of the proposed negotiations had by now leaked out and on May 4th Matsuoka communicated to Germany and Italy in confidence the gist of the plan. They reacted vigorously. To Oshima's opposition and Ribbentrop's protests, Matsuoka guaranteed emphatically that Japan would continue to abide by the terms of the Alliance and that the negotiations could be regarded as supplementary to Axis policy. By the 9th he was attempting to coerce the U.S. into reconsidering her attitude: he instructed Nomura to intimate unofficially that to lessen the tension between the two countries the U.S. must refrain from taking part in the

European War and part company with Chiang Kai-shek (on the 6th the U.S. Government had extended 'lend-lease' to China), and that if the U.S. provoked Germany by her hostile action, Japan would fulfil her obligations under the Tripartite Alliance (i.e. Japan would attack the U.S.).

None the less Germany continued to press the Japanese Government. On May 17th Ott handed Matsuoka instructions he had received from his government:

> Germany considers that the best way to keep the U.S. out of the war is to refuse to negotiate. The German Government regrets that the Japanese Government did not wait for her views before replying to the American proposal. The alliance concluded last year signified a political and moral union between the three countries. Its main object was to prevent any other country participating in the war.

The telegram was in conformity with the terms of the Alliance and Matsuoka's own policy had been in agreement therewith. German pressure, brought to bear through the channel of Ambassador Oshima, shook Japan's nerve-centre, the Army, considerably. It should not be overlooked that the opening of negotiations with the U.S. struck at the base of the Tripartite Alliance.

11. THE JAPANESE REPLY TO THE PLAN

The reply to the Secretary of State drafted by Matsuoka was made on May 12th. The gist was that in principle the Tripartite Alliance aimed to prevent the war in Europe from extending and it was suggested that the U.S. should not participate but that Japan and the U.S. should join hands in restoring peace in Europe. With regard to China, the U.S. should mediate in order to bring about a settlement. If Chiang Kai-shek refused to accept advice, then the U.S. should withdraw her support. The reply also referred to a guarantee of security and the principle of equal opportunity in the Philippines but there was no reference to a meeting between Konoye and Roosevelt. In sum Matsuoka was adjusting the terms of reference to bring them into line with his own policy.

The reply was entirely different from what the Americans had been expecting.

With reference to the presentation of the plan, Matsuoka instructed Nomura as follows: 'In replying to the draft plan you should suggest to the Secretary of State a preamble to the effect that, (1) the U.S.

should not participate in the war, (2) the U.S. should urge Chiang's Government to make peace.' But Nomura refrained from mentioning this suggestion. The difference between the standpoint taken by Matsuoka and that of Nomura from the outset of the negotiations is only too obvious.

The Americans considered that whether they chose to fight or not was a question of their right to defend themselves. They proposed to ascertain by negotiation whether the Axis policy of Japan up to that point was sufficiently flexible to recognize the application of this right. Matsuoka's response to the draft, namely that if the U.S. entered the European War, Japan's duty under the Tripartite Alliance left her no option but to fight also, and that, therefore, he proposed that, in order to solve their outstanding problems, neither side should fight, was diametrically opposed to American hopes. Matsuoka appeared unable to appreciate the American contention that a decision to aid Britain by declaring war on Germany must be made on their own interpretation of their right of self-defence. They concluded that Matsuoka was acting in concert with Germany to neutralize this right and that, therefore, he was blocking the negotiations.

12. *NOTE-VERBALE* FROM THE U.S. GOVERNMENT

The split in the Japanese camp over the negotiations was by now an open secret. Criticism of Matsuoka by those who advocated the negotiations, in Tokyo or Washington, was violent. Ambassador Nomura went so far as to explain to the Americans that apart from Matsuoka the Government, the Army and the Navy and the Emperor himself were all in favour of the negotiations and both in Japan and the U.S. there was a feeling that Matsuoka Must Go.

The American reply to the Japanese Note of May 12th was handed to Nomura by Hull on May 31st. Nomura did not report it but continued to negotiate. This was known to the Japanese Government owing to a report from the Japanese Military Attaché and estrangement between the Government and its representative grew. He did, however, formally communicate to his government a revised version of the Note of May 31st which he had received from the Secretary of State on June 21st. (This was the day on which war broke out between Germany and Russia.)

Attached to the Note were additional notes and a questionnaire (Nomura definitely stated that he could not forward these Notes but that they did not affect the sense of the message itself). The Note is to be regarded as the first official proposal of the U.S. Government in reply to the original plan produced by Japanese and American well-wishers. The gist of it was very different from the draft proposal. It maintained American traditional principles: it explained the American right of self-defence (thereby extracting the teeth of the Alliance), it maintained the 'open door', requested the withdrawal of Japanese troops from China and raised the question of Manchoukuo, it merely suggested friendly talks between Japan and China. Japanese hopes were not so much as touched on. Not only so but a serious 'oral statement' was attached.

The oral statement handed to Ambassador Nomura by Secretary of State Hull on June 21st was as follows (telegram from Nomura of June 23rd, translation is his):[1]

> The Secretary of State thanks the Japanese Ambassador and his associates for their sincere efforts to bring about a better understanding between our two countries and to establish peace in the Pacific. He also thanks them for the especial frankness that has characterized the many conferences that have taken place.
>
> The U.S. Government is no less anxious to bring about an amelioration in our relations as well as a state of peace in the Pacific. In that spirit the Secretary of State has carefully studied all the points made by the Japanese.
>
> The Secretary of State has no reason to doubt that the leaders of Japan are in agreement with the above-mentioned views and opinions of the Japanese Ambassador and his associates, and that they support the action taken to achieve these lofty aims. Unfortunately there are clear proofs from the reports of those who have for many years shown sincere goodwill towards Japan and from information that is coming to this government in increasing quantity from all quarters of the globe that among influential leaders in the Japanese Government there are those that have given a solemn undertaking, from which they cannot recede, to follow a course calculated to support Nationalist-Socialist Germany and her policy of conquest and that, further, the sole type of understanding with the U.S. that these persons can accept is one under which, should the U.S., in pursuance of her present policy of self-defence, become involved in hostile acts in Europe, it is to be expected that Japan will fight at Hitler's side.
>
> The theme of recent official statements by a spokesman[2] of the

[1] Slightly condensed.
[2] The word is given in English in the text. It was interpreted in Japan as meaning Matsuoka.

Japanese Government, made for no apparent reason, proclaiming Japan's commitments and intentions under the Tripartite Alliance, illustrates an attitude that cannot be ignored. So long as responsible Japanese leaders maintain this attitude and openly work on Japanese opinion in this way, shall we not be pursuing a mirage if we expect that the draft we are now studying to yield practical results?

Another cause of disquiet is this. Among the terms to be proposed to China by Japan in making peace, the Japanese Government desires to introduce a provision that Japan be allowed to station troops in Inner Mongolia and North China as a measure for concerting counter-action against communism. The policy based on principles of liberty, that the Government of the U.S.A. maintains, would not, it is thought, permit that Government to consent to measures that could be construed as conflicting with those principles.

For these reasons the Secretary of State can only hope that some clearer indication can be given, than has been hitherto, that the Japanese Government is united in a desire to pursue a pacific course to attain the objects of the proposed understanding.

13. SIGNIFICANCE OF THE HULL *NOTE-VERBALE*

The Secretary of State's *note-verbale* was not only a direct challenge to Foreign Minister Matsuoka. It was America's last word. So long as he was Foreign Minister, it was useless to continue the negotiations nor did they hold out any prospect of success if Japan did not radically amend the position she had taken up. The note was a valuable pointer in that it disclosed the rocks on to which the negotiations had run. But the Japanese leaders merely regarded it as a refusal to negotiate with Matsuoka.

At a Liaison Council Conference on July 10th, Matsuoka spoke his mind. He said that the oral statement amounted to interference in the affairs of the Japanese Government and was an affront to the dignity of an independent country. It should be rejected. The negotiations offered no prospect of success but the time and manner of their suspension demanded careful consideration. Nomura had been instructed to return the oral statement but at a conference on the 12th the Navy Minister asked that the negotiations should be continued at least until the occupation of French Indo-China had been completed. For the moment, therefore, the negotiations were at a standstill. They had suddenly reached an impasse and, if any incident were to occur, it would become impossible to maintain diplomatic relations.

The Americans regarded Hitler as an aggressor and an enemy to peace and security. They envisaged entry into the war as an ally of Britain. Early in 1941 reliable reports indicated that war between Germany and Russia was imminent and they were in a position to assess the probable outcome of the European War. The American attitude towards Japan then stiffened and the negotiations offered no prospect unless Japan made substantial concessions.

It would appear that, though Konoye was the man ultimately responsible, he did not attach the same importance to the Alliance as Matsuoka. He still thought that relations with America could be adjusted by negotiations in Washington. He therefore decided to drop Matsuoka and direct them himself. On July 7th, 1941, he resigned with his Cabinet. He was ordered to reform it. It was the earnest wish of H.I.M. the Emperor that negotiations should be continued and that Konoye should carry them to success.

The third Konoye Cabinet, formed on July 18th, left out Matsuoka and replaced him with Admiral Toyoda, who had been Minister for Commerce in the previous Cabinet. The idea was that, acting under Konoye's supervision, Toyoda would combine well with Nomura, who was also from the Navy. The Navy had for a long time opposed the Army's arguments in favour of the Alliance and that attitude still lingered in the minds of the 'moderates' in their ranks. Konoye, who had supported the Army in their demands and had contracted the Alliance, now planned to utilize the influence of the Navy moderates to make a success of the American talks. It did not occur to him that there was any contradiction. It was part and parcel of his struggle to find a way to peace.

But the Army stood by their Axis policy.

CHAPTER NINE

Council Before the Throne (Part 1)

1. GAP WIDENS BETWEEN POLICIES OF JAPAN AND U.S.A.

RUSSIAN participation in the war at once relieved the burden that Britain was carrying and correspondingly strengthened t e American position, which could now be pushed a stage further. There was no longer any need for her to relax her attitude towards Japanese activities in East Asia. The time had come when she could go ahead with the policy that she had consistently maintained ever since the outbreak of the 'Manchurian Incident'. The plan that had provided the basis at the outset of the talks had by now been put on the shelf.

The second Konoye Cabinet had struggled against the current and had found the going hard. The nationalist policy it had adopted had wrecked the talks. The Cabinet had shown no disposition to modify its attitude on either the Alliance or the southern advance, which had between them become the over-riding factors in the talks. The new draft which Nomura presented on June 15th was in no way different from that of May 12th.

2. EFFECT OF JAPAN'S SOUTHERN ADVANCE ON NEGOTIATIONS

The Army and Navy's southern advance was continued regardless of its effect on Japan's foreign relations. Now that Japanese forces were stationed in North Indo-China, their thoughts were no longer concentrated on China. Equally the British and Americans were not satisfied merely to encourage the Chinese in their struggle against the Japanese. It was Japan herself against whom they were bringing pressure by means of economic warfare.

The U.S. had begun by prohibiting the export of munitions to Japan and restricting trade. In July 1939 they had denounced the trade treaty. Britain followed suit and the other powers possessing territories in the south joined in the policy of political and economic encirclement: A (the Americans), B (the British), C (the Chinese), D (the Dutch). To meet this challenge the Army and Navy had come to feel that they must take a serious decision. Not only as a matter of logistics, but to be prepared for an emergency, it had become an absolute economic necessity to lay their hands on oil resources. They must, therefore, station troops also in *southern* Indo-China. According to what Prince Konoye told newspaper correspondents afterwards, the High Commands considered, strangely enough, that this could be done without affecting the negotiations. The home truths that had been repeated time and again in Washington never seemed to penetrate to the minds of those in Tokyo.

The Army for the most part swallowed German talk of taking Moscow in three weeks and disposing of Russia in three months. But, supposing Germany used her victory to extend her influence into Siberia and establish a base in Vladivostok? That might spell greater danger to Japan than the Russian menace. Something must be done about it; at least that is what the Northern School argued. And so, to counter such an emergency, the Army mobilized one million men and sent them to Manchuria. They gave to the operation the name 'Kwantung Army Special Manœuvres'. When Malik, the Russian Ambassador, asked the reason, Matsuoka replied at the time that Japan attached even more importance to the Tripartite Alliance than to Russo-Japanese neutrality. But the German advance did not quite come up to expectations and, accordingly, the troops assembled in Manchuria were sent southward. Once more the Army and Navy thrust to the south was resumed.

3. THE DECISION OF JULY 2ND, 1941

At a Council before the Throne, held on July 2nd, a serious decision was taken: 'If need be, we accept war with Britain and the U.S.'; and troops were to be stationed in South Indo-China. At this conference, while the decision was to advance southward, the supporters of the Northern School were mollified by the promise that at a suitable opportunity the northern problem would be tackled. It seems that, at the time of the Kwantung Army Special Manœuvres, the demands of the Northern School had alarmed Konoye, for he now displayed great satisfaction—'by this decision the cause of anxiety in the north has been removed'.

This decision of the Council finally settled Japan's destiny. Unless the British and Americans gave way, a clash was inevitable.

Nevertheless Konoye still continued the negotiations in the hope that some way or other they would be concluded satisfactorily. One can only suppose that he thought that their success might make it possible to restrain the Army and Navy. It does not make sense but how else can one explain his conduct? If it was not bluff,[1] it was sheer insanity. What he was doing with one hand he was undoing with the other. His intentions may have been good but they were a mass of contradictions.

Though the decision was a top secret, the Americans got wind of it at once and concluded that Japan was negotiating under false colours. The situation, therefore, became desperate.

The Navy plans, based on the decision of July 2nd, were communicated to the Emperor on July 31st by Nagano, Chief of the Naval General Staff. H.I.M. was extremely perturbed by the plan of campaign against the U.S. contained therein. He enquired, in a tone of reproof, whether war with the U.S. could really be contemplated. Nagano replied that war with the Americans could not be conducted longer than one year and a half with any prospect of success and that Japan's leaders did not actually desire it.

---

[1] In English in the text.

CHAPTER TEN

My Advice on My Return

1. MY INTERVIEW WITH MATSUOKA

ON my way home I reached Washington late in June. There I heard for the first time from Nomura about the American negotiations. It came to my mind that friends in the British Government had told me that talks of some sort were taking place. Learning that negotiations had actually begun, I felt that at all costs they must be brought to a successful conclusion and I resolved that I must press my own views on Foreign Minister Matsuoka, even if it entailed my resignation from the service.

I reached Tokyo towards the end of July to learn that the situation had changed; Matsuoka was no longer at the Ministry of Foreign Affairs and it was the Third Konoye Cabinet—the 'Japan-American Negotiations Cabinet'. All the same I called on Matsuoka to put my views before him.

Matsuoka was very ill but he forced himself to explain the situation to me. He concluded with these words: 'I fought hard to adjust our American relations even if it was the last thing I did but it was impossible. Now the odds are that a conflagration will start whether in the north or in the south. Only when Japan has fallen to the bottom of the pit will the nation awake and climb its way back.' His face was ashen and he seemed to have lost his vitality. His policy as Foreign Minister and his present remarks were entirely at variance. Out of touch with developments at home as I was, I could not help wondering whether his wild speech was not the talk of a madman. I had but one thought, that, whatever happened, Japan must not plunge into this Great War. Looking back now, I am convinced that Matsuoka was appalled at the implications of the Army and Navy behaviour at the Council before the Throne. They had broken loose from the halter and the shouting of the crowd only spurred them on faster in their mad career.

2. MY COUNSEL

Both in lectures given in the Imperial presence and at the Liaison Council, to Prime Minister Konoye and to Foreign Minister Toyoda, I gave my impressions and views gathered from all sources. I went also to the General Staff, the headquarters of the Army, and addressed the officers. At other meetings I spoke to various leaders. I considered it my bounden duty.

The gist of what I said was as follows:

I spoke first of conditions in Britain. 'The British have inherited a spirit of indomitable endurance. The greater the difficulty, the stiffer their resolution. Churchill, their leader, is an outstanding fighter with a will of iron. He has mobilized the entire strength of the British Empire. He is the incarnation of the spirit of a united nation and he has won complete American partisanship. British mastery at sea is unquestioned. Her strength on land and in the air is approaching that of Germany as time passes. The German sea blockade has failed while the British blockade of the continent begins to bear fruit.'

Then I went on to give my own assessment of the way in which the war was developing. 'Germany had to abandon her plan of landing in Britain in the summer of 1940, though for some time to come she will maintain her superiority on the European continent. But in the colonies British trained troops have the upper hand. British supremacy at sea is unshakable. The war with Russia cannot be won in a few months as the Germans claim. You may take a parallel from our own war in China. The German war with Russia is bound to become one of attrition. This is not going to be a short war but a long one. When British preparations are complete and the expected American accession is realized, then, just as in the First World War, Germany's fate is sealed.'

Next I referred to international conditions. 'The union between Britain and the exiled powers continues to tighten. The French are gathering round de Gaulle and their belief in final victory is unshaken. The attitude of America is the decisive factor and under Roosevelt's guidance they are already for all intents and purposes in the war. Actual participation is merely a question of time and opportunity. German difficulties in the occupied territories are bound to grow. That Russian, American and British encirclement of Germany will lead to ultimate victory is a foregone conclusion. The war has already passed the crisis.' Such were my views. They were supported by Major-General Tatsumi, Military Attaché in London, from whom I carried a statement of his views to the Military Authorities in Tokyo.

Finally I said: 'Japan must not enter the war. It must be her absolute determination not to enter the war. She must bring her negotiations with the U.S. to a successful termination and go on from there to solve the problem of China and clear up her relations once for all. Non-entry into the war, and a policy of straightening out her difficulties by diplomatic machinery, would bring Japan's standing in Europe after the war to new heights.' I had been for many years serving abroad and I had little information as to the policy of the Japanese Government and of conditions at home. I had no means of knowing in what direction the military mind was moving nor what were the decisions of the Council before the Throne. I could only think that the Japanese would not be so insane as to enter a losing war.

3. RECEPTION ACCORDED TO MY COUNSEL

In my lecture at the Palace I had dwelt on British resolution, the comportment of the Royal Family, the manner in which the people had taken the news of Dunkirk and their calm under the air bombardment. The Emperor instructed me to repeat the talk in the presence of the Empress.

My speech at the Office of the General Staff was delivered to over a hundred officers. To them I stressed the general aspects of the war and expounded my view that Britain would win in the long run, because she refused to accept defeat, and the more serious-minded of the officers were much impressed. But thereafter I was labelled pro-British and pro-American and I was 'tailed' by the gendarmerie. To the Army a German victory was a matter of common sense; devotion to the Axis had become a sort of religion.

Both Konoye and Toyoda gave me the impression that they were in agreement with my views. They were keen on the talks with America. Konoye in particular, in conformity with the Emperor's wishes, staked everything on their success. Many of my listeners among thoughtful people gave me every encouragement, and, so far as I was in a position to do so, I assisted the Prime Minister in his negotiations with the U.S. But the general atmosphere in Japan was far from favourable.

CHAPTER ELEVEN

Negotiations Between Japan and U.S.A. (Part 2)

1. SOUTHERN ADVANCE RESUMED: AMERICAN 'FREEZING' ORDER

THE Cabinet proposed to continue the negotiations, which it regarded as a matter of life and death, and yet it did not cancel the move into southern Indo-China decided on July 2nd. Could anything have been more inconsistent? The Army occupied Saigon and the Navy Kamranh Bay, on which they started to build a big airfield on July 21st. De Coux submitted to *force majeure*. Konoye telegraphed to Pétain, pledging respect for French suzerainty in Indo-China and urging his acquiescence. At the same time Germany was asked to bring pressure to bear on the Vichy Government. Despite American remonstrances, the Japanese demands were accepted and an agreement on joint defence between Japan and France was signed on July 29th.

The military strategy underlying the occupation was obvious. Kamranh Bay faced Manila and Singapore by sea and Siam by land so that British and American bases in East Asia had been brought within striking distance. Japan's intentions were clear to the Americans, British and Dutch. The U.S. at once 'froze' assets of Japanese firms in the States (July 26th, 1941) and trade between Japan and the U.S. came to a standstill; economic warfare had grown to full scale. Britain and the Netherlands took similar steps. Trade, the life-blood of 80 million Japanese, was now lost save in the occupied territories. Economically the U.S. had within her grasp the power to strangle Japan.

The focus of the negotiations now shifted to the restoration of economic relations. The question was what concessions must Japan make in order to be allowed to buy oil from the U.S.

But the Japanese Army acted as though they were 'possessed'. They put blind faith in German victory and worried only how best to secure Japan's share in the spoils when the day dawned.

2. NEGOTIATIONS CONTINUED

Konoye had misgivings as to the Army's judgment but he was curiously optimistic as to world conditions. With his so-called 'brains trust' (among whom was the communist Hozumi Ozaki) as advisers he continued to negotiate.

The negotiations were extremely complicated and confused. In his memoirs Secretary of State Cordell Hull remarks that Nomura not only failed fully to comprehend American arguments but he also had an incomplete grasp of his own country's proposals. Among the Japanese themselves also co-ordination in their policy was wanting. On the occupation of southern Indo-China negotiations came for a time to a full stop. But the Americans thought it best to continue them and on July 24th the President called Nomura to an interview and suggested that, if Japanese forces withdrew, Indo-China could be declared a neutral zone (later Siam was added). On August 8th Nomura put forward fresh proposals. He made suggestions as to the restoration of trade, the China problem, and withdrawal of troops from Indo-China, but he made no reply to the President's proposal. His evasive attitude gave great offence to the Americans.

The negotiations continued but made no progress. Becoming restless Konoye finally proposed that he himself should meet the President to talk matters over (August 8th: the original draft proposals had envisaged such a meeting).

3. PROSPECTS OF A MEETING BETWEEN KONOYE AND ROOSEVELT

In principle the Americans also had no objection to the meeting. The Japanese pinned their hopes on it and had settled in their mind who were to be the Foreign Affairs, War and Navy leaders in Konoye's party. The Navy had no reservations but the Army agreed to the meeting only on condition that the fundamental policy embodied in the Japanese proposals should not be changed and that, if the President failed to appreciate Japan's 'sincerity' and it became evident that the U.S. proposed to go ahead with their present policy, then the Japanese would terminate the meeting and make up their minds to fight.

Since the negotiations had started, no progress had been made. The gap between the Japanese and American points of view had widened and exasperation was growing. The Army was anything but conciliatory.

In fact since the decision of July 2nd their heads were in the air; the die was cast. Supposing Konoye agreed to the meeting under a condition that he must let events take their course, he must be prepared to shoulder grave difficulties at home. He gave me some inkling of his thoughts, with which I sympathized and which I did my best to encourage: he appeared to be thinking that there was nothing for it but to make this the turning-point, to make such concessions at the meeting as would bring the talks to a satisfactory ending, in accordance with the Emperor's instructions, and force the Army to agree willy-nilly. It was true that the Army was in a truculent mood but at least it was something that most persons of intelligence and the general public hoped that the negotiations would succeed.

For a time the Americans had welcomed the idea of the meeting and the President even designated a meeting-place in Alaska. But the State Department, when they reviewed the talks up to that date, decided that before the two leaders met certain important points must be settled. Mindful of Konoye's past record and his character, they felt that a meeting before some sort of general agreement had been reached carried an element of danger; it might mean that the negotiations were approaching a crisis and that the Americans would be throwing away the time-margin that they needed. With them a continuation of the negotiations until some such rough agreement was reached was essential and they so replied on September 3rd, although Japan had pressed hard for the meeting (on August 28th Konoye sent a personal message to the President urging that the meeting need not discuss details but should settle questions on broad lines by a direct conference between the two heads).

The Japanese put forward a fresh proposal on September 6th. Premising that Konoye accepted Cordell Hull's Four Principles, it pressed for an early reply but the Americans would not abate their demands. Once again on September 27th the Japanese put forward fresh proposals but the Americans were deaf to all blandishments. The more eager the Japanese, the more reluctant became the Americans.

CHAPTER TWELVE

The Sorge Spy-ring

1. THE SORGE CASE

I HAVE told how Germany strongly opposed the talks with America. Apart from the official reports from Matsuoka, Ott, the German Ambassador, had another source of information.

In this matter Russian interests coincided with German, and the 'Sorge spy case', which was disclosed by the Ministry of Justice in 1942, affords a rare illustration of the international activities of the Communist Party, of the defects of Japan's political organization, of the lack of perception of Japanese leaders and of their carelessness in the preservation of national secrets. In February 1949 the details of the affair were published in Washington on the basis of a report from the American Army of Occupation.

The leaders of the spy-ring were Richard Sorge, who was adviser to Ott, and Hozumi Ozaki, who had free access to Prince Konoye. Sorge acted as Intelligence adviser and private secretary to Ott, enjoyed his entire confidence and was conversant with German secrets, which he communicated to Russia. Ozaki was a former correspondent of the *Osaka Asahi* newspaper. He worked in the Cabinet Office and was a member of Konoye's brains-trust. He was in touch with national policy, since Konoye spoke freely to him of secrets of supreme importance, so that he was able to furnish Sorge with intelligence of the utmost value to Russia.[1]

2. REMARKABLE ACCURACY OF SORGE'S REPORTS

One of Sorge's successes was in connection with the decision of July 2nd, 1941, to resume the southern advance. Matsuoka had

---

[1] Since the author states that the details he gives do not differ from the Washington account, they are for the most part omitted from this translation.

graphically described to me the possibility of the conflagration starting either in the north or in the south. Sorge was more accurate. He reported confidently that it would start in the south and that there need be no anxiety in the north. He was also kept informed by Ozaki of the state of the American talks at all stages. But his greatest feat was that of reporting to the Kremlin that Germany proposed to attack Russia on or about June 20th. When Stalin signed the neutrality pact with Matsuoka, he already knew the date set for the attack.

3. OZAKI SUMS UP HIS PAST LIFE

On his arrest Ozaki commented: 'My hair has gone white from the struggle to carry on my hidden activities under false pretences. But my campaign to make a "Red" Japan has succeeded. Japan is plunged in the Great War, the country is in chaos and revolution is just round the corner. Nine-tenths of my work is done and my only regret is that I shall not live to see its completion.'

After his resignation Konoye discussed the Sorge case with me one day. Referring to Ozaki's confession, he said that it made him shudder and continued reflectively, 'I had my plans and both the Army and the Navy professed to approve them but, when it came to putting them into operation, somehow or other they never seemed to work out in the way I expected.'

Sorge and Ozaki were executed in 1944.

CHAPTER THIRTEEN

Council Before the Throne (Part 2)

1. CONSEQUENCES OF THE OCCUPATION OF SOUTHERN INDO-CHINA

SAIGON and Kamranh Bay were within striking distance of the British, American and Dutch colonies and across the intervening sea and land the hostile forces faced each other. On both sides public opinion was at fever-heat. Japan had no oil resources and if she just sat down and waited, she might as well surrender. Unless a peaceful solution became visible in the immediate future, little by little she would draw nearer to 'starvation'.

Rather, then, than sit down to await death, why not hasten and determine the Axis victory by taking the plunge? It would pay Japan to accept the German theory that 'this was the Day', the moment that occurred only once in a thousand years. The argument that the formal decision must now be taken acquired irresistible force: Japan must complete her preparations and make war at once. Needless to say it was the Supreme Command that launched the argument.

2. THE SUPREME COMMAND DECIDES ON WAR

It was Sugiyama, Chief of the General Staff, and Nagano, Chief of the Naval General Staff, who submitted the views of the two branches of the Supreme Command to the Emperor. H.I.M. was seriously perturbed. He took the unprecedented step of summoning the Prime Minister to the Audience.

The two Chiefs submitted to H.I.M. the opinion that the situation was critical, that the Army and Navy considered that it was unwise to waste time in inaction, that the Japanese must now make up their mind that the American talks were likely to fail and that, therefore, it was necessary to get ready so that, supposing the talks to fail, Japan could make the final decision and resort to arms at a moment's notice. Sugiyama said that it was calculated that the whole of the South Seas could be reduced and the intended areas occupied within some three months of the start of hostilities.

The Emperor thereupon displayed a rare burst of anger. He could not place the least reliance on anything the Army told him. Scornfully he asked whether they had not told him that they could clear up the problem of China within one month and yet more than four years had passed. How then did they propose to dispose of an area more remote and larger in extent within three months?

Admiral Nagano then intervened. He explained that by the capture of the oil reserves of the South Seas, Japan's fighting strength would be vastly enhanced and that, even if the war were long-drawn-out, Japan could still go on fighting.

But the Emperor was dissatisfied with the explanations of the two Supreme Commands. He hesitated to take so momentous a decision. This was not a question for the Supreme Commands alone to decide and he demanded that the Cabinet also should give it careful consideration.

3. CONDITIONAL DECISION TO GO TO WAR, SEPTEMBER 6TH, 1941

After conferring with the Army and Navy chiefs and in other quarters, the Prime Minister convened a Council before the Throne at which the decision to go to war was taken, always provided that the negotiations should be continued in the hope that they would succeed. It was, so to speak, a two-way decision: (1) to make war, (2) to continue the negotiations, a decision to do two things that were mutually incompatible. But, regardless of the inconsistency, Konoye had not yet lost hope of the success of the talks. He felt in his heart that the Supreme Command and the Government were two independent entities so that political questions and military operations could be kept separate. Hence he acted, as it were, automatically. The establishment of the independence of the Supreme Command had brought the country to this pass: the will of the nations was split in two. Critics gifted with common sense, who did not breathe the atmosphere of those days but study the phenomenon dispassionately today, will find it wellnigh incomprehensible.

The Council of September 6th was held by agreement between the

Supreme Command and the Cabinet. If the negotiations were not brought to a satisfactory conclusion by October 10th (inclusive), then the decision was to go to war. This was one step further than the decision of July 2nd that, if needs be, a clash with the U.S. and Britain would be accepted. It was a definite decision to fight. Moreover a limit was set beyond which concessions would not be made in the American negotiations. To questions posed by the President of the Privy Council, the two branches of the Supreme Command returned stereotyped replies.

The Emperor was stricken with grief at the decision. Gazing round the assembly, he produced a poem composed by the Emperor Meiji, which he read out from the Throne :[1]

> The seas stretch to all quarters from our shores
> and my heart cries out to the nations of the world :
> Why do the winds thrash the seas and disturb
> peace between us ?

He counselled them to take the meaning to heart and to act accordingly. In so doing, he was asking that assembly of Japan's leaders of the moment—the Cabinet and the High Commands—to search their hearts and reflect. And yet, though H.I.M. had thus told them his wishes, the decision of that Council before the Throne was taken as already arranged.

That is to say, preparations were taken in hand to engage in war with Britain, the U.S. and other countries involved, provided only that if the negotiations with America were successful, the preparations would cease.

The details leaked out almost at once and foreign envoys in Tokyo lost no time in reporting to their governments.

---

[1] I cannot hope to render the rhythm or the beauty of the original. I can only convey the general sense.

CHAPTER FOURTEEN

The Last Days of the Konoye Cabinet

1. WHY SIT DOWN AND STARVE TO DEATH?

By the decision of September 6th the Japanese Government surrendered its hold on the ship of state, which continued to plunge on rudderless into the tempest.

The trouble was that, when the Navy saw how difficult the negotiations were, they became more vociferous than ever in their argument that so long as Japan sat down and did nothing, the U.S. and the Netherlands would deny her oil, and the import of other materials essential to the life of the people would also be impossible. If Japan drifted like this, the time would come when her ability to make war would be gone and she would have to come to terms with the British and Americans. Now, then, was the time to strike the blow and seize the natural resources of the South Seas. Then, Japan would be strong enough to carry on a long war with all its hardship. She must make up her mind before it was too late.

The argument spread. The negotiations must be completed one way or the other without delay, a decision must be taken as to their prospects of success. Under such conditions the result was a foregone conclusion. The talks were doomed from the start.

To this dangerous argument neither Konoye nor the Cabinet had any effective answer. They might almost have been in agreement with it, judging from the manner in which they allowed themselves to be swept onwards by the current. Not for them to accept failure of the negotiations, if it came, and wait for another opportunity, which would have been the calm, commonsense path of the true statesman. They devoted all their attention to the one question—were the talks going to end in success or failure? In the latter case Japan had to take to arms. That was the line of action to which their Japanese way of thinking had conditioned them and on which the seal of the highest possible sanction had now been set. Thus they decided and in so doing created a condition of peril for the country, since there was no hope that the negotiations could be concluded by the date set—the tenth of October.

The Army and Navy then proceeded a stage still further. They urged upon the Cabinet that, if the talks were not concluded by the end of October, they must be broken off and war started then and there. The Cabinet, therefore, in sending a fresh draft, impressed on Ambassador Nomura that they were now entering on the last stage in the negotiations (September 27th), and Foreign Minister Toyoda himself interviewed Ambassador Grew and presented a draft of his views with a time-limit attached. But by now world conditions and the American attitude were settled and no progress was gained. An actual rupture in the negotiations was avoided only because the Americans were playing for time.

2. LAST EFFORTS IN THE NEGOTIATIONS

I have no hesitation in stating categorically that in the American talks Konoye was throughout acting with the best of intentions in accordance with the wishes of the Emperor. Even when he contracted the Tripartite Alliance, he honestly believed that he could clear up relations with the U.S. and Britain. After the decision of July 2nd he still ardently desired an understanding with the Americans. That is why, in spite of the Emperor's misgivings, he light-heartedly came to an understanding with the Army and Navy on the war decision. Logically it cannot be explained unless one makes a minute study of the control of the political situation exercised by the Army and Navy and of the state of public opinion.

Actually Konoye hated war. It cannot be gainsaid that in his heart he yielded to no one in his desire to fulfil the Emperor's hopes for peace by bringing the negotiations to a successful termination. He had previously told me that, if he and President Roosevelt could meet and talk matters over, he was convinced that he could restrain the fighting services. His suite was arranged. In addition to Admirals and Generals, there were to be the Vice-Chiefs of the Army and Navy General Staffs and the Directors of the Bureaus of Military and Naval Affairs. From the Foreign Office there were to be the competent heads of sections and as his own personal adviser I myself was to be nominated.

The American decision that a previous agreement on essentials was a prerequisite blocked the meeting but Konoye still continued wholeheartedly to negotiate. When he and Toyoda had exhausted every effort, Konoye asked me to go to the U.S. to assist Nomura in finding a way out and he went so far as to invoke Grew's assistance to reserve me a seat on a Clipper. But I insisted that, if the talks in Washington were to succeed, it was essential that Japan herself be ready to compromise and should decide on the line to be taken.

3. COMPULSION EXERCISED BY THE ARMY AND NAVY

The Army and Navy were becoming, however, still more uncompromising. The two Supreme Commands wanted a date-line for the commencement of hostilities. They waved aside as a political device any suggestion that, if the talks failed, they could be dropped for the moment. If the negotiations failed that meant war—a typically Japanese way of thinking; in the same way one did not waste time for, if one did, then from a military point of view a chance might be lost that could never be recovered. The Army, represented by Sugiyama, Chief of the General Staff, and Tojo, the Minister for War, were adamant. They maintained that the decision of September 6th was a decision to make war.

The Navy themselves had set the signal for war by their talk of slow starvation. And yet, when the time came, they were not quite ready. War with the U.S. and Britain meant that the Navy must fill the leading role. The Army said that, if the Navy had not the courage to go ahead, all the plans would have to be changed; it all turned on the Navy. So the Navy were cornered and they did not find it easy to shoulder the responsibility. Furthermore, it was the Navy's advocacy of the 'Advance to the South' that was the very essence of Japan's present action. Once the Navy had approved the Tripartite Pact, their 'southern' policy had dragged the country to the edge of the precipice. And they themselves had pressed for the decision of September 6th. True enough, but when it came to the eleventh hour, our Navy, headed by Nagano, Chief of the Naval General Staff, and Oikawa, Minister for the Navy, could not make up their minds. They decided to place the momentous decision in the hands of Prime Minister Konoye.

Their action placed Konoye in a most embarrassing position. Hitherto the independence of the Supreme Command had been the very reason why the Prime Minister had not been allowed to take part in naval discussions. If ever there was one subject in which the Naval Supreme Command was most directly and most seriously concerned, it was this question whether or not to make war. Even, therefore, if the Navy itself deferred to him, he felt that as Prime Minister he could do nothing about it. He spoke bitterly of the Navy's irresponsibility. He wanted the Navy to express its own views and be responsible for them. And who can blame him?

The situation was such that the problem could not be solved merely by shifting the responsibility.

4. CABINET RESIGNS *EN BLOC*

A meeting of Cabinet Ministers was held at the Premier's official residence on October 12th but resulted in a deadlock. The fact was that to succeed in the negotiations Japan must revise her continental policy and withdraw her troops from China. But to this the War Minister was utterly opposed. He said that it was essential to decide at once whether the talks held out any prospect of success and asked the Foreign Minister whether he hoped to conclude the talks by the 10th of November but Toyoda could only reply that, if Japan made concessions as to the withdrawal of troops and other matters, success was not out of the question. Konoye also maintained his attitude that it was desirable to continue negotiating. But Tojo stood to his guns. As War Minister he insisted on a time-limit and an answer Yes or No to his question.

The Prime Minister then offered to talk matters over with him personally but Tojo declined. Japan's policy had already been decided in the Imperial Presence twice over. There was no need, therefore, for a further exchange of views. That being his attitude, Konoye and Toyoda had no confidence in their ability to conclude the negotiations within a fixed time-limit. Where, now, was Konoye's vow that, while he still drew breath, he would bring the negotiations to a successful conclusion? Finally driven into a corner, he threw in his hand and resigned with his whole Cabinet.

BOOK EIGHT

The War of Greater East Asia

The Tojo War Cabinet

CHAPTER ONE

Formation of War Cabinet

1. SIGNIFICANCE OF PRINCE KONOYE'S RESIGNATION

KONOYE'S action in casting aside office and bringing down the Cabinet, at a time when the country was faced with a crisis, was strongly criticized by Kido, Lord Keeper of the Privy Seal.[1] The master of a ship did not abandon it when it was in the midst of a storm and in danger of sinking. As Household Minister he felt that, even if it meant advising the Emperor to dismiss Tojo, the nation should be told in plain terms where the responsibility for the crisis lay.

The fever of impatience of the Army and Navy was at its height and public opinion was fanatically exalted. But the Americans and British on their side were stiffening in their attitude. Unless Japan gave way, there was no hope that the talks would succeed. The question was—could Japan make a fundamental change in her policy? To put it in concrete terms, was she prepared to withdraw her troops from China, if that were the only way in which peace could be preserved? Failing that, it should not have been impossible simply to drop the negotiations.

But to pull up the maddened horse that was galloping towards the precipice was a task that called for no ordinary self-sacrifice. None the less I believe that, however determined the Army and Navy, if Konoye had been steadfast in the pursuit of his convictions, if he had shown an iron will, reliant on the support of the nation, and had stood up to the Army and Navy, even at the danger of bloodshed, he could have won through, for he would have been able to mobilize the whole political influence of Court circles and of all those who possessed intelligence and discernment. It was not I alone that trusted he would act in this way. In this hour of crisis the views of the other State Ministers should have been disclosed in the clearest possible terms. Verily the Army did not enjoy the trust of the whole nation.

[1] The holder of this office was an adviser to the Emperor only second in importance to the Genro, when there was one.

Again, though the Cabinet had resigned, Konoye and the senior statesmen should have studied conditions at home and abroad in detail, they should have combined to preserve peace, as the Emperor desired, and should have had the strength of mind to form a new Cabinet to enforce their views. If only they had had the necessary courage, there might for a time have been civil disturbances but Japan's disaster might have been averted. Even the Army would have hesitated to oppose an Imperial Edict loyally observed by the majority of the upper classes. A Fourth Konoye Cabinet including the senior statesmen, formed in the teeth of Army and Navy opposition, to stand in a body at the side of the Emperor, prepared to go steadfastly forward, regardless of the consequences to themselves, would have been one way out.

But Prince Konoye, who himself had had a hand in bringing about the circumstances, threw in his hand when his immediate path was blocked, just as if it were a mere political upset. Face to face with a crisis greater than any in her history, Japan set about the formation of a new Cabinet as though it were a matter of ordinary routine. Not one step was taken to cope with a situation that was in process of transformation. Attention was concentrated on preventing a new revolt, the Army must be kept quiet at all costs. Ever since the 'Manchurian Incident' the nation had been in the grip of the overwhelming power exercised by the Army. Public defeatism where the Army was concerned ultimately led the country to disaster.

2. POLICY IN FORMATION OF NEW CABINET

Among the upper circles no one really wanted war. How could it be avoided?—that was the question. Everyone was convinced that the Emperor felt the same. It was only those influences that centred in the Army that wanted war. Unhappily it was asking too much to expect the senior statesmen,[1] worn out as they were by the worries of those times, to band together to restrain the Army and enforce the wishes of the Emperor. They had scant knowledge of international conditions and they thought of diplomacy as an art, the skilful use of which would suffice to win over one's opponent. In their blindness they thought it should still be possible to lead the negotiations to a successful conclusion. Surely it was easy enough for a diplomat! It never occurred to

---

[1] Note that the last of the Genro died on November 24th, 1940. No one was appointed in his place though of the existing older statesmen the most likely candidate would possibly have been the Marquis Kido who is mentioned in s. 1.

them that the diplomat has to deal with hard facts. They shut their eyes to realities.

Their minds working on familiar lines, instead of actually checking the Army in its wild career, they attached more importance to finding means of exercising some measure of control over it. Some thought of a Cabinet headed by a member of the Imperial Family. But experience showed that, so far from the Imperial Family controlling, it was they who were used by the Army. It was hopeless to look for a member of the Imperial Family who had the personality to impose the wishes of the Emperor on the Army. Supposing such a Cabinet to become its tool, the Imperial Family would be the target of public resentment. If, on the other hand, it did endeavour to restrain the military, the Imperial Family lacked the requisite power. A struggle in the teeth of Army opposition might bring disaster on the Imperial Family. Nothing could be more dangerous than for one of its members to nourish political ambitions or to utilize those that had them. This was the view of Marquis Kido, and most of the senior statesmen agreed with him that the best plan was to choose a man of character who could exercise control over the Army.

3. CONFERENCE OF THE SENIOR STATESMEN

Under instructions from the Emperor a conference was held of former Prime Ministers to recommend a new Prime Minister. Marquis Kido, the Lord Keeper of the Privy Seal, was to submit the result of their deliberations.

The conference was opened in a tense but hopeful atmosphere. Its members included Count Kiyoura, Baron Wakatsuki, Admirals Okada and Yonai, General Abe, Mr. Hirota, General Hayashi and others. Marquis Kido and the President of the Privy Council were also present. Kiyoura, now aged, needed all his resolution to attend under the ministrations of a nurse. Baron Hiranuma had been injured by a would-be assassin and was not yet sufficiently recovered to attend.

This was an opportunity that might have been taken to scrutinize unreservedly the past policy and behaviour of the Government and the Supreme Command, to expose to the light of day the opinions of statesmen of the highest rank. This, if ever, was the supreme opportunity, armed as they were with the Emperor's wishes, to give a clear lead to the Government. There was, it is true, some discussion of the actual policy of the Government, but it was the general sense of the assembly that the business of the meeting was limited to the recommendation to the Throne of a successor to the post of prime minister, so a discussion of the fundamental question whether or not the country should be led into war was continued no further. Peace or War was not touched on. Attention was focused on the discussion how not to upset Army discipline. Their energies were devoted to the amicable formation of the next Cabinet.

Before the meeting the Army had proposed that H.I.H. Prince Higashi-Kuni should form the Cabinet and War Minister Tojo expressed this view to Konoye, Kido and ex-army Prime Ministers. But Kido considered the proposal highly dangerous. At the conference the suggestion was repeated by the soldiers but was not pressed after General Ugaki had stated that the Prince would be unable to control the Army. Finally the conference accepted Kido's view that Tojo was the only man strong enough to control the Army and to work for the realization of the Emperor's wishes. The conference, therefore, without further ado, completed their business in that one session and Kido submitted Tojo's name to the Emperor.

H.I.M. the Emperor thereupon summoned War Minister Tojo to the Palace. Never before had a servant of the Throne been entrusted with so grave a responsibility to the state.

4. PRIME MINISTER TOJO, OCTOBER 18TH, 1941

In ordering Tojo to form a Cabinet, H.I.M. instructed him that the decision of September 6th might be regarded as invalid, that he was not bound by it and that, with his Cabinet, he should examine the situation from all angles and then determine the policy of the country. Further, he enjoined the Minister for the Navy[1] to work in harmony with the Army and see to it that there was no lack of cohesion. Before this, Kido also had criticized the interpretation put on the decision of September 6th and had argued the absolute need of its cancellation in order that the Emperor's desire for peace should be realized. Tojo, therefore, was given *carte blanche* to re-examine the country's policy. It was indeed the main duty with which he was entrusted.

Tojo's Cabinet was formed at once. He himself was promoted to General; he retained the Ministry of War and for a time held the office of Home Minister also. Admiral Shimada, only recently appointed Commander-in-Chief of the Yokosuka Naval Station, was made Minister for the Navy. Other Ministers of State were Togo, Foreign Affairs; Kaya, Finance; Lieutenant-General Suzuki, Head of the

[1] See next paragraph.

Planning Board and Minister without Portfolio; Admiral Terajima, Communications. Thus a balance was struck between the Army and the Navy. Naoki Hoshino was appointed Chief Secretary to the Cabinet. He had played a part in the establishment of Manchoukuo and had collaborated with Tojo, when the latter was Chief of Staff of the Kwantung Army.

Thus came into being a powerful military Cabinet such as had never been seen before. The Army, which Tojo was to control, had hitherto stoutly demanded war. And this was the Cabinet that was the best the senior statesmen could evolve, a Cabinet that was to produce a successful outcome of the American negotiations by some feat of diplomacy—in other words, if it was lucky, it might!

5. SIGNIFICANCE OF THE ADVENT OF THE TOJO CABINET

At home and abroad it was generally thought that the new Cabinet was a War Cabinet and that Japan was heading straight for war. It was common knowledge that the Konoye Cabinet had fallen because the attitude of Tojo as representative of the Army had made it impossible to go on with the American talks. And now it was Tojo that had stepped forward to form the new Cabinet.

But the new Cabinet announced that it was not committed to past policy, that it was going to subject it to a careful scrutiny and that the negotiations would be continued. The public in general could not quite fathom what the change betokened and those who did still clung to a faint hope and kept their eyes fixed anxiously on the negotiations. But the average person agreed that this was a War Cabinet while the Americans regarded talk of a clean sheet and a fresh start as pure trickery, a smoke-screen to hide the war preparations that were being made.

My duties as consultant over the negotiations had ended with the fall of the Konoye Cabinet. I now confirmed the resignation I had tendered on my return to Japan.

CHAPTER TWO

Attitude of the U.S. Towards the Problem of East Asia

(Note by Translator. Exigencies of space make it necessary to omit five sections in which the author traces for his Japanese readers the growth of the U.S., the development of its vast resources, the gradual change in the interpretation of the Monroe Doctrine from 'hands off the N. and S. American continents' to a broader conception of her duty as a democratic nation to defend other nations throughout the world from the aggression of countries aiming at the domination of their weaker neighbours, coupled with the corresponding feeling that their activities threatened the security of the U.S. itself. The concluding section of this chapter follows.)

AMERICAN POLICY TOWARDS EAST ASIA

IT was the American policy to prevent the establishment by other powers of spheres of influence in China; the policy took its stand on the doctrine of the 'open door and equal opportunity for all'. The aim was to interpose a barrier against 'colonization' in East Asia. It had, therefore, become a positive policy that sounded a warning against power diplomacy and expressed sympathy with racial aspirations.

When Japan defended Manchuria from Russian inroads, the Americans sided with her. But when Japan herself adopted a forward policy in China, the attitude changed to one of firm opposition to 'aggression'. American policy had always as its objective the liberation of China. She sympathized with the revolutionaries and in view of her own past history carefully watched the awakening of the Chinese people. Her policy, therefore, was all too different from that of Japan, which thought only of temporary advantage and was swayed by the ideas of the party or faction in power at the moment.

Since the Opium War, Britain had enjoyed a paramount position in China and controlled East Asia. When Japan emerged as a Great Power, it became advantageous to join hands with her; hence the Anglo-Japanese Alliance. But the U.S. was not so well pleased that the Alliance should buttress Britain's vast possessions and enable Japan to make a forward move in China. The First World War caused a change. In East Asia Britain now had to collaborate with the U.S. and not with Japan, because this had become a first principle with America. The Alliance was abrogated and thenceforward Britain and the U.S. adopted a common policy in China.

After the 'Manchurian Incident' the Stimson doctrine declared that the U.S. could not recognize this alteration of the *status quo ante*. America announced her support of China and her opposition to Japan. As Japan plunged further and further into China, the U.S. attitude stiffened. She denounced her treaty of commerce, and enforced the 'freezing' order. During the Washington negotiations, the American attitude towards East Asia never wavered.

The American world policy under Roosevelt relied on her national strength to enable her to realize her ideals both in the East and in the West. She decided that the Axis powers were aggressors and joined forces with Britain, France, Russia and the Netherlands to resist them. Neither would she come to terms with aggressors nor yield ground to them.

As Japan advanced southward, so the A.B.C.D. encirclement was drawn tighter and left Japan no option but to state whether she wanted Peace or War.

CHAPTER THREE

Opening of Hostilities

1. THE CABINET'S ATTITUDE TO THE NEGOTIATIONS

THE world was waiting for the storm to break in the Pacific. The U.S. mustered her fleet in Pearl Harbour. The British and the Dutch hastened their preparations. In Japan the 'starvation' theory prevailed. The new Cabinet and the Supreme Command spent night and day at Headquarters studying and re-studying that important decision taken in the Imperial Presence and their talks revolved round the Washington negotiations.

The Government drew up two draft proposals, A and B, which were carried at a Council before the Throne on November 5th. Based on a resolve to make war, orders were issued that the negotiations were to terminate on November 25th, later postponed to November 29th.

In order to assist Nomura, the Foreign Minister sent Kurusu, former Ambassador to Germany, and, by the good offices of Ambassador Grew, he was enabled to catch a Clipper from Hong Kong. Thereafter the negotiations were conducted by Nomura and Kurusu conjointly.

Even so, as I have already observed, there was no hope of turning the negotiations into favourable channels unless Japan radically changed her attitude.

2. 'DO OR DIE'

In the negotiations the Japanese Government had more than once repeated the same proposal in a different form but the two parties were thinking on different lines and their aims were so diametrically opposed that this method had not brought the American attitude any nearer to the Japanese. The Americans had broken the Japanese cyphers and the

Secretary of State knew the Japanese intentions in advance and could plan his response accordingly.

War fever had grown in Japan and Nagano, Chief of the Naval General Staff, who had at one time said that war was out of the question, had been converted to the view that, if an initial victory led to the capture of oil and other resources from the Dutch East Indies, then Japan need not fear a long war. Since to an island country victory or defeat rested on mastery at sea, the Navy's estimate of prospects and its decision had a decisive bearing on the question whether or not to fight. The bold policy won the day—there was nothing for it but to go all out for a final victory. Now that the Navy had stepped out of the confines of military strategy and invaded the field of politics, there was no one left to combat their views. The Army itself had long resolved on war and welcomed the Navy's new attitude.

As for the negotiations, there were limits to the concessions Japan could make. So long as the Army and Navy were confident of the issue, they could see no reason to compromise at the expense of their self-respect. The Japanese Government, therefore, made its last proposals to the U.S. Government, while in the Diet the Prime Minister and the Minister for Foreign Affairs adopted a firm attitude and indicated that there were limits beyond which concessions could not be made.

3. FINAL NEGOTIATIONS

Proposal A[1] made to the Americans was a final attempt at agreement on the lines of the preceding talks. If an understanding was not reached under A, then B[1] proposed that Japan should withdraw her troops from South to North Indo-China, the U.S. should cease supporting Chiang Kai-shek and cancel the freezing order and a new point of departure could be found in the more cordial atmosphere that would result. In accordance with instructions, therefore, Nomura presented A.

There was a sense of urgency, since a time-limit had been decided upon. Nomura and Kurusu did their best and on November 20th presented B, as to which Togo had telegraphed them that it did not admit of compromise. The unconciliatory attitude was at once reflected in the American reaction and Cordell Hull, who understood the Japanese attitude from his intercepts, placed no faith in the protestations of the two diplomats. The Americans concluded that Japan was conceding nothing; in fact, judging from her deeds, she was becoming more

[1] *Vide* Chapter Three, s. 1.

stubborn than ever. Moreover they entertained doubts as to the reason why Kurusu had been sent, did not trust him and redoubled their suspicions (Cordell Hull's *Memoirs*, p. 1064 *et seq.*).

The Secretary of State consulted with the signatories of the Nine Power Pact. By now the U.S. had abandoned procrastinating tactics and proposed to make certain of Japan's hostile intentions. They handed a reply on November 26th. It summarized the views of the associating powers and was firmer in tone than any previous communication. A *modus vivendi* had been drawn up at the request of the American Army but, in deference to the wishes of China and of Britain, this reply was presented instead. To put it briefly, the American reply demanded that the situation before the 'Manchurian Incident' should be restored. Japan had understood that she was being asked to withdraw her troops from China Proper but now she was being asked to withdraw her troops from Manchuria also. Neither Roosevelt nor Hull imagined that Japan would comply. Indeed they both had a distinct impression that for Japan it would be the signal for war.

4. THE EVE OF WAR

The vital point of the negotiations was really recognition of the state of Manchoukuo. That was the very minimum of what Japan had hoped to gain. Withdrawal of troops from that country meant the dissolution of Manchoukuo. The Cabinet's attitude had already been determined in the Liaison Conference of November 15th and the Japanese Government interpreted the latest American proposal as an ultimatum demanding the impossible.

The negotiations had culminated in a crisis. According to official documents, the Americans regarded their proposal as the final stage in the negotiations, they anticipated that Japan would reject it and they ordered all Army and Navy stations in the Pacific to be alerted. Churchill announced that, if war broke out, Britain would join in within the hour. In Japan the Supreme Command and the Government had also made their decision.

From the beginning there had been fundamental misunderstandings on both sides. Many who took a hand in the negotiations had ideas different from those of Japan and their efforts had only added to the complications. The U.S. was determined to assist Britain to crush Nazi Germany and was prepared to go to war for the purpose. Had Japan been willing to liquidate her commitments under the Tripartite Alliance, to change over to a policy of collaboration with America and Britain and to withdraw her troops from China and Indo-China, then the U.S. might have made concessions in regard to Manchoukuo and striven for an understanding.

There is no reason to doubt the good intentions and zeal of Japan's representative,[1] but the Army and Navy would not budge an inch from the stand they had taken. The Americans played for time to complete their preparations against attack. The Japanese Army and Navy bided their time to resort to direct action. From start to finish the negotiations were cumbered with contradictions and cross-purposes.

5. EXPLANATION GIVEN ME BY THE FOREIGN MINISTER

About this time, although I did not know the inner details of the negotiations, nor yet the decision of the Liaison Conference, I still felt that, if only Japan kept out of the war, a brighter day would dawn. I *must* do my best to save Japan from a course inviting disaster. After mature deliberation, I called at the Ministry of Foreign Affairs for the first time since the formation of the Tojo Cabinet. In the absence of the Foreign Minister I was interviewed by the Vice-Minister, Nishi.

To him I said: 'I have not called today to ask you to divulge anything that is confidential. What I would like to say is that, however often the Minister may be changed, this is no time for Minister for Foreign Affairs to take the responsibility for going to war. We all appreciate the difficult position in which the Minister is placed but please be so good as to give him my message.' I then withdrew. If the Minister resigned, the Prime Minister would probably take over the Ministry in order to carry out his intentions. Yet, none the less, I thought that the stand taken by a Foreign Minister who had the courage of his convictions would remain as a landmark for the future.

Shortly after the opening of hostilities I was invited to go to China as Ambassador and I took the opportunity to ask Minister Togo why he had voted for war. He explained that the calculations produced by the Army and Navy chiefs and the Planning Board led to the conclusion that Japan would win and he could not combat their arguments nor did circumstances permit him to oppose them. I contented myself with saying that of national issues the decision whether or not to go to war was the most serious and was not one to be taken on a balance of probabilities. This discussion took place after Japan had won amazing successes at Pearl Harbour and in Malaya and the people were intoxicated by the belief in victory. The nation as a whole approved the declaration

[1] Or representatives. There were two at the end.

of war and were in a mood to make any sacrifice required in its conduct.

As expected, the American reply of November 26th confirmed Japan in her attitude. Even the hesitants in the Navy and the dissidents in the Government agreed that Japan could not accept the American demands. Flagging public opinion came to life again.

On December 1st a Council before the Throne deliberated upon a proposal to make war on the U.S., Britain and the Netherlands and finally decided on war.

6. SQUADRON SETS OUT; FINAL NOTIFICATION[1]

A plan of operations was decided. A squadron was ordered to assemble at the Kuriles. 'If the U.S. remains obdurate and there is finally no hope of settlement, war opens on X Day and the enemy is to be "at once attacked".' The squadron would carry secret instructions but was to return if the negotiations were concluded satisfactorily. On X Day Nomura and Kurusu were to interview the Secretary of State before the attack and on Government instructions were to notify him that the negotiations were closed.

The Foreign Office regarded it as essential under The Hague Treaty that advance notice should be given of the opening of hostilities. The Supreme Command had no objection but the Navy insisted that the interval should be as short as possible in order to increase the advantage of a surprise attack. The point was left in the hands of the Supreme Command and the Foreign Minister; on the insistence of the Naval General Staff, the interval was reduced to thirty minutes. The Foreign Office was to telegraph instructions to the Ambassadors by the close of the previous day. The notice was to be confined to a formal statement that the negotiations were closed and the essential details were to be telegraphed last. The Americans, however, read all the Government's important telegrams and knew beforehand.

Nomura and Kurusu were instructed to request in advance an interview at 1 p.m. on December 8th.

---

[1] Note that in Japanese phraseology there is a distinction between *saigo no tsukoku*, 'final notification', and *saigo no tsucho*, 'ultimatum'. Japan never presented an ultimatum to the U.S.

7. CONFERENCE OF SENIOR STATESMEN

Preparations were made secretly and with despatch. A Military Council was held and, also, on November 29th, a conference of the senior statesmen. To the latter the Government explained the general circumstances and the course of the negotiations. Wakatsuki expressed concern at the economic situation but no particular questions were asked. Thereafter, the senior statesmen were summoned to an Audience and requested to give their views.

At this important meeting in the Palace no one opposed the war, no one advanced any considered views as to the future of the country. Public opinion was inflamed and thinking people had for days been dreading the outcome. In summoning the statesmen to the Palace and explaining the situation, the Government were already doing something out of the ordinary. The summons to an Audience at which they were invited to express their views was a complete break with precedent. Was it not because the Emperor was anxious to ascertain their views? They could not have doubted it. And yet, though the highest authority in the land, their Emperor, had given them this wonderful opportunity of expressing their views, why, if any one of them opposed the war (and actually they did), did not one single person summon all his courage and tell the naked truth? Perhaps they thought that they must go through with it now, that a *volte face* was impossible. Shall we say that they were impelled by the spirit of defeatism towards the Army?

Before this, H.I.H. Prince Takamatsu had suddenly, at the eleventh hour, informed the Emperor that the Navy still had misgivings and was opposed to war. H.I.M. had at once summoned the Minister Shimada and the Chief of the N.G.S. Nagano and had earnestly enquired what the Navy really thought. Both replied that the Navy's decision for war and its conviction of victory were exactly as had been decided by the Liaison Conference. Everything, therefore, was carried out as anticipated by the Liaison Conference, the Conference in the Imperial Presence was convened on December 1st, all arrangements were determined and the Emperor eventually approved the War Declaration.

8. THE SURPRISE ATTACK OF DECEMBER 8TH, 1941

In the early dawn of December 8th telephones in Tokyo were busy. The great success of the attack on Pearl Harbour was already known to those in the inner circles and communicated to their friends. The radio announced the outbreak of war and read the Imperial Decree. The citizens listened respectfully. They rejoiced at the good news and breathed a sigh of relief. It was not entirely due to the good news. They had been held in a state of suspense so long and now that waiting was over they sighed with relief, as a Japanese might well do, and as Japanese they resolved to go through with it to the end and smash the enemy. Nobody had time to reflect what it all meant.

The night before, Ambassador Grew had received a personal message from the President to the Emperor urging peace and had requested Foreign Minister Togo to present it. But it was all too late. In the depth of night Togo went to the Palace and delivered the President's telegram. By that time the attack had already begun. As the fateful day approached, delivery of telegrams to the British and American Embassies, including the President's appeal, had been delayed under instructions from Supreme Headquarters.

Togo called Grew to the Foreign Office at the same time as he had instructed Nomura and Kurusu to deliver the notice that negotiations were closed and handed him a copy. At that moment Grew thought that it was the reply to the President's appeal since he had not yet heard of the Pearl Harbour attack. When he returned to the Embassy outside communications had been cut.

9. THE FINAL NOTIFICATION

Unhappily, delivery of the notice in Washington had taken place later than intended. Owing, it is said, to disorganization in the Japanese Embassy, preparation of a fair copy of the telegram had taken too long. When Nomura and Kurusu met the Secretary of State (at 2.20 p.m.) it was already more than an hour later than arranged (such hitches were an unfortunate blot on Foreign Office efficiency). Cordell Hull had already read the telegram and knew the purpose of the Ambassadors' call. What was worse, a telephone message from the White House had advised him that something untoward had happened at Pearl Harbour. The Ambassadors were coldly received by the Secretary of State. Having listened to their business, he said that in fifty years of public service he had never met with such deceitful, double-faced dealing, and pointed to the door. The two Ambassadors, with a strained expression on their faces, took leave and returned to the Japanese Embassy, there to learn for the first time that war had started.

10. THE WAR OF GREATER EAST ASIA

Hitherto the story has been one of 'incidents'. Now I have to speak of War. The Navy proposed to call it the 'War of the Pacific'. The Army preferred the 'War of Greater East Asia' since it was a fight for the crown of leadership there, and so it came to be called.

The Army and the Navy each regarded the war from its own point of view. But for the country it was neither the one nor the other. It was a World War into which Japan had been drawn. The Asian and the European campaigns, the struggles in the Pacific and the Atlantic, were not separate wars; they were closely interconnected parts of one war. Japan, with her limited vision, might call it the Greater East Asia War but what matters a name? It was precisely this narrow outlook of Japan's leaders, their ignorance of world conditions, that brought Japan to disaster.

Germany and Italy gave their blessing on Japan's adherence to the Alliance and immediately declared war on the U.S. Churchill, who had welcomed the Russo-German War, now exclaimed 'the war is won'. He meant that the spiritual and material strength of the U.S. had been enlisted without reservation on the side of the Allies.

CHAPTER FOUR

Japan's Plan of Campaign (Part 1)

1. FUNDAMENTAL MISTAKES AND LACK OF CO-ORDINATION

THE tale I have to tell is one of tragic defeat, the culmination of the political bankruptcy of the preceding decade. The country or the individual that thinks only of self is like a blind man rushing into the unknown. In the present-day struggle for existence the wisdom of the sages is required. The future of the country that sums up world conditions incorrectly is determined from the beginning. Unhappy Japan! She not only misunderstood: she was impatient and intolerant of restraint. Always it was 'glory' that mattered. In national policy, in the plan of campaign, it was 'glory' that decided. This it was that moulded the mentality of the people in time of war. It was splendid, but endurance and wisdom would have been more valuable.[1]

After the European War had begun, Japan contracted the Tripartite Alliance. When the outcome of the Russo-German War hung in the balance, she still persisted in her southern venture. As the pattern of the war in Europe was beginning to take shape, she quarrelled with the two most powerful nations in the world and thrust herself into the World War. Verily this precious stone was doomed to be shattered.[2]

Two factors together determined Japan's defeat: lack of co-ordination in the plan of campaign and miscalculation of Japan's physical resources. The course of war was ruthlessly to disclose that her leaders suffered from a lack of calm, scientific judgment in administration, in economics, in psychology, in everything.

---

[1] The translation does not do justice to the text. Japanese precepts often appeal to the emotions rather than to reason. The underlying thought is that it is better to die in the moment of glorious success than to live ingloriously: 'One crowded hour of glorious life is worth an age without a name.' See also note on the code of military honour in the Translator's Foreword.

[2] *Cf.* 'This precious stone set in the silver sea.'

2. REFLECTIONS OF GENERAL TOJO

In Sugamo Prison General Tojo gave his reasons for the defeat. 'Basically it was lack of co-ordination. When the Prime Minister, to whom is entrusted the destiny of a country, has not the authority to participate in supreme decisions, it is not likely that the country will win a war. Then, again, the Supreme Command was divided between the Army and the Navy—two entities that would not work in unison. I did not hear of the Midway defeat till more than a month after it occurred. Even now I do not know the details. There was no proper unity in operations right up to the finish.'

What must have been the depths of feeling of one who maintained dead silence so long and only disclosed his thoughts at the very end! General Tojo began as Minister for War, then as Prime Minister he doubled the offices, he directed the war and at the end took over the post of Chief of General Staff, assembling all authority in his own person in his endeavour to co-ordinate the administration and the Supreme Command. His reflections in the hour of death have enormous value.

Hereafter I attempt to give a record of the general plan of campaign, based on accounts given to me by associates in Sugamo Prison, collated with material disclosed at the Tokyo Tribunal.

3. THE BASIS OF JAPAN'S MILITARY STRATEGY[1]

Japan's strategy took for granted German victory. It was hoped that Russia might be induced to join the Alliance but when that plan failed, and Germany opened war on Russia, wishful thinking induced the belief that Germany would smash Russia and strike down through the Caucasus to Persia and India. Japanese strategy, therefore, aimed at the destruction of the British Empire and the occupation of Singapore, whence the Navy could advance into the Indian Ocean to join hands with Germany coming east from North Africa or from central Asia, and then win the war by combined Japanese-German operations.

4. NAVAL STRATEGY

The Navy's first thoughts were concentrated on the Pacific with the American fleet as its prime objective. Strategy was based on an effective

[1] Ss. 3 to 6 and Chapter Five are very much abridged.

reply to American naval tactics, which planned to cross the Pacific via bases strung on a curve, to relieve the Philippines and then turn north to attack Japan. The problem was how to destroy this fleet. The Pacific islands held by Japan lay between America and the Philippines and would serve as bases from which to do so. But this plan took only the U.S. into consideration. There were also Britain and other nations to reckon with. Though the Japanese Navy had increased enormously in recent years, to hold a line stretching from the Pacific to the Indian Ocean, and to maintain it intact against air attack, was beyond the powers of the Navy.

The solution was to deliver a stunning blow to either the U.S. or Britain and the surprise attack on Pearl Harbour was chosen for the purpose. The secret intelligence gained by the enemy from their ability to decipher our telegrams and the consequent state of preparation of this naval base make the great success of the attack all the more outstanding, for the raiding squadron had a vast ocean to cross; a bold attack indeed. The enemy were caught napping. Even so the result speaks volumes for careful planning and rigorous training.

The attack made American blood boil and united the nation. Foreigners, and particularly the Americans, hold that the watchword 'Remember Pearl Harbour' led America to her victory over Japan. It may be that had the Japanese Navy kept to its original strategy, it might in the long run have paid better though the initial difficulties would have been far greater.

However that may be, the success, while rousing the American people to fighting pitch, gave the Japanese people overweening confidence, and subsequent naval defeats stem from that fact.

5. A VAST AREA OF OPERATIONS

The Army thought mainly of the war of Greater East Asia. It wanted to join hands with Germany and force Britain to surrender. The aims of the Army and the Navy, therefore, differed. It is only natural that, while acquiescing in military plans, the Navy should desire to protect its flank by putting the American fleet out of action. But after Pearl Harbour and subsequent successes in the South Seas, the Navy, proud of its invincible fleet, expanded its ideas. Extremists embraced the vast Pacific in their vision; Hawaii was to be captured and the sphere of operations was to be extended over the whole area. The Army on the other hand wished to concentrate its forces in South-East Asia. These divergent aims made cohesion difficult. When it came to carrying into effect this jumble of discordant ideas, there was a lack of co-ordination and the field of operations was extended to its extreme limit.

In general, strategy took no count of distance and time. Planners pored over maps and indulged in day-dreams that ignored material and practical factors. The naval belief that it could retain mastery at sea and in the air over the Pacific against the two most powerful air and maritime nations in the world is a phenomenon for history to marvel at. As the war continued, mastery was gradually yielded to the enemy and at the end our forces spread over the Pacific Islands and the mainland were left to their fate, to fight until they were overwhelmed.

The Japanese forces fought well. In no instance was their record for courage tarnished. They showed the world of what the 'Japanese spirit' was capable. When the public were informed on April 30th, 1943, that the garrison on Attu in the Aleutians under its commander Yamashita had fought on until not one man remained alive, they wept tears of pride and sorrow. They poured out their gratitude and emotion at this supreme sacrifice. But this tragic battle to a finish was only one example of the 'death or glory' struggle to which the country was committed and could not affect the war situation as a whole.

6. A HOLLOW VICTORY

To the Army and Navy the surprise attack was both an article of faith and an art. Within one year Japan had accomplished all she set out to do. Her success astounded the world: the Navy air-arm in particular was matchless, the Army's skill in jungle warfare was incomparable. The Army and Navy vied with each other in their exploits. That initial success had exposed the Western Pacific, the South Seas and South-east Asia to her conquests as far as her arm could reach.

Supply by sea to these far-flung forces, even with the shipping Japan possessed at the outset, could scarcely have been adequate. Once Japan lost mastery at sea and in the air, her forces became isolated targets for attack and were crushed one by one. Before the year was out the tide was beginning to turn and they were doomed.

CHAPTER FIVE

Japan's Plan of Campaign (Part 2)

1. FIRST FRUITS OF VICTORY

THE Pearl Harbour success had more or less destroyed the American Pacific Fleet assembled there. Meanwhile the Army was moving on Singapore. Siam was drawn into a treaty of alliance and some of our forces waiting in Indo-China entered the country, while others were landed at Khota Bharu in North Malaya. An army under General Homma landed at Lingayen for the conquest of the Philippines.

The pride of the British Navy, the largest battleship in the world, the unsinkable H.M.S. *Prince of Wales*, on which Churchill and Roosevelt had drawn up the Atlantic Charter, was sunk off the coast of Malaya with another battleship, H.M.S. *Repulse*, by an air squadron from Indo-China. Within two months Singapore had fallen to the Japanese Army under Commander-in-Chief Yamashita (February 15th, 1942). Branching out, the Army occupied Rangoon (March 8th), Java (March 9th), the Andaman Islands (March 23rd), Manila (January 3rd), Corregidor (April 4th). The Navy in the meantime had sunk navy and merchant ships in the Indian Ocean, had shelled naval stations in Ceylon and Madagascar and had made a surprise sortie on Sydney, Australia.

The conquest of the Philippines had taken longer than anticipated. The American forces on the Bataan Peninsula and on the island of Corregidor at the entrance to Manila Harbour put up a desperate fight and additional troops had to be sent. The Commander-in-Chief, General MacArthur, escaped at the last moment, leaving behind a message, 'I shall be back.'

2. CO-PROSPERITY SPHERE REALIZED: MILITARY 'HUBRIS'

The Navy's first line ran through the Luchus,[1] Formosa, the Philippines, Borneo and Sumatra. A second line ran from Tokyo Bay, via the Marianas, Caroline Islands, Bismark, New Britain, to a point on the east of New Guinea, and there were still further outposts on Wake Island, the Marshall, Gilbert and Solomon islands. It seemed as though the Navy were merely crossing a no man's land, so completely did it extend its area of conquest before its enemies had time to prepare their defences. Sumatra and Borneo oil-wells were captured undamaged (at Palembang a Japanese air-borne unit came into action for the first time).

The first stage in the plan of campaign was complete and essential sources of supply had been captured. The foundations of the 'Greater East Asia Co-prosperity Sphere' had been laid and the resources required for a long war had been acquired. They had only to be retained and utilized to win the war! The Germans went so far as to envy Japan her successes. The Army and Navy preened themselves on the way their plan of campaign had worked out. Their pride was overweening and a certain Hirade, a naval propagandist, announced on the radio that the U.S. would be forced to capitulate on the steps of the White House. The mistaken impression that the war had already been won gained ground. The public lost their heads and any hope of their realizing what a world war entailed was dispelled. Contrast this mood with the American 'Remember Pearl Harbour'.

3. BATTLE OF THE CORAL SEA

In the Southern Pacific our field of operations extended beyond New Britain to Guadalcanal at the South-east tip of the Solomons. Southward again the capture of New Hebrides and New Caledonia would threaten sea-lanes between Australia and the U.S. and guard the stepping-stones behind them. Further, in order to cross from Timor to Port Darwin in North Australia, it was necessary to have a firm grip on Papua (Australian territory in New Guinea), for this would not only provide a useful base but would prevent the enemy counter-attacking from Australia. Port Darwin had already been twice attacked by bombers and as a military station had been abandoned by the Australians.

The capital of Papua was Port Moresby, which could be attacked both by sea and by land. The plan was for a task squadron to escort

[1] Also written Loochoos; in Japanese, Ryukyu.

troopships from Rabaul round the eastern corner of New Guinea into the Coral Sea in order to attack Port Moresby from the sea. At this point it ran into an enemy aircraft-carrier squadron.

The landing operation was thereby frustrated. Our squadron under Rear-Admiral Hara discovered the enemy squadron, led by the *Lexington* and the *Yorktown* under Rear-Admiral Fitch, and attacked. The *Lexington* was sunk (May 8th). The *Yorktown* also was seriously damaged but escaped, and after hasty repairs at Pearl Harbour was in time to take part in the subsequent battle of Midway. Our squadron also was badly damaged and the sea attack on Port Moresby was abandoned.

Later, an attempt was made to capture Port Moresby by land but this effort also failed. The plan to attack Northern Australia was thwarted and, to make matters worse, the rear of our Solomon Island expeditionary force was harassed by the American counter-attack that developed.

The battle of the Coral Sea was in itself a hard-won victory but strategically it not only marked the turning-point of the war but it also led to a severe reverse sustained in the battle of Guadalcanal.

The Coral Sea battle and the attack on Midway were the last offensive actions by our Navy.

4. NAVAL STRATEGY: SECOND PHASE

Preparations for the American counter-attack were made in Australia in close concert with the Americans. Ports on the Pacific Coast served as subsidiary bases for the Australian and American forces that were being equipped and trained by MacArthur.

To meet this counter-attack the Navy's plan of campaign had to be extended to cut communications between the U.S. and Australia. The Navy, therefore, embarked on the second phase of its plan of campaign.

5. DEFEAT AT MIDWAY, JUNE 5TH, 1942

The Americans anticipated the attack on Midway. As the Yamamoto combined squadron, with the Minami aircraft squadron in the vanguard, openly approached, escorting troopships carrying in all one brigade, an American aircraft squadron was lying in wait for them.

The battle opened with an attack by American fleet aircraft, which had had word of the approach. While our own aircraft were attacking Midway, the *Yorktown* and other vessels of the fleet in charge of

Admiral Spruance launched the unexpected attack from the flank. Our squadron opened fire but valuable time was lost in switching over from a land attack to a sea battle. A number of the attacking aircraft pierced the barrage and scored hits on the aircraft-carriers, which blew up from the fire that spread to their own explosives. In the space of a few minutes our aircraft squadron was shattered.

Commander-in-Chief Yamamoto called off the attack and the squadron withdrew in confusion. One by one the aircraft-carriers sank. Meanwhile the land-based American aircraft, warned by radar, were circling the airfield and the attacking aircraft returned, after accomplishing little, only to find their 'mother-ships' had been destroyed.

In this battle the Navy lost all but four of its best aircraft-carriers and a great number of its most experienced flyers. Many captains went down with their ships. Minami was rescued, to die at Saipan. The Americans had avenged Pearl Harbour.

By the battle, parity with the U.S. Navy was lost and in succeeding defeats mastery of the sea and air was soon transferred to the Americans. 'Midway' was in fact the turning-point. American squadron-training developed and skill improved; American technique and industrial capacity caused the gap between the relative strength of the two countries to grow ever wider. Japan could never catch up again.

This defeat shattered Japanese plans. The details were never divulged either to the nation or to the Cabinet. They were even kept secret from all but a few in the Navy itself. The Japanese Army and Navy do not admit defeat. The public announcement left it to be inferred that American losses were greater than ours. This refusal to acknowledge a reverse is a firmly rooted weakness—a relic from feudal times. It is not a sign of strength.

The attack on the Aleutians succeeded and Attu and Kiska were captured. But in the south plans to attack the Fiji Islands and New Caledonia were abandoned. None the less we clung to our outposts on the Solomon Islands, Guadalcanal and Bougainville. An unfavourable war of attrition developed and despite numerous heroic battles the ability of the Navy to keep the forces supplied declined steadily. And when Commader-in-Chief Yamamoto flew on an inspection tour from his Headquarters on Truk, he was shot down and killed. The enemy knew in advance from their Intelligence that he was coming.

In the talk above recorded[1] Tojo said: 'That was the time when our plan of campaign should have been entirely revised. But the Navy was a law unto itself.' Though our naval and air power was impaired, the Navy made no attempt to contract its line of battle but clung on to the

[1] Chapter Four, s. 2.

Solomons. Many people think that had Japan done then what she did over a year later—withdrawn to the Mariana, Caroline, Rabaul line and consolidated their defences—she might have gained time to recover.

The name 'Midway' is apposite. We reached that point some six months or so after the war started.

6. WAR OF ATTRITION IN GUADALCANAL

Guadalcanal at the tip of the Japanese forward line threatened communications between America and Australia; accordingly it was the first objective of the counter-attack. The Japanese land forces fought well but the Navy was now inferior in the air and supply by submarine failed. Nothing was left but to 'amend the line of advance' (official announcement of February 9th, 1943), i.e. to withdraw.

Some months later Bougainville met the same fate. The extreme endurance of the Japanese forces, left to fight on rations eked out by what they could cultivate on the spot, was magnificent but tragic. Here Japan threw away the brightest jewels in her crown;[1] the tragedy was to be repeated elsewhere. The war of attrition was fought to the bitter end on Guadalcanal and Bougainville. Here an important part of Japan's fleet air arm was expended. Mastery at sea and in the air was lost. Intended reinforcements were sunk *en route*. Japan's outpost troops lived on roots and tree-bark, on snakes and rats. The greater part starved to death.

American forces now resorted to 'island hopping' and 'by-passing' and in their advance took New Britain, Admiralty Islands, Halmahera, Leyte, Luzon. MacArthur had come north again.

In the meantime German forces had been routed in North Africa and had been halted at Stalingrad. Both in the East and in the West Axis fortunes had taken a decisive turn for the worse. The hope of clasping hands in the Indian Ocean had been but a dream. The time had come for Japan to pull back her far-flung battle-line—if she could. The Japanese Army was adept at advancing but did not know how to retreat. It was past-master at the surprise attack but was not so skilled at collecting its winnings.

---

[1] *Gyokusai*. See '7. The Code of Military Honour' in the Introduction.

CHAPTER SIX

A New China Policy (Part 1)

1. JAPAN'S LIMITED RESOURCES

IN one sense the motive of the 'Manchurian Incident' could be regarded as self-defence. We could argue that Japan had valuable rights in Manchuria, which China set herself to destroy, and that to feed her growing population those rights were a matter of life and death to Japan. But her use of military power is difficult to defend. She pretended that Manchoukuo was an independent state but it is impossible to deny that it was an old-style military government controlled by the Japanese Army.

Economically Japan was strong enough to control Manchuria but she had no reason for going further nor were her resources sufficient for the task. But, under the military theory that finance was a matter of printing notes, her economic burden went on growing *pari passu* with the extension of her military burdens. Bureaucrats and scholars sheltered themselves behind the military theory. In season and out of season the Army preached that their ventures strengthened Japan's economy and added to her natural resources.

If, economically, Japan was not strong enough to solve the problem of China, how could she hope to carry the burden of the newly occupied territories?

2. FALLACY UNDERLYING ECONOMIC OPERATIONS IN CHINA

Japan's hold on China amounted to no more than the occupation of key-points in North, Central and South China. For the purpose the army of occupation consisted of one million troops or less in the midst of a hostile population. The lines of communication were insecure and the area was vast.

None the less the Army's policy was merely a copy of the political, cultural and economic measures tried out in Manchuria, though the conditions were entirely different. Results were poor because Japan's strength was unequal to the task. Cultural efforts need not detain us: the outstanding failure was in the economic field. In Manchuria Japan was the alms-giver. In China she was the taker and that antagonized the Chinese. It was all very well to talk of Sino-Japanese undertakings and of mutual benefit. In fact what began as 'acquisition of resources' ended as 'economic exploitation'.

As a result of the economic blockade,[1] Japan had to concentrate on trade with neighbouring countries. In return for raw materials she sent manufactured goods. Hence the Japanese-Manchurian-Chinese 'co-prosperity sphere'. The manufactured goods or single articles, such as gold, paid for the raw materials. But the latter were turned into munitions and little went towards the livelihood of the Japanese people. Furthermore, since imports of materials from other countries had ceased, the available volume of exports to China decreased until Japan was unable to pay for the materials she received. The Army then resorted to the printing of 'military notes'. Inflation followed and this unpopular measure had to be backed up by the display of power.

The formation of Sino-Japanese companies was, therefore, not merely designed to acquire rights. It was partly forced on the Army as the only direct means of attaining its ends.

3. MISTAKES IN ADMINISTRATION MADE BY OCCUPATION FORCES

In the occupied territory the administration of the Cental Government and of district offices was subject to threefold control: (1) internal direction by Japanese advisers and employees; (2) indirect supervision by the Asia Development Board;[2] (3) the general supervision of military and naval representatives of the occupation forces. Japanese officiousness accorded ill with the strong aversion of the Chinese to interference. In North China a People's Association, on the model of the *Concordia Society* of Manchoukuo, was formed with a Chinese President and a Japanese Vice-President. It professed to be a movement in support of the Government but the people held aloof.

This policy, so opposed to the needs of the time, was extemporized to assist in the task of holding the key-points and their lines of communication. The Chungking Government and the Communist Party

[1] By the U.S. and other countries.
[2] *Vide* Book Four, Chapter Seven, s. 1.

were able to combat it with ease. In order to defend the railways, the Japanese Army built a system of trenches alongside with fortifications at intervals. In central China large areas, with the towns and villages within them, were designated 'clearance districts' and enclosed in bamboo palisades. The local inhabitants were then interrogated and unwelcome elements were dealt with.[1] This childish effort rarely succeeded in its object. In Yenan, Headquarters of the Communist Army, the leader of the Japanese Communist Party, Nosaka, and other Japanese, imbued Japanese prisoners with communist principles and laboured to cause dissension in the ranks of the Japanese Army. As for the Chinese associates in Japanese enterprises, they bent their energies to building up a path for the future of China and the Chinese people. They were by no means the tools of the Japanese Army.

4. MOTIVES UNDERLYING THE NEW CHINA POLICY

When I went to Nanking as Ambassador early in 1942, Japan's prestige was at its height owing to her recent victories and the economic situation was tranquil. Communications between Japan and China were normal, trade was uninterrupted and the notes of the Chinese Federal Banks were readily interchangeable into Japanese currency, a fact of which the astute Chinese were quick to take advantage and lay in stocks of Japanese commodities.

I hoped that I could effect a radical change in our China policy while relations were favourable. This, I thought, was the opportunity to put into operation the policy I had desired so ardently for years. Leave to the Chinese the actual control of their government and economy. Let Japan stop interfering in China's internal affairs and instead give her every assistance in recovering her sovereignty. In other words treat China as an independent country, abolish unequal treaties, establish mutual relations as equals, and offer political and economic assistance without attaching any reservations. Then again, so soon as the progress of the war permitted, withdraw every Japanese soldier from China and restore all vested rights. Whether Japan won or lost the war, there was no other way to adjust relations with China (the state of Manchoukuo was now recognized by her).[2]

These were the aspirations that I had nursed when I served in China before. Now unless Japan approached not only China, but all countries in East Asia, in a spirit of respect for their sovereignty and their equal

[1] Method is not stated.
[2] By the Nanking Government, not by Chiang Kai-shek.

rights, the war itself was meaningless. If only I could put my plans into operation, then I felt that my own previous efforts in China had borne some fruit.

I had frequently explained these views of mine to the central authorities, to influential circles and to the Army and Navy. The Emperor accepted them wholeheartedly. Prime Minister Tojo also was gradually won round and set himself to convert the Army. But a valuable year was lost before the Japanese Government finally decided to put the whole plan into operation.

Such was the plan that I have called the 'new China policy'.

5. BASIS OF THE CHANGE IN POLICY

Although it took Tojo a year to get the Army to change its stand, the time was not entirely wasted, for in the meantime the situation was coming to a head.

(a) Since 1937 close on a million young Japanese soldiers had been fighting in China. They were beginning to ask themselves what they were fighting for and the question was difficult to answer. They could not help feeling that Japan and China should be friends and not at daggers drawn. It might mean that much that had been gained in the past must be written off but at least a Japanese could feel that he was on the right track at last;

(b) Japan's horizon had been enlarged by the war. Her mission lay in Asia but it was no part of that mission to extract temporary advantages from an unwilling China by force of arms. China also had the same mission, the same responsibilities. In the long view Japan was merely butting her head against a wall in China. She should be a pioneer but at the same time she should march shoulder to shoulder with the people of Asia in establishing common ideals and common prosperity. Japan began to awake from an evil dream. Her mission was to liberate Asia, to raise Asia to her feet again;

(c) The Army's plan to acquire raw materials in China had come to a dead end. Japan's output had dropped, shipping had declined and communications were difficult. For a time Japanese goods had flowed into China, but the proceeds had not been made available for the purchase of materials and inflation had resulted. The willing co-operation of the Chinese was necessary if Japanese munitions factories were to be fed. There were obvious limits to the efficacy of power diplomacy. And the argument did not apply only to economic questions. The Japanese Army was beginning to see that a Chinese attitude of willing co-operation was essential. And this was what the Chinese also wished.

6. FORMATION OF THE GREATER EAST ASIA MINISTRY

About this time it was proposed to form a new ministry. After the 'Manchurian Incident' the Army formed a Manchurian Bureau to handle Manchurian questions independently of international affairs generally. Similarly after the 'China Incident' the Asia Development Board was formed to handle Chinese questions. Now, the Army had cast its net over a wide area outside China but few of these territories were under military government. Mostly they remained under their own administration, though subject to military control. Many, however, had not actually been 'occupied'. Siam was an outstanding example.

Manchuria, China and countries in the south did not fit into the category of ordinary international relations. The Army maintained that the affairs of these partners in the co-prosperity sphere, being of a special nature, had to be taken out of the jurisdiction of the Ministry of Foreign Affairs and handed over to a Greater East Asia Ministry, into which the Manchurian Bureau and the Asia Development Board could be absorbed. The Cabinet concurred.

What the proposal amounted to was this. Greater East Asia was to become an area in special relationship to Japan and a species of Colonial Office was to be established. Foreign relations were to be divided into two parts: (1) East Asia and (2) the rest of the world. Diplomacy was to become a two-headed monster. There were to be two Ministers for Foreign Affairs.

Since China was included in the area to receive special treatment, the plan ran counter to the 'new China policy'. Strong protests by the Ministry of Foreign Affairs and by the Privy Council were brushed aside and the new Ministry came into being. Foreign Minister Togo resigned in consequence.

I also made up my mind to resign. But in urging me to stay the Prime Minister took a different line. He said: 'The new Ministry has been formed to carry out your policy. The Minister is to be Mr. Kazuo Aoki, who has been adviser in Nanking to Wang Ching-wei and subscribes to your views. The new Minister for Foreign Affairs is the former director of the information board, Masayuki Tani, who has a thorough understanding of the policy and will assist the operations of the Greater East Asia Ministry. Since you are the central figure in this policy, I sincerely trust that you will remain at your post to carry it out.'

I agreed to do so. But in our understanding of the new policy Tojo and I had undoubtedly divergent points of view. I had, however, set my heart on carrying out the policy as I understood it.

7. PROBLEM OF PEACE AS AFFECTED BY THE NEW POLICY

In my conduct I was impelled by the belief that, whatever the outcome of the war, the new policy would in the main be of benefit to Japan. Our attitude towards China had been our first step on the wrong path in our foreign relations. The China problem must, therefore, be settled purely as a question of our relations with another country. The revolution in our foreign relations, started by the 'Manchurian Incident', could scarcely be set right by treating such questions as domestic problems. If we were to put our house in order, we must be able to derive strength from our foreign relations. Then the spirit underlying the new policy could permeate our home administration and Japan herself might set out afresh on a new path.

Thus the new policy was not directed solely towards China or East Asia; it also had its bearing on domestic politics. Abroad it was to be pursued first in China, then in the whole of East Asia. Popularize the Idea, then introduce it at home, so that it may extend its rays to our own administration. So might the mistaken aims of the Army and Navy be corrected and peace restored to a country shaken by the '*Showa* upheaval'.[1]

The new policy had features that China had for many years hoped for in vain; had it been in operation, the clash between the two countries need never have occurred. But if it could be put into effect now that we had the Wang Ching-wei Nationalist Government to deal with in Nanking, Chiang Kai-shek's Government in Chungking would no longer have cause to fight Japan. The question of an understanding between Chiang and Wang could then be tackled and finally the hope of peace between China and Japan would come into view. I regarded the policy, then, as not only the prerequisite to an understanding between Chiang, Wang and Japan, but a means of building up the necessary background. That was the tremendous significance of the policy. A radical transformation of Japan's outlook would remove the cause of war and might prove the key to international peace.

Merely to say that Chiang Kai-shek had no longer cause to fight Japan would not of itself lead to an understanding with him because he was backed by the U.S., Britain and their allies. But the reform of

[1] The Japanese title of the book.

Japan's foreign policy would bring it into line with their hopes also, as publicly declared; we should be back again on the international highway; and we could prepare the ground for an understanding not only with China but with the U.S. and Britain. Had the reform taken place during the American negotiations, they could have been brought to a successful conclusion. To put it briefly, the new policy was to be the foundation on which world peace could be built. The Atlantic Charter might be reinforced by a Greater East Asia Declaration.

I believed that at home political consciousness could be awakened, mistakes in the system of government could be rectified, we could anticipate the result of the war and prepare for the final settlement.

CHAPTER SEVEN

A New China Policy (Part 2)

1. THE EMPEROR'S WISHES

THE Emperor fully appreciated the importance of the new policy and desired to see it put into effect. He encouraged Tojo and approved the transfer of H.I.H. Prince Mikasa[1] to Army Headquarters in China. The Prince met officers and Civil Servants in Shanghai, he reiterated the Emperor's interest in the policy and gave instructions for its implementation.

In compliance with the Emperor's wishes Tojo enthusiastically promoted the project and himself went to Shanghai and Nanking to explain it and issued orders for its fulfilment. How deep did his convictions go? I could not say. He took the policy under his guidance mainly because he felt that it was the Emperor's wish. But at least one can say that his appreciation of the policy went far beyond that of any of the other military leaders. He certainly wished to place the war aims on a high level and he worked hard for the purpose. That is clear from his declaration and conduct at the Greater East Asia Conference.[2]

2. IMPLEMENTATION OF THE NEW POLICY

Implementation began early in 1943. The Wang Ching-wei Government welcomed it and sprang to life. But on the Japanese side many obstacles and misunderstandings were encountered. These arose mainly because of the cleavage between the new policy and old military ideas as enframed in the Basic Agreement between Japan and China. Nor were orders emanating from Tokyo taken to heart by troops at the front. For instance, the intention was to return to the Chinese what belonged

[1] Younger brother of the Emperor.
[2] *Vide* Chapter Eight, s. 4.

to them but factories were turned over with the greater part of the machinery unusable.

I turned my attention to political questions and began with the foreign settlements. The return of our settlements in Suchow, Hangchow, Hankow and Tientsin was taken in hand and this time the Privy Council raised no objections. The settlements at Shanghai and Amoy were international, involving, therefore, other interests beside our own, but Japan took charge of Italian interests.

Progress was made with the problem of extra-territoriality. The problem of the customs tariff had already been settled. The stationing of foreign troops between Peking and Hankow under the Boxer Agreement was to be abolished. Thus complete agreement between Japan and China[1] was reached on the question of the unequal treaties.

3. I BECOME FOREIGN MINISTER

In April 1943 I returned to Tokyo in order to discuss the next stage and was requested by the Prime Minister to join the Cabinet as Minister for Foreign Affairs. I urged that it was necessary to stay in China to promote the new policy. But Tojo said that he wanted me in Tokyo to guide its prosecution from the centre and to lend a hand in its application to East Asia.[2] With this aim in view, he proposed an exchange of posts between myself and Tani, the present Foreign Minister. I therefore accepted the appointment.

On numerous occasions the Emperor charged me to carry through the new policy. H.I.M. also expressed his longing for the restoration of peace. Tojo was well aware of the fact.

I conferred with Tani, the new Ambassador, and went ahead with my task. I looked forward to a time when we could ally ourselves with China on terms of real equality. In Japan the procedure required for the formal abolition of all 'unequal treaties' was complicated. There were difficult problems and various hitches. That I was able to overcome them was due to the change in the prevailing sentiment of which I have spoken. I felt as though I had stepped into a new country when Tojo declared that so soon as peace with China was made, our troops would at once be withdrawn completely.

I then set about introducing the new policy to the whole of East Asia. I did my best to bring about a nation-wide understanding through the

[1] The word 'China' is to be understood in a limited sense—China as represented by Wang Ching-wei's Government in Nanking.
[2] In effect this would subordinate the Greater East Asia Ministry to the Ministry of Foreign Affairs.

medium of the Diet. Thus I was able to proclaim 'war aims' that had never been very clearly explained to the people—the liberation and rebirth of East Asia, the emergence of its nations from 'colonialism', all countries to be on an equal footing as a bulwark of world peace. This alone would completely satisfy Japan.[1]

4. BASIC SINO-JAPANESE RELATIONS AS AFFECTED BY THE NEW POLICY

The return of the foreign settlements, the abolition of the unequal treaties and the formation of a new partnership between the two countries, were formally completed and the relationship had become as one between equals. A formal declaration was made that Japanese troops would be withdrawn without delay. The problem now was reconciliation between the Nanking and Chungking Governments. Once China was reunited, peace between Japan and China could be made, paving the way to peace with other nations (the Americans and the British).

At a time when Chiang Kai-shek was completely under the domination of the Americans and British, it was out of the question to expect him to make peace with Japan if they were opposed to his doing so, nor was he in a strong enough position to act as a mediator. The fates were not propitious. Chiang was heavily engaged in the war with Japan, particularly since the declaration that followed the meeting between Churchill and Roosevelt in Cairo. As a practical question, therefore, there seemed no immediate hope of Chiang lending his name to a peace between Japan and China, or an all-round peace, unless Japan capitulated.

None the less I was convinced that, whatever the outcome of the war, the restoration of good relations with China was absolutely essential; I believed that the active pursuit of the 'new deal' with the Chinese people would show that Japan's actions and aims were founded on ideals of justice. If the world could be brought to appreciate this fact, then we should obtain one fundamental requisite for the attainment of peace.

The Army attitude to China had been too Machiavellian.[2] Japan's aim, then, must be to demonstrate to the Chinese people that the Japanese national spirit was a just one. The new policy was not merely for the edification of the Nanking Government, nor yet was it a bar-

[1] I.e. the new Japan that the author envisaged.
[2] English word in the text.

gaining counter with the Chungking Government. Japan was to show the Chinese people as a whole what were the real intentions of the Japanese nation.

5. OUR DIPLOMATIC POLICY

Whatever the Army and Navy might say, the war was going badly. The nation was of course bound to strain every nerve in the war effort, but there was no reason why they should close their eyes. So far as I could, I analysed objectively reports as to world conditions and supplied material for a critical assessment to the Cabinet, the Diet, the Privy Council, the Imperial Rule Aid Association, to business men and to the nation. I need hardly say that under a strict military censorship this was no light task.

I never ceased to marvel at the listlessness of the Diet, but it was my only medium. I should have welcomed a serious discussion but all I heard from start to finish was the old cry of weak diplomacy: it seemed that I lacked fighting spirit! At that time diplomatic functions were circumscribed. Legally the Foreign Minister's powers were so limited that many pitfalls beset the path of constructive diplomacy. But I did my best to put forward a coherent policy. My speeches in open and closed debates in the Diet may be summed up as follows:

> The new policy towards China must be carried to its logical conclusion; it is even more important that it should operate in any area where Japan's influence is paramount. It should become a new policy for the whole of Greater East Asia. Its object is the awakening of the peoples of Asia, their liberation and their future progress. I pray that it may become a contribution to the cause of world peace. For Japan it means the establishment of the 'good-neighbour' policy and the improvement of our international relations.
>
> We have a treaty of neutrality with Russia; it must be respected and strengthened as part and parcel of our good-neighbour policy. Japan must give a solemn declaration of her war aims, viz. that she is fighting in self-defence in support of the principles I have just mentioned, not in any bellicose spirit, and not for any special claims. When, and only when, these fair and just aims are clearly understood by the people, the war will have a meaning and their fighting spirit will be enhanced.
>
> We must be prepared to make peace so soon as our aims have been attained. The emphasis on our war aims and the limits we

assign to them will provide the groundwork for the restoration of peace. Now that we are at war, we cannot abandon them half-way. We must continue to pay the price. But, as individuals or as a nation, it is both a sacred duty and a source of strength to discover for ourselves what is the ultimate reason for our existence.[1] Let the result of the war be what it may, that is the most splendid quest for us, whether as a nation or as individuals. Let us not be laggard in that sacred duty.

Such was the gist of the speeches that I made to the Diet and at every available opportunity, so long as I remained Minister for Foreign Affairs.

[1] I.e. what should be our goal.

CHAPTER EIGHT

The New Policy in Greater East Asia

1. ASIAN NATIONALISM AS AFFECTED BY JAPAN'S WAR-AIMS

THE First World War was a struggle for the liberation of the nations. It was fought between the white races of Europe, and at the Paris Conference the principle of 'self-determination' was proclaimed. But the principle did not apply to countries outside Europe. Asia remained colonized or semi-colonized. The Second World War was a war in which the Asians might recover their sovereignty. They were roused by this cry and were prepared to fight for their freedom.

Only by the liberation of Asia and of Africa and their rehabilitation can the peace of the world be promoted and its progress assured. My contention was that Japan's war-aim was to liberate the Orient. She had no designs other than this. Once this end was attained, she was ready to end the war at any time.

In pursuance of this aim, Japan decided to recognize the sovereignty of nations that had not yet achieved independence, one by one. The Prime Minister himself visited the countries of East Asia in turn in order to prepare the ground. The independence of Burma was recognized. Then came the turn of the Philippines and steps were taken towards recognition of Indonesia. In Japan's own dependencies of Korea and Formosa thought was given to the people's participation in the government, and to autonomy. Assistance was also given to the independence movement in India and the Provisional Government of Free India was recognized.

Needless to say these measures met with many obstacles at home.

2. POPULAR LEADERS OF EAST ASIA

Since the Russo-Japanese War the tide of nationalism had been rising throughout Asia. In East Asia, also, champions of the cause had appeared in each country. Their representatives were Laurel (Philippines), Dr. Bhamo (Burma) and Sukarno (Indonesia). From Annam patriots had flocked to Japan. These enlightened leaders were zealous to rescue their peoples from colonial status. Their lives were dedicated to the cause, which was calculated to rouse even the most faint-hearted, and even in defeat their spirit was a beacon light in East Asia.

When Japan recognized the independence of the Philippines, Laurel, Chief Justice of the Supreme Court, was installed as President. He had a strong will and his outstanding personality made him an ideal leader. In Burma Dr. Bhamo was installed in recognition of his long fight for independence; it was his indomitable spirit and wisdom that had laid the foundations. Indonesia was not ready for independence but Sukarno had led the movement for many years and was an ardent patriot. With Japan's assistance his efforts were nearing fruition.

But no one can speak of racial movements in Asia without calling to mind Chandra Bose, the great Indian leader.

3. CHANDRA BOSE

The Indian independence movement had a long history. Gandhi preached non-co-operation but Chandra Bose said that independence could not be won that way; force must be met by force, and accordingly he endeavoured to terminate British domination in that way.

He had received an English education and studied political economy at Oxford. His life was dedicated to the cause of Indian independence. Though filled with burning zeal, he was not a fanatic. His resolute will combined an ardent temperament with great intellectual ability: he could plan well and he had foresight. His sincerity was manifest in his expressive face, his demeanour and his gestures. No one could listen to him unmoved.

The British had imprisoned him many times. But when war broke out he escaped to Afghanistan and with Japanese assistance reached Germany. He threw in his lot with the Axis, considering that the war gave India her chance. In Berlin he succeeded in getting together a battalion from among the Indian prisoners of war but, realizing that he could not hope for quick results in Germany, he decided to put his trust in Japan. He was conveyed by German submarine to the Indian Ocean, transferred to a Japanese submarine and so reached Malaya, where he proceeded to enrol the Indian Army of Liberation.

He paid three visits to Tokyo, the first to make contact with the Japanese authorities, the second to attend the Greater East Asia

Conference and the third for final consultation when the war was going badly. In speaking at a meeting arranged in his honour, his voice would break with emotion. It was the voice of a patriot calling on the heavens to witness his sincerity.

At his earnest request the only portion of Indian soil occupied by the Japanese Army—the Andaman and Nicobar Islands—was placed under the administration of the Provisional Government of Free India, of which he was the head. The Army's Imphal campaign was ill-devised but to Chandra Bose it was the first step towards India's freedom. On March 30th, 1944, his Government addressed a manifesto to the Indian people that is an imperishable monument to his name. The Imphal campaign had attempted the impossible. It began well but petered out. Many thousand Japanese soldiers starved to death but their sacrifice was not in vain because it served to open the eyes of the Indian people.

In anguish after the final defeat Chandra Bose was flying back to Japan when his plane crashed in Formosa, but even in death he still fought for his country because his people could not believe that he was dead.

When the war ended, his subordinates were tried by court martial in India, it being claimed that he was merely an agent of Japan, but three Ministry of Foreign Affairs officials testified that he was nothing of the kind but a true Indian patriot. The British judges decided that the accused were all loyal to India and acquitted them.

Later Britain recognized Indian independence, an act that speaks volumes for British statesmanship.

4. THE GREATER EAST ASIA DECLARATION, 1943

The historic Conference of Greater East Asia was convened in Tokyo in November 1943. It was attended by representatives of China, Manchoukuo, Siam, the Philippines, Burma and 'Free India'.

The conference issued a Declaration, in which the assenting countries declared their mutual respect for each other's independence and equality, agreed to co-operate in the advancement of East Asia, in conformity with the principles of co-existence and co-prosperity; they gave their word to promote free trade and cultural exchange and pledged themselves to fight until they had gained the liberty and rehabilitation of Asia.

The Declaration bears some resemblance to the Atlantic Charter. In its spirit it included many ideas common to both. But, whereas the

Charter is a simple statement of principles, the Declaration proclaims the policy to be followed by the assenting countries.

It was an extension of the new China policy. It supplied an explanation of the true Spirit of Japan as embodied in the declaration of her war-aims. Enshrined in it was the principle of racialism which the U.S. proclaimed during the war and which inspires the United Nations—and for which Asia strives.

For the peoples of Asia the battle is not yet over. It is not sufficient that they should demand their freedom. They themselves must offer a positive contribution to their own rehabilitation and to the peace of the world. It is no light task for them to serve the cause of international intercourse with the same experience and qualifications as shown by the West. They must never forget that a prodigious development of their physical and mental capacity is required.

CHAPTER NINE

War-time Diplomacy (Part 1)

1. POLICY *VIS-À-VIS* RUSSIA

A WAR-TIME preoccupation was our relations with Russia. We had a treaty of neutrality, which, so long as it was observed, guaranteed peace. In the war between Germany and Russia Japan remained neutral as did Russia in our own war. We decided on a policy that faithfully observed the Treaty and publicly said so more than once. Though Japan was at war, whenever trouble arose between us on sea or on land, we hastened to come to an agreement. In the War Tribunal Russia labelled Japan the aggressor in the border disputes that had occurred before the war, but she had no complaints to make as to our action during the war.

Our problem was this. Would Russia continue to observe the Treaty? We did our best to strengthen it. When Matsuoka signed the Treaty, Russia expressed the wish that we should return our oil and coal concessions in North Saghalin. Japan on her side wished to revive the negotiations for a Fisheries Treaty that Russia had dropped when Japan entered into the anti-comintern pact with Germany. As it was, a temporary agreement had to be negotiated with difficulty every year. I took up the whole question with Russia. The relinquishment of our North Saghalin concessions raised difficulties at home while the fisheries talks were long drawn out; but agreement was reached at last and an agreement was signed in Moscow by Ambassador Sato and Molotov in the spring of 1944.

2. QUESTION OF PEACE BETWEEN GERMANY AND RUSSIA

When Japan had contracted the alliance with Germany, she had hoped that Russia could be induced to join. Her hope now was that the war between Germany and Russia could somehow be brought to an end. As part of their war plans, the Japanese Army also would have liked to see peace between Germany and Russia, much in the same way as it wished to contrive some sort of an agreement with Chungking. The Army naively thought of diplomacy as a means of manœuvring another country into war or peace overnight. But to translate strategic conceptions into diplomatic action is not quite so simple. The great thing, however, was to build sound foundations for the return of universal peace. Just as it was desirable to create conditions in Chungking favourable to peace, so, if only for the betterment of relations between Japan and Russia, it seemed advisable to take up the question of Germany and Russia.

For the purpose I had it in mind to send Hirota, the former Prime Minister, on a special mission to Moscow. He was to be given authority to proceed from Moscow to Berlin and to do his best to restore amicable relations between the two countries and to set on foot a move towards general peace.

I secured agreement in Japan to the plan. But the Russians looked upon it merely as a proposal to send an envoy to act as intermediary between themselves and the Germans, and declined the proposal. I put forward the plan more than once. But, in their own view of the way in which the general situation was developing, the Russians made it quite clear that they did not consider that the time was ripe (American records show that the Russians kept the U.S. informed of the Japanese plan).

3. RUSSIAN ATTITUDE TOWARDS A TREATY OF NEUTRALITY

Molotov, the Soviet Foreign Commissar, was profuse in his declarations of Russian respect for the Treaty of Neutrality, but when Japan proposed that its terms should be extended he replied that there was plenty of time to think of that and when, in April 1945, Russia denounced the Treaty, Molotov pointed out that it had still a year to run.

When I took over as Foreign Minister (March 1943), Russia had turned to the offensive and thereafter won victory after victory. During this time I could not but see that her attitude towards Japan was taking on a threatening look. It was clear that Russian calculations were turning to the consequences of the war. Regardless of Japan's protests, they were giving facilities for American flyers who had bombed Japan to land in Russian territory and were sheltering them. American and British action in requesting Russia to flout the Treaty of Neutrality, and in paying her a big reward to open war on Japan, provides an interesting sidelight on their respect for a treaty.

A student of Russia's materialistic diplomacy will experience no difficulty in judging her attitude. Her aims in East Asia should be clear from the result of my efforts for a better understanding. After Yalta, American and other newspaper reports were sufficient to indicate that Russia was preparing to enter the war against Japan. Once she denounced the Treaty of Neutrality, there could be no question but that this was her intention.

4. RELATIONS WITH GERMANY AND ITALY

War-time relations with Germany and Italy were simple. The three allies did their best to be of mutual assistance to each other but, when I was Foreign Minister, the two war fronts were separated and co-operation was out of the question. There was nothing left but the natural duties incumbent on an ally. That the Axis powers were thus compelled to conduct two separate wars by the failure of the attempt to join hands in the Indian Ocean was the principal cause of defeat.

In view of her own lack of success, Germany pressed Japan to attack Russia. The German Ambassador constantly passed on to me intelligence of Russian infringements of the Treaty—her offer to the U.S. of bases for aircraft and submarines, her hospitality to American flyers, her vast imports of munitions for Soviet troops in the Far East; to prevent any misconception, however, I always made it quite clear to him that Japan herself had no intention of violating the Treaty of Neutrality. I also pointed out to him that Axis strength was already taxed to its utmost and that the war front should be contracted rather than extended.

Stahmer had been a colleague of mine in Nanking and had approved my new China policy. Through him I urged the German Government to institute a similar policy in the occupied territories. It seemed to me that a modification of the policy of repression was essential if peace were ever to be restored. I learnt only at a later stage that it was impracticable. Hitler despised the Slav and other races and he had entrusted the administration to the fanatic Rosenberg. He refused to consider my plans either for peace with Russia or for a total peace. Victory or death! The tragedy was that he could not envisage a middle course.

5. RELATIONS WITH FRANCE AND PORTUGAL

In East Asia France was in a delicate position. In China she had, like Britain, extensive rights in the settlements, in the Leased Territory and in the railways. French Indo-China was on the route of the Japanese Army's advance.

Ambassador Arsène-Henri had died at his post and had been succeeded by Cosmë, former Ambassador to China. Typically French, Cosmë had keen perception and I admired the manner in which he discharged duties that cannot have been easy. Everywhere in the Far East the French had to consider conditions in their own homeland. There the Vichy Government was subject to German domination while de Gaulle, who had thrown in his lot with the British and Americans, claimed that it was he who represented the French. In the Far East they faced entirely different relations with Japan.

French officials could not adopt a hostile attitude towards Japan; they sought, therefore, to prevent further inroads on their rights by passive resistance. But when, towards the end of the war, de Gaulle re-entered Paris, de Coux, the Governor in Indo-China, at once swore allegiance to him, and, the French administration having become hostile, Japan had no option but to make an end of it. At the same time Japan, while guaranteeing the security of Annam, gave approval to the initiation by Annam and Cambodia of steps towards the recovery of their independence.

Relations with Portugal called for careful handling; she had a 'factory'[1] at Macao in South China and she owned half the island of Timor in the Pacific. Macao was almost the only neutral zone in China and the Western allies used it as an intelligence centre. Timor was strategically important since it lies half-way between the Netherlands East Indies and Australia. The Japanese Army occupied the western half belonging to the Dutch and their pursuit of the enemy created various problems. Relations with Portugal became difficult when she permitted the use of the Azores by the British and Americans. Fortunately we were able to maintain diplomatic relations throughout the war.

Spain was friendly to the Axis but at the very end her attitude changed. She then made an issue of Spanish rights in the Philippines and severed relations.

---

[1] Merchant trading station.

CHAPTER TEN

The Quest for Peace (Part 1)

1. TREATMENT OF THE QUESTION OF PEACE

As Foreign Minister I considered my most important duty was the quest for peace; I came indeed to feel that in itself alone the task justified my position in the Cabinet. When I was sworn in, Prime Minister Tojo confirmed my belief that the Emperor longed for peace.

But this struggle was not like the Russo-Japanese War. It was a 'total war': kill or be killed. The Army was resolved to fight to the very end. If anyone spoke of making peace before that, he was ruthlessly punished. The War Minister rigidly enforced the autocratic powers of the Army and used the gendarmerie as state police. To them a peace advocate was a pacifist and anyone who mentioned defeat was a rebel and such people were to be suppressed. The Army thought that this was the way to win the war. So the gendarmes kept watch on senior statesmen, members of the Cabinet, Diet members and people of 'liberal' turn of mind. Nor was I free from their surveillance.

Under such conditions it was extremely difficult to handle the question of peace, since the Army leaders were themselves in charge of political procedure. Times had changed from the Russo-Japanese War when Count Hirobumi Ito[1] had collaborated with the Cabinet and considered with them the question of peace.

Though the powers of the Army and Navy had by now extended to all branches of the administration, constitutionally there had been no outward change. The power to declare war and to make peace was still vested solemnly in the Emperor. Under the constitution, again, the discharge of the Emperor's diplomatic authority came within the duties of the Minister for Foreign Affairs as the competent adviser. The Minister, therefore, was entitled to learn the Emperor's wishes from him personally in order that he should be in a position to plan and act

[1] Later Prince Ito.

accordingly. Naturally the actual execution must be discussed with the Prime Minister and Cabinet, and carried out with their approval, but it would not be practicable to consult with a military Prime Minister on each detail of the preparatory action that would lead up to the final peace. I need hardly say that the utmost circumspection was required under the prevailing conditions.

2. CONDITIONS PRECEDENT TO PEACE NEGOTIATIONS

Soon after becoming Foreign Minister I learnt the Emperor's wishes from Kido, Lord Keeper of the Privy Seal. Thereafter I frequently made my humble report to H.I.M., was duly questioned and expressed my views. The Emperor's will was crystal clear: he desired peace at the earliest moment. So long as Japan's good name were maintained, the question of her overseas possessions was immaterial.

If these peace discussions at the fountain-head were to become known, there was no knowing what internal disturbances might break out. Kido and I therefore kept them for the moment locked up in our breasts, while we awaited the right moment for action.

In May 1943 he and I discussed the question of peace in detail. Kido had a number of ideas. He gave his own views on an offer to make certain concessions in the South Seas as an opening to negotiations. I said that the struggle had now developed into total war and that we were pitted against the entire strength of the Western allies. As the fortunes of war were trending, we must be reconciled to complete acceptance of their demands. While the battle continued, no intermediary could bring the opposing sides together at a conference table. We had got to accept that hard fact. The British-American leaders had at Casablanca declared their intention to fight until the unconditional surrender of the Axis (January 1943; subsequently the Cairo decisions were announced in November).

Under ominous war reports from day to day the year 1943 sped by.

3. GERMAN ATTITUDE TOWARDS THE QUESTION OF PEACE

One question demanding careful thought was that of a separate peace; on the outbreak of war the three allies had adopted a proposal from Japan that peace was an issue that concerned the Axis as a whole and must be agreed upon by all three powers together. When, however,

Italy defected in the summer of 1943, the issue lay between Germany and Japan alone.

Inducement of Germany to make peace with Russia would have been a step forward. But, though Stahmer himself was not opposed, his Government would not hear of any such suggestion and declined to allow Japan to take up the question with Russia. Further, as already stated, Germany would not consider milder treatment of her occupied territories. Meanwhile Hitler continued to talk of victory to Oshima.

Since a combined peace was impossible, then if Japan wanted peace, she could but wait for a German collapse to absolve Japan from her promise.

I continued anxiously to watch the progress of the German war.

4. MY COVENANT WITH THE LORD KEEPER OF THE PRIVY SEAL

At the Cairo Conference, which was attended by Chiang Kai-shek, a decision was announced to reduce Japanese territory to that held before the Sino-Japanese War.[1]

In company with Kido, permanent adviser to the Throne, I constantly conferred with the Emperor on the subject of the war situation and the restoration of peace. I put forward a suggestion that regular meetings of the senior statesmen should be convened in the Palace; those favourable to peace might be confirmed in their views and their influence might be beneficial. But it was felt that their individual character and background were scarcely calculated to further the cause. Nor was a Cabinet directed by the Army the place to discuss peace before the end of the war. If the militarists got wind of a peace movement, it was all over. There was nothing for it but to await the moment when the Emperor gave an absolute command that the war must cease (between ourselves we called it the Voice of the Sacred Crane[2]). It must be the moment when Japan was absolved from her obligations under the Alliance. That was the time when the people would understand.

Kido and I took upon our shoulders the entire responsibility, he in the Palace and I in the Government. We made a covenant together and strove to perfect our plans, each in his own department.

---

[1] 1894–95.
[2] Possibly a reference to an old saying that, even when the crane was hidden from sight, its voice was heard in heaven.

5. THE WAR: CHANGE IN NAVAL STRATEGY

By the second half of 1943 the tide of war was definitely running against the Axis. In the Pacific the Yamazaki detachment in Attu had been annihilated, our forces in Guadalcanal and Bougainville had been wiped out, New Britain and the Admiralty Islands had been lost. Lines of communication were menaced by enemy submarines and aircraft. Our fleet- and air-arm had suffered shattering losses.

The Navy were compelled to draw in their line of defence and Imperial Headquarters revised its plan of campaign: the new line was to run from the Bonin Islands via the Marshall and Caroline Islands to the north of New Guinea and was to be held to the death. A Council before the Throne was convened on September 30th, 1943, at which Hara, President of the Privy Council, asked the Supreme Command whether they could guarantee this line, seeing that they had frequently revised their plans already. Nagano, Chief of the Naval General Staff, answered that in war no one could be absolutely certain of anything. This reply caused a storm and was withdrawn, but the general impression was that the Navy itself had little confidence in the new line.

When it was realized that the war situation was grave, discussions began among persons who thought that the war should be terminated as to the most hopeful means of attaining this object.[1] Various ideas were mooted. Yoshida (later Prime Minister), for instance, suggested that he and Prince Konoye should go to Switzerland in order to seize any opportunity that occurred. When it came to discussing concrete plans, however, it was evident that the only way of getting to Europe was by submarine.

Among the senior statesmen the most interested in peace was Prince Konoye, who kept in close touch with Kido and myself.

---

[1] Reference appears to be to a group of senior statesmen who desired peace.

CHAPTER ELEVEN

U.S. and Britain at War

(Translator's note: This chapter gives a résumé of fighting on the different fronts in the Second World War. Only those campaigns in which Japan was directly concerned are translated here.)

1. THE QUEBEC CONFERENCE, AUGUST 1943, AND AFTER

In the summer of 1943 it was hoped to hold a conference at Quebec between the three leaders—Churchill, Roosevelt and Stalin—but the latter declined the invitation and the meeting, therefore, took place between Roosevelt and Churchill. It was finally decided to set up a 'Second Front' in the summer of 1944; for the time being the main attack was to be directed against Germany. The U.S. Secretary of State was sent on a mission to Moscow, together with the British Foreign Secretary, to explain the Quebec decisions (end of November). At this meeting Stalin did not seem so keenly interested as formerly on the Second Front but surprised Cordell Hull by volunteering the statement that he proposed to take part in the war against Japan. This was at a time when Russia was assuring Japan of her fidelity to the Treaty of Neutrality.

2. RELATIVE IMPORTANCE OF THE EUROPEAN AND THE PACIFIC CAMPAIGNS

The U.S. was fighting on two fronts: in Europe there was the joint campaign with Britain against Germany, in the Pacific there was the war with Japan, in which America bore the brunt of the fighting. Which was to come first? Sentiment said that the Pearl Harbour account should be settled first, but Roosevelt took the broad view that the European War took precedence. That did not mean that the attack on Japan must be postponed. While the emphasis must be placed on the European War, the fight against Japan must be continued with might and main.

After the Midway battle a conference of the allies took place in Washington in October 1942. Thereafter the U.S. turned to the offensive. By the second half of 1943 the battle had crossed the Great Divide and Japan was being pushed back. But, though the war of attrition was in full swing, Japan still held on to the greater part of the conquered territories. In China Japanese forces broke through the gap between Hankow and Canton, and threatened an attack on Chungking. The Army was also able to stage the Imphal campaign.[1] The Japanese Navy might be defeated but the overthrow of the Army could not be achieved in the near future. A final reckoning with Japan might, it seemed, take several years. In the meantime it was necessary to give all possible aid to China, urge Russia to come into the war and so tighten the grip on Japan.

In China, however uncertain the position might be, the Chungking Nationalist Party and the Communist Party were at least holding together. It was scarcely likely, therefore, that China would drop out. But to raise the morale of the Chungking Government and enlist the co-operation of the Chinese people, it was necessary to publicize the lead that the U.S. and Britain were taking in the Far Eastern war. It was necessary to convince China, who was vitally interested in the Pacific, but it was also an integral part of their united war effort.

3. THE CAIRO CONFERENCE, 1943

Roosevelt, Churchill and Chiang Kai-shek met in Cairo in November 1943. Chiang had cause to be satisfied with the decisions. Japan was to be stripped of the Pacific islands she obtained after the First World War[2] and of the Chinese territory she had acquired—Manchuria, the Kwantung Leased Territory, Formosa and the Pescadores, all of which were to be returned to China; Korean independence was to be restored.

Not wishing to give away her own intentions, Russia was not represented at the Conference but she confirmed the decisions later at Potsdam.

4. U.S., BRITAIN AND CHINA AT WAR WITH JAPAN

Britain's war against Japan was directed from bases in Australia and India. In India Wavell, who had been C.-in-C. in North Africa and later

---
[1] *Vide* Book Eight, Chapter Eight, s. 3.
[2] In theory she had acquired only a Mandate from the League of Nations.

in India, had been made Viceroy. Communications with Britain were difficult but munitions works were organized in India itself. Imperial considerations entered into Britain's strategy. Malaya was to be the pivot and the offensive was to be in stages from Australia via Singapore and Hong Kong. This was a slight difference from American strategy, whose aim was to strike straight at Japan.

Similar differences of opinion in the war-direction developed in East Asia, particularly in the British and American attitude towards air transport between India and China. General Stilwell wanted aircraft and materials sent to Chungking both to reinforce the Chinese Army and in order to make it possible for American flyers to bomb Manchuria and Japan from the Chinese mainland. He stressed the need to destroy the Japanese war potential. Britain on the other hand wanted first to recapture Burma, Malaya and Singapore, a strategic plan in which the Americans were not interested.

General MacArthur commanded land, sea and air forces advancing north from Australia; Admiral Nimitz led his fleet and air-arm from Hawaii. MacArthur began with Guadalcanal and proceeded via New Guinea, the Philippines, Formosa and the Luchus to Japan. Nimitz took the Marshalls and Guam and made towards the Bonins for a direct air bombardment of Japan. Stilwell wished to advance his airfields in China for the same purpose. The British-Australian forces proposed, as stated, to turn north when Singapore was captured.

In the final stage of Japan's surrender, MacArthur was appointed representative of all the armies.

The Chinese Nationalist and Communist Armies also had played their role in resisting the Japanese Army from the beginning.

5. DEATH OF ROOSEVELT

On his way home from Yalta,[1] Roosevelt announced that countries that did not participate in the World War, nor lend their aid in the struggle, would after the war be struck out of the list of participants in the international organization of the United Nations. This threatening language was a call to Turkey and other neutrals. Many took the hint to declare war on the Axis at the eleventh hour. This statement of Roosevelt's explains the true nature of that war product, the United Nations.

While the war was still proceeding, the U.S. and Britain devoted

---

[1] *Vide* next section. Events in Europe leading up to the Yalta Conference (February 25th, 1945) are omitted from this translation.

attention to post-war administration. An international organization has several branches: there is of course the political field but it is also concerned in international economics and culture and there are in addition food and labour problems to be considered. Preparatory work on the U.N.O. included the Brentwood Conference on international currency (July 1944), the Dumbarton Oaks Conference on post-war security (August 1944) as well as other conferences. In the San Francisco Conference of April 1945 it was understood that the victors in the war would determine the machinery to be used in the new organization. In order to obtain the full co-operation of Russia, the Americans had strained every nerve, because the operation of this world organization was to form the basis on which the U.S. would plan its future international policy.

After Yalta President Roosevelt, worn out by his exertions and already a sick man, suddenly collapsed and died on the eve of Germany's final defeat.

6. YALTA: SECRET AGREEMENT REGARDING EAST ASIA

After Roosevelt's death, at the end of the war a 'secret agreement between the U.S.A., Britain and Russia relating to East Asia' was published for the first time by the White House. It caused a world-wide sensation.

Up to that time the existence of such a document had been known to no one in the U.S. outside Roosevelt, who signed it. This secret agreement, exchanged by those three heads of the three great powers, was signed by Roosevelt at the request of Stalin as consideration for Russia's participation in the war against Japan, as desired by his military advisers. Russia claimed the succession after the war to each and every right enjoyed by Japan on the Far Eastern mainland.

In this secret agreement Russia obtained the approval of the U.S.A. and Britain to the following concessions: Russia recovered the rights in Manchuria originally enjoyed by Czarist Russia, which she herself relinquished to China in July 1919; Russia acquired the right to establish a naval base at Port Arthur, in addition to paramount rights over the Manchurian Railways extending to the port of Darien; Outer Mongolia was to be taken away from China and established as an independent country; Japan was to cede Southern Saghalin and the Kurile Islands to Russia.

To this document Roosevelt and Churchill attached their signatures at the request of Stalin. In effect, as consideration for Russia's participation in the war against Japan, the U.S.A. and Britain conferred on Russia paramountcy on the Far Eastern mainland.

In return Stalin agreed to make war on Japan within three months of Germany's capitulation; he was in fact confirming what he had already announced to Cordell Hull at the end of 1943 and to Roosevelt at the Teheran Conference. This secret agreement, which violated the Treaty of Neutrality between Japan and Russia and set at naught Chinese sovereignty, was contracted on the 21st of February, 1945. Rights that were a matter of life and death to an independent country and one which moreover was a war-ally—China—were secretly sold to Russia by, of all countries, the U.S.A. and Britain. Imagination boggles at the thought.

It is a commonplace to anyone handling Chinese problems that the country that controls Outer Mongolia and Manchuria controls North China and is in a position to extend its influence over the whole of China. The problem was for many years a bone of contention between Japan and Russia before and after the Revolution.

It would never do for the secret to be divulged prematurely to China and so it was for a long time hidden from her. Finally a newly appointed special envoy, Hurley, broke the news. China was astounded and affronted but Chiang Kai-shek owed much to American and British aid and was powerless. On the advice of the U.S. President, T. V. Soong, Chairman of the Administrative *Yuan*,[1] went to Moscow and there, having no option, accepted the Yalta Secret Agreement on August 15th, 1945.

The troubles that arose in Manchuria and East Asia after the war may for the most part be attributed to this agreement, which was of a nature to influence the destiny of the whole of East Asia, including Japan.

---

[1] *Yuan* = Board, the equivalent of a Ministry.

CHAPTER TWELVE

Fortune of War Turns Against Japan

1. THE CODE OF 'GLORY' ON TRIAL[1]

INITIATIVE passed into the hands of the Allies in 1943. After the defection of Italy, Germany retreated in the face of the advancing Russians, Americans and British; Japan was fighting a losing battle in the Pacific. Since lines of communication were cut, Japanese military and naval forces could no longer receive reinforcements or munitions, food or medical supplies. Everywhere they fought to the last man. The enemy said that it was the courage of despair rather than natural courage. But they showed the world of what stuff the Japanese are made. They may have their detractors but they were the flower of the Japanese race. They withstood every hardship. They fought until they died. Surely the spirits of these heroes will eternally watch over and guard the Japanese people!

From the Aleutians in the far north to Guadalcanal in the extreme south, south-westwards to the Andaman and Nicobar Islands in the Indian Ocean, those outposts in the distant seas, the Greater East Asian War had thrust out its battle-line until it had become a war of the Navy and the Air Force. Japan, a remote archipelago, naturally looked abroad for supplies but she had extended her battle-line over one-fifth of the globe to find them. It was inevitable that she should experience difficulty in keeping the life-line open. To supply her forces she resorted to convoys but her losses only increased. The shipping pool of some seven to eight million tons soon dried up and her transports, with their valuable freight of lives and munitions, sank to the ocean bed.

Ever since Pearl Harbour and Midway the decisive importance of aircraft had been demonstrated. The Army, which had lagged behind, and the Navy, which had suffered great losses at Midway, now devoted every effort towards increasing the air-arm.

[1] See Note 7, 'The Code of Military Honour' in the Introduction.

2. CHAOS IN THE PRODUCTION OF MUNITIONS

Both the Army and the Navy had their own arsenals for the production of essential arms. The Navy manufactured men-of-war, guns and other essential munitions at Kure and Yokosuka and made good any deficiencies from civilian factories. But aircraft were for the most part made in the latter.

In the production of aircraft Japanese manufacturing capacity had to compete with the output of American industry so that superhuman efforts were required. At conferences at Imperial Headquarters (conferences of war-chiefs) the problem was an almost routine subject of discussion, together with that of the Army and Navy competition for the use of shipping.

In the hope of raising the standard of efficiency, the Cabinet adopted a system of inspectors—military and civilian experts—to explain technique, to increase output, to remove bottle-necks and generally to heighten efficiency. A Munitions Ministry was set up, in which industrialists were employed, to concentrate on the manufacture and supply of munitions, particularly aircraft. To all outward appearance results were most satisfactory but the fact was that the industry was already working to capacity. Moreover, neither the inspectors nor the Ministry could interfere with any output that was directly controlled by the Army or Navy; they were even considered to be poaching on such supplies as the latter were obtaining from civilian works. In practice war-time improvisations could not overnight perfect the somewhat halting machinery of peace-time. But the fundamental reason why output did not come up to expectations was the shortage of materials and the lack of sufficient manufacturing capacity.

Imports of iron-ore from China were interrupted and the transport of oil and bauxite from the South Seas was difficult. Since the output of aluminium fell off, the supply of material could not keep pace with the increase in aircraft building capacity.

One way and another the efficiency of the aircraft industry was brought to a high pitch but the demands of the Army and Navy went up by leaps and bounds. They began at 30,000 planes yearly, rose to 50,000 and then to 70,000. The Liaison Council set the target at 40,000. But the struggle to produce this number led to a decline in standard, machine failure in mid-air increased until the low percentage of safe arrival of air transport was alarming.

At the end, the failure of supplies of gasoline was more serious than the question of available planes. A suggestion was made to collect the roots of pine-trees and distil oil from them. But when the country-people had dug up the roots by the sweat of their brow and quantities were collected, distribution of the necessary cauldrons broke down, and the roots dried up and were useless.

After Saipan (June 1944) air-raids became frequent, communications were cut and factories were destroyed. The supply of munitions to the front was entirely disrupted.

3. SOCIAL AND ECONOMIC CHAOS OWING TO DEFEAT

War costs were treated as extraordinary expenditure and passed by the Diet without comment. Munitions plants expanded rapidly, though the growth could not keep pace with the needs of the Army and Navy, nor for that matter was the supply of materials adequate.

In order to find the wherewithal, it was always the practice of the Army and Navy to compete with each other instead of working in unison. In the Budget, each received an equal share, the amount of which was greater than Japanese industrial capacity could cope with. In their use of the money, again, the Army and Navy habitually competed in buying up civilian supplies and troubled little about cost. The pressure of an insistent demand on an inadequate supply spelt inflation. Price control opened the door to a black market, to which the arsenals, leading factories and eventually the populace themselves were forced to resort. Chaos reigned: the national economy sickened and died.

To live at all, the people reverted to a primitive existence. Lack of foodstuffs increased year by year; women and children were driven to distraction in their search for the essential minimum. The Government did its best to distribute fair rations but the supply was insufficient to keep body and soul together. Inevitably the people grew what they could and tried to buy what they lacked. They had never quite understood what the war was all about. To them the war was not theirs but a military war. Thinking people had known this but now the people at large were realizing it.

The Army and Navy for their part thought that, since it was they who had to carry on the war, so they should be treated accordingly. They must have sufficient food, clothes and other necessaries; in everything they had their privileges. But in the different ranks it was the higher that had the better of it so that discipline suffered, while public resentment against the Army and Navy grew apace.

As these social disturbances grew, the gendarmerie and police went ruthlessly about their task of enforcing the powers of the Army in order to whip the people on to further exertions.

CHAPTER THIRTEEN

Fall of the Tojo Cabinet

1. SURRENDER OF SAIPAN, JUNE 1944

BY the beginning of 1944 the fall of Germany was in sight and the offensive against Japan was intensified.

Before the Japanese forces in East New Guinea had been starved out, the Americans landed at Byak in the north-west and carried out a diversionary movement while their main fleet set about an attack on Saipan, a key-point in the Marianas (June 1944). If the Mariana-Caroline defence-line were broken, our whole Pacific campaign would collapse—Saipan was the decisive battle of the Pacific.

Our fleet had suffered grievous losses at Midway and Guadalcanal but was still a fleet in being. Great hopes were centred on Saipan. The fleet, which used a corner of Sumatra as its oil-supply base, was now waiting off the Sulu Islands to the west of the Philippines.

When landing operations began, the American fleet, split into squadrons, patrolled the western approaches. At the same time enemy flyers bombed our bases in Iwojima to thwart attempts to relieve the beleaguered garrison. The *Yamato*, which had been despatched to Byak, was brought north again and with aircraft-carriers joined the main fleet. Spirits ran high: the moment had come to crush the American fleet now tied down at Saipan.

As soon as it had been located, the battle began (dawn of June 19th), when a long-range air-attack was launched against the main group of enemy carriers. Unfortunately our flyers failed to make contact and were forced to come down at the nearest landing-ground, which was Saipan. They were attacked at once and all but wiped out. Having lost its air-arm, our fleet was at a grave disadvantage and, though continuing to fight, drew off westward. Air- and submarine-attacks caused irreparable losses. Saipan was abandoned to its fate and the garrison perished, fighting like animals of the jungle.

Saipan, being one of the mandatory islands, had become a centre of sugar cultivation, and refineries had been established. There were, therefore, a great number of Japanese settlers. On the eve of the crisis several thousand women and children had been evacuated by boat, but before the vessels could reach Japan they were sunk without discrimination and the occupants drowned. Civilians left on the island died with the garrison to a man.

Afterwards, Tinian, Guam and Kwajalein suffered the same fate as Saipan.

2. CRITICISM OF THE ARMY AND NAVY

The Mariana line that was to have been defended to the last had fallen at one blow and our Pacific strategy had been overturned. Still worse, the knowledge that the homeland was left wide open to air-attack came as a thunderbolt to the whole nation.

As the air-attacks increased in violence, defence of the main islands became the overriding factor in the plans of the Army and Navy. The Cabinet had stripped civilian supplies to find the food, shipping and munitions that the Supreme Command demanded. The latter had preached that the great moment was approaching—and had been defeated at Saipan; thereafter one reverse followed another.

Criticism mounted: the Army and Navy were too interested in political manœuvres to attend to their own business and home defences were riddled with holes. In vain the Army and Navy proclaimed that enemy losses were far greater than ours and ultimate victory was assured. Public confidence was waning. There was a great gulf between the fighting men and the rest of the nation.

The war chiefs had food for thought.

3. CO-ORDINATION OF WAR LEADERSHIP

One man stood out in the public eye as the leader of the Government, the man who issued the war commands—General Tojo. But the war was not turning out as he wished. To him, the chief reason was that war leadership never followed one line. The Cabinet was kept in the dark as to what was happening. The Supreme Commands kept under their exclusive control both the main plan of campaign and particular engagements, so that the Cabinet was no more than a Government organ charged with the duty of satisfying the demands of the Supreme Command. To win a total war it was necessary that it should be pursued in one undeviating line. Otherwise it was lost. Control must be gathered into one hand; better late than never.

The Army and Navy were directly responsible only to the Emperor. They admitted Tojo to consultation but brooked no interference. They were independent, rival organs. At a pinch the air forces of the Army and Navy might be combined, and the plan had its advocates, but there was much to be said for and against, and time pressed. But at the very least complete control of the Army was essential, so Tojo took the drastic step of combining the offices of War Minister and Chief of the General Staff; Sugiyama, the Chief at the moment, resigned. Tojo took over this post and thus had supreme command of the Army. The Navy followed suit and the Navy Minister, Shimada, took over the post of the Chief of the Naval General Staff. The result was that Tojo and Shimada divided between them control of the Army and Navy. Tojo now held authority over every activity except that of the Navy, where he had no status.

To some extent the change was a move in the right direction. Relations between the Supreme Commands and the Government improved. But the decline in the fortune of war was the result of Japan's weakness when pitted against powerful enemies. This was one infirmity for which there was no cure. For Tojo himself, the concentration of power in his own hands brought on his head the indignation of the people at the abuse of government by the gendarmerie.

The resentment of the people at war-time hardships increased daily. Propaganda by the left wing took advantage of the worsening conditions and became more effective as the violence of the air-raids grew. People were looking for scapegoats. Lack of unity was only too evident: it was each one for himself. Under such conditions the gendarmerie suspected everybody. A retired statesman named Seigo Nakano, thought to be shielding himself behind a mask of Nazi beliefs, made a public speech attacking Tojo and was for a while detained by the gendarmerie. He was promptly released but for some unknown reason committed suicide. Public disquiet grew.

Tojo made a stand against any signs of defeatism in the Cabinet and pacifists received short shrift. He exhorted the public to unite as one man in the prosecution of the war but he only aroused opposition. The Japanese may be a docile people but at all times there is an undercurrent of revolt against oppression. In Tojo's last days as Prime Minister the pent-up feeling of resentment at the arrogance of the Army ever since the 'Manchurian Incident' came to a head. The more the people were repressed, the more the spirit of defeatism grew, and the more it grew, the stronger the reaction against the Government.

4. CRITICISM OF PRIME MINISTER TOJO

In the inner circles of the Army and Navy at this last stage, opposition to one man holding two such important posts as those of War Minister and Chief of the General Staff became overwhelming. Those responsible for the men serving overseas were united in their criticism, though it may well be that their feelings were not entirely uninfluenced by their own hopes of advancement.

Two or three members of the Imperial Family who were soldiers or sailors by profession submitted to the Throne that this duplication of posts was undesirable. It was hinted that it was iniquitous that such an able man as General Umezu, for instance, should be left in the comparative backwater of Manchoukuo.

By nature Tojo was straightforward and impulsive, traits that did not commend him to the senior statesmen. Tojo himself did not particularly mind who they were. He would not put up with anyone who aired opinions that were bad for the country, still less anyone who campaigned for peace or strove to overthrow the Cabinet at such a time as this.

Most of the senior statesmen felt that the Cabinet did not enjoy the confidence of the people. They met from time to time and eventually started a movement to overthrow the Cabinet. They began with a definite attack on the Navy Minister, who duplicated the post of Chief of the Naval General Staff. A whispering campaign in the General Staff said that Shimada was nothing more than Tojo's automaton. Outside the General Staff it was said that he was not the man to cope with a dangerous crisis like this.

Up to then the Navy had never disclosed the fact that Midway was a defeat nor that Saipan had revealed the weakness of the Navy. Now the public were beginning to realize these facts and demanded Shimada's head on a charger; he it was, said they, who was mainly responsible for all the reverses suffered by the Navy since the outbreak of war.

The Emperor drew Tojo's attention pointedly to the load of responsibility carried by Admiral Shimada and Tojo was compelled to act.

5. TOJO RESIGNS

The unpopularity of the Tojo Cabinet was the topic of the day; some of his Ministers urged resignation. But he stood to his guns: when the battle was at its height was no time for a soldier to retreat. To soften criticism, however, he relinquished the post of Chief of the General Staff and appointed the C.-in-C. of the Kwantung Army, General Umezu, to replace him. Admiral Soemu Toyoda, while remaining C.-in-C. of the Combined Fleet, became Chief of the Naval General Staff. A little later Shimada's resignation was accepted and Admiral Nomura,[1] who had been serving as Naval Attaché in Berlin, was appointed Minister of the Navy.

Continuing, Tojo wished to bring in, as Minister Without Portfolio, two ex-Prime Ministers—General Abe and Admiral Yonai. The latter had retired from active service to become Prime Minister and would have been only too pleased to be connected with the service again but a civilian post had no attractions for him. He therefore declined the offer. Tojo's attempt to regain popularity had failed.

Tojo still hesitated to resign. His was the responsibility for starting the war in the first place. He was afraid, therefore, that to resign while the war continued would be construed as a confession of defeat. But he could not fail to see that popular sentiment was dead against him.

He abandoned any further attempt to bolster up his Cabinet and resigned.

---

[1] Tadakuni Nomura is to be distinguished from Kichisaburo, Ambassador to the U.S. 1941–42.

BOOK NINE

The War of Greater East Asia (*continued*)
Koiso-Yonai Coalition Cabinet

CHAPTER ONE

The Koiso Cabinet: Supreme War Council

1. THE KOISO-YONAI COALITION CABINET

ON July 18th a Council of Senior Statesmen was convened to find a way out of the perplexing political situation.

The statesmen had overthrown the Tojo Cabinet but their positive action ended there. They had neither the resolution nor the ambition to undertake the task of finding a way out of the predicament in which the country was placed. The Emperor had requested them to propose a new Prime Minister and that was the task on which they concentrated, carefully avoiding any discussion of either the course to be adopted in the conduct of the war or of the international situation. They resorted to the familiar practice of tinkering with the internal situation and left it at that.

Since it was war-time, the Prime Minister must be a soldier or a sailor: otherwise how could the Army and Navy be directed? The unanimous decision was that it should be a soldier. One on active service was out of the question and after some searching they found their man in the Governor-General of Korea, General Koiso belonging to the first reserve of officers (first choice had been the bellicose General Terauchi but he could not be spared from the southern campaign).

Koiso is generally regarded as having been the mainspring of the 'Manchurian Incident' and the March[1] and October[2] 'Incidents', but since some time before the war he had been out of politics and he had had no direct connection with the conduct of the war. Prince Konoye was not happy about his past record and put forward Admiral Yonai as a counter-balance. Against the wishes of the Navy, Yonai was restored to the active list by Imperial Decree and made Minister of the Navy. Sugiyama became Minister of War and I was retained as Foreign

[1] Book One, Chapter Two, s. 4.
[2] Book One, Chapter Six, s. 1.

Minister, duplicating the post of Minister for Greater East Asia. Two politicians, Yonezo Maeda and Toshio Shimada, who were friends of Koiso, were brought in, their appointments testifying that the influence of the Diet had revived since the war reverses.

Though, like Tojo, a soldier, Koiso was on the retired list, had no authority over the Army and had for some time lived outside the mainstream of Army life. He was a stranger to party politics. Altogether, as a 'lone' Prime Minister he had to rely on the assistance of those who had the necessary connections.

I accepted my own appointment because I was strongly inspired by the same views as those of Court circles. I attached great importance to the necessary link between our general foreign policy and our policy in Greater East Asia. I was convinced that there must be no tampering with the new policy towards China.

2. SUPREME COUNCIL FOR THE DIRECTION OF THE WAR

The Koiso Cabinet was well received by the public; it was not all-powerful like Tojo's Cabinet nor had it the same despotic air. It was none the less purely a war cabinet, concerned only with the effective and successful conduct of the war; peace did not come within its purview. As always, peace formed no part of its charter; that would have to be planned outside the Cabinet, if at all (Kido's *Diary*, June 26th, 1944, *cf.* also his written testimony).

In order to add to the importance of the Liaison Conferences at Imperial Headquarters, Koiso succeeded in getting the title amended to 'Supreme Council for the Direction of the War'.[1] Apparently his aim was to use his own high rank in the Army to take into his own hands the actual direction of the war. But its conferences were by their nature merely councils of the Supreme Command; the members of the Cabinet, even the Prime Minister himself, had no authority to speak on any matter other than their own affairs, nor were the Cabinet given the power to so much as touch upon war directives. The Army and Navy dissociated themselves entirely from the Cabinet. As for the Prime Minister and the War Minister, they were outside the charmed circle. The Prime Minister might be a soldier but he was not on the active list.

The name had changed but the Council functioned in the same way as before. The standing members were: the Chiefs and Vice-Chiefs of the two General Staffs, the Prime Minister, the Ministers of War, Navy and Foreign Affairs (in Tojo's time the Minister of Finance and the

[1] Hereafter called the 'Supreme War Council'.

President of the Planning Board also attended). Other Ministers attended when matters within the competence of their ministries were discussed. As a steering committee, the Chiefs of the Military and Naval Bureaux and the Chief Secretary to the Cabinet attended. In the agenda there was no reference to the conduct of the war. One could not help feeling that the Prime Minister was held at arm's length.

At the end of each meeting, the Ministers attended talks given by the Army and Navy Liaison Officers and on occasion by the Chief of the Bureau of Political Affairs (Ministry of Foreign Affairs). The agenda of the conference itself was occupied mostly by the demand on the Cabinet for shipping, aircraft and munitions generally. Other questions discussed were foreign and home affairs. In practice Cabinet Members spent their time fighting a rearguard action against demands, the reasons for which were far from clear but which were of serious political import.

War reports were closely followed but they covered only non-confidential matters; Japanese losses were concealed. In fine the War Council decided the manner in which decisions of the Supreme Command were to be carried out, considered the demands made on the Cabinet and made the best bargain possible; that was all.

In turn the Koiso Cabinet devoted all its energies to carrying out the orders it received from the Council.

3. ADVERSE WAR REPORTS

Despite the utmost efforts of the Cabinet to meet military demands, the war was a succession of misfortunes. Since the fall of Saipan, the Japanese had been studying where the next blow would be struck. A direct line to Japan suggested Iwojima in the Bonin Archipelago, which could provide an airfield. It was generally agreed that this would be MacArthur's next objective. Post-war accounts reveal that Admiral Nimitz proposed to bypass the Philippines and capture Formosa in order to ensure communications with China and cut the line between Japan and the South Seas as a prelude to a direct attack on Japan itself. But at a meeting in Hawaii in July 1944 between Roosevelt and MacArthur, the President agreed that the Filipinos should not be left thus to wait their turn and a landing in the Philippines received his assent.

For the purpose MacArthur had chosen the island of Leyte, lying south-east of Luzon and by its conformation forming a link between the north and south islands. A powerful mixed force of

x

marines and land forces began the landing in November 1944 after a naval bombardment.

General Yamashita in Manila had already reinforced the garrison at Leyte. Saying that the landing there was just where he wanted it, he continued to send troops in support. Our combined fleet also, under Commander-in-Chief Toyoda, had been waiting for this. Both the Army and Navy proclaimed that this was an excellent opportunity for a decisive battle and the Cabinet Ministers, therefore, pinned their hopes on it. Leyte made great demands on our shipping, for the Philippine army had already used up most of the available local transport. The Cabinet cut down civil needs to the absolute minimum to meet the call. The Prime Minister pronounced that this was the battle of battles on which victory or defeat hung. It was to be another Tennozan.[1]

Reserves from Luzon were sent and the Navy set out from its southern base in battle array.

4. THE BATTLE OF LEYTE

Our fleet had been badly mauled at Saipan but it was still fairly strong. Now that America had mustered its forces to recapture the Philippines, it must be given battle with all our might. The nation waited in suspense for the deeds to be expected of its incomparable Navy, which they had been taught to believe had emerged unscathed from its previous encounters.

The fleet was divided into two squadrons; one was to make straight for the landing-place and strike confusion into the bridgehead; the other was to come round the north of Leyte to attack the enemy and obstruct the landing operations. A diversion was to be made by the Ozawa squadron coming from the Inland Sea towards the north-east of Luzon.

The southern squadron was attacked by air and submarine but held on its course and inflicted great loss on the enemy before dying game. The northern squadron also sank a number of enemy ships but called off the attack and, returning on its course, fell in with the Ozawa squadron; it then came south again, only to be destroyed by the main air force of the enemy fleet.

For all practical purposes our Navy was destroyed at Leyte. That we learnt after the war was ended. In this battle was sunk the *Musashi*.

---

[1] Tennozan: a hill commanding the approach to Kyoto from Osaka. Here Hideyoshi overthrew the rebel Akechi who had killed his master Nobunaga. The battle was decisive since it established Hideyoshi as dictator. He is regarded as Japan's greatest military strategist—the Napoleon of Japan.

It was completed during the war, was of 64,000 tons and mounted nine 18-inch guns.

The Council was given detailed accounts of the progress of the battle. The final report announced that the odds had been too great and, most regrettably, it had been necessary to call off the engagement. But much greater losses had been inflicted on the enemy than we ourselves had suffered. The enemy had in fact shot his bolt. The story was on the old familiar lines. The further the enemy advanced, the more favourable were our prospects. It sounded plausible. It must have been an unenviable task to talk in this way. But the nation believed and even Cabinet Ministers were deluded into hoping for the best.

The Ministry of Foreign Affairs did its best to enlighten the Army and Navy on the basis of enemy *communiqués* but the soldiers and sailors simply denied that there was any truth in enemy reports.

5. THE BATTLE OF LUZON

The enemy, that was thought to have been so hard hit at Leyte that he could not stage another advance, carried out a landing operation in the Lingayen area on January 9th, 1945, in force. The operation, which could bear comparison with the landing on the Normandy beaches, was successful and by February Manila was already in enemy hands.

The Army had said that Manila possessed adequate defence equipment and ample stores of munitions. The gallant General Yamashita was in command; this then was to be the decisive battle. Koiso proclaimed that this time it was really going to be Tennozan[1]—the turning point. The Government produced all the shipping it could lay its hands on. The public hoped against hope.

It was not to be. Our Navy had received its death blow at Leyte; our transport was exhausted. Isolated in a distant sea, Yamashita was condemned to fight a full-scale campaign to its inevitable end. His forces fought in vain against overwhelming odds. And though this was a fight to the death, there was friction and disunity between the naval and military detachments under his command.

Japan had formally recognized the Government of Manila. President Laurel fled to the north of the island and presently took refuge in Japan, together with the Ambassador, Murata.

Yamashita was supposed to have been fully prepared. But Muto, his Chief of Staff, informed me in Sugamo Prison that when he took up his

[1] See s. 3.

post he was appalled at the weakness of the defence measures. Who was responsible?

The army of occupation had not taken to heart our policy for Greater East Asia. In the fury of their fight to the death they resorted to conduct contrary to ethical decency. They left in the Philippines an evil record of which we may well be ashamed.

6. FALL OF IWOJIMA, MARCH 31ST, 1945

After Saipan, Nimitz moved in to attack Iwojima. This brought home to the Japanese that the war was at their doorstep, because the island is administratively part of Greater Tokyo. It proved impossible to send help either by sea or by air but the Tanahashi garrison sold their lives dearly. They had ingeniously turned an inhospitable volcanic island into an armed camp which they defended valiantly. They inflicted great losses on the American forces, struck a chill to the heart of the enemy and died to a man.

Air-raids had been started by B29s as soon as they had captured the airfields on Saipan and Tenian. Aircraft based on Iwojima became a powerful support and the island was an excellent place for an emergency landing. Raids on Japan, therefore, increased in violence.

Bombers from Saipan approached Japan in waves. Fujiyama gave them their bearings so that by night they could bomb industrial areas in Nagoya or the Tokyo-Yokohama district. During the day they flew at a great height and plotted the country.

They also came up the Kishu and Bungo Channels and laid waste industrial centres in the Osaka district, the islands of Shikoku and Kyushu. They side-stepped to bomb cities in central Japan. Others again struck North-East Japan. Nor were cities and towns on the Sea of Japan overlooked.

Finally, the enemy air forces in China gradually advanced their airfields. They bombed the Anshan Iron Works in Manchuria, inflicting serious damage and causing a panic. They also bombed the Yawata Steel Works in Kyushu.

The Japanese skies were at the mercy of the American bombers.

7. AIR BOMBARDMENT

The air-raids were the most frightful experience the Japanese people have ever undergone. On the grounds that Japanese production of munitions was parcelled out among home industries, the raiders systematically burnt out the whole of large and small cities and towns. These were mostly built of wood and it was comparatively easy to set them on fire with oil-incendiaries. These were invented by the Americans and, as they improved, were extremely powerful. Their use was perfected to a fine art. The first wave dropped bombs round a town and set up a circle of fire. Nights of strong wind were chosen and bombs were dropped to windward in great quantity. The area encompassed by a wall of flame then became the target for the next wave which systematically bombed the whole. The area became a sea of flame. Such was carpet-bombing.

Large cities such as Tokyo and Yokohama were attacked by one formation after another throughout the night. For small towns one formation was ample. Picked towns received a baptism of fire; as fire called up wind and wind called up fire, fierce conflagrations arose, in which parks and streams availed nothing as places of refuge. The populace had no means of escape and were burnt to death.

Raids on the low-lying districts of Tokyo in March 1945 killed over 100,000. Sumida River's waters were at one time converted into a Turkish bath covered with burnt corpses. Not even the Great Earthquake could equal the inferno. Over the whole of Japan tens and tens of thousands were burnt to death. Day by day Japan turned into a furnace, from which the voice of a people searching for food rose in anguish. And yet the clarion call was accepted. If the Emperor ordained it, they would leap into the flames. That was the people of Japan.

8. THE NAGOYA EARTHQUAKE

As though the cup were not already full, the Nagoya industrial district was visited by a great earthquake, which did far greater damage than even the air-raids. Toyohashi[1] was destroyed; works producing precision instruments were damaged beyond repair. The combination of raids and this earthquake dealt a death-blow to our munitions industry. The Minister of Munitions, the inspectors, managements and hands worked like demons to overcome these calamities. A suggestion was mooted to construct underground aircraft works and a start was made, but it was all too late.

Aircraft, shipping and munitions generally, manufactured with sweat and blood, were despatched from the works but, before they could reach the front, they were sunk at sea or destroyed from the air.

[1] Forty-five miles south-east of Nagoya.

CHAPTER TWO

War-time Diplomacy (Part 2)

1. OVERTURES TO CERTAIN FOREIGN COUNTRIES

KOISO strained every nerve to work in close co-operation with the Supreme Command. As the tide of war swept nearer to Japan, he frequently brought up the important question of overtures to Chungking and Russia at War Council Conferences: 'If we do not make them now, we shall always regret it.' He meant that Chungking should be detached from the Anglo-American camp and that Germany and Russia should make peace so that Russia might be won over to the side of the Axis. That was what the Supreme Command thought also.

These plans had already been tried out by the Tojo Cabinet but I had no objection to another attempt. I thought, however, that such proposals, expedient though they might be, held out no prospect of success unless they were founded on the principle of justice such as would satisfy the honour and dignity of the state. If they were not such as reason would approve, we should be merely adding to the tale of our losses. In my eyes the war was lost. There was nothing left but to make the best of it. Any approach to Chungking should be made with the consent of the Nanking Government, which had made common cause with us. Any offer to mediate between Germany and Russia must be made with the consent of Germany, which had most at stake.

2. OVERTURE TO CHUNGKING

Wang Ching-wei's Nanking Government had been fostered by Japan, which had formally recognized it as the Government of China. When Wang visited Japan, he was treated as the Head of a State. The Government's avowed aims were twofold: to bring peace to a reunited country and to combat communism. Wang himself had stated that once these objectives were attained, he would leave the question of his future role in Japan's hands. To ignore the Nanking Government, therefore, or to conduct secret negotiations with Chungking behind Wang's back, would conflict with the principle of which I have spoken and could not be considered for a moment.

Before recognizing the Nanking Government, Japan had failed in every attempt to come to terms with Chungking, and the Government had decided to make no further effort. But the Army had secretly made moves from Peking and Shanghai to get in touch. The Chinese go-betweens had been mainly concerned to safeguard their own future and did not seriously contemplate any new development in the situation. Roughly speaking there were two channels. One was personal contact with friends in Chungking. The Chinese, in return for their services, looked for favours from the Army of Occupation. The agents either paid visits to Chungking, going overland or making a detour round the coast, or, with the connivance of the Army, maintained contact by wireless sets of their own. The other channel was provided by Chinese business men in Shanghai. They became interested when the war went against Japan. In the hope of protecting their own interests, they attached more importance to keeping Shanghai out of the fighting zone than to actually bringing about a peace.

Most of these go-betweens secretly kept in touch with the Nanking Government and, even if they did not do so, the Government was in a position to find out what they were up to. It was easy to see, therefore, that any attempt to negotiate secretly would be a cardinal error which might have disastrous results.

The Tojo Cabinet had been working to secure Wang's assent and the Koiso Cabinet redoubled its efforts. The Supreme War Council determined to engage in active peace negotiations through the channel of the Nanking Government and Shibayama, the Vice-Minister of War, was sent as special envoy to Nanking (he had previously been Military Adviser there). To prevent any possible misunderstanding, he was to see Chen Kung-pao, Acting Chief of State in the absence of Wang, who was in hospital in Nagoya, and to lose no time in securing his assent.

3. CONFLICT OF OPINION WITH THE PRIME MINISTER

Unfortunately a serious difference of opinion arose about this time between the Prime Minister and myself.

As Colonial Minister General Koiso had voiced no objection to the move to win over Wang Ching-wei but he had never really approved.

The antagonism continued when he became Prime Minister. It might be Japan's policy to respect the Nanking Government but he himself had other ideas. He had his own particular views with regard to China. He thought that a study of China's topography and history indicated that it could not be administered as one unit; it should be divided into several administrative areas to be administered under Japan's control. He had concrete plans for the purpose. He disclosed them at the first conference of the War Council in December and invited the urgent consideration of the members.

I was at a loss to understand his purpose. As Foreign Minister I could not accept the suggestion. I said that at this stage of the war Japan could not go back on her established policy. She could not abandon her aim of appealing to the Chinese people through the Government that she had recognized. The Vice-Chief of the General Staff, who was representing his Chief, expressed regret that the point had been raised. Thereafter I was unable to see eye to eye with the Prime Minister.

Even the Ministry of War disagreed with Koiso on the point. On one occasion Sugiyama, Minister of War, said to me:

'Koiso's methods fill me with alarm. When I was Vice-Minister he was Director of the Military Affairs Bureau. About the time of the 'Manchurian Incident' he was, without my knowledge, engaged in various plots. It was the same later on. His associate at the time was Ninomiya, the then Vice-Chief of the General Staff and now a Cabinet Minister. General Matsui, Lieutenant-General Tatekawa and Colonel Hashimoto, together with the "Asia Development League" and the Young Men's Association belonging to the Imperial Rule Aid Association, form an active wing of the Cabinet. Look out, for anything might happen.'

I did not display particular interest at the time but Sugiyama said much the same thing whenever we met. I felt that he knew more than he said and I was put on my guard.

4. A SUGGESTION OF CABINET RECONSTRUCTION

One Sunday (December 17th, 1944) the Prime Minister asked me to see him and broached the subject of Cabinet reconstruction. He said that the Minister of Munitions needed a rest, and one or two other changes were desirable. He proposed to appoint the present Minister of Education, Lieutenant-General Ninomiya, to the post that I was duplicating, viz. Minister for Greater East Asia. The persons concerned, other than myself, were willing.

I reserved my reply since an important question of policy was involved. After mature consideration I decided to oppose the suggestion. As the war was tending, it was more than ever necessary that the Ministry for Greater East Asia should act in perfect harmony with Japan's general policy. An independent Minister might follow a policy directly opposed. That was a danger that I could not countenance. I therefore made it clear to the Prime Minister that I had no intention of continuing in the responsible position of Foreign Minister unless he changed the views he had expressed in the War Cabinet and his present intention to separate the two ministries.

Yonai, the Minister of the Navy, lent his good offices and various compromises were suggested but at this stage of the war I could not budge from the stand I had taken on the main issue. Eventually reconstruction of the Cabinet stopped at the Ministry of Munitions, to which Shigeru Yoshida (at the moment Governor of Fukuoka Prefecture) was appointed.

5. PROMOTION OF THE NEW POLICY IN GREATER EAST ASIA

Under my guidance every effort was made to promote the 'new policy' not only in China but also in the other countries of Greater East Asia, but the severance of communications made the task always difficult and in some cases impossible.

Wang Ching-wei died. He was succeeded by Chen, who was ably seconded by his associates. These men were true patriots and laboured to bring to reality the dreams that China had nursed so long. We did all we could to help them.

The economic side of the new policy had hitherto been neglected, but now that I had control of the G.E.A. Ministry once more, I announced a new economic plan as part of the general policy. I summoned local officials to Tokyo to discuss the project. There were difficulties. All played their part but, as the war position worsened, the troubles we encountered were beyond imagination.

The independence of Indonesia was approved by the War Council and announced by the Prime Minister in the Diet. I gave every encouragement to Sukarno, who had come to Tokyo for discussion. Kyujiro Hayashi was appointed adviser (he had been Consul-General in Mukden at the time of the 'Manchurian Incident'). Under Hayashi's assistance Sukarno's plans made great headway.

6. THE PROBLEM OF FRENCH INDO-CHINA

Indo-China also presented difficulties.

French officials passively resisted but, being under the authority of the Vichy Government, made a show of collaboration. Japan's misfortunes, however, caused a sudden change in their attitude. They were better able than the Japanese to read the omens and they were in a ticklish position. When the German Army withdrew from France, the new de Gaulle Government revived the original declaration of war against Japan. De Coux then proclaimed his allegiance and made it clear that Indo-China also was at war with us.

Indo-China was the base for Japan's expeditionary forces in Malaya, Burma, Java and Sumatra and had to be held secure at all costs. Nor could Japan tamely submit to a declaration of hostility.

France's colonial policy had always been violently reactionary. She had put down independence movements with a strong hand. Refugees had flocked to Japan and the Second World War gave impetus to the movement.

It was a basic part of Japan's new G.E.A. policy that, should the Japanese Army, for its own security, throw out the French authorities, racial aspirations should be recognized and an independent government set up. When, therefore, on instructions from Imperial Headquarters, the Japanese Army disarmed local French forces, steps were taken to hand over the administration to such governments.

The support given to the independence movement in Annam and Cambodia was about the last positive action Japan took in Greater East Asia.

7. KOREAN AND FORMOSAN AUTONOMY

Chosen[1] and Taiwan[2] had long been under the administration of the Colonial and Home Ministries. They were treated as extensions of the Japanese mainland and were outside the sphere of foreign diplomacy. From the beginning the aim had been to assimilate their peoples and successive Governors-General had laboured to that end.

In Chosen the policy had been implicit in Admiral Saito's administration, but under Generals Ugaki, Minami and Koiso it had been followed more actively. One of the last steps had been to render family

[1] Korea.
[2] Formosa.

names by their Japanese pronunciation[1] and to adopt conscription.

Both in Chosen and in Taiwan Japanese cultural institutions were introduced. Thus Universities were established, with the result that Korean political understanding had shown a notable advance; industry had developed greatly. Koiso showed marked sympathy with the Korean desire to be given a share in government and strongly advocated that Chosen should send representatives to the Imperial Diet. Tojo had already agreed in principle. Now under Koiso a bill to allow Chosen to send representatives was passed and became law.

The proposed system resembled the former practice of sending Irish Members to the House of Commons. It did not, therefore, imply independence but was one step towards autonomy. It would hardly satisfy local aspirations but I welcomed it as a move in the right direction. I believed that, however inadequate, it might be brought into line with our policy for Greater East Asia.

8. THE MIAO PING AFFAIR

Unfortunately I found myself in disagreement with the Prime Minister over the question of China once more.

At Shibayama's request[2] the Nanking Government had made peace overtures to Chungking but had not yet received a reply. Koiso secretly invited one Miao Ping to Tokyo with the intention of using him to intrigue with Chungking direct.

Miao Ping had been expelled from the Nationalist Party by Chiang Kai-shek and had been shielded by the Army of Occupation for purposes of their own. For a time he was President of the People's Association in Peking[3] and then, on Wang Ching-wei's installation, he was pushed into the position of Deputy Chairman of the Legislative Board. Having found him guilty of treacherous conduct, Wang would have had him executed but for the intercession of the Japanese Army. He continued, therefore, at his post but he had no love of the Nanking Government and spent most of his time in Shanghai, where he plotted with friends of his in Chungking. The Japanese Army used him to collect intelligence and acquiesced in his use of a wireless set. On his side Miao was in close contact with those Japanese civilians who were antagonistic to the Nanking Government, with whom he curried favour on the score of his Chungking activities.

[1] Place-names had always been rendered in Japanese. Thus Pingyang became Heijo.
[2] *Vide* Chapter Two, s. 2.
[3] Book Eight, Chapter Six, s. 3.

Miao wished to ensure his own safety. He acted as a 'broker' in Shanghai for the overtures to be made to Chiang Kai-shek. He planned the suppression of the Nanking Government in return for the withdrawal of Japanese troops. His reward was to be his reinstatement in the service of Chiang Kai-shek.

One of Miao's 'contacts' was General Tsai Liu, Chief of the Chungking secret police, who was in touch with agents behind the lines of SACO (Sino-American Co-operative Organization), a secret American Intelligence organization. Tsai was a born intriguer but no one trusted him. Tani, the Japanese Ambassador, and the local Japanese Army chiefs were agreed that he could accomplish nothing. Koiso, however, suddenly called a meeting of the Supreme War Council one Sunday (March 21st, 1945), reported that he had invited Miao to Tokyo and disclosed a plan to employ him: he was to use a wireless set at the inn where he had been installed, to get in touch with Chungking and sound out the intentions of Chiang's Government.

The assembly were astounded at Koiso's sheer folly.

I strongly combatted the plan. It was a flagrant violation of the decision we had already taken. It was an intrigue behind the back of the Nanking Government and an affront to all decent principles. It was playing into the hands of the Chungking Government. It would not bring about peace.

The Minister of War also opposed the plan. Umezu, Chief of the General Staff, agreed with him: he expressed concern at the delicate position in which the Supreme Command would be placed if it did succeed.

Since the exchanges of opinion that followed resulted in agreement that Miao should be sent back to China forthwith, I regarded the affair as settled.

9. THE MIAO PING AFFAIR (CONTINUED)

I was soon disabused. On April 3rd I was summoned to the Palace. The Emperor informed me that the previous day, in a political report, the Prime Minister had referred to his invitation of Miao to Tokyo and explained that he would like to be given authority to employ him as an intermediary in his approach to Chungking. H.I.M. had advised Koiso that peace negotiations could not be furthered by people like Miao nor was it right at such a time to adopt means that savoured of intrigue. But the Prime Minister would not listen to advice. The Emperor had accordingly asked the Minister of War for his views, which were unfavourable to the plan. H.I.M. had further consulted the Minister of the

Navy, who was strongly opposed and expressed regret that any Prime Minister should resort to such tactics. What did I think?

At first I endeavoured to reassure the Emperor: the whole question had been threshed out and Miao should now be on his way home. 'That is not so,' said H.I.M., 'he is still here and is far from inactive.' I then recounted to the Emperor what I had said at the War Council and continued: 'At this juncture, when the war may be considered to have turned decisively against Japan, we can but ascertain Your Majesty's views and strive for the best termination that we can achieve. All unfitted as I am, I shall strain every nerve. But in this hour of her peril Japan must tread the path of honour. If we do not stray from that path, Japan may fall but she will rise again. If we turn to pursue devious ways Japan may be lost for all time.'

The Emperor said, 'I quite agree.'

It transpired later that it was Miao who induced Koiso to ascertain the Emperor's wishes at first hand; Miao knew that Chiang Kai-shek had no confidence in anything said by Japanese officers or civilians. The Palace was well acquainted with the Miao Ping affair because certain confederates had sounded H.I.H. General Higashi-Kuni. The Prince had, after minutely questioning them, passed on the information to Marquis Kido.

At the Tokyo Trial Koiso declared that he had planned to further the cause of peace with the U.S. and Britain through the mediation of Chiang Kai-shek but that the attempt had been blocked by the orders of the Emperor, who had been influenced by the opposition of the Ministers for Foreign Affairs, Army and Navy. It is a pity that neither the Minister for Foreign Affairs, nor the Emperor, nor Marquis Kido, received any inkling, whether during the Miao episode or at any other time, that Koiso had any such plans for making peace.

At the end of the war Miao Ping was arrested by the Chinese Government and executed as a traitor. At his trial Tsai Lin denied that he had had any traffic with Miao Ping.

CHAPTER THREE

The Quest for Peace (Part 2)

1. INITIATING STEPS TO END THE WAR

Our plans to restore peace premised that we must await the right moment when the Emperor could issue a direct command. Meanwhile we should foster a state of mind in the Army and Navy ensuring obedience thereto, in order that no serious obstacle should arise. This was the most difficult problem, since it savoured of a domestic campaign.[1]

I strove to enlist the aid of Sugiyama, Minister of War. I sought him out time and again until gradually he began to display interest in a termination of the war. With Admiral Yonai, Minister of the Navy, it was plain sailing. But what was all-important was not the Army and Navy Chiefs, but the attitude of the 'senior staff officers'. I therefore instructed my Chief Private Secretary, Toshikazu Kase, to get in touch with Marquis Yasumasa Matsudaira, Chief Secretary of the Lord Privy Seal, and Colonel Matsutani, Private Secretary to the War Minister. Together they prepared the ground. These men were not defeatists. They put aside the question of their careers and volunteered unreservedly for the task of bring back peace to their beloved country. Even after I had relinquished my post as Minister, they continued their efforts to secure a sympathetic understanding in all quarters.[2]

In the Army the overwhelming body of opinion was that Hondo[3] must be defended. One version of the idea was that the fighting hitherto had been merely outpost skirmishes; the enemy must now be lured ashore and destroyed, just as the Mongol invaders had been wiped out.[4] It was rumoured that several thousand special attack planes[5] were held

[1] Cf. Book Eight, Chapter Ten, s. 4.
[2] Kase's own account of the part he played can be read in *Eclipse of the Rising Sun*.
[3] Or Honshu—the Main Island.
[4] 1281. Kublai's attempt to conquer Japan was the last previous invasion of Japan.
[5] Popularly known as suicide planes.

334

in readiness. The war-chiefs proposed to transfer the Emperor and essential Government organs to a refuge near Kategawa in Nagano Prefecture, where the foundations of an underground 'Palace' were begun. Meanwhile new recruits were issued with bamboo spears and wooden guns for drilling purposes.

'Defence of the mainland' became synonymous with the earlier 'Death or Glory'. As the 'starvation' theory had heralded the outbreak of war, so the conviction that there was no escape from a fight to the death gradually took hold of the people. They were too exhausted to think clearly.

2. IF THE PEOPLE SEEK A GLORIOUS DEATH, WHAT BECOMES OF JAPAN?

Many a time I turned over in my mind this military concept of death in the hour of glory.[1] Human beings are at one and the same time individuals and members of the state. It rarely happens that death is the only alternative to dishonour but there are occasions when the soul can survive only if the body dies. We Japanese know that well. And, now, here were we in our archipelago in the Pacific Ocean fighting out this battle that could have only one end—death, stage by stage. Devoted men in their storm planes and torpedoes attacked the enemy and died shouting '*Banzai*' at the moment they struck home. Living in their mother-country Japan, every Japanese from the Emperor down could have no hesitation when there was no alternative but death if the Japanese people were to preserve their honour and attain everlasting life.

In the summer of 1940, when Germany had rolled up the map of France, I had witnessed the heroic resolution of the British people. At any moment now Japanese soil was to be trodden underfoot by the enemy. Would that we might show the same resolution! And yet! The British resolution was the will to live. Japan today needed that same will. It was for life that the British went on fighting. Japan must now have the will to stop fighting! That conclusion was to me indisputable. I pursued my course, more determined than ever.

One had only to study the whole course of the war to realize that the Army's talk of destroying the enemy on our own soil did not deserve credence. After Iwojima would come the Luchus and then Kyushu, or Shikoku, or Hondo. With their overwhelming strength, the enemy would not find it too difficult to seize key-points throughout Japan.

[1] *Gyokusai*. See earlier allusions.

In 1940 the British had counted on the Navy and the Air Force, which were in good heart. The people too were united as well as resolute. The U.S. was at their back. Their decision, therefore, was based on cool, calm calculation of the odds. But Japan unfortunately had no prospect of victory. It had never been the people's war. If Japan went down in ruin, and her whole mode of life as a state were lost, how could she ever recover a position of honour in the world? Japan could only stand up with other nations as equals against the background of her own precious traditions.

The reason for the war was beyond the understanding of the people, who at heart would have liked to avoid it. They had had ten years of war since the 'Manchurian Incident'. They had but one wish—that the war would end. Military propaganda was pure camouflage.

Many thought that the Emperor was not kept well informed; H.I.M. should summon senior statesmen in turn and invite them to speak frankly. He did so, but only one—Prince Konoye—offered what amounted to a considered opinion. The gist of this was that Japan was in danger of going communist, the consequences of which would be worse than surrender. The Emperor enquired, 'In that case what would you advise?' but Konoye had no remedy to suggest.

The Emperor knew well enough what the position was and approved the search for peace in speech with both Kido and myself.

A written copy of his speech that Konoye had drafted was stolen and photographed by gendarmes, who found it in the house of Ambassador Yoshida (later Prime Minister). Yoshida was arrested but Konoye escaped arrest.

3. MY STATEMENT TO THE SENIOR STATESMEN

Kido and I were agreed that, in view of our commitments to Germany, her collapse should be the signal for Japan to end the war. I find from my records that I placed it about April or May; I had made my own plans accordingly. I had explained my views at Cabinet meetings and, through a Foreign Ministry representative, to the Supreme War Council. But I felt that it was necessary also to inform persons of importance who were not in office, such as the senior statesmen, in order that they too should give serious thought to the future of Japan.

Many other notable men, who were becoming increasingly alarmed, came to see me and I now felt that the time had come when I must speak my mind openly. Certain of the senior statesmen had been meeting in private. On March 23rd I was asked to receive a delegation and readily agreed. Wakatsuki, Okada, Hiranuma and Konoye appeared.

As spokesman Baron Wakatsuki posed the question: were there any diplomatic means by which Japan could be rescued from her hopeless position; could Japan, for instance, invoke the services of Russia, with whom she still had a treaty of neutrality? I replied that, according to my own information, Russia herself was likely to attack Japan at any moment. All that Japan could do was to approach the U.S. and Britain direct, and that she could do only if she faced up to the position in which she was placed. The question was: had Japan the courage to admit her predicament and decide accordingly?

Okada said at once, 'I understand you perfectly and entirely agree.' He meant of course that Japan should make up her mind to end the war and take the necessary steps.

To give the senior statesmen further food for thought, I explained the international situation at length and left them in no doubt as to Japan's peril.

4. MY ADDRESS TO THE PRIVY COUNCIL

My address to the senior statesmen created a stir among influential circles. A week later I was invited to address the Privy Council. The gist of my talk was as follows:

(a) The German war has entered its last phase. Her leaders still proclaim their confidence in ultimate victory and pin their hopes on the use of secret new weapons. But it appears to me that when a continental country becomes enfeebled on land and in the air, the war is nearing its end; the same argument applies to an island country when it loses mastery at sea and in the air (the allusion was to Japan). In these days of mechanized, mass warfare, the defeat of the weaker country comes very suddenly. My estimate is that Germany's collapse may be expected about April or May;

(b) In spite of Japanese urging, Hitler maintains that a peace move is unnecessary since, as he says, Germany will win the last battle. He proposes to fight it out and, if necessary, to 'die a glorious death'.[1] Reports that Germany is planning to make a separate peace are not to be believed. In any case she could not do so. The position of Nazi-Germany differs from that of Japan with her Imperial Throne.

[1] *Gyokusai.*

(c) An assessment of reports-to-hand indicates that, since Yalta, Russia has been making her preparations to attack Japan, whenever it suits her best. We must be prepared for her to descend on Manchuria in overwhelming strength. Her protestations of neutrality mean nothing.

The time has come when Japan must give grave consideration to her future course of action.

5. REVERBERATIONS IN THE PRIVY COUNCIL

I had nerved myself up to these talks, which were designed to arouse influential circles; I wanted to give them a true picture of the situation in the hope that they might arrive at the right frame of mind. At this particular meeting few questions were asked after my address, so that I was left uncertain as to the impression I had made.

But, as the meeting was breaking up, the President, Admiral Suzuki, and a few others drew me into a corner. Suzuki was, surprisingly for him, eloquent. He reminded me that Iyeyasu, founder of the House of Tokugawa, had been beaten time and again but had gone on fighting until he won the last battle, which made him ruler of Japan.[1] He recalled, further, that as C.-in-C. of the Training Squadron he had visited San Francisco many years ago and that at a welcome meeting he had expressed the view that, if Japan and the U.S. ever fought each other, it would be the end of both, to which opinion the Americans present agreed. It seemed to me that the Admiral wished to infect me with his own combatant spirit; his attitude was that Japan must fight to the last.

I was profoundly disappointed. I had spoken for more than an hour and this was all I had gained! My associates and I had already lost all faith in the War Cabinet and had hoped that Suzuki could be induced to form a new Cabinet to end the war. Actually Suzuki did become Prime Minister shortly afterwards and in his first speech in the Diet expressed the same views as he had given me.

6. APPEAL FOR ASSISTANCE TO NEUTRAL COUNTRIES

The Axis sun was sinking. Germany was at her last gasp, though she would not sue for peace. The time was fast approaching when Japan *must* take steps to end the war.

[1] The Tokugawa Shogunate lasted from the close of the sixteenth to the middle of the nineteenth century.

But to whom was she to turn? Russia was too dangerous. To make a direct appeal to the British and Americans, an intermediary who could be trusted must be chosen. I played with the idea of Madrid, where many influential British of Cabinet rank resided, but the project came to nothing. Of neutral envoys in Tokyo the only two suitable were Bagge, the Swedish Minister, and the Papal Delegate.

Bagge had long resided in Tokyo, knew Japan well and had a high reputation for sincerity. He was shortly returning to Sweden and readily offered to assist, saying, 'I cannot bear to think of the ruin of Japan, which has such a "glorious past".' After careful thought, I asked him to ascertain what peace terms the U.S. and Britain had in mind and to inform me through Okamoto, our Minister in Stockholm. I stipulated only that the terms must be consonant with the honour of Japan.

CHAPTER FOUR

Deterioration of the War Situation: Fall of the Koiso Cabinet

1. SPECIAL ATTACK UNITS

AIR and sea attacks on Formosa and the Luchus greatly increased. In Japan servicemen and people alike were keyed-up: the time was fast approaching when the homeland must be defended. To that end the Army and Navy made their final preparations. The tactics of the fight to a finish—the *gyokusai*, whether in a set-battle or in single combat—were employed. *Kamikaze*[1] squadrons were formed; the aviator aimed his plane, charged with explosives, straight at his enemy target in the hope of inflicting the maximum damage; in night attacks one man guided a midget torpedo-boat itself aimed at an enemy ship. These were all young men who sacrificed their lives for their country. Most were servicemen but many were volunteers just out of school.

Let no man belittle these 'suicide battalions', and call them barbaric. We know that young French soldiers in the First World War attached a flower to their rifle-barrels before going forward to their death at Verdun and Lens. In the Second World War, when the enemy was poised for the invasion across the English Channel, young flying men, barely out of school, clambered into their fighters humming a song and plunged into the midst of the German raiders. Under leaders such as Clemenceau and Churchill respectively they fought, in firm belief of final victory. In Japan the situation was all too different; Japan was fighting a losing battle. Does that lessen the value of their sacrifice? Nay, it increases it, for their souls shall live, to watch over the Japanese race for all time.

---

[1] Wind from heaven. The gods had aided the Japanese in repelling the Mongol invaders by bringing down a storm that dispersed their armada.

2. RESENTMENT AGAINST THE ARMY AND NAVY

The aerial bombardment of Japan from the north-east of the mainland to the south of Kyushu, together with the Nagoya earthquake, had wrought havoc among her munition factories. Communications were interrupted. In short the machinery of production had been dislocated while enemy squadrons freely approached Japan's shores and bombarded key-points.

The Army and Navy extended their supervision of civilian factories, and simple-minded officers subjected the workers to moral lectures and exhortations, as though they were on the parade ground. Normal organization within the works was shattered. Resentment against the arrogance and ruthlessness of the Army and Navy reached its height. Vigilance defeated its own end and the flow of production was thrown out of gear. The nation was worn out with all this ceaseless activity.

And yet, in spite of all, the people did their utmost to discharge their war-time duties.

3. BATTLE OF LUCHU ISLANDS; DEFENCE OF MAINLAND

When the enemy had broken through the Kyushu–Luchu–Formosa line, where would they strike next? Would it be Saishuto,[1] or Kyushu or the Main Island? In any case plans for the defence of the mainland must be speeded up. But the Army with all its arms and ammunition was in the South Seas or on the continent. Japan's own strongholds were bare. The Navy no longer counted. Japan had the remains of her air-arm and her recruits, who were not properly armed, and that was all.

The Army hastened to bring home troops from Manchuria and Korea, some of whom had to march most of the way. Trenches were dug and forts thrown up. That meant the confiscation of valuable rice and arable land. The Army was setting up the battlefield for the last struggle but the people were having their source of food taken from them and they seethed with indignation. Home defence meant the destruction of their means of livelihood.

In its last battle for the Luchus and Formosa the Navy asked for the support of the Army air-fleet but the military authorities replied that it was needed for the defence of the homeland. In May the

[1] Island at west end of the straits between Japan and Korea.

Americans landed on Okinawa[1] in force and completed the conquest in a month.

To meet the coming invasion, the Army established Western Headquarters at Hiroshima and Eastern Headquarters at Tokyo.

4. KOISO RESIGNS

General Koiso was profoundly depressed by the war situation and did his best to retrieve it. Like Tojo he tried to co-ordinate the work of the Army and the Government. But he was hampered by the fact that he was not on the active list. He obtained an Imperial Decree authorizing him to attend conferences of the Supreme Command but that alone was unsatisfactory because he was still only an observer. To overcome this difficulty he submitted to the Emperor that he should be returned to the active list, take over the post of Minister of War and be given positive authority to conduct the war.

Army and Navy chiefs, who were not on the best of terms with retired officers, such as Koiso, strenuously objected. They were prepared to consider the case of Admiral Yonai, who had merely retired to join Koiso's Cabinet, but Koiso himself had retired in the ordinary course of events. They refused, therefore, to allow his return to the active list. Against his wishes, they replaced Marshal Sugiyama at the Ministry of War by General Anami, who had just returned from the front, made Sugiyama C.-in-C. of the Eastern Headquarters, and Marshal Hata, newly returned from China, C.-in-C. of the Western Headquarters. These moves received Imperial Sanction.

Baulked of his desire to play a decisive part in the direction of the war, Koiso resigned with his Cabinet.

---

[1] The main island of the Luchus.

CHAPTER FIVE

The Problem of Prisoners of War

1. CONFLICT BETWEEN THE FEELINGS OF HOSTILITY AGAINST AN ENEMY AND THE DICTATES OF HUMANITY

RESENTMENT against British and Americans had sprung originally from the 'Manchurian Incident' and mounted as friction between Japan and their countries grew. Japanese susceptibilities were deeply wounded by the anti-Japanese attitude of the U.S. and Britain. At the same time the sudden access of power to the Army and Navy coincided with the growth of a feeling of hostility towards foreigners generally, which newspapers, magazines and books spread among the people. International communism fanned the quarrel.

Naturally this bitter feeling was accentuated by the outbreak of war. Propaganda whipped it up. Reports were current of inhuman handling, and of lynching, of Japanese in the U.S. Specious conversations were retailed imputing malicious treatment of repatriated Japanese when their ship called at British Indian ports. Great indignation was also caused by the Doolittle air-raid, which had no military significance but in which small school-children were killed and wounded.

Presently there appeared reproductions from American magazines showing toys made of human bones, and caricaturing Japanese war heroes, which had a great vogue in the U.S. Pictures were shown of Japanese burned to death by weapons that shot liquid flame in the fighting in the south. Then came the air-raids in which cities and towns were systematically burned to the ground. In this 'carpet-bombing' the inhabitants perished with their homes. The rage of the people boiled over.

Behaviour in battle and treatment of prisoners are two entirely different problems. Under no circumstances whatsoever should the Japanese fail in their humanity. Should they do so, the Japanese would disgrace their traditions and must hide their faces from their ancestors in shame. This was an even greater problem than that of victory or defeat, for I was convinced that, whatever the outcome, the Japanese spirit would rise triumphant, if only she conducted the war magnanimously. Thus would our international relations be restored. After the war with Russia Japanese travelling in that country were pleasantly surprised by the welcome they received. That was the reward of the spirit of the Japanese shown during the war. Similar results followed the war with Germany.[1]

It is terrible to think that after the Second World War many wrongful acts involving inhumanity were brought to light, so that our good name was lost and an impression was created abroad that the Japanese people are cruel monsters. It behoves the Japanese to study carefully how this came about. None the less, can it be fairly said that it is a common characteristic of the Japanese people to commit atrocities? War conditions were peculiar, food and materials were scarce, communications had broken down and the number of prisoners was greater than there were officials to deal with them. It would indeed be lamentable if instances of misconduct were allowed to overshadow the true spirit of the Japanese people. This unfortunate impression abroad may hinder the restoration of good relations for some time to come and put back Japan's rightful development.

I may add that it became clear at the Tokyo Tribunal that the most thorough investigation failed to show that Government leaders had ever ordered, or planned, any inhuman treatment of prisoners.

It was currently said that when General Matsui, commanding officer at Nanking, learned what had happened there, he was overcome with grief and burst into tears. After the war many instances were recorded of kindly treatment by Japanese in individual cases and a number of letters of thanks were received from ex-prisoners of war and persons who had been in concentration camps.

2. EXCESSES CAUSED BY HOSTILE FEELINGS

There is always danger that in the height of battle the wrought-up feelings of the combatants may lead to excesses. Even when this does not occur, actual fighting may result in hardship to the local inhabitants. During the first battle of Shanghai, I urged on the Army and Navy the need to do all possible to mitigate the sufferings of Chinese who had taken refuge in the foreign settlements,[2] and on occasion they delayed

---

[1] A considerable number of Germans were taken prisoner in the capture of Tsingtao.
[2] Presumably the Japanese 'Concession' is intended.

military action for the purpose. It can well be imagined that it was difficult to obtain such concessions. After Pearl Harbour Americans and British, residing in the occupied territories in China where I was Ambassador, were temporarily confined. Then enemy aliens were unavoidably put into concentration camps, but I am glad to say that the Chinese guards respected my wishes and treated them well.

From April 1943 I was Japan's Foreign Minister. A year and a half had elapsed since the opening of hostilities. Ordinances had been promulgated for the treatment of prisoners of war and of enemy aliens in accordance with the terms of The Hague and Geneva Conventions and the necessary orders had been issued. In accordance with past practice, the Army established a Prisoners' Control Bureau and a Prisoners' Intelligence Section.

This question of the treatment of prisoners and enemy aliens was one of the most serious I had to handle. I think that the conditions will be readily understood by anyone who understands Japanese legislation. The officials directly in charge were Army officers and the police; since everything was under the control of the Army, no one else could interfere.

It was the duty of the Foreign Minister to safeguard Japanese subjects who were detained abroad and at the same time to satisfy foreign countries that Japan herself was behaving correctly. Naturally I was most anxious on the point, particularly when I thought of Japan's position after the war. No one could be more concerned than a diplomat that our treatment of prisoners and enemy aliens should leave no cause for complaint. It is his duty to leave no stone unturned to rectify any cause of complaint to which his attention has been drawn.

I myself am convinced that I did all that was possible. The Tokyo Tribunal adjudged me guilty on the point. It is not for me to question their verdict.

3. THE TREATMENT OF PRISONERS

I was alarmed by the rancour displayed by the Army authorities. I was, further, disturbed by the popular indignation against the air-raids. This was not merely because I received many protests from the countries with which we were at war. I was dismayed by the gap between my own ideals and the realities of war.

At a Cabinet meeting an influential colleague, who had been formerly a Political Party member, challenged my views. When a brutal enemy murdered non-belligerents, why, he asked, should they receive better rations than the Japanese themselves, who were short of food? When flyers shot down innocent people, why should they not be tried as murderers? But the Minister of War supported my views.

My attitude was assailed in the Diet. It was said that I was half-hearted in my protests against the repeated sinking of hospital ships. Would the Minister explain, I was asked, what was my objection to the term 'American devils' used by his own colleagues? Most of my mail consisted of questions why enemy prisoners, guilty of inhuman conduct, should receive favoured treatment when they burned people to death together with their homes, while those who escaped had nowhere to live and nothing to eat.

In such an atmosphere my task was not easy. Although I had no actual authority in the matter, I did my best to prevail on the Army Chiefs to do their best to ensure correct treatment. Senior officers agreed with my view that it should be beyond reproach. But among the middle-ranking officers as well as the troops at the front were many who were imbued with Nazi ideology. As usual they paid little heed to the orders of their superior officers and appear to have disobeyed them frequently.

To reply to the complaints of enemy countries I had to rely on data supplied to me by the Prisoners' Intelligence Section. The section showed more disposition to second my efforts than did other sections of the Ministry of War. If it failed in its duties, that was because the Army at the front, and the prisoner-of-war camps, withheld the truth.

4. JAPAN'S SHAME: THE ATTITUDE OF THE ARMY

As the war went on, the flood of enemy protests grew. The Foreign Ministry forwarded them to the Prisoners' Intelligence Section and Ministries concerned and received stereotyped replies. The protests were various—brutal treatment of prisoners employed on the Burma railway, atrocities on Wake Island, wrongful treatment of prisoners in the South Seas, the question of permission to visit prisoner-of-war camps, the sinking of hospital ships. Many of the instances were not merely morally wrong, they could not be defended on the score of belligerent law. They were acts of which the Japanese must feel ashamed.

Enemy countries learned of the disgraceful treatment meted out to prisoners from those who escaped, and were stirred to action. In the British House of Commons Foreign Secretary Eden disclosed what was happening and said that when he heard the word *bushido* he felt nauseated. I was filled with anguish at his disclosures, many of which were new to me. I asked the Military Authorities to make strict investigation and was assured that they would do so. I frequently renewed the request but the replies I received usually denied the facts or merely said that any action taken had been quite proper. The Army said that the enemy was inventing incidents to slander Japan. They persisted in declaring that their repeated instructions ruled out the possibility of anything wrong occurring.

I then drafted a plan for a special Commission of Enquiry and put it up to the Military Authorities but they turned it down.

I also brought the matter up in Liaison Conferences.[1] The Army Chiefs merely replied that treatment was in accordance with the laws but that they had no objection to making careful investigation. The fact was that they would not believe that anything was wrong.

I still felt, however, that I must make one further effort. I thought of an appeal to the Emperor. At the same time I forwarded the whole dossier to Marquis Kido.

At an Audience I explained the serious nature of the subject and begged that the Emperor would issue the necessary order to the Army. H.I.M. was already acquainted with the details. He said that if there was any truth in the reports, it was a serious breach of duty and reflected shame on Japan. He was deeply concerned and would instruct the Army to put the matter right.

It is within my knowledge that the order, which was duly issued, had an excellent effect.

5. IMPROVEMENT IN TREATMENT

The shortage of food and materials at the front made the treatment of more prisoners than had been anticipated no light matter. Nor was it easy to make changes in the midst of war. But the Minister of War succeeded in putting through a number of reforms. Conditions disclosed after the war show that they were far from satisfying the requests made by the enemy, who expected the treatment to be in accordance with the terms of the Conventions. The fact that Japan acquired this dishonourable reputation must remain as a slur on her history. That the Japanese Army in the Philippines and the South Seas behaved with an utter disregard of the spirit of the new policy in Greater East Asia is a reproach that cannot be blotted from the memory. In Sugamo Prison Tojo told me again and again that he could not forgive himself for his

[1] Of the Supreme War Council.

failure to carry out the Emperor's wishes. The fact is stated in his last testament also.

The request made by the countries that had taken over charge of enemy interests, that they should be allowed to visit detention camps, was now liberally met. Facilities were given for the distribution of parcels. In particular Red Cross parcels were sent from designated ports in the Russian Maritime Provinces via Japan and distributed through the whole of the South Seas area.

I had difficulty in persuading the Army to spare shipping from its supplies, which were woefully short, but I succeeded in extracting a considerable tonnage. One case was that of the *Awa Maru* (17,000 tons). This vessel sailed from Japan as far as Singapore. The enemy had granted an unconditional safe passage both for the outward and the return journey. It successfully discharged its mission and started back, homeward-bound. In the Formosan Straits it was sunk by an enemy submarine. With it perished some 2000 civilians, who went down with the ship. Among them were many whose services would have been invaluable in rebuilding the future Japan. The enemy submarine rescued one single person, in order that he might be interrogated.

This was the last event in my tenure of office. The date was early in April 1945.

6. HUNT FOR WAR CRIMINALS

The war pursued its course relentlessly to its end. Life itself, which had been considered man's most valuable asset, was of no more consequence than a blade of grass. Air-raids became ever more violent. Finally, atom-bombs were dropped on Hiroshima and Nagasaki to test out their efficiency and at one blow more than 200,000 non-combatants were sacrificed. At that moment Japan had already decided to surrender and was taking preliminary steps.

The United States, Britain, China, the Philippines, the Netherlands, France and Russia, sometimes in union and sometimes separately, punished those guilty of atrocities. The trials reflected the characteristics of each nation. I have no desire to record them in detail. Each displayed only too completely the characteristics of a court martial by the victor. Some indeed were mediaeval in their outlook.

Even the American Tribunal awarded heavy sentences on the basis of written statements by prisoners and detained persons, which were accepted as they stood without further question, no opportunity of cross-examination being afforded.

Up to date (June 1949) more than 4000 persons have been sentenced, of whom more than 700 have been condemned to death. Not only so. Though some four years have elapsed, Japanese, not only prisoners of war but also civilians, are still detained by the conquerors and are employed in hard labour. The number published amounts to many tens of thousands.

It has hitherto been generally accepted that acts of war end with the Armistice. Many years have elapsed since the end of the Second World War and yet today the relations are still those of a vendetta. The slaughter of an opponent after the war has ceased may be cloaked by legal procedure but religion condemns it. On September 2nd, 1945, on board the *Missouri*, I attached my signature to a document that witnessed the end of the war. For the sake of a restoration of amicable relations in future, in the cause of humanity I trust that the victors will now cease punishing the conquered and will re-establish peace and goodwill on a foundation of liberty and equality.[1]

---

[1] It should be remembered that the book was published in 1952. The author recorded such facts as were available to him at the time.

BOOK TEN

Surrender

Suzuki and Prince Higashi-Kuni War-end Cabinets

CHAPTER ONE

The Suzuki Cabinet: Final Stages of the War

1. FORMATION OF SUZUKI CABINET

THE senior statesmen assembled to choose the leader of the new Cabinet. As usual it was a conference as to who should be designated, but as matters stood they could scarcely make a definite choice without deciding the problem whether to terminate the war or to fight to a finish. In addition to those who had met before, General Tojo was also present.

The meeting decided that a soldier or a sailor would be most suitable. One or two, who, like Tojo, were soldiers and contended that it was necessary to go on fighting, maintained that a soldier was required. Others, again, particularly those who had held informal meetings and were alarmed at the outlook, considered that Admiral Kantaro Suzuki, President of the Privy Council, was more suitable. He had for many years been Grand Chamberlain. He would, therefore, prove the most trustworthy mouthpiece of the Emperor's views. Marquis Kido hastened to submit his name to H.I.M.

In forming his Cabinet (April 7th), Suzuki wished to retain the Ministers of War, of the Navy and of Foreign Affairs, but my appointment was dropped in consequence of the strong opposition of Koiso, the previous Prime Minister. Until Togo was appointed in my place, there was a gap of one or two days, during which I handed over to the Vice-Minister and left office.

Thinking people hoped that this would be a Peace Cabinet.

2. DESTRUCTION OF JAPANESE ARMY

A month later Germany collapsed.

Japan was in no better case. Since she had lost command of the sea and air, the Army, scattered on the continent and over the Pacific

Ocean, thousands of miles away, was useless to her. The enemy could pick his objectives and attack in overwhelming strength. Profiting from experience, he had no hesitation in 'by-passing' and advancing boldly.

During January and February, 1945, the American Army completed the conquest of Luzon and seized key-points such as Palao and Pelew. Nimitz captured Iwojima in March and used it and Saipan as bases for the air bombardment of Japan. Japan was cut off from her own Army and her defences were destroyed. The occupation of Okinawa as a prelude to the landing in Japan began in April.

For the Navy Okinawa was the climax. If it could not be defended, then Japan itself was defenceless. The Navy, therefore, mustered its 'special attack squadrons' and sent them in at intervals of a few days in waves of ten or more. They disabled more than half the air-carriers, men-of-war and craft and damaged others. The garrison too fought gallantly and inflicted heavy losses. But the enemy knew also that this was a decisive battle and poured in troops regardless of losses.

This was the time when, as I have related, the Navy appealed to the Army to use its remaining aircraft in support, but the Army declined because, it said, they were needed for the defence of the mainland. Even to the very last the Army and the Navy were rivals and not partners.

The odds were too great and Okinawa fell—one more Aceldama.

The scene was now set for the battle for the homeland. The Army declared that it had still 7000 aircraft, which it would use to gain the final victory. It planned to lead the nation into battle and busied itself laying in stocks of bamboo spears and wooden guns.

3. FOREIGN DIPLOMACY OF SUZUKI CABINET

The new Cabinet at once summoned a special session of the Diet, in which it made its aims clear. There were no signs, such as thinking people had envisaged, of any intention to stop fighting. The talk was all of defence against an enemy landing and of the fight to a finish.[1] The Prime Minister himself explained the measures he was taking to ensure victory and adjured the nation to put its shoulder to the wheel. Cabinet Ministers said much the same thing.

It mattered not that Germany had disappeared and that Japan must now fight alone; moreover the war was going from bad to worse. Having disposed of her war with Germany, Russia was transporting troops to East Siberia night and day.

Foreign Minister Togo had always been an advocate of closer

[1] *Gyokusai.*

relations with Russia. Even after notice of Russia's denunciation of the Treaty of Neutrality had been received (April 7th), his views did not change. He invoked the services of a fellow-thinker, ex-Prime Minister Hirota, to sound out the Russian Ambassador, Malik, who had taken refuge in Hakone; he was to enlist the goodwill of Russia by offering a transfer of certain Japanese rights on the continent. Malik evinced interest in the suggestion but there was no reaction from Moscow. Prince Konoye also tackled Malik privately; his reception was chilly.

Minister Bagge, who had agreed to mediate on his return to Stockholm, enquired of the Japanese Minister there whether the Foreign Minister held the same views as his predecessor. Togo put a stop to any possible activities by saying that the Cabinet had changed in the meantime. Presumably he had more faith in a continuation of existing relations with Russia.

But the latter's attitude was such as I have already explained. She was preparing to attack Japan, though Malik professed interest in the talks with Hirota, and Molotov continued to assure Ambassador Sato that Russia still proposed to respect the Treaty of Neutrality.

CHAPTER TWO

The Quest for Peace (Part 3)

1. THE EMPEROR PROMOTES PEACE

THE Prime Minister now admitted that the war situation was far worse than he had thought. Okinawa left little room for doubt as to the outcome of the war.

On June 13th Marquis Kido called on Yonai, Minister of the Navy, and asked him if he had given thought to a termination of the war. Yonai replied: 'What can I do? Suzuki is very set in his views.' Kido, therefore, called on Suzuki and enquired, 'Have you any ideas as to the restoration of peace?' To his utter amazement he got the answer: 'What can I do? Yonai is very stubborn.' He suggested that they should get together and thrash it out. A similar enquiry made to Togo elicited the reply, 'What do you expect me to do when the Council before the Throne only the other day came to the decision to continue the war?'

It was Kido's alarm at this decision (June 8th) that had aroused him to action. It was worded: 'The war must be prosecuted to the end. Thus only can we hope to preserve Japan's integrity, defend her Imperial soil and attain the object of this "Sacred War".' A further clause read: 'In the sudden changes that are taking place in world conditions it behoves us to seize any opportunity that may occur of conducting the war under more favourable circumstances. Suitable measures should be devised that can be actually pursued, for instance in China or in Russia.' Kido, therefore, obtained Imperial assent to his embarking on the project to bring the war to an end. Anami, the War Minister, had maintained a stalwart attitude but, at a conference of the Supreme War Council on June 18th, he went so far as to speak of making a study as to which country should be asked to conduct peace negotiations.

Shortly afterwards the Emperor gave fresh instructions to the Prime Minister to prepare plans for terminating the war. On June 22nd H.I.M. summoned the members of the War Council to a tea-party and made his views known to them. Time passed and little was done. Then again on July 7th the Emperor urged the need for haste.

The fact was that only Japan's surrender would end the war. And that the Army would not countenance. It maintained that the war must be fought out on the homeland before there was talk of peace. Both the Chief of the General Staff and the War Minister, therefore, opposed peace. The Navy, under Yonai's guidance, did not oppose it. Suzuki ran from one to the other, and finally, on a suggestion from the Army which accorded with the Supreme War Council decision, decided to send a Special Envoy to Moscow armed with a letter from the Emperor requesting Russia to mediate; Konoye was to be the envoy.

Prince Konoye was received in Audience and was entrusted with the Imperial instructions. He was affected to tears by the Emperor's words and vowed to lay down his life in this great mission. But when Ambassador Sato spoke of the visit to the Russian Government and on being pressed explained its purpose, Molotov said that his reply would have to be postponed, since he was on the eve of a journey.

On July 17th Molotov left Moscow in company with Stalin, who was proceeding to the Potsdam Conference.

2. THE POTSDAM DECLARATION

The Conference opened on July 17th but Stalin did not arrive till the following day.

Half a year had passed since Yalta. In the meantime the U.S. had carried the main burden of the war against Japan, which was in its last stage. The participation of Russia, obtained at such a sacrifice, no longer seemed essential, and neither the Americans nor the British were very keen on it. Russia on the other hand had made up her mind.

Just at this juncture Secretary of War Stimson handed President Truman a report that the experimental trial of the atom bomb in New Mexico had been successful. Stimson thought that, before the bomb was used, Japan should be advised to make peace and warned that the U.S. possessed bombs of terrific destructive power. It was his draft that formed the basis of the Potsdam Declaration. The report was shown to Russia and, though she demurred, the declaration was published to the world, thereby drawing Japan's attention to its contents.

3. FIRST REACTIONS TO THE POTSDAM DECLARATION

The terms of the Potsdam Declaration were that, in the first place, Japanese troops must surrender unconditionally at once. Politically the terms of the Cairo Declaration were to be followed: Japanese territories were to revert to those held before the war with China; Korea was to be independent; Formosa and the Pescadores were to be restored to China; the Mandatory Islands in the Pacific were to be withdrawn from her administration. Further, references were made to reparations; ban on the munitions industry; rejection of military government; adoption of democracy; punishment of war criminals, etc. In one respect the terms differed from those imposed on Germany —the continued existence of the Japanese Government was allowed and Japan was guaranteed a viable economy with access to sources of supply.

In Japan first reactions were divided between acceptance and refusal of the terms, but before any decision could be taken Prime Minister Suzuki came out with a statement that the Potsdam Declaration should be treated with silent contempt. The Public Relations Section echoed his view in the newspapers. His attitude was, however, simply that of the Army. Foreign Minister Togo heard the statement with indignation.

My own house had been burned out and I was living in Nikko but I had heard indirectly of Marquis Kido's activities. When Germany collapsed, it flashed across my mind that Russia would now attack Japan. Although communications between Nikko and Tokyo were broken, I managed to get through in order to call on Kido. It was now already August. He told me of the proposal to send Konoye on a special mission to Moscow. I was overjoyed: here at last was the 'Voice of the Sacred Crane'![1] But the Keeper of the Privy Seal went on to tell me that no reply had yet been received from Russia though three weeks had elapsed. It was obvious that he was worried. Did I think that the Russians would answer? 'Yes,' I replied, 'you may be sure that they will, but what they will say will be the opposite of what Japan expects.'

I also called on Matsumoto, Vice-Minister, and the heads of departments in the Ministry of Foreign Affairs, and expressed my appreciation of their efforts for peace. I begged them to maintain their solidarity and to continue to work for the good cause.

---

[1] *Vide* Book Eight, Chapter Ten, s. 4.

4. THE ATOM BOMB. RUSSIA ENTERS THE WAR WITH JAPAN

While Japan was still debating what response to make to the Potsdam Declaration and was torn with anxiety as to Russia's reply to her appeal, August 6th came with the news that a strange bomb had fallen on Hiroshima, the Western Army Headquarters, that the city was wiped out, that Governor Otsuka had perished with the citizens, but that Hata, the C.-in-C., had escaped unhurt. Declaration of war by Russia followed and her Army began to pour into Manchuria.

On August 8th Molotov interviewed Ambassador Sato and handed him Russia's reply to the suggestion of Konoye's special mission—a declaration of war. Since Japan had rejected the Potsdam peace proposals (he used Suzuki's statement as a pretext for this announcement), it would be impossible for Russia to mediate. Since Japan was so intractable, therefore, Russia declared war in the interests of world peace and joined forces with the U.S. and Britain.

The U.S. announced that the missile dropped on Hiroshima was an atom bomb, that an area of some ten square miles was destroyed, within which no human being could live. The Army *communiqué* endeavoured to minimize the disaster: the bomb was of a special nature but its effects had been exaggerated, in fact there was no need for alarm. The U.S. Government, however, knew quite well the nature of the bomb and travellers from the West brought news of the tragedy that had occurred; the city had been entirely destroyed at the moment of explosion and over a large area scarcely a living thing survived.

5. POTSDAM DECLARATION: THE EMPEROR AGREES TO INTERVENE

For a long time past the Emperor had decided that the war must stop and had instructed the Supreme Command and the Government to take steps. Knowing this, the Army could not openly oppose the Emperor's wishes. They had, therefore, agreed to Konoye's mission and they now agreed to accept the Potsdam Declaration on the following four conditions: (1) the position of the Emperor must be retained as a national institution; (2) the enemy must not land in Japan or attempt to occupy it; (3) Japanese forces abroad should be withdrawn by Japan on her own initiative; (4) war criminals were to be tried and punished by Japan herself.

In their nature these 'conditions' were far from consistent with the aims of the Potsdam Declaration. Even if presented, they could scarcely call for a reply. The enemy was in a position to invade at any moment now. The populace, watching recruits drilling with wooden cannon and rifles, were filled with apprehension. On the 9th the second atom bomb was dropped on Nagasaki and, in effect, a breach was made in the defence of Kyushu.

At the Supreme War Council conference (August 7th) the four conditions aroused little argument. Prince Konoye was filled with gloom. If the Government adopted the Army's conditions as they stood and the enemy rejected them, then a war of extermination was likely. He asked me for my views. I replied that the presentation of such conditions would merely stiffen the enemy demand for unconditional surrender, if indeed they did not impose still stiffer terms. Since, sooner or later, we had to accept them, the longer we delayed, the worse it would be for us; meanwhile it was our people who were paying the price.

It had come to Konoye's ears that the Government lacked the strength to stand up to the Army. Only an Imperial decision would meet the situation. But I gathered that Kido was hesitating. Accordingly I went once more to call on him.

Marquis Kido was not in the best of humours. He had already taken it upon himself to induce the Emperor to order that the war should be brought to an end; he hesitated to worry H.I.M. a second time in order to ensure that his wishes were carried out.

I exerted myself to persuade him. One false step and there would be a struggle between the Army and those who opposed it. Who but the enemy would benefit? We were hovering on the verge of an irretrievable disaster: rather than leave matters in the hands of a Government that was too weak to restrain the Army, it was right and proper to invoke an Imperial decision. Finally, Kido agreed with me. Meanwhile Russia was overrunning Manchuria, was invading Southern Saghalin and the Kuriles, and showed every sign of crossing into Hokkaido.

The Emperor accepted Kido's recommendation and signified his readiness to issue an Imperial order as soon as the Government desired him to do so. H.I.M. so informed the Prime Minister in person. The problem had now narrowed down to a draft, prepared by the Foreign Ministry, dropping the four conditions and accepting the Potsdam Declaration, provided only that the 'Imperial Prerogative' institution be retained.

6. COUNCIL BEFORE THE THRONE: THE EMPEROR'S DECISION

Suzuki, the aged Prime Minister, at once convened a Council before the Throne for that same evening (August 9th). He also notified the Supreme Command. In addition to the Supreme Command and the War Council, Baron Hiranuma, President of the Privy Council, was also summoned in accordance with the usual practice.

The Prime Minister raised the question of the Potsdam Declaration and suggested that Japan had no option but to accept it. Representatives of the Army moved that it should be accepted with the four conditions attached. The Government on the other hand maintained that the retention of the 'Imperial Prerogative' should be the only condition attached. Since unanimity was unobtainable, it was proposed that H.I.M. the Emperor should make the decision.

Having called for further elucidation of the two proposals the Emperor gave his decision in favour of the draft prepared by the Foreign Ministry and so took the final, serious decision to end the war.

The stipulation that the 'Imperial Prerogative' be retained was phrased originally in the Foreign Ministry draft that 'the position (of the Emperor) under the laws of the country' should not be changed. Baron Hiranuma, however, remarked that the Emperor's authority to exercise the Supreme Command stood above the laws of the country, this being the Kokutairon,[1] and the phrase was amended to 'Imperial Prerogative'.

The Army representatives had displayed no special objection to the Imperial Decision at the time but in military circles alarming passions were aroused. In the morning of that same day no one had voiced opposition to the four conditions. And yet that evening a Council before the Throne had been convened on the spur of the moment, at which the morning's decisions had been overthrown. The malcontents decided that it must have been a plot and they suspected that the Cabinet were the culprits.

The air-raids went on day after day. News from Manchuria and Saghalin was confused. The people wandered about aimlessly, a prey to despair.

---

[1] See note in Introduction (Political terms).

7. SURRENDER: THE EMPEROR'S RIGHTS OF SOVEREIGNTY

Japan's reply in acceptance of the Potsdam Declaration was presented to the U.S. and Britain by Switzerland; there was a general feeling of happiness that the Second World War was ending in a complete victory for the Allies. Russia, however, paid no heed and went straight ahead with her design to occupy Manchuria, Korea and Saghalin. Halsey, the American C.-in-C., also continued his operations.

In the U.S. Army circles were inclined to accept Japan's desire to retain the 'institution of the Emperor'.[1] But the Secretary of State, Byrnes, himself drafted a reply, which was forwarded with President Truman's approval. The gist was that the Emperor's rights of sovereignty would be subject to the overriding authority of the Supreme Commander of the Army of Occupation and that ultimately the form of Japan's Government would be determined by the nation itself. From a study of the messages that had been exchanged it was obvious that the terms of the Potsdam Declaration were moving in the direction of unconditional surrender.

On receipt of the American reply, sent in the name of the Allied Powers, there was much argument among the Japanese. The Army said that the reply could not be accepted, for the reference to the 'institution of the Emperor' constituted an infringement of Japan's political constitution; the War Minister was strong on the point, the Chief of the Army and Naval General Staffs took the same stand and it was the view of the President of the Privy Council[2] also.

The Minister for Foreign Affairs, however, just as stoutly maintained that the reply was satisfactory and the Government agreed. Marquis Kido, Keeper of the Privy Seal, held that on a question of the interpretation of a diplomatic document the opinion of the Minister of Foreign Affairs must be accepted and pronounced in favour of that interpretation. He succeeded in overriding Baron Hiranuma and Army circles.

Meanwhile the enemy dropped leaflets explaining the Potsdam Declaration in the hope of winning over public opinion. The situation did not brook delay. Finally the question was left to an Imperial Decision.

The last Council before the Throne was convened on August 14th. In addition to the Supreme War Council the entire Cabinet attended.

---

[1] The phrase used by Cordell Hull in his *Memoirs*. See note in Introduction (Divine right of the Emperor).
[2] Baron Hiranuma.

The Prime Minister recounted in detail the progress of this question of acceptance of the Potsdam Declaration, which he said had resulted in a difference of opinion between the Army and other parties concerned. The meeting was then open to discussion. Army representatives contented themselves with a brief statement of their views, but there was no general debate.

The Emperor then gave his decision. H.I.M. adopted the view of the Minister for Foreign Affairs and announced that the American reply should be accepted.

The final decision was taken to accept the Potsdam Declaration.

On the following day, August 15th, the Emperor himself broadcast to the nation that the war was at an end.

The Suzuki Cabinet then tendered its resignation. In the concluding stages there had been complete disagreement between Suzuki, the aged Prime Minister, and Togo, the Minister for Foreign Affairs.

CHAPTER THREE

The *Coup d'état* That Failed

1. OPPOSITION FROM THE SENIOR STAFF OFFICERS

EXTREMISTS in the Army and Navy, who had always contended that the war must be decided on the Main Island, were extremely dissatisfied with the decision to stop fighting. Their pride would not allow them to acquiesce. Anami, the War Minister, had raised no particular objections at the Council before the Throne and had attached his signature to the Imperial Decree, but, in the stormy atmosphere prevailing, found the task of restraining the senior staff officers more than he could manage. These were in fact the men who had exercised the real power in the Army throughout the 'Showa upheaval'.

The plan of these staff officers was to carry out a *coup d'état* by a military operation; to set aside the Emperor's advisers and Government officials who had advocated the termination of the war; to take the Emperor under their protection and to continue the war. Then they would oppose the enemy landing and decide the issue—victory or defeat. If by any chance they were defeated, then the nation must go down fighting.[1] In any case they would not consider peace before that. Had they not already prepared a refuge for the Imperial Family, and made arrangements for the transfer of Government to Nagano Prefecture?

2. ATTITUDE OF ARMY CHIEFS

On his way home from the Council on the 14th, the War Minister, Anami, called on Umezu, the Chief of the General Staff, with a face registering indignation. Here was a pretty pass, he said; there was nothing for it but for the Army to take the Emperor under its protection

[1] *Gyokusai.*

by a *coup d'état*, to establish military government in order to continue the war. He asked Umezu to take part.

Umezu had had a shrewd suspicion what was toward. When he had heard out Anami's request, made at the instigation of his Staff, he quietly pointed out the duty of a loyal soldier. Once the Emperor had given his Imperial Decision in Council before the Throne, a loyal servant obeyed. He urged the Minister of War to control his unruly staff.

Anami made no comment and left in silence.

During the morning of that day, and before the Council meeting, the Emperor had summoned the top-ranking officers—Fleet Admiral Nagano and Marshals Hata and Sugiyama—had announced that the war must be ended and invoked their best efforts. That day arrangements had been made for the Army Chiefs to lunch together at the War Ministry. Umezu, Chief of General Staff, proposed that those present (viz. himself; Anami, War Minister; Doihara, Inspector General of Military Education; Marshal Sugiyama, C.-in-C. Eastern Headquarters; Marshal Hata, C.-in-C. Western Headquarters) should sign a covenant swearing to carry out the Emperor's wishes. All had agreed and had signed. Anami had then moved heaven and earth to persuade his staff officers to agree but had failed.

He expiated his failure by committing suicide (disembowelment) at the Ministry of War before daylight on August 15th.

3. THE *COUP D'ETAT* FAILS

The revolt was set in motion at once. Major Hatanaka and other officers from the Bureau of Military Administration formed the vanguard. It was their idea to attack the Palace. In company with staff officers from the Imperial Guards Division, they proposed as a first step to prevent the Emperor's broadcast to the nation on the ending of the war.

They called on Mori, Commander of the Guards Division, and tried to talk him over but, finding that they could not do so, dispatched him on the spot, together with his Chief of Staff. They then forged an order in his name, armed with which they led out a detachment from the Division and attacked the Palace. They proposed to put the Emperor's advisers under restraint, take the Emperor under protective custody and proceed to direct action to attain their object.

The private residences of the Prime Minister and of the President of the Privy Council were burned at the same time.

But, though they searched the Department of the Imperial Household from top to bottom, they could not lay their hands on the record on which the Emperor's broadcast had been taken nor yet on the Keeper of the Privy Seal. One detachment, therefore, seized Radio Broadcasting House. But the record was duly broadcast from a station that they failed to discover.

General Tanaka, Commander in charge of Tokyo Defences, had by now arrived at the Palace. He harangued the staff officers leading the revolt. His voice broken with emotion, he reproached them for their outrageous behaviour and adjured them to desist. Realizing that they had shot their bolt, the rebel leaders committed suicide.

That was the end of the *coup d'état*.

Tanaka assumed responsibility and, having satisfied himself that all was in order, himself committed suicide with his own sword.

It will be noted that this theme of *coups d'état* runs through the whole of the '*Showa* upheaval'.

4. THE EMPEROR'S BROADCAST

The whole nation listened respectfully to the Emperor's Broadcast. Troops at the front and people abroad also heard it. Thinking people were prepared for it. To the masses, however, who had no means of knowing the inner workings of government but had simply been told that they must fight to the death, it came as a bolt from the blue. But when it dawned on them that their Emperor had graciously decided that this tragic war must cease, their hearts were filled with gratitude. It seemed too good to be true.

Nevertheless many people could not bring themselves to acquiesce. Many Army and Naval officers signalized their opposition by committing suicide: Onishi, Vice-Chief of the Naval General Staff, was one such. Among the people, also, those who had put their faith in that divine wind that had once routed the Mongol invaders accounted surrender a national shame. Fanatics crowded the Niju-bashi[1] and addressed their lamentations to the Palace; many indeed in their frenzy committed suicide.

Taken in conjunction with Army resentment, the situation looked extremely threatening.

It is reported that one group, belonging to a right-wing organization, gathered on the Yoyogi Parade Ground.[2] There they prostrated them-

---

[1] The bridge forming the approach to the main entrance of the Palace compound.
[2] To the north-west of Tokyo.

selves before the Rising Sun and ten or more young men ceremoniously registered their protest by disembowelment. Rioters assembled on Atago-yama.[1]

In the midst of this alarming depression, the Cabinet of Prince Higashi-Kuni was formed to carry out measures for ending the war.

---

[1] A small hill north of Shiba Park. Atago is an avatar of Izanami, the consort of Izanagi. By their union they created Japan.

CHAPTER FOUR

The Task of the 'Cabinet of the Imperial Family'

1. A THREATENING OUTLOOK

THE decision to end the war had been taken by the Suzuki Cabinet, but its resignation had left the task of carrying it into effect to the incoming Cabinet. Here again, just as the Emperor had taken the decision, so the actual fulfilment depended on H.I.M.'s wishes. It was Marquis Kido's recommendation, therefore, that on this unique occasion a member of the Imperial Family could best undertake the duty of forming a Cabinet. There was no time to convene a conference of senior statesmen, since Japan was face to face with a crisis unparalleled in her history.

Prince Konoye undertook the position of Deputy Prime Minister in order to advise Prince Higashi-Kuni, who was to be Prime Minister. As War Minister, General Shimomura, who had lately been C.-in-C. in North China, was appointed; Admiral Yonai remained as Navy Minister; I became Foreign Minister. As Cabinet Offices the foreign-style Akasaka Detached Palace, which had been left standing in a burned-out area, was selected. The formal installation took place in the Department of the Household, which is within the Palace compound.

At Atsugi[1] was an airfield which formed the headquarters of the Naval Special Task Units. Here had been assembled the 'Divine Wind Squadrons' and it was here that the last squadron of all was waiting to show its mettle when it came to the final battle. Keyed-up as they were, these young flyers could not lightly accept a decision to give in. Day by day they broke all regulations in flying over the capital. They flew ominously low; they gave threatening demonstrations over the Palace and Government buildings; they showered leaflets proclaiming that this was Armageddon.[2] It was true that the attempted *coup d'état*

[1] Some twenty-five miles south-west of Tokyo.
[2] *Gyokusai*.

planned with Army Headquarters had failed. But the scenes taking place in front of the Palace and on Atago-yama were none the less alarming.

There were still considerable forces in Japan itself, in Manchuria, in China and in the south. No one could tell what would be their reaction to the decision to lay down their arms. Army Headquarters viewed the task of getting the order obeyed throughout the islands of the Pacific with the gravest concern. But the Emperor had given the word; whatever the difficulties, the authorities concerned could but do everything possible to carry matters through, properly and without disaster, and hope for the best.

For the most part the masses now appreciated the situation and welcomed peace with all their hearts. That was the saving grace.

2. PREPARING TO BRING THE WAR TO AN END

The task of the Cabinet fell into three stages: (1) to bring the Emperor's Decree home to the troops and the nation and to get it obeyed; that was the *raison d'être* of the Cabinet; (2) to complete the necessary administrative arrangements; (3) to carry out the terms of the Potsdam Declaration.

The Emperor issued a Cease-fire Order. At the same time three or four Members of the Imperial Family were chosen to visit points in Japan and Military Headquarters in China and elsewhere, in order to communicate the Imperial wishes and to see that they were carried out.

At military headquarters in Tokyo, once the *coup d'état* had failed and diehards had committed suicide, conditions became normal. Army and Navy officers in Tokyo and at the front realized that the Decision had been taken by the Emperor, their Supreme Commander; they swallowed their bitterness and obeyed. The only exception was that on isolated islands in the Pacific troops went on fighting for months, even for years, simply because they had not received the Order.

This was indeed the 'Voice of the Sacred Crane' but it had also become the will of the nation. The Atsugi flights were suppressed. The Army and Navy central authorities had at last abandoned their creed,[1] and threw themselves heart and soul into winding up the war. Demobilization was in fact a far more ticklish task than starting the war.

Little by little the agitation before the Palace subsided and the crowds on Atago-yama dispersed. The main anxiety of the people now was to find food and to wait in suspense for the return of husbands and

[1] *Gyokusai.*
2A

sons from the front. Otherwise the hearts of those who had been concentrating on the war-effort were drained of emotion, except for that carking fear—what was to become of Japanese women and children non-combatants stranded in Manchuria and China?

The first of the three tasks was completed under the wholehearted guidance of Prince Higashi-Kuni.

3. CONCLUDING PROCEDURE

The second task of the Cabinet was to complete the necessary administrative arrangements to bring the war to an end.

The Supreme Commander of the Allied Powers, General MacArthur, was in the Philippines. His first act was to request Japan to send delegates to discuss procedure. Japan sent General Torashiro Kawabe, Vice-Chief of the General Staff, a Foreign Ministry representative and others. On their return they brought back a copy of the Instrument of Surrender and Directive No. 1. The first was in accordance with the Potsdam and Cairo Declarations and required the signatures of the Emperor and representatives of the Government and of Military Headquarters. Directive No. 1 was stern. It contained detailed orders for the unconditional surrender of the forces; complete cessation of operation of munition works; rapid disarmament of troops; evacuation of military establishments and cessation of flying. In Japan it was regarded as a Japanese version of the Morgenthau plan, envisaging the return of Japan, confined within four small islands, to the agricultural economy existing before the Meiji Restoration.

The Instrument of Surrender was much what had been expected but the complete closure of munition works under Directive No. 1 created a serious problem because, in the way munitions were made in Japan, it meant the closing down of nearly every factory in the country. Nonetheless, in its determination to abide by the terms to which it had agreed, the Government complied with this as with other clauses of the Directive.

Since the surrender the people had lapsed into inertia. But disquiet lingered; there was no knowing what further trouble the extremists might be planning.

CHAPTER FIVE

Signature of the Instrument of Surrender

1. ARRIVAL OF THE ARMY OF OCCUPATION

IT had been announced that the Instrument of Surrender was to be signed at the end of August but the date was changed to September 2nd and the ceremony was to take place on the deck of the *Missouri* off Yokohama. The Americans had their own delicate questions of protocol between the Army and the Navy. As Supreme Commander, MacArthur represented the Navy as well as the Army, but the designation of the flagship *Missouri* as the venue represented a graceful recognition of the tremendous sacrifices made by the Navy in the Pacific War. The *Missouri* is named after the state from which President Truman came.

American (Allied) Forces were brought by air to Atsugi on August 28th as the forerunners of the Army of Occupation. MacArthur arrived by the same route a few days later and set up his headquarters at Yokohama. At the same time the American Fleet occupied Yokosuka. Tokyo Bay had been designated as the first stage in the occupation with Yokohama as the centre.

Atsugi had been only lately the home of the Special Task Squadron. Accordingly the Japanese Navy were hard put to it to get it ready in time to hand over at one or two days' notice.

2. CHOICE OF DELEGATES TO SIGN THE DOCUMENT
OF SURRENDER

The choice of delegates to sign the Document of Surrender presented the greatest difficulty. They must be persons who accepted full responsibility for terminating the war and who would inspire confidence in Japan's sincerity. As the first step to be taken by a defeated Japan, the slightest false move would be fatal. Japan had laid down her arms. Her enemy was now entering, with blood-stained sword held at the ready, the country of those Japanese who they thought only yesterday fought like beasts of the field.

The feeling of Japan's leaders, now that the war had ended so suddenly, was characteristic. They abhorred, as an unclean thing, the act of shouldering responsibility for the deed of surrender and they did their best to avoid it. To sign the deed of surrender was, for a man in the public eye the end of all things, for a soldier or sailor virtual suicide.

I myself had longed with all my soul for the end of the war and, behold, it had come to pass. It was my duty to carry through the last decisive act. I summoned all my resolution and determined to set the final seal on my services to the Throne. For all I knew, a bomb might be my reward, but that counted for little. I hoped and prayed that surrender was to be the dawn of a brighter era in which Japan might live.

3. DUTY OF THE DELEGATES

I had thought that the Army and Navy should each choose a representative and I suggested that the Emperor and the Government should be represented by one or two delegates. My idea was that, in addition to myself, the Prime Minister or the Deputy P.M. should be the Emperor's personal delegate, but this plan was not accepted. Finally it was agreed that the Minister of Foreign Affairs should represent the Emperor and the Government, and that the General Staff should nominate either its Chief or Vice-Chief. Accordingly I was nominated to accompany Umezu, Chief of the General Staff. The Emperor summoned us separately to Audience and solemnly entrusted us with our serious mission.

As Minister for Foreign Affairs, and as representative of the Emperor and Government, I was entrusted as a Minister Plenipotentiary with the duty of signing the Instrument of Surrender at an unprecedented event in the history of Japan. At my Audience I ventured to submit the following advice:

> 'Signature of the Instrument of Surrender is an event that is entirely new in our history. It is a regrettable tragedy. But it is the one and only means by which the Japanese race can be saved from destruction and our unbroken history and culture can survive. It is, therefore, an unavoidable necessity.
>
> Throughout her history Japan has been a united nation—one

people, one Sovereign. When such as I are permitted to enter Your Presence, we feel that the will of the people and the will of our Emperor are one. It is only because those who have been clothed in authority have at times gone astray that Japan has fallen into this lamentable predicament.

The democracy on which the Potsdam Declaration insists is not in itself inconsistent with the institutions of this country. I even think that under its influence they will be enhanced. With this thought in my mind, I feel that if, having signed the document, we follow it faithfully and completely, we shall promote a happier destiny for this country. I verily believe that that is an entirely possible consummation.'

The Emperor appeared to approve my sentiments. H.I.M. said, 'I entirely agree with you,' and he was graciously pleased to encourage me to persevere with the policy I had outlined.

4. THE INSTRUMENT OF SURRENDER SIGNED

At dawn on September 2nd, Umezu and I and our suite gathered at the official residence of the Prime Minister. Having bowed to the Palace, we set out for Yokohama. Not a soul was on the streets. As far as the eye could see, we traversed a burnt-out scene of desolation, in which survivors were to be seen here and there picking over the ruins. The scars of war were vividly presented before our eyes.

From Yokohama Pier we embarked on an American destroyer and for an hour threaded our way through the American and British men-of-war that filled Tokyo Bay, before arriving at Nimitz's flagship *Missouri*. The previous day had been 'day 210'[1] but the ocean lay calm under the rays of the rising sun. We clambered up the gangway and were saluted by the guard. As we made our way to the upper deck, where the ceremony was to take place, it was just short of ten o'clock.

The enclosure was thronged with enemy onlookers. It was filled to overflowing with newspaper correspondents and photographers. Prominent were General Percival, who surrendered at Singapore, and General Wainright, who surrendered at Bataan. Facing us across the table were the Allied representatives. The C.-in-C., MacArthur, entered; in his speech he declared that the war was over and requested us to sign the Instrument of Surrender. I signed first and Umezu after me.

[1] The period between the 210th and the 220th day after the planting of the rice is critical because of the danger of a typhoon ruining the crop.

MacArthur then signed in acknowledgement of our surrender, followed by the national representatives. The U.S. was represented by Admiral Nimitz and Britain by Admiral Fraser. Russia and China were also represented.

It was a wonderfully fine day. As we stood on the deck Fujiyama appeared, towering over Tokyo Bay and reminding us that we were saying good-bye to summer. But, though the *Prince of Wales* had sunk off Singapore, her sister-ship, H.M.S. *George V*, lay proudly before us, spruce in shining silver.

We returned to the pier and drove back to Tokyo, to report to the Government and the Emperor. Our serious task had been accomplished. This day a history of thousands of years had ended. This day a new epoch dawned. Nay, more. It was only by this day that our history could continue. Japan was born anew, though the *Showa* revolution, that was to rebuild Japan, was still in progress. The future of this new Japan depends on the ability and the perseverance of the Japanese race.

There are people who say 'From defeat comes victory.' But, if Japan were to behave as she has behaved in the past, then victory would turn to ashes once again. Only if she turns over a new leaf will she prosper and life be worth living. Her journey through hell will have had a meaning if she emerges worthy of herself. I tried to look into the future but grief came flooding into my thoughts.

CHAPTER SIX

After the Instrument of Surrender

1. ALARM CAUSED BY THE THREAT OF MILITARY GOVERNMENT

Hot on the heels of the Instrument of Surrender, on the evening of September 2nd, came the copy of an order, issued by MacArthur's Headquarters, to the Foreign Ministry's Yokohama Agent, Minister Suzuki : the whole of Japan was to be placed under military government. The report shocked the Japanese Government and the people. It seemed that Japan and the Allied Powers interpreted Japan's acceptance of the Potsdam Declaration in a radically different manner. The Allied Powers' interpretation was that Japan's unconditional surrender signified that, just as in the case of Germany, the country would on occupation be governed by the Army of Occupation. Japan's interpretation was that her surrender was different from that of Germany, which had disintegrated. Japan was surrendering under the terms of the Potsdam Declaration. According to that declaration, the Japanese forces were required to surrender unconditionally but the existence of the Japanese Government was recognized and the reciprocal nature of the functions of the Army of Occupation and the Government were clearly recorded.

I spent that whole night turning the question over in my mind and the following morning (September 3rd) returned to Yokohama to interview MacArthur ; Sutherland, the Commander's Chief of Staff, was present at the interview. I detailed Japan's decision and her preparations for the surrender and then requested that he would think twice before instituting military government. The gist of what I said was as follows :

The decision to end the war was taken by the Emperor himself in consideration of the wishes of the nation. H.I.M. has declared that the spirit of the Potsdam Declaration must be faithfully

375

observed and to ensure its observance he has taken the unusual step of appointing an 'Imperial Family Cabinet', which has taken all the necessary steps. We consider that this is the way in which the Potsdam Declaration can be most loyally enforced. But that Declaration assumes the existence of the Japanese Government and we did not anticipate that you would substitute military government for it. Japan's case is different from that of Germany. If the Allied Powers wish to see the Potsdam Declaration operating satisfactorily, they cannot do better than carry out their plans through the agency of the Japanese Government. On the other hand, if the Army of Occupation adopts a system of military government and assumes direct responsibility for the administration, they are claiming powers greater than envisaged by the Potsdam Declaration. Not only will they be doing something never anticipated by Japan but they will be relieving the Japanese Government from the responsibility of seeing that the Occupation policy is faithfully carried out. It may well be that utter confusion will result, the responsibility for which will not be that of the Japanese Government. The latter has already taken steps to put the Directive No. 1 into effect. It has begun the disbanding and disarming of Japanese troops on all fronts. Orders have already been issued for the cessation of operation of all factories that have any connection with the manufacture of munitions, etc., etc.

I laid particular stress on the Emperor's decision to carry out the terms of the Potsdam Declaration. Above all I emphasized H.I.M.'s love of peace, even so far back as the time of the 'Manchurian Incident'.

The Commander-in-Chief listened with sympathy and interest, and agreed to suspend operation of military government. He instructed Sutherland to take the necessary steps at once.

What appeared to surprise the Commander-in-Chief was that Japan had already closed munition works in accordance with Directive No. 1. It was obvious that a literal observance of that directive would jeopardize the livelihood of the people. He questioned me closely on the point and declared that, provided munitions were not manufactured, the production of necessary articles could be restored and that there was no reason why factories should not operate normally. In this talk I was able to obtain MacArthur's understanding of many of the questions with which we were faced.

It was thus arranged that SCAP[1] would issue the necessary directives for the execution of Occupation policy by the Japanese Government

[1] Supreme Commander Allied Powers.

as established under the Japanese Constitution. In the U.S. there was considerable dissatisfaction at MacArthur's magnanimity and there was some tightening up of the Occupation policy but the principle remained unchanged. The Japanese Government, which had continued through the ages, and the nation, set themselves to honour the pledge they had given in the Instrument of Surrender and to carry out the Potsdam Declaration. On these foundations was built the success of MacArthur's Occupation policy.

2. SHALLOWNESS OF PUBLIC SENTIMENT

For a time all went well. The Emperor's instructions were carried out effectively by the Cabinet and the nation co-operated in an understanding spirit, while the attitude of the Diet, of the Press and of the Cabinet itself was liberal. But once the war was ended, politicians and business men took it for granted that Japan had reverted to the normal conditions existing before the war. Many deluded themselves that international relations also were the same as before and that foreign trade could be resumed without hindrance. They thought in terms of old-world wars such as those with China and with Russia and imagined that this war too was over and done with. Few had any understanding of the results of a total war. They listened happily to pleasing rumours that implementation of the Potsdam Declaration implied understanding of Japan's food problem and a sympathetic handling of the problem of supplies of raw materials for Japan's industries. The harsh result of defeat, namely that Japan's fate lay in the hands of their conquerors, never dawned on them, so irresponsible were many of them.

That was not all. Those who had fawned on the Army and Navy, and hastened to anticipate their wishes, now turned their coat. They loathed their Army and Navy and sang hymns of praise of the Army of Occupation. These were the men who had shouted for a strong policy abroad and reviled the weak-kneed diplomat. Hey presto! They were now moderates. They loved peace. They thought nothing of harming others so long as they saved themselves. Toadyism was rampant. However natural and inevitable this was in the hour of defeat, it sickened the heart of thinking people. Those who were content with the golden mean—behaving properly to all but fawning neither on military circles nor on the Army of Occupation—gradually disappeared from public life.

When SCAP's pronouncement that the operation of industries necessary to the livelihood of the people could be continued just as in normal times, business men fancied that they could resume trade with the U.S. and other countries. Oblivious of the fact that Japan was a defeated country, they pestered the Authorities with requests that showed an entire misunderstanding of the situation in which they were placed. Even in the Government itself were many who indulged in wishful thinking; they imagined that SCAP would give favourable consideration to any application that the Japanese submitted. In my interviews with the Press I was forced to reiterate time and again that the only way to put Japan on her feet was first to realize that we had lost the war and then to study where our previous actions had been wrong.

3. WINDING UP THE WAR; FUNCTIONAL MACHINERY

It came hard to the Japanese to use the word 'surrender'. Military circles contended that in translation it should be rendered *Kyusen*.[1] But whatever you call it, 'surrender' is 'surrender'. Japan's rebirth depended on her realization that she had surrendered as a result of defeat. The Ministry of Foreign Affairs insisted that she must give up glossing over unpleasant realities.

The Ministry proposed to set up a small bureau to be called 'End of War Liaison Office' to take charge of relations with SCAP. The proposal, however, met with strong opposition in the Cabinet; liaison with SCAP was a serious matter, it was claimed, and demanded a large-scale organization within the Cabinet under the control of the Prime Minister. My own view was that the business of winding up the war affected nearly all national affairs and was, therefore, the function of the whole Cabinet, each Ministry handling the particular affairs with which it was concerned. No special Government Organ was required. All that was needed was a liaison office in the Ministry of Foreign Affairs to maintain relations with the Army of Occupation. Such machinery would underline the independence of the Japanese Government. It might be said that there was nothing to prevent each Ministry from corresponding direct with SCAP but the resulting lack of co-ordination would certainly involve serious disadvantages.

This desire for a large-scale Government Organ, to which influential civilians would have the entrée, was really inspired by business vested interests. I had no particular objection to a Government Organ, whether in the Ministry of Foreign Affairs or in the Cabinet Office, to consider civilian proposals; I had even thought of it myself. But I was

[1] Suspension of hostilities, armistice or truce.

determined to preserve Japan's sovereignty, however restricted it might be. That being so, the Ministry of Foreign Affairs, standing as it were on Japan's threshold, was the proper body to exercise jurisdiction over liaison with SCAP. My stand was comparable to my opposition to military government. But practically no one grasped my point of view. Most of the Cabinet Ministers looked on the question as part and parcel of the same old game of the division of the spoils of office. Prince Konoye approached the issue as though it concerned an organ that would be useful in playing off government and civilian interests, the one against the other.

The atmosphere in the Cabinet had covered up the harsh realities of the Instrument of Surrender. The Cabinet had been formed with the definite aim of enforcing faithful compliance with the Potsdam Declaration, but the moment it had completed the first two stages—surrender and signature of the document—it declined to face the resulting situation, which was that Japan was under the occupation of the same enemy forces against which it had so recently been fighting.

4. ARREST OF WAR CRIMINALS

There was no particular reason why the Army of Occupation should show mercy towards Japan. General MacArthur certainly displayed the magnanimous attitude of a statesman, though most of the persons benefited were sycophants begging for favours. But the American attitude was based on a calm, enlightened self-interest; it was not particularly concerned with altruism. That was only natural.

Before occupation was fully established, American Military Police arrested General Tojo in his residence and, having foiled his attempt to commit suicide, took him to Yokohama. The next day they arrested Admiral Shimada. I at once called on SCAP and pointed out this action ran counter to the promise given me that the Occupation policy would be conducted through the agency of the Japanese Government and it was arranged that in future 'persons wanted' would be arrested and handed over by the Government.

Shortly afterwards SCAP handed such a list to the Foreign Ministry liaison officer. It comprised Cabinet Ministers at the outbreak of war and various members of the right wing. Among them were Hirota, the former Prime Minister,[1] and Ogata, a member of the existing Cabinet. The total number was twenty. On the ground that the arrest of a senior statesman and of a present Minister of State was disquieting, I con-

[1] *Vide* Book Three, Chapter One.

ferred with SCAP and succeeded in getting their names removed from the list. The Army of Occupation took a serious view of the influence of the right wing. They regarded the Genyosha,[1] with which Hirota and Ogata were connected, as its spiritual home.

So far no question had been raised about Konoye and myself.

The other persons named were handed over and were confined, first in the old Yokohama Gaol, and then in the ex-prisoner-of-war camp at Omori. Thereafter certain people were very apprehensive that they also might be regarded as war criminals. Some of Japan's leaders strove to get in touch with SCAP; others employed intermediaries who secretly visited SCAP and paid homage to MacArthur.

The Army of Occupation ransacked Yokohama, Tokyo and the neighbourhood for buildings and suitable houses still standing and requisitioned them without scruple. A large proportion of the trams and trains were commandeered, though the existing services were crammed with people; the commandeered vehicles were then operated half empty. Communist Party members, gaoled for criminal offences, were all released, to carry on, openly and with the connivance of the Army of Occupation, a communist campaign against the Government and the 'Emperor Institution'. The Army of Occupation encouraged the public to criticize the 'Institution of the Emperor' and many newspapers and broadcasting stations fell under the control of the communists.

Japan seemed to be on the eve of a revolution. The Army of Occupation made it clear that it would do whatever it wished and the Japanese vied with one another to curry favour.

5. SUBMISSION OF ADVICE AND RELEASE FROM OFFICE

It seemed to me that, quite apart from the domineering attitude of the Army of Occupation and the subservience of the populace, the general 'set-up' of existing Government offices was merely a replica of the old pattern. Defeat had brought about entirely new conditions but I could not discern any trace of a corresponding change in mental outlook. All that people wanted to do was to get the old peace-time machinery working again.

The Army of Occupation was thinking on lines that were radically different from any mere compliance with the Potsdam Declaration. They proposed to remodel Japan from top to bottom. It was not beyond average intelligence to guess what they would request next. They had demanded the handing over as a war criminal of a leading

[1] *Ibid.*

figure in the present Cabinet. True, they had suspended the demand but their action was an indication of their distrust of the Cabinet. Their act had undermined the competence of the Cabinet to carry out the terms of the surrender.

The primary purpose of the 'Imperial Family Cabinet' had been to bring the war safely to an end. That task at least had been fulfilled. It was possible to argue that, the policy of faithful observance of the Potsdam Declaration having been clearly defined, its duties were at an end. The need now was to make a clean sweep of those who represented the old order and to form a fresh Cabinet that could co-operate with the Army of Occupation, smoothly and in keeping with the new order of things.

After careful thought, therefore, I submitted my views with some firmness to the Prime Minister, who was attended by Konoye, the Deputy Prime Minister. I proposed that, apart from H.I.H. Prince Higashi-Kuni himself, the Cabinet Ministers should resign in a body in order to make way for a new Cabinet.

My advice was rejected. At the request of the Prime Minister I handed in my own resignation. Within ten days SCAP requested the immediate discharge from office of the Home Minister, in view of his necessary connection with senior police officers, together with the Chiefs of Prefectural Police throughout the country.

The Cabinet then resigned *en bloc*.

Envoi

Japan has at last attained peace some six years after she signed the Document of Surrender. She is now engaged in the task of recovering the rights of independence and sovereignty.

While in prison, I put together this record of the events that marked the turbulent course of the *Showa* era up to the present day, and now publish it in book form.

The record was compiled during the two years that I spent in Sugamo Prison between the end of 1948, when the Tribunal closed, and November 1950, when I was released. For a year after my release I was engaged in verifying the facts from the lips of my colleagues in our old diplomatic service. I also studied history in public records and books of reference. Such errors as may still remain I trust that readers will point out in order that they may be rectified in a future edition.

THE AUTHOR

March 1952

INDEX

ABE, General, 163, 201, 257, 315
Admiralty Islands, 302
Aizawa, Lieutenant-Colonel, 102, 103
Aleutian Islands, 277, 308
Amau Declaration, 99–101
Amoy, 148, 287
Amuletic Use of Words, The, 9
Amur River, 67
Anami, General, 342, 364, 365
Andaman Islands, 274, 293, 308
Anfu military faction, 41
Anglo-Chinese Treaty of Nanking (1842), 56
Anglo-Japanese Alliance, 25, 26, 43
Annam, 209, 292, 298, 330
Anshan Iron Works, 324
Anti-Comintern Pact, 122 et seq., 127, 151, 152, 168, 171, 177
Aoki, K., 201, 283
Araki, Sub-Lieutenant, 45, 68, 70, 72, 85, 102, 106, 108, 146, 163
Arima, Count Y., 199
Arita, Hachiro, 154, 163, 168, 169, 170, 182
Asakai, Koichiro, 9
Asama Maru, 182
Asia Development Board, 154, 183, 280, 283
Asia Development League, 199
Associates of the Sacred Wind, 69
Atlantic Charter, 274, 285, 293, 294
Atsugi, 368, 371
Attu, 302
Awa Maru, 348
Azores, 298

BARNBY Mission, 97
Bataan Peninsula, 271, 373
Bhamo, Dr., 292
Dias Day, 142, 149
Birobijan, 94
Bismark, 275
Blood Brotherhood, 69, 75, 81
Bonin Archipelago, 302, 305, 321
Book of the Tiger, The, 93, 108
Borneo, 275
Bose, C., 292–3
Bougainville, 277, 302
Boxer Agreement, 287
Braithwaite, G. B., 9
Brentwood Conference, 306

Bungei Shunju Press, 14
Burma, 291, 305
 route, 183, 190
Butler, R. A., 182
Byak, 311

CAIRO, 300, 301, 304
Cambodia, 209, 210, 298, 330
Canton, 45, 142, 304
Caroline Islands, 275, 302
Carpet-bombing, 325, 343
Casablanca, 300
Central China Business Promotion Company, 155
Chahar, 118
Chamberlain, Austen, 57, 182, 183, 188
Changkufeng, 142, 173
Changkufeng incident, 158 et seq.
Chen-ting, Wang, 44
Cherry Society, 68, 159
Chiang Kai-shek (*see* Kai-shek, Chiang)
Chientao, 158
Chi-jui, T., 41, 44
China
 and Japanese expansion, 37–8
 anti-Japanese agitation, 74
 communism in, 44–5, 56
 German advisers withdrawn from, 150
 Japanese aggression in North, 117
 demands on, 39
 economic difficulties in, 279–80
 errors in, 279–85
 full-scale war against, 154 et seq.
 military designs on North, 136
 U.S. sympathy with, 40
 war in North, 140
China School, 136, 146, 154, 183
Chinchow, 67
Chinese Book of Rites, 49
Chinese Communist Party, 74, 101, 124, 137, 138
Chinese National Government, 155
Chinese Revolution, 165
Ching-wei, Wang, 147, 155, 164, 165 et seq., 183, 201 et seq., 217, 283, 284, 326, 327, 329, 331
Chosen, 330, 331
Chuken, 21
Chungking, 142, 147, 155, 166, 304, 305, 326, 331

INDEX

Chungking Government, 183, 207, 280, 288, 289, 304, 327, 332
Chungking Nationalist Party, 304
Chuo Koron Co., 13
Churchill, W. S., 183, 187–8, 191, 204, 216, 217, 239, 264, 269, 274, 288, 303, 304, 306
Ciano, Count, 212
Communism
  in China, 44–5, 56, 74
  in Japan, 32–3
Concordia Society, 93, 184, 199
Control, School of, 71, 147
Coral Sea, 276
Corregidor, 274
Craigie, Sir R., 182, 190
Czechoslovakia, 171

DAIREN, 38, 60, 64, 306
Dan, T., 70
Daniels, F. J., 9
de Coux, Governor-General of Indo-China, 207, 241, 298
de Gaulle, General, 239, 298, 330
Disturbed Years of the Showa Era, The, 13
Document of Surrender, 371–2
Doihara, Colonel, 65, 67, 73, 118, 119, 137, 365
Drought, Father, 219, 222
Dumbarton Oaks Conference, 306
Dunkirk, 187, 188
Dutch East Indies, 263

Eclipse of the Rising Sun, 14, 216
Eden, Anthony, 191, 346

FALKENHAUSEN, General, 146
Fiji Islands, 277
First World War, 14, 39
Fisheries Treaty, 295
Fitch, Rear-Admiral, 276
Formosa, 148, 149, 275, 291, 304, 305, 321
Four Power Pacific Treaty, 25, 43
France
  Japanese diplomacy during war, 298
  reactionary colonial policy, 209
Fraser, Admiral, 374
French Indo-China, 207
  invaded, 209
Fuchow, 148
Fukuzawa, Y., 37

Furness, George, 15
Furusho, General, 142
Fushimi, Prince, 82

GAIKO Kaisoroku, 14
Gandhi, Mahatma, 292
Genro, 20, 50, 72, 81, 85 128, 133, 170, 204, 256
George V, H.M.S., 375
Germany
  absorbs Czechoslovakia, 171
  attacks Russia, 213, 217
  Britain declares war on, 171
  collapse of, 353
  declares war on U.S.A., 269
  invades Poland, 171
  Japan's belief of victory, 189
    diplomacy during war, 295–6, 297
  mediates in China-Japanese War, 145
  reasons for *rapprochement* with Japan, 148
  retreats in Europe, 308
  seeks Japanese gratitude, 150
  withdraws military advisers in China, 150
Gil, Yun Tae, 78
Gilbert Islands, 275
Gobi Desert, 172
Greater East Asia Conference, 286, 292–4
Greater East Asia Declaration, 285
Greater East Asia Ministry, 283
Grey, Sir Edward, 39, 41
Guadalcanal, 275, 276, 277, 302, 305 308, 311
Guam, 305, 312

HABAROVSK, 95
Hague Treaty, 266
Hailar, 172
Hainan Island, 149, 164
Halahen River, 172
Halifax, Lord, 182, 190, 191
Hamaguchi, Y., 62, 81, 90
Hanaya, Major, 66
Hangchow, 62, 287
Hangchow Bay, 141
Hankey, Lord, 15, 182
Hankow, 45, 142, 287, 304
Hankow Government, 165
Hanoi, 166, 207
Hara, K., 44, 81
Hara, Rear-Admiral, 276, 302
Hara Party, 43

INDEX

Harada Diary, 50, 51
Harbin, 67
Hashimoto, K., 35, 68, 328
Hata, General, 142, 181, 192, 342, 359, 365
Hatanaka, Major, 365
Hawaii, 272, 305, 321
Hayashi, General S., 66, 88, 102, 119, 127, 128, 129, 257
Hayashi, K., 329
Higashi-Kuni, Prince, 258, 333, 367, 368, 370, 381
Hiranuma, Baron, 18, 32, 163, 171, 178, 197, 199, 200, 212, 257, 337, 342, 348, 359, 361
Hiranuma's Cabinet, 155, 163, 169, 177
Hirohito, Emperor, 19
Hirota, K., 87, 88, 107, 135, 144, 145, 147, 257, 296, 355, 379, 380
Hirota Cabinet, 111–12, 127, 148
Hirota's Three Principles, 99
Hitler, A., 123, 150, 170, 212, 215, 216, 234, 297, 301
Homma, General, 274
Hondo, 334, 335
Hong Kong, 190, 191, 305
Honjo, General, 97
Hopei, 118
Horiuchi, K., 108
Hoshino, N., 259
Hsuchow, 142
Hsueh-liang, Marshal Chang, 49, 59, 63, 94, 137, 138
Hull, Cordell, 19, 219, 223–4, 226, 227, 229, 231, 232, 242, 243, 263, 264, 268, 303, 307
Hulutao, 60
Hunchen, 158

IMPERIAL Rayon Company, 87
Imperial Rule Aid Association, 198 *et seq.*, 289
Imperial Rule Political Association, 200
Imperial Way, 136
Imperial Way School, 70, 71, 72, 73, 147, 199
Imphal Campaign, 304
India, 291
Indian Army of Liberation, 292
Indian Ocean, 308
Indo-China, 166, 207, 210, 235, 236, 241, 242, 263, 274, 298, 330
Indonesia, 209, 291, 329
Inner Mongolia, 95, 120, 137, 172
Inouye, J., 40, 70

Inouye, N., 69
Instrument of Surrender, 373, 374
International War Crimes Tribunal, 11, 12, 160
Inukai, T., 72, 73, 80, 81
Ishiwara, Colonel, 66, 106, 128, 144, 146, 147
Isobe, I., 103, 104
Isoya, Lieutenant-General, 119, 173
Itagaki, Lieutenant-General, 66, 67, 73, 118, 128, 146, 147, 153, 159, 163
Italy
 declares war on U.S.A., 269
 defeated, 301
 joins tripartite pact, 151
 rivalry with Britain, 152
Ito, Count H., 299
Ito, M., 90
Ito, Prince, 135
Iwakuro, Colonel, 220, 222, 223, 227, 229
Iwojima, 311, 321, 324, 335, 354

JAPAN
 after First World War, 25 *et seq.*
 after surrender, 375 *et seq.*
 and China, 11
 army indiscipline, 52–3
 army on German model, 122
 basis of military strategy, 271
 belief in German victory, 185–6, 189–92
 causes of defeat, 270–1
 Changkufeng incident, 158 *et seq.*
 China incident, 139 *et seq.*
 clash with Russian troops, 172–3
 code of military parties, 21–2
 constitution, 18–19, 50, 51, 52
 Defence State, 127–9
 deification of Emperor, 50–2
 Diet abolished, 127
 diplomacy during war, 295–8
 economic difficulties, 156, 279 *et seq.*
 economic war against, 208, 235–6, 241, 280
 elder statesmen, 20
 end of party government, 81, 82
 errors in China, 279–85
 failure in munitions production, 309
 fear of Soviet, 122 *et seq.*
 fear of U.S. and Britain, 151
 First World War, 26–7
 food shortage, 310
 full-scale war with China, 154 *et seq.*
 Greater East Asia Conference, 294–5

388   INDEX

Japan—*cont.*
 hostilities with Russia, 142
 lack of political responsibility, 195
 Manchoukuo, 67, 86 *et seq.*
 Manchuria crisis, 11 *et seq.*
 Manchuria incident, 37 *et seq.*
 March incident, 36
 Marxism, 32
 military hierarchy, 20
 military incidents, 21
 misses opportunities for leadership in Far East, 178–80
 nationalist theories, 19
 naval strategy, 271–2
 Navy's co-operation with Army, 148–9
 need for oil, 246
 negotiations with U.S.A., 218–34, 241–3, 263–5
 new China policy, 281–90
 North China adventure, 117 *et seq.*
 October incident, 68–72
 Pacific strategy defeated, 311–12
 political background, 18
 political parties, 22
 population problem, 60–1
 Potsdam Declaration, 357–80
 rapprochement with Germany, reasons for, 147–8
 reforms, 33–4
 revises treaties with China, 58
 Russia declares war on, 359
 secedes from League of Nations, 86
 Showa era, 11, 12
 Supreme Command decides on war, 246–8
 surrender, 362–3 *et seq.*
 treatment of prisoners, 343–9
 treaty with Russia, 212–13
 tripartite alliance, 150 *et seq.*, 168 *et seq.*, 202 *et seq.*
 war trials, 348–9
 war with U.S.A., Britain and Netherlands, 266
 U.S.A. occupation forces, 371 *et seq.*
Japan Society, 9
Japan-China War, 138
Japanese Government Railways, 155
Java, 274
Jehol, 80
Jiken, 21

KAGESA, Lieutenant-General, 183
Kai-shek, Chiang, 45, 47, 48, 54, 56, 100, 137, 138, 142, 144, 146, 147, 152, 155, 164, 165, 166, 190, 207, 228, 230, 263, 281, 284, 288, 301, 304, 307, 331, 332, 333
Kamranh Bay, 241, 246
Kanaya, General, 35, 81
Kaneko, K., 90
Kanin, Prince, 82, 102
Kasawara, Major-General, 153
Kase, T., 14, 216, 334
Kasega, Major-General, 166, 201
Kategawa, 335
Kato, Admiral K., 89
Kato, Y., 39, 40
Kawabe, General T., 370
Kellogg-Briand Pact, 25, 65
Khota Bharu, 274
Kiaochow Bay, 26, 39, 43
Kido, Marquis, 20, 133, 163, 195, 198, 255, 257, 258, 300, 301, 302, 333, 336, 347, 353, 356, 358, 360, 362, 368
Kita, Ikki, 31, 34, 103, 104, 106
Kiyoura, Count, 257
Ko-a-in (Asia Development Board), 143
Kohmoto, Colonel, 49
Koike, C., 39
Koiso, General, 35, 118, 319, 320, 323, 326, 328, 330, 331, 332, 333, 342, 353
Koiso Cabinet, 327
Koiso-Yonai Cabinet, 319 *et seq.*
Kokuhonsha, 163, 199
Kokutairon, 18
Konoye, Prince, 106, 113, 129, 133–5, 144, 145, 146, 153, 167, 184, 192, 195, 197, 198, 200, 202, 204, 213, 214, 217, 219, 220, 222, 224 *et seq.*, 302, 319, 336, 337, 355, 357 *et seq.*, 368, 380, 381
Konoye Cabinet, 139, 154, 155, 157, 163, 164, 196, 211, 235
Korea, 148, 158, 159, 291, 304, 319, 330–1
Ku-min, Wang, 167
Kung-pao, Chen, 327
Kuomintang, 47, 48, 59, 155, 165, 201
Kure, 309
Kurile Islands, 306
Kurusu, S., 185, 203, 262, 263, 264, 266, 268
Kwajalein, 312
Kwantung, 304
Kwantung Army, 49, 65, 66, 67, 142, 149, 172, 173
Kwantung Leased Territory, 38
Kyushu, 324, 335, 360

INDEX

LAUREL, President, 292, 323
League of Nations, 25, 42, 60, 61, 64, 65, 77, 78, 86, 100, 208
Lexington, 276
Leyte, 321, 322, 323
Liaison Conference, 264, 265, 267, 347
Lin, General Tsai, 323, 332
Lingayen, 274, 323
Litvinov, M., 158
Lloyd, Lord, 182
London Conference (1935), 91
London Naval Agreement, 87
London Naval Retrenchment Conference, 54
Luchus, 275, 305, 335
Lunghai Railway, 142
Lu-san, Li, 61
Luzon, 321, 322, 354
Lytton Mission, 86

MACAO, 298
MacArthur, General, 274, 305, 321, 370, 371, 373, 374, 375, 377, 379
Machino, Colonel, 49
Maeda, Y., 320
Mainichi Press, 14
Malaya, 265, 274, 292, 305
Malik, V., 236, 355
Manaki, Colonel, 145
Manchoukuo, 67, 86, 154, 172, 201, 264, 281
Manchuria, 260, 279, 304
 China's intentions over, 58–9
 Japan's rights in, 38 *et seq.*
 Tanaka Memorandum, 46
Manchuria School, 147
Manchurian Bureau, 283
Manchurian Crisis, 11
Manchurian Heavy Industries Company, 93
Manchurian incident, 36, 64
Manila, 241, 274, 322, 323
March incident, 36, 65
Marco Polo Bridge, 138, 139
Mariana Islands, 275, 311
Marshall Islands, 275, 302, 305
Masaki, General, 70, 102, 106
Matsudaira, Marquis Y., 334
Matsui, General, 141, 328, 344
Matsuo, Captain, 104
Matsuoka, Y., 86, 196–7, 202, 203, 204, 206, 210, 211–7 *et seq.*, 295
Matsutani, Colonel, 334
Meiji, Emperor, 133, 135, 248
Meiji Government, 27, 37

Mein Kampf, 123
Mekong, River, 210
Memoirs, Cordell Hull, 19
Midway, battle of, 271, 276, 277, 304, 314, 388
Mikasa, Prince, 286
Minami, General, 66, 68, 118, 330
Minami aircraft squadron, 276, 277
Minobe, Professor, 91
Minsei, 22
Minsei Cabinet, 128
Missouri, 349, 371, 373
Mitsui, Lieutenant-Colonel, 103
Mitsukawa, K., 34
Molotov, V., 173, 215, 295, 296, 357
Mongolia, 95 (*see also* Inner and Outer Mongolia)
Monroe Doctrine, 219, 260
Mori, T., 46, 72, 74, 81, 365
Mukden, 48, 64, 66
Murai, Consul-General, 78
Muranaka, Lieutenant, 103, 104
Musashi, 322
Mussolini, B., 152, 212
Muto, Major-General, 192, 220, 323
My Struggle for Peace, 14

NAGANO, Admiral, 108, 237, 246, 247, 251, 263, 267, 302, 365
Nagasaki, 348, 360
Nagasaki Maru, 76
Nagata, Lieutenant-General, 65, 102
Nagoya, 324, 325
Nakamura, Captain, 63
Nakano, Seigo, 313
Namba, D., 32
Nanking, 45, 47, 54, 74, 142, 146, 201, 281, 283, 286, 326
Nanking Government, 54, 165, 217, 288, 327, 328, 331, 332
Naval Disarmament Conference, 88
Nemoto, Lieutenant-Colonel, 68
Netherlands, 209, 210
Neurath, Baron von, 123
New Britain, 275, 302
New Caledonia, 277
New Guinea, 275, 276, 305, 311
New Hebrides, 275
Nicobar Islands, 293, 308
Nimitz, Admiral, 305, 321, 324, 354, 373, 374
Nine Power Treaty, 25, 43
Ninomiya, Lieutenant-General, 35, 328
Nippon Times, 14
Nishida, C., 34

INDEX

Nishihara, Major-General, 207
Nishihara Loan, 41, 56
Nissan Company, 93
Nomonhan, 172-3
Nomura, Admiral K., 77, 78, 180, 197, 220, 222 *et seq.*, 242, 250, 251, 262, 263, 266, 268
Nomura, Admiral T., 315
North China Development Company, 155
North Saghalin, 295
Northern School, 236

OCTOBER incident, 68-72
Oikawa, Admiral, 196, 202, 251
Okada, Admiral, 85, 87, 104, 105, 181, 257, 337
Okawa, Professor S., 34, 35, 36, 65, 68, 93
Okinawa, 342, 354, 356
Okuma Cabinet, 39
Opium War, 260
Osaka, 324
Osaka Asahi, 244
Oshima, Major-General, 116, 122, 124, 125, 146, 151, 152, 153, 169, 170, 185, 197, 216, 228, 229, 230, 301
Osumi, Admiral, 72, 85
Otsuka, Governor, 359
Ott, General, 145, 146, 203, 217, 230
Ottawa Agreement, 61
Outer Mongolia, 95, 172, 306, 307
Oyama, Lieutenant, 140
Ozaki, H., 151, 157, 242, 244, 245

PALAO, 354
Palembang, 275
Papua, 275
Patriotic Industrial Crusade, 199
Peace, Japan's quest for, 299-302, 334-9
Pearl Harbour, 262, 265, 267, 268, 272, 274, 276, 303, 308
Pei-fu, Wu, 155
Peking, 44, 54, 287
Peking-Hankow Railway, 142
Peking-Mukden Railway, 137
Peking-Suiyuan Railway, 142
Pelew, 354
Percival, General, 373
Pescadores, 304
Pétain, Marshal, 241
Philippines, 149, 272, 274, 275, 291, 305, 321, 322, 324, 347, 370
Piggott, Major-General, 9

Ping, Miao, 331, 332, 333
Poland invaded, 171
Politics, Trials and Errors, 15
Port Arthur, 38, 306
Port Darwin, 275
Port Moresby, 275, 276
Port Stanley, 199
Possiet Bay, 158
Potsdam Agreement, 375, 376, 377, 379
Potsdam Conference, 357-8
Pratt, Sir John, 57
Prince of Wales, H.M.S., 274, 374
Prisoners, treatment of, 343-9
Production League, 199
Pu Yi, Emperor, 67, 73, 86, 165

QUEBEC Conference, 303

RABAUL, 275
Ranam, 158
Rangoon, 274
Repulse, H.M.S., 274
Ribbentrop, J. von, 123, 124, 152, 153, 170, 203, 212, 216, 229
Roosevelt, F. D., 213, 223, 225, 229, 230, 239, 242, 250, 261, 264, 274, 288, 303, 304, 305, 306, 307, 321
Russia
 advisers in China, 45
 anti-comintern pact, 122 *et seq.*
 clash with Japanese troops, 172-3
 continues war against Japan, 362
 Germany attacks, 213, 217
 hostilities with Japan, 142
 Japanese diplomacy during war, 295, 296-7
 menaces Manchoukuo, 94
 secret agreement with Britain and U.S.A., 306-7
 takes possession of Chankufeng peak, 158
Russia School, 136
Russo-German relations, 203
Russo-German War, 269
Russo-Japanese Treaty of Neutrality, 211 *et seq.*
Russo-Japanese War, 291, 299

SABURI, S., 44, 54, 55
Saigon, 241, 246
Saionji, Prince, 20, 50, 73, 104, 106, 133, 134
Saipan, 310, 311 *et seq.*, 322, 324, 354

INDEX

Saito, Admiral M., 85, 104, 203, 330
Sakai, Major-General, 119
Sakurakai, 35
San Francisco Company, 306
Satsuma School, 37
Seiyu, 22
Senhan Saiban no Sakugo, 15
Shanghai, 48, 74–9, 140–1, 286, 287, 327, 344
Shanhaikwan, 48
Shantung, 39, 55
Shidehara, Baron K., 42, 44, 54, 55, 58, 62, 66, 81, 90
Shigemitsu, A., 14
Shigemitsu, Mamoru
  address to privy council, 337–8
  ambassador in China, 11, 281–5
  in England, 11, 153, 178, 182, 190–1, 215–16
  in U.S.S.R., 11, 158
  counsel on Britain, 239–40
  death, 13
  efforts to restore relations with Nanking, 55 *et seq.*
  faith in British victory, 186
  foreign minister, 287 *et seq.*, 368 *et seq.*
  resigns office, 259
  returns to Japan, 238–40
  tribute to British people, 187–8
  view of Konoye's resignation, 255–6
Shikoku Islands, 324, 335
Shimada, Admiral T., 258, 267, 313, 314, 315, 320, 379
Shimminkai (People's Party), 184
Shimomura, General, 368
Shirakawa, General, 77, 78
Shiratori, Toshio, 146, 153, 168, 169, 197
Showa, Emperor, 133, 134
Showa era, 11, 12, 134, 150
Showa no Doran, 13, 14
Showa Research Institute, 157
Showa upheaval, 50, 51
Siam, 210, 241, 274, 283
Siberian Expedition, 45
Singapore, 183, 202, 211, 214, 215, 216, 241, 271, 274, 305, 348, 373
Sino-Japanese War (1894–5), 301
Society of the Sword of Heaven, 29, 30, 31, 69, 70
Solomon Islands, 275, 276, 277
Soong, T. V., 63, 64, 307
Sorge, Richard, 216, 217, 244, 245
Sorge-Ozaki spy ring, 95
South Manchuria Railway, 38, 137, 142, 155
Southern School, 202

Spruance, Admiral, 277
Stalin, J., 213, 214, 216, 245, 303, 306, 307, 357
Stimson doctrine, 223, 261
Suchow, 62, 287
Suetsugu, Admiral, 89, 128, 146
Sugamo Nikki, 14
Sugano, Chochi, 73
Sugiyama, General, 35, 128, 135, 142, 144, 146, 147, 246, 247, 251, 313, 319, 328, 334, 342, 365
Sukarno, President, 292, 329
Sulu Islands, 311
Sumatra, 275, 311
Sun Yat-sen, 54, 73, 165
Supreme Council for the Direction of the War, 320
Suzuki, Admiral K., 338, 353, 356, 358, 361, 363, 375
Suzuki, Lieutenant-General, 258
Suzuki, President, 91, 104
Suzuki, T., 197
Suzuki Cabinet, 353 *et seq.*

TAIKOKAI, 34
Taisho, 27
Taiwan, 330, 331
Takahashi, Colonel, 85, 104, 119
Takamatsu, Prince, 267
Tanahashi, 324
Tanaka, General, 42, 45, 47, 48, 49, 50, 72, 73, 366
Tanaka Memorandum, 46
Tangku Truce, 118, 119
Tani, M., 75, 283, 287, 332
Tatekawa, Major-General, 35, 66, 197, 212, 328
Tatsumi, Major-General, 239
Teh, Prince, 120
Teheran Conference, 307
Tenian, 324
Terajima, Admiral, 259
Terauchi, General, 41, 108, 127, 140, 142, 319
Tientsin, 67, 73, 182, 287
Tientsin–Pukow Railway, 142
Timor, 275, 298
Tinian, 312
Togo, S., 173, 265, 268, 283, 353, 354, 356, 358, 363
Tojo, General, 103, 147, 196, 202, 251, 252, 255, 258, 259, 263, 271, 277, 282, 284, 286, 287, 299, 312, 313, 314, 315, 342, 347, 379
Tojo Cabinet, 311–15, 319, 327

INDEX

Tokyo Bay, 275, 371
Tokyo bombed, 325
Tokyo Tribunal, 344, 345
Tora-no-mon incident, 163
Toyoda, Admiral, 234, 239, 240, 250, 252, 315, 322
Toyohashi, 325
Treaty of Neutrality, 296, 297, 303, 307
Treaty of Versailles, 25, 43
Tripartite Alliance, 150 et seq., 164, 168 et seq., 196, 202–5, 221, 225, 230, 231, 250, 264, 270
Truman, President, 357, 362, 371
Tse-tung, Mao, 137
Tsinan, 48, 142
Tsinan incident, 48–9
Tsingtao, 48, 167
Tsitsihar, 67
Tso-lin, Chang, 47, 48, 49, 50
Tsuji, Lieutenant, 103
Tsurumi, S., 9, 19
Tumen River, 158
Turkey, 305
Tzu-wen, Sung (see T. V. Soong), 63, 65

UCHIDA, Count C., 64, 85, 86, 87
Uchida, N., 91
Ueda, General K., 77, 78, 173
Ugati, General, 26, 35, 36, 68, 128, 146, 153, 154, 258, 330
Umezu, General, 119, 173, 314, 315, 332, 364, 365, 372, 373
Umezu-Ho Yung-chin Agreement, 119, 137
United Nations, 294, 305
U.S.A.
    destruction of Japanese Pacific Fleet, 274
    economic warfare against Japan, 235–6
    Japanese negotiations with, 263–5
    negotiations with Japan, 218–34, 241–3
    policy towards East Asia, 260–1
    proposals to Japan, 219
    revises treaties with China, 57
U-ting, Yang, 59

VERSAILLES Peace Treaty, 14
Vichy Government, 207, 241, 298, 330
Vladivostok, 158

WAINWRIGHT, General, 373
Wakatsuki, Baron R., 90, 257, 267, 337
Wakatsuki Cabinet, 36, 62, 67, 72
Wake Island, 275
Walsh, Bishop, 219, 222, 228
Wang, C. T., 44, 48, 58, 61
Wang Ching-wei (see Ching-wei, Wang)
Washington Conference, 25, 42, 89
Washington Treaty, 44
Wavell, Lord, 304
White, Oswald, 9, 13
Wuhan, 160
Wusung, 141

YALTA, 297, 305, 306, 357
Yamagata, Marshal, 37, 123
Yamamoto, Admiral, 37, 85, 106, 168, 276, 277
Yamanashi, General, 26, 47, 49, 128
Yamashita, General, 273, 274, 322, 323
Yamato, 311
Yanagawa, Lieutenant-General, 199
Yangtse River, 142
Yasuoka, S., 34
Yawata Steel Works, 324
Yenan, 94, 281
Ying-chin, Ho, 119
Yokohama, 26, 325, 371, 373
Yoksuka, 309, 371
Yonai, Admiral, 128, 135, 141, 153, 163, 164, 168, 170, 181, 257, 315, 319, 329, 334, 342, 356, 368
Yonai Cabinet, 181–6, 192
Yorktown, 276
Yoshida, Admiral T., 197
Yoshida, S., 108, 153, 196, 202, 302, 329, 336
Yoshizawa, K., 47, 49, 72, 73, 74, 75, 209
Youth Association, 199
Yunnan Railway, 190, 207
Yu-shang, Feng, 44, 58